Second Edition

Atlantic Canada

A History

Margaret R. Conrad   James K. Hiller

OXFORD
UNIVERSITY PRESS

OXFORD
UNIVERSITY PRESS

8 Sampson Mews, Suite 204, Don Mills, Ontario M3C 0H5

www.oupcanada.com

Oxford University Press is a department of the University of Oxford.
It furthers the University's objective of excellence in research, scholarship,
and education by publishing worldwide in

Oxford   New York

Auckland   Cape Town   Dar es Salaam   Hong Kong   Karachi
Kuala Lumpur   Madrid   Melbourne   Mexico City   Nairobi
New Delhi   Shanghai   Taipei   Toronto

With offices in

Argentina   Austria   Brazil   Chile   Czech Republic   France   Greece
Guatemala   Hungary   Italy   Japan   Poland   Portugal   Singapore
South Korea   Switzerland   Thailand   Turkey   Ukraine   Vietnam

Oxford is a trade mark of Oxford University Press
in the UK and in certain other countries

Published in Canada by Oxford University Press

Library and Archives Canada Cataloguing in Publication

Conrad, Margaret

Atlantic Canada : a history / Margaret R. Conrad and James K. Hiller. — 2nd ed.

Includes bibliographical references and index.
ISBN 978-0-19-543160-5

1. Atlantic Provinces—History—Textbooks. 2. Atlantic Provinces—Economic conditions.
I. Hiller, J. K. (James K.), 1942– II. Title.

FC2005.C65 2010   971.5   C2009-906133-3

Cover image: VA 21-18, The Rooms, Provincial Archives, VA 21-18/R.E. Holloway.

This book is printed on paper which has been certified by the Forest Stewardship Council.

Mixed Sources
Product group from well-managed forests
and other controlled sources
www.fsc.org   Cert no. SW-COC-000952
©1996 Forest Stewardship Council
FSC

Printed and bound in Canada.

1 2 3 4 — 13 12 11 10

Contents

Introduction

A Region in the Making

This book is designed to provide university students and general readers with an updated and expanded version of *Atlantic Canada: A Concise History*. In this new edition, we offer an extended discussion of the notion of 'region' and place the region more broadly in its Atlantic and global contexts. We also elaborate on our discussion of social and cultural developments and include more biographies, primary documents, and elaborations of important themes discussed in the main body of the narrative. A list of Further Readings and Recommended Websites at the end of each chapter and a Selected Bibliography of monographs, essay collections, and websites at the end of this volume offer additional resources. Each chapter also features Food for Thought, where we highlight articles that have had a significant impact on the way scholars understand the history of the region.

In the precursor to this text, *Atlantic Canada: A Region in the Making* (2001), we noted the difficulty of writing a cohesive history of the space called Atlantic Canada.[1] While the concept of region has enabled Canadians to come to terms with the physical, cultural, and historical differences in their enormous country, what constitutes a region is always fluid, subject to shifts in migrations, trade patterns, political regimes, and communications systems.

Inevitably, the term 'Atlantic Canada' sits awkwardly with many scholars, who have trouble imagining such a place. Writing in the 1980s, Alan Wilson concluded that, apart from fog and underdevelopment, the Maritime provinces of New Brunswick, Nova Scotia, and Prince Edward Island shared very little with Newfoundland and Labrador.[2] In a much-admired two-volume history of the Atlantic region, Newfoundland and Labrador is an integral part of the pre-1867 volume, but is largely absent from the second volume until it joined Confederation in 1949—as if it had been expelled from the regional fold for its failure, however brief, to conform to its predetermined political destiny.[3] Literary scholars are similarly confounded by the Cabot Strait, with the result that two studies—Patrick O'Flaherty's *The Rock Observed* and Janice Kulyk Keefer's *Under Eastern Eyes*—are required to convey developments in Newfoundland and Labrador and the Maritimes respectively. Taking a political perspective in the late 1970s, J. Murray Beck could find no regional identity at all—only provincial ones.[4] Others have gone even further, claiming that identity exists primarily in Atlantic Canada's own untidy regionalisms. Mi'kma'ki, Acadie, Africadia, Cape Breton, and Labrador are only the most obvious examples of regions that exist within, across, and beyond provincial boundaries.

A shared location is obviously the cornerstone of any region, but even geography is an uncertain ally in the quest for definition. Consisting of islands, peninsulas, and fringes of the North American continent, the Atlantic region is not defined solely by its exposure to the North

Atlantic. If it were, the Magdalen Islands, Saint-Pierre and Miquelon, and the Gaspé would all be integral parts of Atlantic Canada, but politics and economics determined otherwise.

Although formal criteria relating to geography, history, and economic conditions can be used to define Atlantic Canada, it is above all the region's functional relation to the rest of the continent that now fixes its identity. This was not always the case. Nor has the region always been treated as a single geopolitical unit. In the seventeenth and early eighteenth centuries the British and French empires carved overlapping spheres of influence in the Atlantic region, and between 1867 and 1873 the Maritime colonies (with varying degrees of reluctance) all became provinces of Canada, while New-foundland and Labrador resisted the modern continental drift. It was only in the second half of the twentieth century, after Newfoundland and Labrador joined Confederation, that 'Atlantic Canada' became the convenient shorthand term referring to all four of Canada's easternmost provinces.

In this volume we work with the current political definition of Atlantic Canada—the some-times controversial, often artificial boundaries marked on a map—but we do not argue for a quintessential Atlantic Canadian regional culture. Instead we chart formal and functional regional identities and consider the imagined sense of place that has evolved over time among a diverse people. In the documentary evidence left behind by shamans and tourism promoters, poets and photographers, novelists and statisticians, it is possible to catch glimpses of regions of the mind in Atlantic Canada that have often had a greater impact on human motivation than more tangible political and economic structures.

These regions of the mind offer a curiously contradictory and often dated picture of Atlantic Canada. In Kulyk Keefer's view, one lens frames 'white clapboard church in scarlet autumn dale, dories in the very shape of indolence nesting in placid harbours, the subtle rot of grey-shingled shacks in dense spruce groves'; another captures 'senile, ruined faces, large families in two-roomed shacks'.[5] Both ancient and modern bards have often emphasized the Arcadian quality of the At-lantic landscape, but flint-eyed critics such as O'Flaherty have shunned such romanticism, noting the brutal geographical legacy that in Newfoundland and Labrador makes it impossible for 'one generation to tame the environment for the benefit of the next'.[6] O'Flaherty's comment may be less applicable to the Maritimes, where the landscape has been more receptive to human industry, but it touches on a problem that pollsters suggest is endemic in the region: a low sense of efficacy. Atlantic Canadians, past and present alike, have combined regional pride and relentless optimism with a Sisyphean resignation to the idea that it may well be their lot to strive rather than to suc-ceed. The title of Edward MacDonald's history of twentieth-century Prince Edward Island—*If You're Stronghearted*—captures the essence of this ongoing struggle.[7]

Notions of failure and backwardness are never far from the surface of scholarly and journalistic commentary on Atlantic Canada. 'To be a scholar of Atlantic Canada,' Ian McKay has observed, 'is to wrestle, often at the very outset of one's inquiries, with a subtle, pervasive and durable language of disparagement and marginality.'[8] Barry Cooper, a political scientist at the University of Calgary, has gone so far as to argue, as a matter of 'fact', that 'stagnation and decadence remain the most prominent features of pre-modern communal life to have survived into the present' in the Mari-times (by which he meant Atlantic Canada).[9] Cooper offers little evidence to back up his assertion, but such comments inevitably serve as a means of consolidating second-class citizenship.

It is unclear whether accusations of conservatism and backwardness hold much weight. If Atlantic Canadians are more conservative than other North Americans, how does their conservatism manifest itself? Scholars who would confirm the conservative stereotype point to the comparative reluctance of Atlantic Canadians to support radical political movements, the tendency of the region's artists and creative writers to cling to realism, and a commitment to the notion of 'social good' in law and social policy. Scholars who dispute this view draw attention to the region's leadership in the movement for responsible government; its early commitment to higher education for women; pitched battles between capital and labour in mining and steel-making communities; and the outrageously radical efforts of the region's governments, in the second half of the twentieth century, to impose modernization through wholesale resettlement programs, sweeping municipal reform, and state-run enterprise. For our part, we contend that emphasizing radical departures serves the region no better than belabouring the conservative ones. The wiser course is to concede that Atlantic Canada is a complex region with a history long and deep enough to accommodate most academic prejudices.

Even the interpretation of the region's history during much of the twentieth century may have helped to sell the region at a discount. In his provocative book *The Quest of the Folk*, McKay traces the processes by which in the difficult interwar years (1919–39) Nova Scotians succumbed to the myth of a golden age when innocent fisherfolk lived in harmony with an idyllic rural landscape.[10] Romanticized notions of pre-industrial utopias have been common enough in Western societies, McKay argues, but they have proved particularly pernicious in Nova Scotia (and by implication in all of Atlantic Canada), reducing real people to static essences represented by stereotypical figures, such as Glooscap, Rugged Fishermen, and Scottish Bagpipers. In Newfoundland and Labrador, celebrations of outport life have been dangerously combined with a long-standing sense of victimization, with a parade of historical scapegoats—from the fishing admirals to Water Street merchants—used to explain relative backwardness and failure. At the beginning of the twenty-first century, fictional characters—Evangeline, Anne of Green Gables, La Sagouine—seem to loom larger on the region's historical landscape than do more complex realities.

When they venture outside their natural habitat, Atlantic Canadians often find that such 'folk' images work against them, the first impression being that they are quaint rustics in a modern world of sophisticated go-getters. At the same time, it seems, nothing so becomes the Atlantic region as the leaving of it. Writing in 1912 from Leaskdale, Ontario, the popular writer L.M. Montgomery conceded that her new home was 'a very pretty country place—would be almost as pretty as Cavendish if it had the sea. . . . At times—generally in the winter twilight—I am very homesick and feel as if I would exchange all the kingdoms of the world and the glory thereof for a sunset ramble in Lover's Lane.'[11]

Gary Burrill argues that the idea of leaving home is inseparable from the Atlantic regional identity.[12] As the 'light infantry of capital', Atlantic Canadians have sailed the oceans of the world and criss-crossed the continent in search of work and greener pastures. This phenomenon has inspired 'leaving' songs in both Prince Edward Island ('Prince Edward Island Adieu') and Nova Scotia ('Farewell to Nova Scotia') that are now canonized in folklore. The 'Ode to Newfoundland' is sung with as much enthusiasm in the taverns of Toronto and Fort McMurray as in the province that so many of its sons and daughters have left. Such evidence of social cohesion notwithstanding, Atlantic Canadians have generally been quick to assimilate to other North American cultures and have left little permanent record of a distinctive legacy from a beloved homeland. This should come as no surprise. Despite their nostalgia for the 'home place', Atlantic Canadians have been full participants in creating a shared continental culture.

Identities are not inbred; they are learned. Moreover, they vary over time and are constrained by social and cultural factors. In his 1970s study of identity formation in Cape Breton, Stephen Ullman discovered that pride in the island (as opposed to pride in Nova Scotia or Canada) increased with age, was stronger among Mi'kmaq than Euro-Canadians, and was also more pronounced among the working than the middle class.[13] Had he included gender among his variables, he would have likely found that, given their socialization to separate spheres, women and men also would have revealed differing levels of regional awareness. Marilyn Porter's work on outport Newfoundland suggests that family and community concerns among women may well have a bearing on the findings of many quantitative studies purporting to measure regional or provincial traits.[14]

The foregoing suggests that 'region' and 'regionalism' are slippery concepts, ones that should be understood as reflecting shifting cultural and historical contexts rather than fixed and static 'truths'. The two terms also need to be distinguished. While the Atlantic 'region' can be easily found on a map, 'regionalism' implies a political stance, a consciousness of a shared outlook that can be summoned up when other structures—familial, communal, provincial, national, global—fail. Such a regionalism may manifest itself as friendliness in distant ports, but it has not been the stuff of political cohesion at home. Over the years, calls for a union of the Maritime or Atlantic provinces have been voiced by policy-makers desperate to find a quick fix for real or imagined ills. That no such union has ever materialized suggests not only that there are other powerful identities in Atlantic Canada competing for dominance but also that regionalism has limited value as a vehicle for common action.

Although Atlantic Canadians have so far rejected political union, they have increasingly come to share an angle of vision regarding the world they inhabit. This common perspective derives in large measure from being economically poor and politically weak relative to much of the rest of North America. It might well be asked why 2.3 million people inhabiting a resource-rich area that is larger than most of the world's nation-states are not wallowing in wealth. Small countries off the edges of continents—among them Great Britain, Japan, and most Scandinavian countries—have proven that economic success is possible without vast hinterlands or favoured climates. What caused the Atlantic provinces to forsake their destiny?

Fish, fur, timber, minerals, and agricultural land provided Atlantic Canadians with the material conditions for a degree of economic well-being, but these resources and their dispersal along an extensive North Atlantic littoral have also nurtured dependency and diversity. With no internal metropolitan centre to impose a homogenizing influence, Atlantic Canada has historically been loose-jointed and vulnerable to outside forces. In the eighteenth century the region became the site of a struggle between France and Great Britain for imperial domination. The losers in this contest were Aboriginal peoples and Acadians—the region's first European settlers—who were marginalized and saw most of their lands taken over by immigrants from Europe and the Thirteen Colonies/United States, who settled in the Maritimes between 1713 and 1867.

While there have been many efforts to explain the region's plight in the Industrial Age, most scholars point to the vagaries of federal policies and capitalist exploitation. E.R. Forbes and Donald Savoie have demonstrated convincingly that national policies have been deficient in addressing the needs of the Atlantic provinces.[15] This outcome, Sean Cadigan argues, is a result of dependency relationships in a capitalist society that 'produced places that have enjoyed disproportionately economic benefits and concomitant power while other places have suffered disproportionately from exploitation.'[16]

Taking a slightly different perspective, Savoie has also argued that community life in Atlantic Canada is richer than modern statistical analyses, based on narrow notions of economic well-being, suggest.[17] It is, after all, a moot point whether wage earners forced to spend most of their annual income on survival in more favoured regions of the continent are any better off than their counterparts in the Atlantic region, where the scale of living is smaller but may be equally rich in material and psychological well-being.

David Alexander, who perhaps contributed more to the understanding of his adopted region than any scholar of his generation, suggested that 'a new notion of happiness' based on the idea of regional self-reliance was emerging.[18] This idea has yet to be fully realized, but the rising tide of globalism and threats of environmental and financial meltdown may well advance the process of regional co-operation and reduced expectations of economic growth more rapidly than even Alexander could have imagined.

Along with offering students an updated and concise history of Atlantic Canada, our primary goal in writing this book is to make this diverse region better known to its citizens. We also hope that it will appeal to readers who are unfamiliar with the region and its people. Making available a synthesis of the region's long and remarkable history may increase awareness and understanding, while helping Atlantic Canadians to develop a more accurate and assured sense of who they are.

Further Readings

Friesen, Gerald. 2005. 'Space and Region in Canadian History', *Journal of the Canadian Historical Association 2005* New Series, 16: 1–22.

Hiller, James K. 2000. 'Is Atlantic Canadian History Possible?' *Acadiensis* XXX, 1 (Autumn): 16–22.

McKay, Ian. 2000. 'A Note on "Region" in Writing the History of Atlantic Canada', *Acadiensis* XXIX, 2 (Spring): 89–101.

Widdis, Randy William, Margaret R. Conrad, Jean Barman, Bill Waiser, and Sean T. Cardigan. 2006. 'Round Table on Re-Imagining Regions', *Acadiensis* XXXV, 2 (Spring): 127–68.

Food For Thought

Forbes, E.R. 1978. 'In Search of a Post-Confederation Maritime Historiography', *Acadiensis* VIII, 1 (Autumn): 3–21.

Matthews, Keith. 2001. 'Historical Fence Building: A Critique of the Historiography of Newfoundland', *Newfoundland Studies* 17, 2 (Spring): 143–65.

Recommended Websites

Atlantic Canada Portal
http://atlanticportal.hil.unb.ca

Newfoundland and Labrador Heritage
http://www.heritage.nf.ca/home.html

Nova Scotia Archives and Records Management
http://www.gov.ns.ca/nsarm/

Prince Edward Island Public Archives and Records Office
http://www.gov.pe.ca/cca/index.php3?number=1004626

Provincial Archives of Newfoundland and Labrador
http://www.therooms.ca/archives/

Provincial Archives of New Brunswick
http://archives.gnb.ca/Archives/Default.aspx?culture=en-CA

Part I

The Atlantic Region, 1500–1867

.

*I*n the late fifteenth century Christopher Columbus and John Cabot encountered the Americas. They were not the first Europeans to explore the western shores of the Atlantic Ocean, but their voyages set in motion an extraordinary chain of events. Over the next three centuries Europeans traded, plundered, and ultimately began to settle on the fringes of their 'new world'. The Aboriginal peoples who had been living in North America for millennia gradually accommodated the intruders who brought with them not only valued trade goods but also devastating diseases, new flora and fauna, intermittent warfare, and a world view that often contrasted sharply with their own.

What is now the Atlantic region of Canada was on the front line of these developments. The fish and fur found in abundance in the region attracted public and private investment, and soon European monarchs were vying with each other for dominance of the North American continent and its peoples. Although Great Britain ultimately triumphed over France in the Seven Year's War (1756–63), it soon lost 13 of its North American colonies, which declared independence as the United States of America in 1776.

The colonies that had once been claimed by France remained part of 'British' North America. In this space, peoples from Europe, Africa, and other areas of North America mingled in new colonial societies that by the mid-nineteenth century were well on their way to developing their own strategies to survive and thrive in a world being transformed by the Industrial Revolution.

Chapter 1

Beginnings

In 1855, J. William Dawson, a native of Pictou County, Nova Scotia, published a book entitled *Acadian Geology*. In it he reflected on a time 350 million years earlier when 'multitudes of large animals now extinct' inhabited the Maritimes and 'submerged tropical forests' laid the foundations for the region's rich coal deposits. Dawson was a pioneer in the emerging fields of geology and paleontology, two of the sciences that, in the nineteenth century, were transforming everything people had hitherto believed about the earth and its inhabitants. A strict Presbyterian, he refused to accept the theory of evolution as expounded by his famous contemporary Charles Darwin. Dawson nevertheless helped to advance new scientific ideas about the origins of the earth and the emergence of an 'Atlantic region'.

The Making of the Atlantic Region

In Dawson's time most people living in the British North America subscribed to a biblical interpretation of the origins of the universe. They believed that God had created heaven and earth in six days—some thought 4004 years before the birth of Christ—and placed Adam and Eve in the Garden of Eden, from which they were eventually expelled to people an imperfect world.

Aboriginal creation stories also attributed the earth's origins to powerful gods. According to Mi'kmaq beliefs, Kji-kinap made the world and breathed life into a large, flat stone that he named Kluskap (Glooscap). With the help of a young man and a young woman, Kluskap cleaned out the silt-choked river beds, made the trees grow, summoned birds and animals from the Sky World, and shaped various geological features. Like the Christian God, Kluskap established a gendered social order. 'I am going to marry you together,' he told the pair who helped him to form the earth. 'You will live together and have children, and they will have children. Go and make yourselves a wigwam. The man can go out into the forest and hunt animals. The woman can cook them.'[1]

The implications of the scientific view of creation that now dominates most textbooks also take a leap of faith to grasp. In the 1830s, Abraham Gesner, another Nova Scotia-born scientist, discovered fossils in the Bay of Fundy region. These drew the attention of Charles Lyell, the British founder of modern geology. In 1852 Lyell and Dawson explored the cliffs around Joggins on Chignecto Bay, where they found the earliest reptilian remains discovered in North America to that time. These findings helped to confirm the view that the earth and its inhabitants were far older than the Book of Genesis suggested.

Scientists now think that the earth is at least 4.5 billion years old, and explain the creation of continents and oceans in the framework of plate tectonics. According to this approach, continents are in constant movement, colliding and breaking apart as they float on the planet's soft, molten interior. When a supercontinent breaks apart into smaller continents, oceans form

Table 1.1 Timeline	
1 billion–750 million years BP	Supercontinent Rodinia dominates the earth.
350–200 million years BP	Supercontinent Pangaea, with its coal-forming swamps, dominates the earth; fish and reptiles flourish.
200 million years BP	Pangaea begins to break up, creating the Americas, Eurasia, and Africa.
66 million years BP	Mass extinction of earth's species, including the dinosaurs, perhaps as a result of the impact of an asteroid or meteorite.
2 million–10,000 years BP	Ice Age grips the earth.
20,000 years BP	Glaciers from the last ice age begin to melt.
10,600 years BP	Approximate date of the Paleo-Indian site at Debert: the first known human habitation in the Atlantic region.
10,000–2500 BP	Archaic cultures inhabit the Maritimes and Newfoundland.
4000 BP	Paleo-Eskimos arrive in Labrador.
2500 BP	Woodland (Ceramic) cultures begin to dominate the Maritime region.
2000 BP	Dorset people arrive in Labrador and spread to the island of Newfoundland.
1250–1450 CE	Thule culture arrives in Labrador.

between them; when those continents collide, the earth's crust buckles to form mountain chains, and pieces of ocean crust, arcs of volcanic islands, and continental fragments litter the landscape. These redistributed elements are called 'terranes'. The Atlantic region represents a collage of such terranes, welded to each other over millions of years of continental movement.[2]

The eastern part of the Canadian Shield dates from the period when several continental fragments came together to create the supercontinent of Rodinia. While all of Labrador is composed of ancient rocks from a mountain-building collision, known as the Grenville Orogeny, the southern boundary of this landform also slips into the Gulf of St Lawrence and parts of Newfoundland. The recent discovery of a fragment (called the Blair River block) of the Grenville Orogen near the northern tip of Cape Breton testifies to the dramatic geological processes that have occurred in the region over billions of years. Indeed, Atlantic Canada boasts some of the earth's oldest landforms: at Saglek Bay in Labrador, for instance, rocks have been found that date back some 3.6 billion years.

Rodinia broke apart into smaller continents about 750 million years ago. As the cycle of continental drift continued, the Atlantic region took shape at the centre of a continent named Pangaea, which itself was formed when ancient continental plates—Laurentia to the west and Gondwana to the east—collided. Evidence of the collision can be seen in many parts of the Atlantic region, most notably in the section of the Appalachian mountain chain that includes Gros Morne National Park, on the west coast of Newfoundland. In 1987 UNESCO declared Gros Morne a World Heritage Site in recognition of its geological importance.

Two hundred million years ago, the two plates that had formed Pangaea separated, and the space between them was filled by the present Atlantic Ocean. In the breakup, fragments of Gondwana remained attached to Laurentia, including the Eastern Zone of Newfoundland, much of Nova Scotia (the Megumba Zone), and parts of New Brunswick and the northeastern United States. The terrain stretching from northern Africa to Scandinavia bears striking resemblances to the Atlantic shores of the Maritimes and Newfoundland because they were once part of the same land mass.

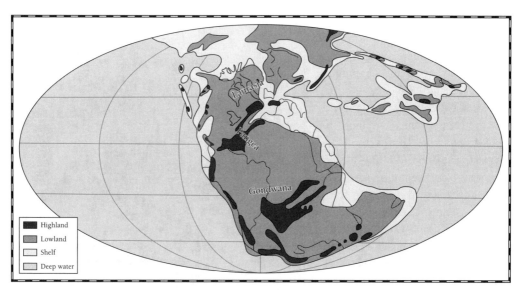

Global paleontology about 215 million years ago. Atlantic Geoscience Society, *The Last Billion Years: A Geological History of the Maritime Provinces* (Halifax: Nimbus Publishing, 2001), p. 126.

| | | | | millions of years | | | | | | | |

Paleontological timeline. Atlantic Geoscience Society. *The Last Billion Years: A Geological History of the Maritime Provinces* (Halifax, Nimbus Publishing, 2001) p. 126

In the 200 million years since Pangaea divided and the North Atlantic continent began drifting northward, adjustments of the earth's crust and the forces of erosion have eaten away the once rugged mountains of the Appalachian chain and built up the continental shelf, with its rich reserves of oil and natural gas. Water flowing from mountains along the coastal margins and the interior of the continent created the Gulf of St Lawrence, carved out the Cabot Strait and Strait of Belle Isle, and laid down the iron-rich sandstone deposits that are responsible for the red soils of Prince Edward Island. Where water drained into basins creating lakes, life forms emerged. One such lake occupied what is now Albert County in New Brunswick. Lake Albert once teemed with fish and algae, and it is their remains, locked up in the lake sediments, that are the source of the hydrocarbons still being extracted from an oil and gas field near Moncton.

The exposed rocks along the Bay of Fundy reveal dramatic evidence of the last 360 million years of the earth's history. During the Carboniferous period (360–286 million years ago), the region was subjected to repeated buckling and faulting. When the buckling and sediment accumulation were slow, the vegetation that grew on the river flood plains was preserved as coal beds; when these processes occurred more rapidly, forests were drowned, trapping reptiles in hollow tree stumps. The reptiles that Dawson and Lyell discovered in drowned forests were the ancestors of the dinosaurs that would dominate the region for nearly 200 million years until they suddenly became extinct—perhaps as a result of an asteroid or meteorite hitting the earth—some 66 million years ago.

The final shaping and scraping of the Atlantic landscape occurred during the last Ice Age, which gripped the continent from 2 million to 10,000 years ago. During the Wisconsinan glaciation (75,000–10,000 years ago), the Laurentide Ice Sheet gradually expanded to cover most of what is now Canada, including Labrador and the tip of Newfoundland's Northern Peninsula. The rest of Newfoundland and the Maritimes were covered by another ice cap, which formed part of the Appalachian Glacier Complex. Ice flowed over earlier river valleys, cut deep

'Reptiles of the Coal Period', an illustration from the 1891 edition of J. William Dawson's *Acadian Geology*.

valleys and fiords, and dumped boulders, gravel, and fine sand throughout the region. Erratics—glacial debris dropped by the moving ice cap—still litter the landscape in some areas, including along the road to Peggy's Cove, Nova Scotia.

About 20,000 years ago the glaciers of the last ice age began to melt. The sea level rose, fell, and rose again as the ice retreated and the land rebounded from the weight of the glaciers. Prince Edward Island began as three islands and was later connected to the mainland by a land bridge. In periods when the sea level was low, sections of the continental shelf and much of what is now the undersea coast, including the Bay of Fundy, lay exposed. The Atlantic region took the geological form we recognize today as recently as 3,000 years ago.

Joggins: The Earth's History Written in Stone

The Joggins Fossil Cliffs in Nova Scotia, which attracted the attention of J. William Dawson in the nineteenth century, were declared a UNESCO World Heritage Site in 2008. Described as the 'coal age Galápagos' due to their wealth of fossils from the Carboniferous period, the rocks found at this site include the remains and tracks of very early animals and the rainforest. The site bears witness to the first reptiles in earth history, which are the earliest representatives of the amniotes, a group of animals that includes reptiles, dinosaurs, birds, and mammals. Upright fossil trees (together with animal, plant, and trace fossils) are preserved at a series of levels in the cliffs, providing evidence about the forests that dominated the land in this period, and are now the source of most of the world's coal deposits. The Joggins site played a vital role in the development of basic geological and evolutionary principles, including the work of Sir Charles Lyell and Charles Darwin.

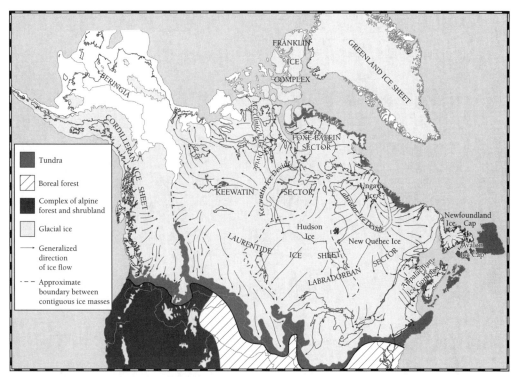

The Last Ice Age (Wisconsonian). R. Cole Harris, ed. *Historical Atlas of Canada I: From the Beginning to 1800* (Toronto: University of Toronto Press, 1987), Plate 1.

Where is Here?

What exactly is Atlantic Canada today? Geographic diversity rather than homogeneity is the region's most obvious feature. Extending over 17 degrees of both longitude and latitude, Atlantic Canada contains 539,101 square kilometres of land and fresh water, and 16,000 kilometres of saltwater shoreline. At 1,652 metres, Mount Caubvick in Labrador's Torngat Mountains is the region's highest point, while no part of Prince Edward Island rises above 142 metres. In western Newfoundland, New Brunswick, and Nova Scotia, the Appalachian range dominates the landscape. These mountains are so old that they have been eroded into stumps, the highest of which is Mount Carleton in New Brunswick (820 metres). In Cape Breton and Newfoundland the Appalachians rise steeply from the sea, helping to make the Cabot Trail and Gros Morne National Park two of the most spectacular tourist attractions in the world. Several millennia ago, the Atlantic region was much larger than it is today, and its ancient contours can be seen in the rough outlines of the continental shelf. The relative shallowness of the shelf has, until recently, provided a rich habitat for fish and still makes it possible to extract undersea deposits of oil and natural gas.

Climate also ranges widely in the region, from the subarctic conditions of northern Labrador to the temperate ranges of southwestern Nova Scotia. Although weather is influenced primarily by continental systems moving eastwards, these are modified by the ocean, which gives Atlantic Canada warmer winters and cooler summers than areas of North America in the same latitudes farther west. Most of the region lacks the warming influence of the Gulf Stream that keeps Great

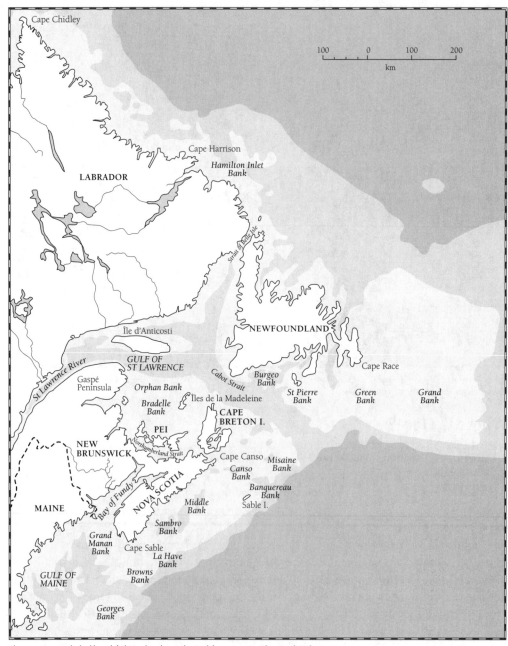

The continental shelf and fishing banks. Adapted from Innis, *The Cod Fishery*, 7.

Britain pleasantly mild compared to Newfoundland and Labrador, though the two regions are in roughly the same latitude. When the Gulf Stream meets the cold Labrador Current carrying ice from the north, it produces the fog for which the Grand Banks are infamous.

Labrador makes up 54 per cent of the total land mass of the Atlantic region, but its rugged landscape, which is part of the Canadian Shield, has never supported a large population. By contrast, the rich soils of Prince Edward Island and the valleys of the St John and Annapolis-Cornwallis rivers invited settlement and yield agricultural crops in modest abundance. Most of the region sustains a forest cover, much of it a mix of deciduous and coniferous trees. Over the past 500 years, the forests have been so thoroughly exploited that few old-growth stands are left. By contrast, the mineral wealth of the region, with the exception of the coal deposits of Nova Scotia and New Brunswick and the iron and nickel deposits of Labrador, has yet to be fully exploited.

The First Peoples

The early history of human habitation in the Atlantic region is difficult to determine because many areas of coastal settlement have sunk below sea level, and the region's acidic soils tend to destroy any organic materials that have not been submerged. As a result there are few sites that offer evidence of continuous occupation over long stretches of time. Archaeological discoveries in recent years have enabled us to imagine the broad outline of the region's early human history, but we may never know the full story.[3]

Scholars call the earliest North American peoples Paleo-Indians. Hunting species such as mammoths, mastodons, and longhorn bison, they moved across the continent from the south and west as the retreating glaciers permitted, adapting their culture to the changing climate, animal species, and vegetation. The oldest discovered remains of human settlement in the region were found in the 1960s near Debert, Nova Scotia. Dated to about 10,600 years ago, the site is believed to be a seasonal encampment near a caribou trail passing through the Cobequid Bay region. Although these Paleo-Indians may have relied primarily on caribou for survival, their descendants pursued diverse hunting, fishing, and gathering subsistence patterns, gradually making their way to the rich maritime life of the Strait of Belle Isle, where archaeological evidence dating back nearly 9,000 years has been found at Pinware Hill in southern Labrador.

Paleo-Indian culture, based on chipped stone technology, gave way to a sequence of what are termed Archaic cultures, distinguished from their predecessors by the fact that their stone tools were ground and polished. While it is believed that Archaic peoples inhabited the region from 10,000 to 2,500 years ago, until recently very little was known about the first 5,000 years of their occupation. Because of evidence found near lakes and rivers and from drowned coastal sites in the Bay of Fundy and off Prince Edward Island, archaeologists now agree that the Early and Middle Archaic cultures they have identified in New England also lived in the Maritimes. Recent findings by archaeologist Susan Blair and a team of researchers at Jemseg Crossing in New Brunswick reveal human occupation extending back more than 7,000 years.[4] This and other new sites currently being researched indicate that we are on the cusp of a more complex understanding of the region's 'ancient' human history.

By the late Archaic period, beginning about 5,000 years ago, there were two distinct groups inhabiting the Atlantic region: the Interior Late Archaic and the Coastal Late Archaic. The Interior Late Archaic peoples represented an eastern version of the Laurentian tradition that extended from the Great Lakes to the shores of what are now Maine and New Brunswick. The Coastal Late Archaic marks a distinct phase in what archaeologist James Tuck calls a Maritime Archaic tradition.[5] With local variants, it extended from Maine to northern Labrador and from Newfoundland to the Gulf of St Lawrence, and reflects a continuous occupation of coastal areas from the Paleo-Indian period to European settlement. There has been considerable debate on this issue, in part because time and tides have eroded areas where these people once lived. B.J. Bourque, for instance, maintains that the Late Archaic in the southwestern Maritimes and Maine represents a separate cultural tradition, which he calls the 'Moorehead phase'.[6]

In Labrador and Newfoundland archaeologists have been able to document an unbroken Maritime Archaic tradition running from 7,500 to 3,500 years ago. Surviving artifacts from sites such as L'Anse Amour and Port au Choix indicate that a Northern Branch of that tradition—now referred to as the Labrador Archaic—spread from the Strait of Belle Isle along the coast of Labrador, eventually reaching Saglek and Ramah bays. The Southern Branch people occupied southern Labrador and were the first humans to colonize the island of Newfoundland, where they established themselves some 5,000 years ago (perhaps even earlier), spreading around the entire coastline, with the possible exception of the Avalon Peninsula.

About 6,000 years ago, the Labrador Archaic abandoned southern Labrador and focused their activities between Hamilton Inlet and Nachvak. They also abandoned their traditional single-family dwellings for large rectangular longhouses, which could be up to 80 metres in length, and accommodate up to 100 people. These structures suggest that the Archaic came together in large groups at certain times of the year to quarry chert, hunt caribou, and carry out their elaborate mortuary rituals.

There is also evidence that people belonging to the Broad Point (or Susquehanna) culture, first defined in the mid-Atlantic states of North America, moved into the southwestern extremes of the

Rock formations at Hopewell, Albert County, New Brunswick. These 'flower pots', carved by the exceptionally high tides of the Bay of Fundy, are left exposed at low tide. They became popular tourist attractions in the nineteenth century. PANB, New Brunswick Travel Bureau, P93AL-14.

Maritimes in the late Archaic period. What makes them distinct, apart from the broad points of their artifacts, is that they cremated their dead and buried the ashes and bone fragments in pits. The Broad Point peoples seem not to have penetrated much beyond southwestern New Brunswick and the Yarmouth–Tusket region of Nova Scotia.

Ramah Chert

If they could get it, pre-contact toolmakers preferred to use chert, a silica-rich sedimentary rock that is brittle, flakes easily, and produces a sharp edge. There are two sources of chert on the Labrador coast, in the Cape Mugford and Ramah Bay areas. Ramah chert is distinctive. It is usually light grey, semi-translucent, with black bands. Black and orange dots are also common. Starting at least 6,000 years ago, this chert was used by all indigenous cultures in Newfoundland and Labrador to make knives, spear points, and other tools. It was clearly prized and traded between coastal peoples as far south as Maine, as far west as Trois-Rivières, and in sites west of Ungava Bay.

Archaeologists have wondered why Ramah chert was used so extensively and for so long—from the Maritime Archaic to the Recent Indians and European contact. Why did some peoples prefer it to other, more accessible cherts of similar quality? It is thought that Ramah chert probably had value as a special, exotic stone from a far-distant source. More speculatively, some think that Ramah chert's translucence and colouring gave it spiritual and symbolic importance.[7]

Whatever their specific traditions, all Archaic cultures depended—as had their Paleo-Indian predecessors—on some combination of hunting, fishing, and gathering. Their highly mobile communities consisted of bands made up of a few related families, 50 people on the average. Although they carved out territorial jurisdictions, there was probably significant interaction between the sea-based and interior peoples who shared the region's bounty. The likelihood of a robust trade is suggested by the discovery in sites throughout the region of tools made of much-prized stone such as chert in Labrador or rhyolite on the island of Iona in Cape Breton. Adapting their resources of stone and bone to the job at hand, these cultures developed an impressive array of tools to ensure survival. In the sea-based societies, people fashioned toggling harpoons to spear seals and swordfish, which they then killed using lances tipped with bone and ground slate points. Animals were butchered with stone knives and the skins dressed with bone scrapers. From the bones of small birds and animals people crafted fine needles and awls with which to make shelters, clothing, footwear, and carrying bags. Ground and polished axes, adzes, and gouges were used to fashion wooden spear shafts, traps, and other hunting equipment, as well as wooden bowls, dugout canoes, house frames, and small decorative objects.

Archaic peoples had highly developed spiritual beliefs, burying their dead, accompanied by red ochre, tools, weapons, and decorative objects, in cemeteries. If the surviving carved charms, tokens, and amulets are any indication, the Archaic peoples living in the Atlantic region had great respect for the fish, sea birds, whales, and seals on which they depended for survival. At Port au Choix, for example, some of the graves included the remains of a particular bird species, which may have served to identify family lines.

Climatic Change and Cultural Adaptation

Population movements and cultural evolution in the Maritimes appear to be linked to climatic change. About 3,500 years ago, rising sea levels and cooling temperatures encouraged greater reliance on shellfish and fur-bearing animals and the adoption of new practices and technologies from other cultures. The Maritime Archaic culture as such disappeared. About 2,500 years ago, absorbing influences and perhaps immigrants from the south and west, the Maritime peoples moved into the Woodland (or Ceramic) period, characterized in part by the use of clay pottery. Modern Mi'kmaq, Wolastoqiyik, and Passamaquoddy have almost certainly descended from the Woodland peoples, who predominated in the Maritimes between 2,500 and 500 years ago.

The appearance of ceramics may be an indication that Archaic peoples borrowed technology from adjacent cultures in the New England and St Lawrence regions to meet changing circumstances. The notion of cultural borrowing would allow for more continuous human occupation of the region than has hitherto been considered possible. Such a theory is supported by the Augustine and Oxbow burial mound sites found on the Miramichi River and at Skora, near Halifax. Similar to sites associated with the Adena in Ohio, they suggest either that people from the interior of the continent swept through the region 3,000 years ago or that Maritime Archaic people had learned new ways to inter their dead relatives.

Most Woodland sites are located along the coast or on rivers where fish were abundant. From the available evidence, there seems to have been considerable continuity in the seasonal rhythms. For example, some bands in eastern New Brunswick made regular late-winter expeditions to Prince Edward Island to catch sea mammals. While most bands were highly mobile, the discovery of more than a hundred semi-subterranean pit-houses in the Passamaquoddy Bay area suggests that people living there were based in the same village for most of the year. These pit-houses were conical structures framed with poles or saplings covered with skins or sheets of bark and sometimes banked with a mixture of shells and soil, presumably to keep out the cold.

The peoples of southeastern New Brunswick developed somewhat different cultural patterns, but they shared with their neighbours a dependence on shellfish and the use of clay pots. Shell middens—accumulations of discarded shells of clams, quahogs, mussels, and occasionally scallops or oysters—are found throughout the region and offer valuable evidence about the evolution of Woodland material culture. At a midden site at Sellar's Cove, on the shores of St Margaret's Bay, Nova Scotia, remains from nearly the entire span of the Woodland period indicate that pottery techniques declined, perhaps because people were becoming more mobile. By the time of European contact, both the semi-permanent dwellings along the coast and pottery had disappeared, for reasons that have yet to be fully explained.

Mobility was greatly advanced by the use of birchbark for making dishes, baskets, and especially canoes. Ribs for canoes were made from cedar and thwarts from maple or other hardwoods. Woodland peoples appear to have used their canoes primarily for river and coastal travel, but they were clearly able to navigate the Northumberland Strait, the Strait of Canso, and, some claim, the Cabot Strait as well. Before the arrival of Europeans, the region's Aboriginal peoples had also adopted the bow and arrow.

Newfoundland and Labrador experienced the same climatic shift that affected the Maritimes, but received successive immigrants from the north rather than the south and west.[8] The first of

Major archaeological sites in the Atlantic region. Adapted from Buckner and Reid, *The Atlantic Region to Confederation*, 4.

these were the Pre-Dorset Paleo-Eskimos, who arrived in Labrador approximately 4,000 years ago and whose descendents later spread to the island of Newfoundland occupying regions abandoned by the Maritime Archaic. In turn, their culture was replaced about 2,000 years ago by the Late Paleo-Eskimo, usually called Dorset (after the Baffin Island community of Cape Dorset where their

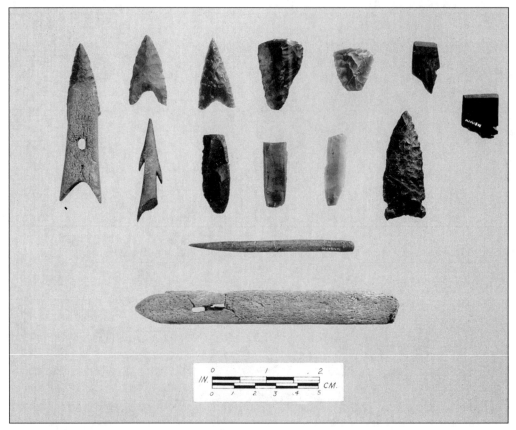

Dorset Paleo-Eskimo artifacts, 1,300 to 2,000 years old, from Port au Choix in northwestern Newfoundland. Clockwise from top left: a bone harpoon head tipped with a stone end-blade, two typical Dorset triangular end-blades, two end-scrapers, two ground nephrite engraving tools, a chipped-stone knife, three microblades, and a bone point. At the bottom is a segment of a whalebone sled-runner, and above that a stone awl. M.A.P. Renouf, Memorial University, St John's.

remains were first identified). They disappeared from the island of Newfoundland by the ninth century and from Labrador by 1300. Skilled in crafting stone, bone, and ivory tools, the Dorset people produced distinctive soapstone lamps and cooking vessels as well as whalebone 'shoes' to protect the runners on their sleds, which they probably hauled themselves.

The direct ancestors of the modern Labrador Inuit were the Thule, the last major group to migrate there from the western Arctic. Adept at catching whales with their large toggling harpoons, kayaks, and umiaks, they moved quickly across the High Arctic. Their success was facilitated by a warming trend, which reduced the sea ice and drew both bowhead and right whales into the northern waters. Arriving in the extreme north of Labrador between 1250 and 1450, they reached Saglek by 1500 and soon after that encountered Europeans in the Strait of Belle Isle.

Since the material culture of the Thule has been well preserved, we know more about their lifestyle than that of most early peoples in the region. Their typical house was an oval-shaped, semi-subterranean structure with three levels, entered through a tunnel leading to a slightly elevated flagstone floor. At the rear was a raised sleeping platform. A low earthen exterior wall supported a whalebone interior frame, which was covered with baleen and sod to create a domed roof. It seems likely that the Thule people also built igloos—although it is impossible to trace their fast-disappearing remains. The Thule had teams of dogs trained to pull their sleds. By 1500 right whales were the mainstay of their diet, supplemented by the sea mammals, birds, fish, land animals, and wild berries that flourished in the region.

The origins of the modern Labrador Innu are imperfectly understood, but have been traced back about 1,000 years to a tradition known to archaeologists as Recent Indian, the remains of which have been found at Point Revenge. On the island of Newfoundland, the Little Passage people, named for the site near Gaultois on Newfoundland's south coast, were also Recent Indians and the direct ancestors of the Beothuk.

Conclusion

The history of the peoples of Atlantic Canada before European contact shifts constantly as new archaeological evidence emerges and gives rise to new theories. Many questions remain unanswered, but it is now possible to trace the main outlines of a story of continuous human occupation beginning with the arrival of Paleo-Indians more than 10,000 years ago. What we can say for certain is that archaeologists have opened a fascinating window on past cultures in the Atlantic region, which has a long history of peoples encountering environmental change, new technologies, and new populations.

Further Readings

Atlantic Geoscience Society. 2001. *The Last Billion Years: A Geological History of the Maritime Provinces*. Halifax: Nimbus Publishing.

Blair, Susan, ed. 2004. *Wolastoqiyik Ajemseg: The People of Beautiful River at Jemseg*, Vol 2: *Archaeological Results*. Fredericton: Archaeological Services, Heritage Branch, Culture and Sports Secretariat.

Colman-Sadd, S., and S.A. Scott. 2004. *Newfoundland and Labrador: Traveller's Guide to the Geology*. St John's: Government of Newfoundland and Labrador.

Davis, Stephen A. 1994. 'Early Societies: Sequences of Change', in Phillip A. Buckner and John G. Reid, eds, *The Atlantic Region to Confederation*. Toronto and Fredericton: University of Toronto and Acadiensis Press, 3–21.

Rankin, Lisa. 2008. 'Native Peoples from the Ice Age to the Extinction of the Beothuk,' in Newfoundland Historical Society, *Short History of Newfoundland and Labrador*. Portugal Cove–St Philip's: Bolder Publications, 1–22.

Food for Thought

Daniels, John D. 1992. 'The Indian Population of North America in 1492', *The William and Mary Quarterly*, 3rd series 49, 2 (April): 298–320.

Recommended Websites

Glacial Ice
http://www.entrenet.com/~groedmed/glaciers.html

Gros Morne National Park
http://www.pc.gc.ca/pn-np/nl/grosmorne/index_e.asp

Joggins Fossil Cliffs
http://www.jogginsfossilcliffs.net/

The Natural History of Nova Scotia
http://museum.gov.ns.ca/mnh/nature/umbrell2.htm

Newfoundland and Labrador Natural Environment
http://www.heritage.nf.ca/environment/ne_contents.html

Chapter 2

Aboriginal Peoples

With the arrival of Europeans in the late fifteenth century, a much more detailed picture of Aboriginal societies began to emerge. Europeans were intrigued by the 'New World' that they had found, and many of them wrote meticulous descriptions of its peoples and their ways of life. While their accounts must be treated with caution, they add an important dimension to the story told by the surviving material culture and the oral traditions of indigenous peoples.

In the Atlantic region the newcomers encountered at least five cultural groups, which they called Eskimo and Montagnais–Naskapi in Labrador, Beothuk in Newfoundland, and Micmac and Malecite in the Maritimes. These were not necessarily the names that those peoples used to identify themselves. In recent years, for example, northern people have objected to 'Eskimo', a term with obscure origins. They prefer to be called 'Inuit', meaning simply 'the people'—a term that many Aboriginal groups used at the time of contact to distinguish themselves from the other creatures with whom they shared the land. More recently, Aboriginal peoples have begun adopting names and spellings that reflect their own language structures rather than imposed Europeanized versions. Thus 'Micmac' becomes 'Mi'kmaq', 'Malecite' or 'Maliseet' becomes 'Wolastoqiyik', and 'Montagnais–Naskapi' becomes simply 'Innu'.

When Giovanni Caboto (John Cabot) embarked on his transatlantic voyage in 1497, the human population of the Americas was no less varied than that of Europe.[1] Natives of the Atlantic region lived on the eastern edge of a world that included complex empires, city-states, confederacies, and chiefdoms, as well as band communities like their own. The Labrador Inuit were the easternmost branch of a culture stretching across the Arctic, while the Mi'kmaq, Wolastoqiyik, Beothuk, and Innu belonged to the Algonkian language group, which occupied an extensive territory from the Atlantic to the Rockies. Essentially communal societies, they were largely self-sufficient, though in contact with each other.

All pre-contact peoples in the Americas shared a world view according to which humans were part of a cosmological order that included the land and its animals, the stars, and the sea. The universe functioned harmoniously only when natural forces were in balance—a condition maintained by elaborate rituals. Because of their strong spiritual beliefs, most of the surviving evidence of pre-contact Aboriginal societies takes the form of burial sites, not monuments to the living. What today would be called the natural and social sciences were highly developed. Before the arrival of Europeans, the American peoples had calculated the movement of the sun and stars and understood a great deal about the medicinal properties of plants.

As primarily hunter-gatherers, the Natives of the Atlantic region followed a seasonal round that allowed them to make the most effective use of the resources around them. They shared

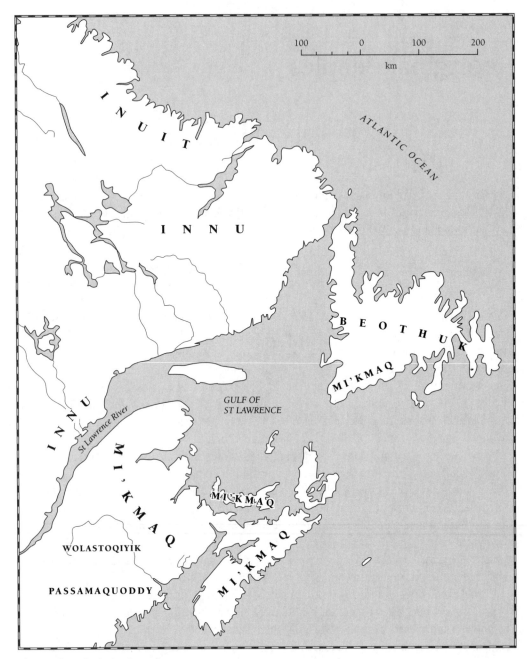

Aboriginal peoples in the sixteenth century.

characteristics with other northeastern Woodland cultures that dominated present-day New England and Quebec, but they also had access to the region's rich ocean resources. Although long winters, especially in Newfoundland and Labrador, sometimes made survival difficult, the Aboriginal peoples of the Atlantic region were relatively affluent by the standards of northern North America at the time of European contact.

The Mi'kmaq, Wolastoqiyik, and Passamaquoddy of the Maritimes

The Mi'kmaq in 1500 lived throughout what are now the Maritime provinces. While estimates of their numbers at the time of contact range from 3,500 to 200,000, the scholarly consensus now suggests a figure between 12,000 and 15,000.[2] The extended family, sometimes supplemented by a few unrelated individuals, was the basic unit of Mi'kmaq society. Headed by a chief, or *sakamow*, this unit formed the summer village that could number as many as 200 people, but broke up into smaller groups during the winter. Summer was also a time for Mi'kmaq leaders to come together to consult on matters of common interest.

By the eighteenth century the Mi'kmaq were divided into seven districts, each governed by a chief who presided over a council of chiefs from each district's communities. This form of political organization may have developed in response to European trade, but the significance of chiefs seems to have been deeply rooted in Mi'kmaq society. Nicolas Denys, a French fur trader who spent several decades in the Maritimes in the seventeenth century, noted that the Mi'kmaq greatly valued the genealogical traditions that linked them to a line of 'ancient chiefs' stretching back more than 20 generations.[3]

Mi'kmaq men were skilled hunters, using dogs to help them track down their prey, which were then dispatched with spears and arrows. Fish were so plentiful that they were easy to catch with three-pronged spears, loosely woven nets, and weirs. The Mi'kmaq method for trapping migrating birds was ingenious. The men would hunt these birds at night, floating their canoes among a flock of ducks or geese and then lighting torches. The light would confuse the birds and cause them to circle the torches, enabling the hunters to knock them down with long poles. The hunters' catch would be cooked in watertight containers made from birchbark stitched with spruce roots and sealed with spruce gum; heated stones from the fire would be placed in the pot until its contents boiled.

Although the Mi'kmaq diet featured fish, fowl, and other animals, the moose played a central role in the Mi'kmaq economy. Every part of the animal was used. Its meat was eaten fresh and dried, its bones rendered a highly nutritious moose butter called *cacamos*, and the skin was fashioned by Mi'kmaq women into clothing, moccasins, carrying bags, and snowshoe webbing. Antlers and bones were turned into tools, weapons, and needles. Moose brains were used in tanning skins, dewclaws became rattles, shin bones were carved into dice, tendons served as thread, hair was used in embroidery, and hoofs yielded an ingredient used to treat epilepsy. While moose were killed throughout the year, they were most easily caught in the winter, when snowdrifts impeded their escape from hunters speeding along on snowshoes.

While Europeans reported on the Mi'kmaq's diet and hunting practices, they also frequently commented on Mi'kmaq gender roles, courtship practices, and family relationships. According to Chrestien Le Clercq, a Récollet missionary in the Gaspé region in the second half of the seventeenth century, the Mi'kmaq were patriarchal, subordinating women and 'mooseless' younger males to the authority of adult men:

Oral History

To preserve the fire, especially in winter, we would entrust it to the care of our war-chief's women, who took turns to preserve the spark, using half-rotten pine wood covered with ash. Sometimes this fire lasted up to three moons. When it lasted the span of three moons, the fire became sacred and magical to us, and we showered with a thousand praises the chief's woman who had been the fire's guardian during the last days of the third moon. We would all gather together and, so that no member of the families which had camped there since the autumn should be absent, we sent out young men to fetch those who were missing. Then, when our numbers were complete, we would gather round and, without regard to age or rank, light our pipes at the fire. We would suck in the smoke and keep it in our mouths, and one by one we would puff it into the face of the woman who had last preserved the spark, telling her that she was worthy above all to share in the benign influence of the Father of Light, the Sun, because she had so skilfully preserved his emanations.[4]

It is now widely recognized that oral traditions are more reliable than historians used to believe. Certainly this account of a Mi'kmaq cultural tradition, recorded in the 1740s on what is now Prince Edward Island, is powerfully evocative. It also reveals more about the problems that a Maritime winter posed for the region's indigenous people than any inert artifact could. At the same time, it leaves many unanswered questions. We have no way of knowing, for example, whether the practice described here was still current in the 1740s, or how widespread it may have been. Moreover, although the account is attributed to Chief Arguimaut (L'kimu), it was preserved for posterity by a Roman Catholic missionary, the Abbé Pierre Maillard. The evidence of ethnographers is rarely accepted without scrutiny today, and we must not lose our critical perspective when we discover a rare archival document. Many of the Europeans who first came into contact with Aboriginal peoples had a Christian world view, a sense of cultural superiority, and a gendered perspective that often led them to misinterpret—perhaps deliberately, perhaps unconsciously—what they heard and saw. For all its seeming authenticity, this oral account must be treated like any other historical evidence: as the product of a particular time and place, with no greater claim to truth than any other kind of text.

The women have no command among the Indians. They must needs obey the orders of their husbands. They have no rights in councils, nor in the public feasts. It is the same, as to this, with the young men who have not yet killed any moose, the death of which opens the portal to the honours of the Gaspesian nation, and gives to the young men the right to assist at public and private assemblies. One is always a young man, that is to say, one has no more rights than the children, the women, and the girls, as long as he has not killed a moose.[5]

Polygamy was practised, Le Clercq reported, and marriages were easily dissolved, especially when no children were involved. The method of carrying infants drew Le Clercq's particular attention. 'In place of a cradle, they make the children rest upon a little board, which they cover with the skins of beaver or with some other furs.' Both the cradleboard and the infant's clothing were adorned with beadwork, porcupine quills, and painted designs, which Le Clercq believed were used 'to beautify it, and to render it just so much the finer in proportion as they love their children'.

Like all Aboriginal peoples in the Atlantic region, the Mi'kmaq had a complex world view that helped them to explain their existence. They considered the sun and moon to be the ancestors of 'People' who lived on the Earth, which was part of a spiritual universe made up of Six Worlds. In addition to the Earth World, there was the World beneath the Water, the World beneath the Earth, the World above the Sky, and the World above the Earth. After death, the People went to the Ghost World, which a very few managed to visit while still living.

The Mi'kmaq universe formed itself out of Power, which was manifested in people, animals, plants, and phenomena such as winds, weather, seasons, and directions. Not only could one form of power change into another—a person into a wolf, or a stone into a person—but the character or state of mind of the power force could also change, from good to evil, for instance, or strong to weak. This notion of power made for an unpredictable universe, but it encouraged people to acquire and use power responsibly through proper behaviour.

At the time of contact, people with special spiritual powers played a major role in articulating the Mi'kmaq sense of the world and the appropriate ways of living in it. Legends helped to remind people of spiritual truths, and signs representing spiritual phenomena, such as the sun, were often incorporated as intricate designs on clothing, adornments, and other material possessions. Believing that dreams and trances helped them to contact spirit powers, the Mi'kmaq placed great emphasis on developing ways to achieve altered states of consciousness and paid close attention to the knowledge revealed in their dreams.

The Wolastoqiyik, who lived in what is now southwestern New Brunswick and northeastern Maine, shared many characteristics with the Mi'kmaq. According to Mi'kmaq lore, the Wolastoqiyik were a breakaway tribe, but evidence suggests that their differences were rooted in deeper cultural patterns. In the early contact period, the Wolastoqiyik were distinguished from other Aboriginal groups in the Atlantic region by their practice of growing corn, which they might have done even before the arrival of Europeans.

Both Native oral history and early European records report that there was conflict between the Wolastoqiyik and their Mi'kmaq neighbours, but we have no way of knowing the extent of the enmity in the pre-contact period. What is clear is that when the Mi'kmaq gained access to European weapons, they used their military advantage to expand their control over the Gaspé Penin-

This engraving of an 'homme Acadien' shows a Mi'kmaq marked with various symbols, including both a sun and crosses. LAC, c-21112.

sula as well as portions of the St John River watershed, which had traditionally been Wolastoqiyik territory.[6] By the seventeenth century, the Mi'kmaq were scoring victories over the Abenaki, an Algonkian tribe, as far south as the Saco River in Maine. The Passamaquoddy occupied the north shore of the Bay of Fundy, the Gulf of Maine, and the St Croix River and its tributaries. Their seasonal rhythms were much like those of the Wolastoqiyik, with whom they also shared a common language.[7] With seafood as their main source of survival, the Passamaquoddy were skilled in catching such species as porpoises and pollock with their well-aimed spears. The name is an anglicization of the Passamaquoddy word *peskotomuhkati*, which means 'pollock-spearer' or 'those of the place where pollock are plentiful'.

When the boundary was drawn between British North America and the United States following the American Revolutionary War (1775–83), the Passamaquoddy found themselves living under two political jurisdictions, neither of which recognized Native claims. The Passamaquoddy eventually received an Indian Township Reservation in eastern Washington County in Maine, but those who live in Charlotte County, New Brunswick, have no First Nation status. Some Passamaquoddy continue to seek the return of territory now situated in St Andrews, New Brunswick, which they claim as Oonasqamkuk, a Passamaquoddy ancestral home and burial ground.

The Beothuk, Innu, and Inuit of Newfoundland and Labrador

Until recently not a great deal was known about the Beothuk, an Algonkian people who chose to remain apart from Europeans and became extinct in the late 1820s. Perhaps numbering as many as 2,000 in 1500, they were among the first Aboriginal people whom Europeans encountered in North America. Because they painted themselves with red ochre, they may have inspired the term 'Red Indian'. For food and clothing the Beothuk depended primarily on caribou, which they hunted during the herds' fall migrations, although marine resources such as seals, seabirds, fish, and shellfish were also important. Moving frequently to accommodate the seasonal round, the Beothuk travelled long distances in distinctive, light-weight birchbark canoes and lived in easily assembled wigwams (sometimes conical, sometimes oval or multi-sided) covered with hides or birchbark.

The Beothuk were probably in contact with the Innu, who by 1500 were living on the south coast and interior of Labrador, but they tended to stay away from the Inuit. The Innu depended on what the interior could provide, principally caribou and a variety of freshwater fish, which they caught in the winter and spring. During the summer months they gathered on the coast in large groups to hunt whales, seals, and saltwater fish before breaking into small bands to winter in the interior.

Like other Aboriginal groups in the region, the Innu shared the rewards of a successful hunt and encouraged egalitarian values. Open displays of anger were repressed, decisions were made through discussion and consensus, and conformity was encouraged through joking and ridicule. Patience and good humour were considered important virtues. In contrast to Europeans, who practised a harsh discipline aimed largely at breaking children's will, the Innu spared their children physical punishment. Europeans remarked that, although gender roles were clearly defined among the Innu, the group's women appeared to be relatively independent and powerful. They dominated the life-sustaining lodge hearth, controlled the distribution of food, and readily left husbands who were not good providers.

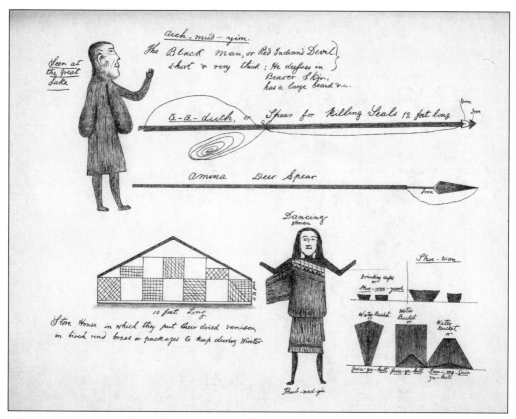

Before her death in 1829, Shawnadithit, the last surviving Beothuk on the island of Newfoundland, drew these images depicting aspects of her culture. LAC, c-28544.

Primarily a coastal people, the Labrador Inuit were based in the area north of Hamilton Inlet. They moved further south on a seasonal basis, especially after Europeans arrived in the Strait of Belle Isle. During the fall and winter the Inuit lived in semi-subterranean sod houses at the mouths of fiords, the men hunting whales and seals from their kayaks and umiaks until the sea froze, when they would hunt seals through the ice. In the spring some fished through lake ice, while others built snow houses on the outer islands and lived on seals, fish, and mussels. In early summer everyone moved to the islands and lived in skin tents. In July the Inuit congregated at places where salmon was plentiful before beginning the inland caribou hunt.

The success of the hunt was assisted by shamans, or *angakut*, who mediated between the human and spirit worlds. In 1772 the Moravian missionaries at Nain reported that a female shaman 'fell into a trance, when her soul took a tour through the inland parts, where she saw a vast quantity of Rain Deer. Upon this the Esquimaux went to the inlet as directed by her, where they saw and got many deer.'[8] Shamans also treated sickness, which was thought to be caused by evil spirits, and in general helped Inuit to make sense of their lives and deaths.

One of the earliest European images of North America is a woodcut of an Inuit mother and daughter, probably from Labrador, who were captured by French fishermen and taken to Europe

The Capture of an Inuit Woman and her Child

Printed in Augsburg, Germany, in 1567, this woodcut is the first known European depiction of Inuit drawn from life. From W.C. Sturtevant, 'The First Inuit Depiction by Europeans', *Etudes Inuit Studies* 4, 1–2 (1980): 47–9.

Europeans frequently took Native people captive and either forced them to work as slaves or put them on display as curiosities. The Inuit woman and child shown in this woodcut were captured in 1566 on the Labrador coast by French mariners and taken to Europe. The text reads (in part):

In this year 1566 there arrived in Antwerp . . . a savage woman (a small person) together with her little daughter, and she is shaped and clothed as this picture shows, and was found in Nova Terra. . . . [T]his woman with her husband and little child were met by the French . . . and the husband was shot through his body with an arrow. However he would not surrender but took his stand bravely to defend himself. . . . Finally he was struck and wounded in his throat so severely that he fell to the ground and died from the wound. This man was 12 feet tall and had in twelve days killed eleven people with his own hand, French and Portuguese, in order to eat them. . . . [T]hen they took the woman with her child and brought her away; and none of the Frenchmen could understand a single word of hers or speak with her at all. But she was taught enough in 8 months that it was known she had eaten many men. Her clothing is made of seal skins.

. . . The paint marks she has on her face are entirely blue [and] . . . cannot be taken off again. . . . Her body is yellow-brown. . . . The woman was 20 years old when she was captured . . . the child 7 years. Let us thank God the Almighty that He has enlightened us with His word so that we are not such savage people and man-eaters as are in this district, that this woman was captured and brought out of there, since she knows nothing of the true God, but lives almost more wickedly than the beasts. God grant that she be converted to acknowledge Him. Amen.[9]

in 1566. That the fishermen killed the woman's husband before taking their captives foreshadowed the hostile relations that quickly developed between Inuit and newcomers. Writing in the early seventeenth century, Samuel de Champlain noted that the Inuit were 'very malicious . . . [attacking] fishermen, who in self defence arm small vessels to protect the boats which put to sea to fish cod'.[10] In later years the French would be slow to establish fishing and sealing stations on the Labrador coast, in part because of their justified fear of the Inuit.

Conclusion

Every Aboriginal group in the Atlantic region would have had dramatic tales to tell once Europeans began to frequent their coasts in the early sixteenth century. In each case the encounter brought disease, death, and social and economic dislocation, even to those who, like the Mi'kmaq, had initially welcomed the Europeans and what they had to offer. The least affected were the most remote, the Inuit and northern Innu bands. Those who lived around the Gulf of St Lawrence bore the brunt of the first European efforts to explore, fish, trade, and spread the Christian faith.

Further Readings

Blair, Susan, ed. 2004. *Wolastoqiyik Ajemseg: The People of Beautiful River at Jemseg*, Vol. 2: *Archaeological Results*. Fredericton: Archaeological Services, Heritage Branch, Culture and Sports Secretariat.

Dickason, Olive P. 2008. *Canada's First Nations: A History of Founding Peoples from Earliest Times*, 4th edn. Toronto: Oxford University Press.

McGhee, Robert. 1996. *Ancient People of the Arctic*. Vancouver: University of British Columbia Press.

Marshall, Ingeborg. 1996. *A History and Ethnography of the Beothuk*. Montreal: McGill-Queen's University Press.

Prins, Harald E.L. 1996. *The Mi'kmaq: Resistance, Accommodation, and Cultural Survival*. Fort Worth: Harcourt Brace College Publishers.

Ray, Arthur J. 2005. *I Have Lived Here Since the World Began: An Illustrated History of Canada's Native People*, rev. edn. Toronto: Lester/Key Porter.

Food for Thought

Martijn, Charles A. 2003. 'Early Mi'kmaq Presence in Southern Newfoundland: An Ethnohistorical Perspective, c. 1500–1763', *Newfoundland Studies* 19, 1 (Fall): 44–102.

Recommended Websites

Aboriginal Peoples of Newfoundland and Labrador
http://www.heritage.nf.ca/aboriginal/default.html

Innu-Aimun (Innu of Labrador and Quebec)
http://www.innu-aimun.ca/modules.php

Mi'kmaq-Maliseet Institute
http://www.unbf.ca/education/mmi/

Mi'kmaq Portraits Collection
http://museum.gov.ns.ca/mikmaq/

Mi'kmaq Resource Centre
http://mrc.uccb.ns.ca/

Pepamuteiati Nitassinat [Innu Place Names]
http://www.innuplaces.ca/index.php?lang=en

Chapter 3

European Encounters, 1000–1598

When there were no people in this country but Indians, and before any others became known, a young woman had a singular dream. . . . A small island came floating in towards the land, with tall trees on it, and living beings. [The shaman] pondered the girl's dream but could make nothing of it. The next day an event occurred that explained all. What should they see but a singular little island, as they supposed, which had drifted near to the land and become stationary there. There were trees on it, and branches to the trees, on which a number of bears . . . were crawling about. . . . What was their surprise to find that these supposed bears were men.[1]

Josiah Jeremy's account of one Mi'kmaq community's first sighting of hirsute Europeans and their tall-masted sailing ships was recorded by Silas Rand, a nineteenth-century Baptist missionary. What encounter this story describes is impossible to determine, but one thing is clear: the meeting of two very different cultures marked the beginning of a new era for both.

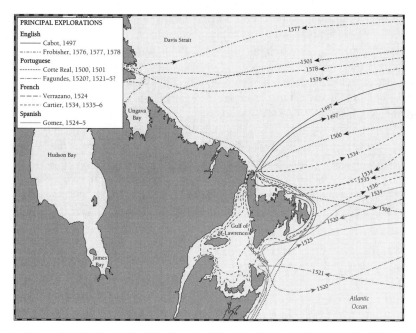

Map covering European exploration in the sixteenth century. Based on Harris, ed. *Historical Atlas of Canada I*, Plate 19.

Across the Atlantic

During the second half of the fifteenth century, Europeans began to look outward from their own continent and from the Mediterranean which had, hitherto, been the centre of European trade, commerce, and culture. Emerging nation-states on the Atlantic littoral—Spain, Portugal, England, and France—began to look for new opportunities and, in so doing, created an Atlantic world within which the American 'New World', Africa, and Europe became firmly interconnected.

This reorientation from the Mediterranean to the Atlantic was driven initially by commercial priorities. As the Middle East increasingly came under the control of hostile Islamic forces, Europeans searched for routes that would allow them to trade directly with Asia. Developments in sea-going technology made such options possible. With better ships and navigational devices, long-distance voyages became possible and ambitious sailors, driven by the lure of economic gain, were prepared to take the risk. International rivalry was another factor driving European exploration. While monarchs generally respected each others' spheres of influence, they were eager not to fall behind in staking claim to overseas territories.

Overseas ventures were also part of a dramatic cultural awakening in Europe fuelled by the Renaissance, a rebirth of interest in the learning and cultural achievements of ancient Greece and Rome. Under the influence of Renaissance thinkers, Europeans began to reflect on broad areas of knowledge and ask troubling questions: Was the Pope's word final on matters religious and political? Could the earth be round instead of flat? In the middle of the fifteenth century Johannes Gutenberg invented the mechanical printing press, which made it easier to disseminate new ideas, and Europe quickly became a hotbed of intellectual ferment. It was in this context that exploring new frontiers geographically and intellectually became more relevant.

The Portuguese and the Spanish on the Iberian peninsula of Europe were the first to establish seaborne empires and were soon entrenched in central and south America and the Far East. France and England followed later and more cautiously. Both were preoccupied by nation building and by the religious tensions precipitated by the Reformation, which in the sixteenth century divided Europeans according to Roman Catholic and Protestant beliefs. Moreover, the English began their empire in Ireland, which for a time diverted attention from Atlantic adventures. Nevertheless, by the early seventeenth century what is now Atlantic Canada was firmly enmeshed in commercial networks based in France and England, the Iberians having retreated from North Atlantic enterprises. Increasingly interested in permanent possession and settlement, both France and England began to make claims of sovereignty and to establish plantations in Newfoundland, in Acadia (the present-day Maritimes), along the St Lawrence River, and down the eastern seaboard. Fragile, bound to the metropole, and often dependent on the goodwill of (or alliance with) Aboriginal populations, these settlements were the first tentative steps in the creation of powerful European empires in North America.

The Norse

The first Europeans to reach Atlantic Canada were the Norse. Their arrival in Labrador and Newfoundland more than 1,000 years ago marked the final stage in a process that had begun in Scandinavia several centuries earlier. Waves of migrants, often preceded by the raiders we know as

Vikings, spread across northern Europe and then westward over the North Atlantic. Unlike their successors 500 years later, they were looking not for Asia but for land that they could settle.

Eirik the Red colonized southeastern Greenland late in the tenth century. Shortly thereafter, in 986, a merchant-shipowner named Bjarni Herjolfsson was blown off-course while travelling to the new settlement. Finding himself sailing along an unknown coastline, he headed north and then east to Greenland without taking time to explore, but his voyage was remembered. A few years later, Leif Eiriksson retraced Bjarni's route in reverse. According to evidence from the Norse sagas, Leif found three lands. The first he called Helluland, which consisted primarily of rock and ice (it was probably Baffin Island). The second, Markland, was flat, wooded, and almost certainly part of southern Labrador. Leif then reached a country he called Vinland, with grassy meadows and well-stocked rivers. The expedition wintered there before returning to Greenland.

Table 3.1	Timeline
c. 1000	Greenland Norse reach northeastern America.
1492	Columbus encounters the Caribbean.
1497	John Cabot reaches Newfoundland.
1498	Cabot disappears on his second voyage.
1500	Gaspar Corte Real reaches 'Terra Verde'.
1502	First known English fishing voyage to Newfoundland.
1504	First known French fishing voyage to Newfoundland.
1508–9	Sebastian Cabot looks for the northwest passage.
1520s	Basques enter the Newfoundland fishery.
1524	Giovanni da Verrazzano sails along the North American coast.
1525	Possible Portuguese colony on Cape Breton.
1534	Jacques Cartier's first voyage to the Gulf of St Lawrence.
1550s	French develop offshore bank fishery; Basques develop whaling industry in the Strait of Belle Isle.
1580s	English West Country ports begin to enter Newfoundland fishery; decline of the Portuguese and Spanish fisheries.

Leif Eiriksson made several later expeditions, and others explorers followed. The most ambitious of the known Norse ventures was that of Thorfinn Karslefni, who attempted to establish a settlement in Vinland and remained there for several years. Like at least one of its predecessors, Thorfinn's expedition found it impossible to coexist with the people living in the region, whom the Norse called Skraelings—a highly derogatory term meaning 'wretches' or 'savages'. Largely as a result of conflicts with the Skraelings, Thorfinn retreated to Greenland. The Norse never created a permanent settlement in Vinland and stopped travelling there. Whether this encounter had any impact in Europe is uncertain, but some scholars think that the story lingered on and that later explorers may well have heard rumours of lands to the west.

Europeans on the Move

The possibility of other transatlantic voyages before the late fifteenth century has generated enormous interest and a large literature of uneven quality. Some think that St Brendan set sail in a curragh from Dingle Bay in Ireland with 17 monks sometime in the sixth century and landed in Newfoundland or some other part of America. Others claim that the Welsh Prince Madoc reached Florida in 1170, or that the Scottish Prince Henry Sinclair landed in Chedabucto Bay on 2 June

L'Anse aux Meadows

The location of Vinland has been debated since at least 1837, when the Danish scholar C.C. Rafn proposed the Rhode Island area. Various other sites along the eastern seaboard of North America were suggested from time to time, including Newfoundland's Northern Peninsula. In 1914 William A. Munn, a local merchant and amateur historian, identified L'Anse aux Meadows as the most likely place. It was there that direct physical evidence of Norse occupation was discovered by Anne Stine and Helge Ingstad in 1961. Since 1978 it has been a World Heritage Site.

It seemed difficult at first to reconcile the L'Anse aux Meadows site (the name is from the French *L'Anse aux Méduses*) with some of the evidence from Norse sagas, especially references to grapes. Furthermore, why had the Norse built in such an exposed location? The consensus today is that Vinland was not a single place, but a region which encompassed the Gulf of St Lawrence. L'Anse aux Meadows may well have been a base camp for exploration and for the transshipment of goods—mainly lumber and wild grapes—found elsewhere. It was never meant to be a permanent colony.[2]

Although similar to other Norse sites of the eleventh century, the settlement at L'Anse aux Meadows differed in several important ways other than its exposure. Unlike most Norse locations, there is no evidence of livestock or other animals, nor of barns or byres. Of the nine buildings that have been excavated at the site eight were sod dwellings and the other was a small forge. The houses were designed for year-round habitation and could accommodate between 70 and 90 people. Although the artifacts and debris that have survived suggest that women were present, most of the inhabitants were men. The main activities seem to have been carpentry, iron manufacture, and smithing, activities associated with boat repair and possibly boat building.

The base camp did not have a long life. Although relations with the local inhabitants were confrontational, it is unlikely that they drove the Norse out of the region. Vinland was a long and difficult journey from Greenland, and its resources were not vital. For some time, however, the Norse continued to visit Markland (Labrador).

1398 (an embellishment has Sinclair burying the holy grail at Oak Island, on the southern shore of what is now Nova Scotia). The more plausible theories limit themselves to suggesting that English vessels from Bristol and Portuguese vessels from the Azores may have reached North America sometime between 1450 and 1492.

The first to undertake the systematic exploration of the Atlantic were the Portuguese, who probed south along the African coast and then began reaching further west. Their goal was to develop new sea routes to India and other parts of Asia, in an effort to share in the lucrative spice trade monopolized by the Italians. By the end of the fifteenth century, the Portuguese had rounded the Cape of Good Hope and reached India, sparking increasing interest all along the European Atlantic seaboard in the possibility of reaching Asia by sailing west.

Europeans had known for centuries that the earth was round, but for good reasons were reluctant to venture too far out to sea. With the development of more seaworthy vessels and improvements in navigational instruments in the fifteenth century, captains were better able to establish their positions, set their courses with reasonable accuracy, and sail for days without sighting land. These advances enabled the Genoa-born seaman, Christoforo Corombo (Christopher Columbus), sailing in the name of the Spanish Crown in 1492, to reach what he (and everyone else in Europe) thought was Asia, but was in fact the Caribbean. Five years later Zuan Caboto (John Cabot) also reached what was assumed to be Asia, where he raised a cross along with the banners of England and Venice.

To John Cabot goes the credit for bringing widespread public attention to the abundance of cod in the northwest Atlantic that ultimately attracted permanent European interest. Commissioned by King Henry VII to 'sail to all parts, regions, and coasts of the eastern, western, and northern sea' and authorized 'to conquer, occupy, and possess whatever towns, castles, cities, and islands, he discovered', Cabot returned to England in August 1497 bringing tales of 'new founde landes' whose adjacent waters swarmed 'with fish which can be taken not only with the net, but in baskets let down with a stone'.

Because the evidence is scanty, the location of Cabot's landfall has been the subject of considerable debate. There are, roughly speaking, three groups of interpretations: those that favour

John Cabot

Cabot's ship *The Matthew*.
Photo: The Newfoundland
Historical Society.

Zuan Caboto, later anglicized to John Cabot, was born in Italy around 1457, but where is uncertain. His family moved to Venice, where he was naturalized as a Venetian citizen in or about 1476. He married a Venetian, and his sons were born there.

Cabot was a businessman and merchant, possibly involved in the valuable spice trade with what we now call the Middle East—modern Lebanon, Syria, and Palestine— where spices arrived overland from the Far East. Given the value of the trade, there was intense interest in finding new, direct maritime routes to Cathay—India and China—where the spices originated. Cabot evidently shared this enthusiasm and by the later 1480s he was in Spain and Portugal. Cabot failed to find patrons, perhaps because of the apparent success of Christopher Columbus's first voyage.

Thus Cabot moved on to England. Mariners from Bristol were already probing into the North Atlantic, and it seems that Cabot had a scheme to reach Cathay by sailing across northern latitudes. He received letters patent from King Henry VII in March 1496, authorizing him to make such voyages on behalf of the English Crown. Backed by Bristol merchants, Cabot made his first attempt in a single vessel in 1496: it was a failure. The second attempt, in 1497 in *The Matthew*, reached an American landfall. The third, undertaken the next year, is shrouded in mystery. It was during this voyage that Cabot disappeared—there is a legend that he met his end at Grates Cove in Conception Bay, Newfoundland.

Cabot's second son, Sebastian, also went into the exploration business. He may have accompanied his father on the 1497 voyage. Until the twentieth century there was confusion about which Cabot had done what, and John's accomplishments were often attributed to the son.[3]

a landfall in the Strait of Belle Isle region; those that argue for the east coast of Newfoundland; and those that champion Cape Breton or points further south. Most Maritime historians used to support the claims of Cape Breton, arguing that Cabot would have been carried south by storms and ocean currents and that cartographic evidence supports their case. Newfoundlanders have consistently dismissed these arguments, holding it as an article of faith that Cabot's first landfall was Cape Bonavista. How, they ask, could he have missed Newfoundland? And does not John Mason's 1617 map bear the legend 'Bona Vista Caboto primum reperta'? Today most scholars lean towards a northern landfall, somewhere either side of the Strait of Belle Isle. Cabot would have sailed north along the Irish coast before turning west, and as a skilled navigator would have been capable of holding that latitude.

Wherever the exact location of the place that Cabot described, Henry VII was pleased by the mariner's apparent success and authorized a larger expedition in 1498, financed by Bristol merchants. Virtually nothing is known about this voyage. It seems likely that Cabot's ships would have returned to the lands found in 1497 and then sailed south, looking in vain for 'Cipango' (China). Information on early-sixteenth-century maps suggests that some of Cabot's men returned to describe their findings. There were a few more voyages from Bristol to the new lands, but the city's merchants were, for the most part, more interested in trade than fishing. It was not until the second half of the sixteenth century that England began to take a renewed interest in what North America had to offer.

Meanwhile, Spain and Portugal had established that the Atlantic was the highway to the immense resource-base of the Americas. In 1494, by the Treaty of Tordesillas and with the blessing of the Pope, they divided the non-Christian world between them. A north–south line was drawn west of the Cape Verde Islands: territory west of the line was awarded to Spain and east of it to Portugal. Although Cabot may have been trespassing, his findings stimulated further exploration. Assuming that the 'new' lands in the North Atlantic lay within his sphere, King Manoel of Portugal authorized a number of voyages by inhabitants of the Azores, sometimes in alliance with Bristol merchants. In 1499 João Fernandes, a small landowner or 'labrador', reached Greenland, which as a result was called 'Labrador' on some early maps. In the sixteenth century the name was transferred to the coast of North America, where it has since remained. In 1500 Gaspar Corte-Real reached 'Terra Verde'—probably Newfoundland. There he captured 60 of the local inhabitants and delivered them to Lisbon, where they attracted widespread interest. According to the Venetian ambassador, the captives were 'tall, well-built' and 'will make the best slaves I have ever seen'.[4] The Corte-Reals were awarded a 'captaincy' in eastern Newfoundland, and Gaspar returned to North America with three ships in 1501, but his vessel disappeared. A similar fate befell his brother Miguel in 1502. A third brother made a futile attempt to find them both in 1503.

Although these voyages provided cartographers with important new information, it was not yet understood that the 'new founde landes' were part of a new continent. Contemporary maps show the 'discoveries' of Columbus, Cabot, and the Portuguese either as islands in the ocean or as connected with Greenland and Asia. An important contribution to a better understanding of North American geography was made by Giovanni da Verrazzano. In 1524, on behalf of France's King François I, he explored the coast between the Carolinas and Cape Breton, and possibly part of Newfoundland as well. His purpose had been to find a passage to Asia, but instead he ascertained the existence of a continuous North American coastline and established the first formal link between France and North America. Similar voyages were made in 1524–5 on behalf of Spain by Estevão Gomes (who kidnapped a large number of Native people, probably on the Nova Scotian coast), and for England's King Henry VIII by John Rut, who in 1527 sailed from Labrador to the Caribbean. It is probable but not certain that the Portuguese navigator João Alvarez Fagundes, who in 1521 registered his discoveries from an earlier voyage to the Atlantic region, led an expedition in 1525 from the Azores to establish a colony, possibly on Cape Breton Island. Its failure has been attributed to the climate and the hostility of the local inhabitants.

In 1534 François I commissioned Jacques Cartier to sail beyond Newfoundland to 'discover certain islands and countries where it is said a great quantity of gold and other precious things are to be found'. From a landfall near Bonavista, Cartier sailed through the Strait of Belle Isle and circumnavigated the Gulf of St Lawrence, thinking that it was an inland sea. He found the north shore of the gulf uninviting, but on sighting Prince Edward Island on a warm summer day he proclaimed it 'the best-tempered region one can possibly see'. He spent little time exploring it and seems not to have determined that it was an island. On his second voyage, in 1535, he found the entrance to the St Lawrence River. He and his men spent the winter of 1535–6 near present-day Quebec City, and in 1541–2 he participated in an unsuccessful attempt to establish a permanent European settlement there.

With Cartier's voyages the first phase in the European discovery of North America came to an end. The coastline from Mexico to Greenland had been explored, described, and mapped. For most of the explorers, who had no intention of staying, their voyages ended in disappointment. They found neither gold nor spices, and the Native people were sometimes hostile. Even the northwest passage to Asia eluded them, although for many years English explorers, beginning with Sebastian Cabot in 1508–09, tried to find it. Nevertheless, the first generation of explorers had located a region that some Europeans thought potentially rich and profitable. John Cabot might not have found spices or precious metals, but he had located a rich new source of fish.

The Fishery

The northwest Atlantic fishery quickly emerged as an exceedingly profitable business. In this period fishing employed more Europeans than any other occupation except agriculture. Fish was an important source of protein, easy to preserve and transport, and often replaced meat on Roman Catholic fast days. Moreover, work in the fishery served to train mariners for service at sea in time of war. Thus the Atlantic region rapidly became a pole of European activity comparable to that of the Caribbean and the Gulf of Mexico,[5] especially as there were opportunities to hunt whales and trade for furs. In the 1580s Spain was annually sending about 100 ships and 4,000 or 5,000 men to central America. Meanwhile, the Atlantic region attracted at least 400 European ships a year, possibly more, carrying approximately 10,000 men. They returned with some 200,000 metric tonnes of cod, and furs besides.

Although the English had sponsored Cabot, they were not the first to make significant use of the new fishing grounds. English markets were adequately supplied by local and Icelandic fisheries. Moreover, their major fishing ports were on the northeast coast—not the best starting point for transatlantic voyages. The ports of northern and eastern France were better positioned, and French markets for North Sea cod were already in place before the Cabot voyage. Vessels from

A reconstructed Basque chalupa at Red Bay, Labrador. Crewed by six men and powered by either sails or oars, shallops such as this one were used for whaling in the Strait of Belle Isle. Photo Kevin Redmond, Parks Canada, 1998.

Channel ports in Brittany and Normandy were therefore the first to fish regularly in Newfoundland waters, possibly as early as 1504. In their wake came fishermen from ports such as Bordeaux and La Rochelle, who after 1520 were joined by Basques from southern France and northern Spain. By the 1520s between 60 and 90 French vessels were crossing the Atlantic each year to the region known variously as 'the new found land', 'terre neuve', or 'terra de bacalhao'.

The role of Portugal in the north Atlantic fishery of the sixteenth century is a subject of some controversy. Certainly there was a Portuguese presence in the region, but whether it included a fishery of any significance is debatable. Given the current state of knowledge, the most that can be said is that the Portuguese sent over relatively few vessels and seem, on the whole, to have been more interested in the region's landward potential than in codfish. Nevertheless, Portuguese-derived place names line the shore south of St John's, among them Cape Spear (Cauo da espera), Ferryland (Farilham), and Cape Race (Capo raso).

While the Portuguese seem to have concentrated on Newfoundland, the French established a presence throughout the region. Bretons and Normans fished at Cape Breton and Gaspé. Later in the sixteenth century they moved along the coast of the Nova Scotia peninsula and into the Bay of Fundy. French and Spanish Basques often fished together off the Gaspé Peninsula, in the Gulf of St Lawrence, and in the Strait of Belle Isle. At Newfoundland, Bretons concentrated on the northeast coast between Cape St John and Cape Bauld (le Petit Nord). French and Basque vessels alike used the island's south coast, from Trepassey to Fortune Bay (la Côte du Chapeau Rouge), and Placentia emerged as the centre of the northwest Atlantic fishery. These were at first shore-based fisheries, but later in the century France also began to exploit the offshore banks—first the Grand Bank, then those off southern Newfoundland and in the Gulf.

Another form of mid-century diversification was the Basques development of a whaling industry in the Strait of Belle Isle. They established stations on the Labrador coast between Cape Charles and the St Paul River, the most important at Red Bay (Butus, or Hable des Buttes), where archaeologists have recently excavated both the buildings and the wreck of the *San Juan*, a galleon that sank there in 1565. At the height of the industry, some 30 Basque ships hunted right and bowhead whales annually, employing about 2,500 men. Although whalers sometimes remained in Labrador for the winter, such sojourns were usually involuntary, the result of delaying departure so long that the ships became icebound. Perhaps it was during one such enforced stay in Carroll's Cove (then known as Puerto Breton) that Joanes de Echaniz dictated his will—one of the earliest in Canada—on Christmas Eve 1584.

By the end of the sixteenth century the Iberian fishery was in decline. The Spanish government imposed new taxes and restrictions on trade and shipping, and inflation increased costs. Moreover, the war with England, which culminated in the disaster of the Spanish Armada in 1588, caused serious disruptions and financial losses. Annexed by Spain in 1580, Portugal saw its fortunes decline as well. Having depleted the whale stocks off Labrador, Basque whalers moved elsewhere. Spanish Basques continued to fish in the Gulf and off southeastern Newfoundland throughout the seventeenth century, but in decreasing numbers. An important result of these developments was that Iberia now needed to import significant quantities of fish.

In response, the French fleet expanded to perhaps as many as 500 vessels in the 1580s, and French fishermen began using the Gulf much more extensively than they had before, steadily moving further west into the St Lawrence River itself. The same market opportunity caught the attention of ports in southwestern England (the West Country) such as Poole, Plymouth, and Dartmouth. Anthony Parkhurst, a merchant who first came to Newfoundland in 1574, estimated in 1578 that no more than 50 English vessels made the trip to the island each year; by the early seventeenth century that number had increased to at least 200.

At first, conflict between the English and French fisheries appears to have been relatively rare. The French, sailing from ports along the coast from Normandy to the Pyrenees, produced both a 'wet' (or 'green') cure, in which the fish was taken into the ship's hold and heavily salted or packed in brine, and a 'dry' cure, in which the fish was split, lightly salted, and then dried on shore. The French market, particularly in the north and east, generally preferred green fish, but in response to demand from Spain, Portugal, and the Mediterranean, French Basques in particular produced dry-cured fish, which kept better in hot climates. By contrast, the English, sailing almost exclusively from West Country ports, produced only a dry cure (known as salt fish) and ignored the domestic market in favour of Iberia and southern Europe. For the English, salt fish was above all an article of trade, a commodity to be exchanged for bullion, fruits, wines, and exotic Mediterranean goods.

The production of salt fish demanded the building of seasonal fishing stations where the catch could be cleaned, salted, and dried. Increasingly, the English began to establish themselves on the eastern shores of the Avalon Peninsula, gradually forcing out other nationalities and extending as far north as Bonavista. Newfoundland's 'English Shore' was the first English foothold in what is now Canada.

Native–European Trade

In the sixteenth century there were no permanent, year-round European settlements in the Atlantic region. The fisheries were seasonal extensions of a European industry, reliant on a European workforce and European markets, and there seemed little need for overseas colonies. One factor that eventually helped to change this attitude was the development of the fur trade. Native people were usually eager to barter with the newcomers, and casual trading was already commonplace well before the 1530s. By the time of Cartier's first voyage, the Mi'kmaq in the Gaspé region were certainly familiar with the rituals of the fur trade. In July 1534 Cartier met a group of Mi'kmaq near the Baie des Chaleurs:

> The next day some of these Indians came in nine canoes to the point at the mouth of the cove where we lay at anchor with our ships. . . . As soon as they saw us they began to run away, making signs that they had come to barter with us; and held up some furs of small value, with which they clothe themselves. We likewise made signs to them that we wished them no harm, and sent two men on shore, to offer them some knives and other iron goods, and a red cap to give to their chief. Seeing this, they sent on shore part of their people with some of their furs; and the two parties traded together.[6]

Basque whaling stations attracted Inuit, Innu, and St Lawrence Iroquoians, all of whom placed a high value on metal objects, especially knives and axes. Local people sometimes pilfered metal items when Europeans were absent, but by mid-century the practice of trading furs had become well established. It was further stimulated after 1580 by the European demand for hats made of felted beaver fur.

Although the 'portage' trade—carried on by fishers, whalers, and sailors on their own behalf—continued, some French merchants began sending out vessels solely to buy furs along the coasts from Labrador to the Penobscot River in present-day Maine, and in the Gulf of St Lawrence. In 1583, for example, Étienne Bélanger of Rouen collected a valuable cargo that included moose, deer, and seal pelts as well as fine furs such as beaver, marten, and otter. Some outfitters had their vessels combine fishing and fur-trading. There was little fur-trading in Newfoundland largely because there were few Natives to trade with.

Seasonal though it was, the European presence had profound consequences for the region's Aboriginal people. European diseases eventually infected even people who had no direct contact with the newcomers, and Native populations diminished as a result, although the size of the decline is a matter of debate. At the same time, the fur trade upset traditional subsistence patterns and created dependence on Europeans for foodstuffs, alcohol, and metal implements, including copper cooking pots, knives, and guns. The Inuit showed considerable hostility to Europeans and the Beothuk avoided contact, but relations with other Native groups were generally good.

The Basques seem to have got on well with the Innu. In the last decade of the sixteenth century, the West Country sea captain Richard Whitbourne reported that the Innu were 'an ingenious and tractable people (being well used)', who worked in the whale fishery, helping to hunt and process the catch. The Mi'kmaq and Wolastoqiyik seem to have been eager to trade from the beginning, and gradually established close relations with the Europeans. Some Native people became middlemen, 'sailing in Basque shallops, wearing various items of European clothing . . . speaking a half-Basque,

DOCUMENT:
The Voyage of the *Grace* from Bristol, 1594

In the 1590s, Bristol merchants became interested in the resources of the Gulf of St Lawrence, particularly whales and walrus. Several expeditions were fitted out, among them the *Grace*, Sylvester Wyet master, carrying a Basque pilot. The voyage was not very successful; the *Grace* failed to find whales and had to catch a cargo of fish instead.

> We departed with the aforesaid Barke manned with twelve men . . . from Bristoll the 4 of Aprill 1594, and fell with Cape D'Espere [Spear] on the coast of Newefoundland the nineteenth of May . . . [and sailed along the south coast of Newfoundland, and then north.]
>
> In this bay of Saint George, we found the wrackes of 2 great Biskayne [Basque] ships, which had bene cast away three yeeres before: where we had some seven or eight hundred Whale finnes, and some yron bolts and chaines. . . . Here we found the houses of the Savages, made of firre trees bound together in the top and set round like a Dovehouse, and covered with the barkes of firre trees, we found also some part of their victuals, which were Deeres flesh roasted upon wooden spits at the fire, & a dish made of a ryne of a tree, sowed together with the sinowes of the Deere, wherein the oile was of the Deere. There were also foules called Cormorants, which they had pluckt and made ready to have dressed, and there we found a wooden spoone of their making. And we discerned the tracks of the feete of some fortie or fiftie men, women and children.
>
> . . . [We then] shaped our course over to that lond Isle of Natiscotec [Anticosti]. . . . Here we . . . found wonderfull faire and great Cod fish. . . . And after wee had searched two dayes and a night for the Whales which were wounded which we had hoped to have found there, we returned backe to the Southwarde . . . and so came to the Bay of Placentia and arrived . . . among the fishermen of Saint John de Luz and of Sibiburo and of Biskay, which were to the number of three score and odd sayles . . . of whom we were very well used. . . . There the men of Saint John and Sibiburo bestowed two pinnesses [pinaces] on us to make up our voyage with fish. Then wee departed over to the other side of the Bay . . . and fished so long, that in the ende the Savages came, and in the night, when our men were at rest, cut both our pinesse and our shippes boate away . . . yet it was our good fortune to . . . get them againe. Then for feare of a shrewder turne of the Savages, we departed . . . and arrived in Farrillon [Ferryland], and finding there two and twentie sayles of Englishmen, wee made up our fishing voyage to the full in that harborough . . . to our good content: and departing thence we arrived . . . in the river of Bristoll by the grace of God the 24 of September 1594.[7]

half-Indian trade jargon', and bartering furs from as far south as the coast of Maine with French or Basque traders in the Gulf of St Lawrence and at Tadoussac.[8]

Conclusion

The European discovery of North America in the late fifteenth century opened a period of encounter and exploration that gradually changed the way the world was perceived and experienced by

Native North Americans and Europeans alike. Fishing, fur-trading, and whaling ensured that the European presence would be permanent, even if it was in this period largely seasonal. Aboriginal peoples adapted in differing ways to the new arrivals, developing relationships that at first were not grossly imbalanced. This fluid, maritime world was the beginning of the modern Atlantic region and set in motion forces that would, over time, create a very different environment.

Further Readings

Fitzhugh, William, and Elizabeth I. Ward, eds. 2000. *Vikings: The North Atlantic Saga*. Washington: Smithsonian Institution Press.

Lewis-Simpson, Shannon, ed. 2003. *Vinland Revisited: The Norse World at the Turn of the First Millennium*. St John's: Historic Sites Association of Newfoundland and Labrador.

Pope, Peter E. 1997. *The Many Landfalls of John Cabot*. Toronto: University of Toronto Press.

Sawyer, P.H., ed. 2000. *The Oxford Illustrated History of the Vikings*. Oxford: Oxford University Press.

Wright, Ronald. 1993. *Stolen Continents: The New World Through Indian Eyes*. Toronto: Penguin.

Food for Thought

Pope, Peter. 2003. 'Comparisons: Atlantic Canada', in Daniel Vickers, ed., *A Companion to Colonial America*. Oxford: Blackwell, 489–507.

Recommended Websites

History of the Northern Cod Fishery
http://www.stemnet.nf.ca/cod/home1.htm

L'Anse aux Meadows Historic Site
http://www.pc.gc.ca/lhn-nhs/nl/meadows/index_e.asp

Newfoundland and Labrador Heritage: Exploration and Settlement
www.heritage.nf.ca/exploration/default.html

Chapter 4

Colonial Experiments, 1598–1632

The success of Europeans in colonizing the Americas is one of the most significant developments in early modern history. Until recently, historians assumed that the outcome was predetermined by the supposed moral, technological, and institutional superiority of Europeans. Now it is recognized that, although their advanced technology and complex governance structures may have been advantages, the newcomers could not colonize a strange new environment until they had learned how to survive in it. This knowledge was obtained partly through experience, but largely from the local inhabitants. Because the Europeans were unable to adapt quickly to the local environment, their colonization efforts in the sixteenth century failed and the small settlements established in the seventeenth century were unstable, subject to attacks from other Europeans and dependent on the tolerance of Aboriginal inhabitants. This situation changed little until the eighteenth century, by which time Europeans had become familiar features of the North American landscape.

Early Colonizers

Early colonization efforts reflected the weakness of the European powers competing for ascendancy in the region—primarily France and England. The rulers of these emerging nation-states delegated colonization and governance to private individuals and companies. This approach, coupled with persistent international conflict, made the region vulnerable to economic, political, and religious rivalries defined in Europe. With the Atlantic Ocean serving as much to link them to Europe as to distance them from it, the eastern margins of North America became a stage on which imperial characters acted out their competing roles.

Colonization efforts between 1578 and 1632 yielded some bold characters, high drama, and meagre results. In 1578 Queen Elizabeth I of England granted Sir Humphrey Gilbert, an early enthusiast for overseas ventures, a patent to explore and occupy those parts of eastern North America not already taken by the Spanish. Gilbert's dream was a colony in some part of what is now Massachusetts. In 1583 a reconnaissance expedition sailed from Southampton. Arriving off Newfoundland, the four ships made for St John's harbour to obtain food and other necessities. After convincing the captains of the 40 or so fishing vessels there that he was not a pirate, Gilbert was allowed to pass through the Narrows, where one of his ships ran anticlimactically aground. On 5 August he went ashore and formally claimed the land for the English Crown. He erected a pillar with the arms of England fixed to it, issued licenses to non-English ships, and appropriated shore premises that he then leased back to those who were using them. Before

Table 4.1	Timeline
1583	Sir Humphrey Gilbert claims Newfoundland for Elizabeth I.
1598	Marquis de la Roche attempts to establish a colony on Sable Island.
1604	Sieur de Monts attempts to establish a base at Ste-Croix.
1605	De Monts and Samuel de Champlain establish Port-Royal.
1606	Champlain founds the Ordre de Bon Temps.
1610	London and Bristol Company founds colony at Cupids; Membertou and his family baptized by a Roman Catholic priest at Port-Royal.
1613	Destruction of Saint-Sauveur and Port-Royal by Samuel Argall.
1621	Sir George Calvert founds the Colony of Avalon at Ferryland; James I of England grants 'Nova Scotia' to Sir William Alexander.
1629	Alexander establishes colonies on Cape Breton Island and at Port-Royal.
1632	England recognizes French claim to Acadia in the Treaty of Saint-Germain-en-Laye.

he reached the mainland of North America, the expedition began to fall apart. Gilbert eventually had to admit failure and decided to return home without reaching his destination. He drowned during the voyage, last seen sitting on board his vessel, a book in his hand, shouting, 'We are as neare to Heaven by sea as by land.'[1] Some historians have interpreted Gilbert's performance in St John's harbour as a significant event in the evolution of the first British empire, but since neither Gilbert's successors nor the English Crown followed up on his assertion of sovereignty, it meant little in practical terms.

It was not the English but the French who began European settlement of the Atlantic region. In 1598 King Henri IV ascended to the throne following a bloody civil war between Roman Catholics and Protestants (Huguenots) that had raged since 1562. Emulating the model established by other monarchs, he tried to restore his own treasury and the glory of his country through overseas ventures financed by private interests. Entrepreneurs were offered a monopoly of the fur trade in French-claimed territories if they would agree to transport settlers and support Christian missions among the local inhabitants. The first settlement attempt was made on Sable Island where, in 1598, the Marquis de la Roche shipped 10 soldiers and 40 settlers from Rouen. Only 11 were left by the spring of 1603, when the settlement was abandoned.

The next, ultimately more successful, initiative was led by Pierre Du Gua, Sieur de Monts, a Huguenot who in 1603 was appointed as Henri IV's viceroy in 'la Cadie', Canada, and 'autres terres de la Nouvelle France'. In return for a 10-year fur-trade monopoly, de Monts agreed to sponsor at least 60 settlers annually and to support efforts to convert Native peoples in the area to Christianity. The next year de Monts set out to establish a colony in 'la Cadie'. His entourage included two Roman Catholic priests, a Protestant minister, several noblemen, masons, and carpenters, a miner, a surgeon, and an apothecary, as well as sheep and hens. It also included seasoned explorers, among them Samuel de Champlain, a veteran of the religious wars and an enthusiastic proponent of European colonization.

After exploring the south coast of Nova Scotia and the Bay of Fundy (named 'la Baie Française' by de Monts), the group finally chose Dochet Island, at the mouth of the St Croix River, as the site for a settlement. The choice seems to have been dictated by a concern for military protection, but it proved disastrous. The harsh climate, lack of firewood, and inadequate provisions brought great hardship. By the spring, 35 of the 79 men who had wintered on the island had died of scurvy.

Port-Royal

All but three of those who survived the ordeal returned to France. One of the few determined to re-main was Champlain, who spent the summer of 1605 trying to locate a better site for a settlement. After exploring the coast as far as Cape Cod, he finally fixed on a sheltered basin on the south shore of the Bay of Fundy. The previous year, Champlain had described Port-Royal, today the Annapolis Basin, as 'the most suitable and pleasant for a settlement that we had seen'.[2] While the natural mili-tary protection, agricultural potential of the soil, and temperate climate were all good reasons for choosing Port-Royal, it had another advantage as well. The Mi'kmaq in the area under their chief, Membertou, were prepared to tolerate the intruders. Having experienced a hostile reception from Natives in the Cape Cod region, the French recognized that friendship with the local inhabitants was a decided asset in any effort to establish a colony.

The would-be colonists established a new base on the north shore of the sheltered basin. More tightly constructed than the one at St Croix, their 'habitation' included a 'very fine cellar, some five to six feet high', so that cider and other supplies would not freeze as they had done on the St Croix. More importantly, the French planted gardens and made friends with the Mi'kmaq in the area, with whom they continued to trade over the winter. The Natives were particularly fond of

Membertou

Membertou, chief of the small band of Mi'kmaq in the Port Royal region, impressed the French colonizers on whose records we must rely for information about his life. Exceptionally tall, Membertou also sported a beard, an unusual feature among the normally smooth-faced Native men. He claimed to be more than 100 years old and to remember Jacques Cartier's visit to the region in the 1530s. Historians are skeptical of this claim to such longevity. In 1607 he led an expedition against the Abenaki living in what is now Saco, Maine—hardly the task for an old man. Nevertheless, there can be no doubt about his willingness to enter into an alliance with the French men in his midst and his genuine affection for them (which seems to have been mutual). Champlain noted, though, that Membertou had the 'reputation of being the most evil and treacherous among all those of his nation'.

On 24 June 1610 Membertou and 20 members of his family were baptized by the priest Jessé Fléché, becoming the first known Aboriginal converts to Roman Catholicism in New France. Membertou received the Christian name of the French King and thus appears as Henri Membertou in many historical accounts, including the *Dictionary of Canadian Biography*. Although he renounced his shamanic beliefs, Membertou's conversion to Christianity was likely undertaken in the spirit of alliance and friendship rather than as a result of a clear un-derstanding of Roman Catholic doctrine. He nevertheless replaced the shamanic bag that he wore around his neck with a cross and agreed as he was dying of dysentery in September 1611 to be buried in the French graveyard rather than with his ancestors.[3]

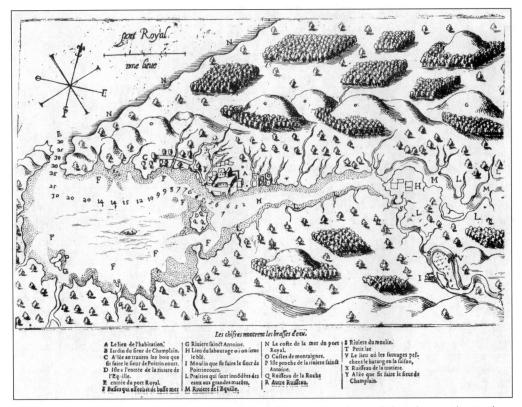

Champlain's map of the first Port-Royal. The habitation is flanked by a trout brook (X) and Champlain's garden (B). The wheat fields (H) would become the site of Fort Anne, and the mill is located on the Allain River (I). LAC, NL 15325.

fresh bread, which the colonists made from corn flour ground with hand mills. Despite these improvements, a third of the 45 men who wintered at Port-Royal in 1605–6 succumbed to scurvy.

In the spring of 1606 Jean de Poutrincourt et de Saint-Just, who had been appointed as lieutenant-governor of Acadia, brought skilled workmen to Port-Royal along with several aristocratic relatives and friends who would play important roles in the development of New France. These included Charles de Biencourt, Poutrincourt's son; Louis Hébert, a cousin from Paris who was an apothecary and horticulturalist; Claude de Saint-Etienne de La Tour, a cousin from Champagne, and Charles, his 14-year-old-son; and Marc Lescarbot, a lawyer from Paris who would later publish an account of the activities of this circle under the title *Histoire de la Nouvelle France* (1618). Determined to succeed in their venture, the gentlemen planted wheat and built a gristmill so that they would be less dependent on supplies from France. Pleased by the relatively warm winters at Port-Royal, they developed innovative responses to the challenges of survival. In 1606 Champlain founded the Ordre de Bon Temps, which obliged each member to take turns providing game and fish for the table. The survival rate improved—only four people died of scurvy that winter.

Notwithstanding his success in establishing the colony, de Monts faced insurmountable challenges. His fur-trade monopoly was impossible to enforce against the attacks of rivals, and in 1607 it was revoked. Financial losses soon obliged him to order the abandonment of Port-Royal. De Monts and Champlain thereafter concentrated their efforts on the St Lawrence, where they established a base at Quebec in 1608, while Poutrincourt—to whom de Monts had given the Port-Royal area—remained committed to Acadia. In 1610 he returned there with his son and some 20 colonists, including the priest Jessé Fléché.

The Mi'kmaq had looked after the habitation while the French were sorting out their difficulties. In short order Poutrincourt collected a shipload of furs, Fléché baptized Membertou and his family, and Biencourt set off for France to obtain support for the enterprise by demonstrating that it could be both financially and spiritually profitable. He managed to find a patron in the Marquise de Guercheville, but her support was tied to the condition that the Jesuits, who had become influential at the French court, would control missionary work in Acadia and become partners in the fur trade. In May 1611 Biencourt returned to Port-Royal with 36 colonists and two Jesuit priests, Pierre Biard and Énemond Massé.

Le Théâtre de Neptune
en la Nouvelle France, 1606

The early European explorers, traders, and colonizers were above all else intrepid sailors who braved the difficult Atlantic crossing to pursue their dreams of fame and fortune. Whatever their country of origin, they were men of the Renaissance who shared a cultural background centred on classical literature. Thus they would all have been familiar with the gods of Greece and Rome, among them Neptune, the god of the sea. Indeed, sea-sickness was politely described as 'yielding up the tribute to Neptune'.

One of the more memorable moments at Port-Royal occurred on a mid-November day in 1606 when Poutrincourt, Champlain, and their crew returned from two months of exploration along the Atlantic coast. As they anchored in the waters adjacent to the habitation, they were approached by 'Father Neptune', complete with silvery locks and flowing beard, in a boat drawn by six 'Tritons'. The sea god, brandishing his trident, drew alongside Poutrincourt's longboat and addressed him in Alexandrine verse:

Halt mighty Sagamo, no further fare!
Look on a god who holds thee in his care.
Thou knows't me not? I am of Saturn's line
Brother to Pluto dark and Jove divine.

After outlining what had been achieved through his command of the oceans—adventure, trade, exotic goods—the explorers were reminded:

If Man would taste the spice of fortune's savour
He needs must seek the aid of Neptune's favour.
For stay-at-homes who doze on kitchen settles
Earn no more glory than their pots and kettles.[4]

Believed to have been the first play written by a European in North America, *Le Théâtre de Neptune* may not be exceptional as poetry, but its existence underlines the rich cultural life that the French brought with them to their 'New World'.

This return proved to be the start of the colony's troubles. While Poutrincourt was in Paris, serious quarrels broke out between young Biencourt and the Jesuits. The Marquise de Guercheville, who was determined to see the Jesuits prevail, obtained control over territories in Acadia outside of Poutrincourt's jurisdiction and financed an expedition to move the Jesuits from Port-Royal to Saint-Sauveur, a new colony established on a site opposite what is now known as Mount Desert Island on the Penobscot River in Maine. Alarmed by these developments to the north, the governor of the English colony of Virginia, established in 1607, instructed Samuel Argall to attack the French settlements.

In the fall of 1613 Argall took the Jesuits prisoner, destroyed Saint-Sauveur, and burned Port-Royal. Returning the following year to find complete devastation, Poutrincourt and most of the colonists returned to France. Only Biencourt, his cousin Charles de Saint-Étienne de La Tour, and a few others stayed on.

Backed by La Rochelle merchants, Biencourt and his partners built a successful business in fur and fish. They developed good relations with the Mi'kmaq and extended their activities into the harbours of Cap Nègre, Cap de Sable, Port Lomeron, and La Hève on the south shore of Acadia. Following the death of Biencourt in 1623, the direction of the colony was entrusted to Charles La Tour, who with his father, Claude, continued to make Acadia his home. Charles married a Mi'kmaq woman (likely a chief's daughter) and their union, later blessed by a Récollet priest, produced three daughters, all of whom were baptized. One eventually entered a convent in Paris.

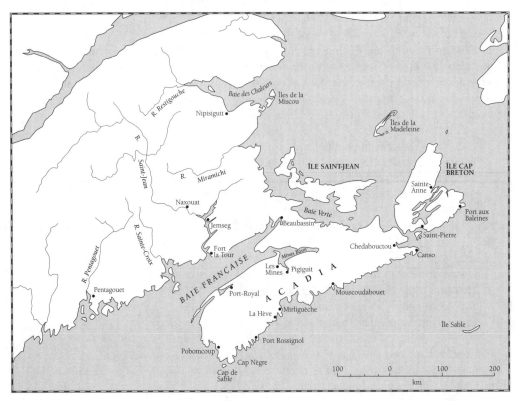

Acadian settlements in the seventeenth century. Adapted from Reid, *Acadia, Maine and New Scotland*, 191–4.

Lord Ochiltree's Short-lived Venture in Cape Breton, 1629

James Stewart of Killeith in Scotland became the fourth Lord Ochiltree in 1615, when he was about 33 years old. He was one of a number of men who saw North America as a place to play out their ambitions and perhaps to reap the financial rewards they needed to live in the grand style expected of the noble class. Like many of the early colonizers, Ochiltree's efforts were frustrated by political manoeuvres in Europe, where the rivalry between England and France increasingly had an impact on North America.

Apparently short of money, he became involved with Sir William Alexander's colonial enterprises. In 1629, in association with the Alexanders and with financial support from King Charles I, he attempted to establish a Scottish colony at Port-aux-Baleines, near the later site of Louisburg on Cape Breton Island. With about 60 Scottish recruits, he built a small fort named 'Rosemar'.

The colony was part of Charles I's policy to out-manoeuvre the French by developing a network of outposts stretching from Newfoundland to Virginia. When the war with France ended in the spring of 1629, the King changed his approach to foreign policy, but Ochiltree did not know this and initially behaved aggressively, as if the war still continued.

A French convoy commanded by Captain Charles Daniel, aware of the peace, attacked and destroyed Fort Rosemar on the grounds that Ochiltree was a pirate. The inhabitants of the fort were marched north to Bras d'Or Bay, forced to build another fortification for the French, and then shipped back to Europe in squalid conditions below decks. Ochiltree and 17 others were then imprisoned at Dieppe before he was repatriated. He died penniless in 1659, after 20 years in prison for falsely accusing the Marquis of Hamilton of high treason.[5]

French claims to Acadia were directly challenged by English and Scottish patents issued in 1620 and 1621. The latter constituted a grant from King James I of England to Scottish nobleman Sir William Alexander of 'New Scotland', defined as extending from the St Croix to the St Lawrence. After his first attempt to found a colony failed, Alexander persuaded the King in 1624 to create 150 knights-baronet who, in return for payment, would each receive a title and a land grant of 30,000 acres (12,150 hectares). There were few takers, but after many vicissitudes a fleet finally set sail for America in the spring of 1629, by which time Charles I (James's son and successor) was King of England and his short, disastrous war with France was just coming to an end. Two colonies were planned: one led by Lord Ochiltree in Port-aux-Baleines, Cape Breton, and another at Port-Royal.

Ochiltree's settlement at Port-aux-Baleines failed, but the colony established at Port-Royal by Sir William Alexander's son (also named William) survived by making accommodations both with the Mi'kmaq and with Claude de la Tour, whom David Kirke, an English adventurer, had captured at sea and taken to England. Willing to switch allegiances, Claude became one of Alexander's knights-baronet and married a Scottish lady-in-waiting to the Queen. Charles I would probably have liked to retain 'New Scotland', but under the terms of the Treaty of Saint-Germain-en-Laye (1632) he was required to return it to France. Port-Royal was abandoned, and France's title to Acadia was left unchallenged for the time being. As for Alexander, his legacies are a name, a flag, and a coat of arms still used by the province of Nova Scotia.

The Newfoundland Plantations

The other, equally precarious, node of European settlement in the region was Newfoundland's Avalon Peninsula. In 1610 the London and Bristol Company decided to establish a plantation at Cupids in Conception Bay. The investors hoped to develop a fur trade with the Beothuk and create a series of permanent settlements that would enable the company to control a substantial proportion of the Newfoundland fishery and trade. On behalf of the company, John Guy, a Bristol merchant, brought out 39 men in 1610, followed by 16 women in 1612. The son born to the wife of Nicholas Guy in March 1613 was probably the first English child born in what is now Canada.

Although the colony's early years were quite promising, problems soon developed. The settlement was harassed by the pirate Peter Easton; the soil and climate proved to be less favourable to agriculture than expected; there was friction with the migratory fishermen; and since the settlers had virtually no contact with the Beothuk, a fur trade failed to develop. These factors, adding to internal dissension, led to the plantation's breakup. A few colonists remained in Cupids, and some moved to Bristol's Hope (now Harbour Grace), but others left Newfoundland behind them.

Cupids may have been a business failure, but it marks the beginning of permanent English settlement on the Avalon Peninsula. To recoup some of its investment, the London and Bristol Company began to sell tracts of land to other potential colonizers. The first of these was Sir

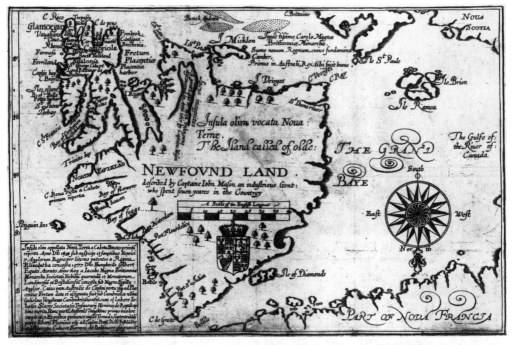

The John Mason Map, 1617. When Mason was appointed governor of the English colony at Cupids in 1616, he was already familiar with Newfoundland. His map—the first English depiction of the island—constitutes an important piece of evidence for those who believe that John Cabot made his landfall at Cape Bonavista. On the left, just below the peninsula named 'North Falkland' (now the Bonavista Peninsula), is the legend *C. Bona Vista a Cabato primum Reperta*. LAC, NMC-21046.

William Vaughan, a Welsh lawyer and scholar who saw in overseas colonization a solution to social and economic problems at home. In 1616 he purchased the Avalon Peninsula south of a line from Caplin Bay (now Calvert) across to Placentia Bay, and called his land 'New Cambriol'. A flimsy settlement was established at Aquaforte, which Richard Whitbourne later moved to Renews. By 1621 the colony was finished. Vaughan sold off sections of his property to Sir George Calvert and Lord Falkland and retired to his library to write *The Golden Fleece* (1626), a fanciful book promoting the colonization of Newfoundland.

Falkland did nothing with his holdings, but the wealthy and influential Calvert established a plantation at Ferryland in 1621. Known as the Colony of Avalon, it became one of the earliest permanent European settlements in northeastern America and was among the best capitalized, with stone houses, a cobbled street, a quay, warehouses, and defences. Calvert, who was named Lord Baltimore in 1625, viewed the colony as a business enterprise, but he also wanted Ferryland to be a haven of religious freedom. Himself a convert to Roman Catholicism, Baltimore allowed both Protestant and Catholic clergy to serve the colonists.

Still the colony failed to meet expectations. Baltimore was disheartened not only by the inhospitable climate but also by a slump in the fishery and the high cost of dealing with French privateers. After an interval in England, he departed for Maryland in 1632, leaving his Ferryland property (in which he had invested more than £20,000—$4 million today) in the hands of agents and a village of some 30 people. At this time the total European winter population on the English Shore was probably not more than 200.

Despite valiant efforts, the European presence in the Atlantic region in the early seventeenth century remained largely seasonal and migratory. Settlement was not necessary for catching fish and trading furs; indeed, much of the good agricultural land was far removed from the best harbours for trading and fishing. If formal colonization schemes in Newfoundland and Acadia were to be successful, they had to generate profits that would satisfy investors and at the same time provide enough resources to support year-round habitation. There also had to be compelling reasons, whether ideological or self-interested, for Europeans to leave their homelands for an unknown and potentially dangerous 'new world'. Religious persecution unleashed in the wake of the Protestant Reformation and population pressures in Europe served as powerful stimuli for overseas migration, but other regions of North America were more easily adapted to European settlement.

After more than a century of contact, it was clear that unfavourable agricultural conditions made Newfoundland unsuitable for extensive colonization, even in the absence of a large Aboriginal population. The emergence of a permanent population on the island was the result of informal settlement, and its viability depended on the ability to import foodstuffs, though locally grown potatoes became an important dietary staple by the middle of the eighteenth century. Even so, in the seventeenth century 'plantations' linked to West Country ports were growing up in Conception Bay and at St John's, which was one of the most important centres of the migratory fishery. A resident fishery was made possible when 'sack' or cargo vessels (at first Dutch) entered the trade and began purchasing the planters' catch. In Labrador there were no European settlers at all. Barren and forbidding, with a subarctic climate and a seemingly hostile Native population, it attracted only migratory fishermen and traders.

DOCUMENT:
Planting a Colony in Ferryland

On 26 August 1621, Edward Wynne wrote to his employer, Sir George Calvert, outlining his activities in planting a colony at Ferryland on the east coast of the Avalon Peninsula:

> The place whereon I have made choice to plant and build upon is . . . the fittest, the warmest, the most commodious of all about the harbour. As soon as the [Mansion] house and fortification is fitted and finished, I shall (God willing) prepare and fence in a proportion of seed ground and a garden, close by the house. It may please your Honour not to send out any cattle next year, because I cannot fodder for them so soon, before there be some quantity of corn [grain] growing, but it may please your honour to send some goats, a few tame conies [rabbits] for breed, as also pigs, geese, ducks and hens. I have some hens already. Some spades from London were necessary, if of the best making, also some good pick-axes, iron crows [crowbars], and a smith, and also such as can brew and bake.[6]

The Ferryland cross. This ornate iron cross was excavated at Lord Baltimore's Ferryland settlement. It was once gilded and embedded with gems. James Tuck, Memorial University, St John's.

A North Devon bowl decorated with intricate *scgraffito* designs. Also excavated at Ferryland, it probably dates from about 1673. James Tuck, Memorial University, St John's.

Like other European colonizers, Wynne was attempting to recreate the old world in the new, a project that proved more challenging than this optimistic letter implied. Baltimore himself spent part of 1627 and the winter of 1628–9 in Ferryland, before deciding 'to shift to some other warmer climate of this new worlde'. As he complained to King Charles I:

> . . . from the middest of October, to the middest of May there is a sad face of wynter upon all this land, both sea and land so frozen for the greatest part of the tyme as they are not penetrable, no plant or vegetable thing appearing out of the earth untill it be about the beginning of May nor fish in the sea besides the ayre is so intolerable cold as it is hardly to be endured.[7]

Acadia

The story in Acadia was quite different. On the periphery of the rapidly developing North Atlantic trading system, Acadia was bypassed by Puritans from England, who fetched up further south in

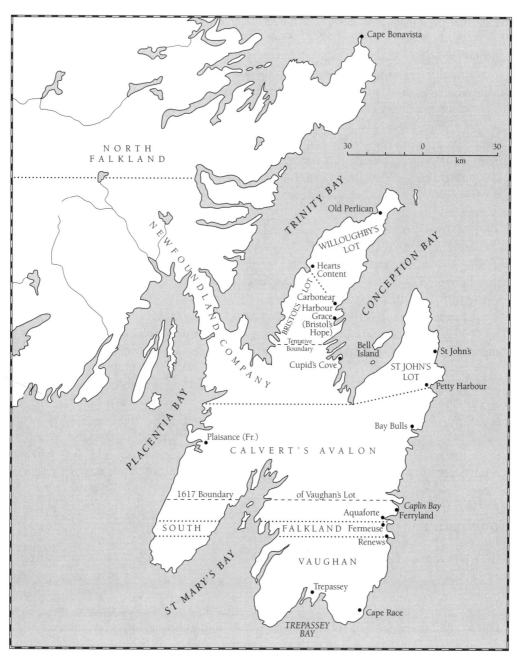

The English Shore of Newfoundland, seventeenth century. Adapted from Gillian Cell, ed., *Newfoundland Discovered: English Attempts at Colonisation, 1610–1630* (London: Hakluyt Society, 1982), 21.

the Massachusetts Bay area, and even by the French, many of them Huguenots, who moved to the West Indies. But Acadia had potential. Although its climate was more extreme than Europe's, with hotter summers and colder winters, Europeans could survive there, particularly with the help of the Mi'kmaq. The sheer abundance of resources—fish, fowl, and fur in profusion, trees growing down to the shoreline, and pockets of potentially productive agricultural land—and relative proximity to Europe commended the region to prospective immigrants.

The French were the first to explore Acadia's agricultural potential. As Ramsay Cook has pointed out, French colonizers in Acadia were determined to cultivate the North American wilderness. Lescarbot, for example, was clearly pleased with his efforts at Port-Royal: 'I can say with truth that I have never done so much bodily work through the pleasure which I took in digging and tilling my gardens, fencing them in against the gluttony of the swine, making terraces, preparing straight alleys, building storehouses, sowing wheat, rye, barley, oats, beans, peas, garden plants, and watering them. . . .'[8] In creating his European oasis, Lescarbot was participating in a crucial part of the colonization process: the introduction of European animals, plants, and, through their very presence, diseases.

By Lescarbot's time, European ecological imperialism was already well underway. Plant seeds (including dandelion) were among the early passengers on fishing vessels, and European diseases were already taking their toll among the Aboriginal population. Père Biard noted in 1612 that the Native people 'are astonished and often complain that since the French mingle with and carry on trade with them, they are dying fast and the population is thinning out. . . . One by one the different coasts according as they have begun to traffic with us, have been more reduced by disease.'[9] Within another century, European rats, cats, rabbits, cattle, sheep, pigs, and deer would be competing with bears, caribou, moose, and mice for the region's resources.

Europeans were notoriously careless of the abundance they found around them. When Sir Humphrey Gilbert arrived in Newfoundland in 1583, Stephen Parmenius, a young Hungarian poet who accompanied the admiral, noted that they considered burning down the forests 'so as to clear an open space for surveying the area'. This ill-conceived plan was apparently abandoned only after 'some reliable person asserted that, when this had occurred by accident at some other settlement post, no fish had been seen for seven whole years, because the sea-water had been turned bitter by the turpentine that flowed down from the trees burning along the rivers.'[10] Whether by accident or by design, Europeans were gradually making their mark on the North Atlantic landscape.

Conclusion

Although Europeans had difficulty forming stable colonies in the Atlantic region in this period, they had staked out the Avalon Peninsula and the area surrounding the Bay of Fundy as potential sites for settlement. They had learned by hard experience what was required to survive through the long winter months and knew that there was wealth to be made in the fisheries and the fur trade. By 1632 the region had also become a pawn in imperial rivalries. As Native populations declined, retreated, or made accommodations with the intruders, the way was paved for settler societies that would gradually transform the Atlantic region into a satellite of western Europe.

Further Readings

Cell, Gillian, ed. 1982. *Newfoundland Discovered: English Attempts at Colonisation, 1610–1630*. London: Hakluyt Society.

Dunn, Brenda. 2000. *A History of Port-Royal/ Annapolis Royal, 1605–1800*. Halifax: Nimbus.

Jones, Elizabeth. 1986. *Gentlemen and Jesuits: Quests for Glory and Adventure in the Early Days of New France*. Toronto: University of Toronto Press.

Pope, Peter E. 2004. *Fish into Wine: The Newfoundland Plantation in the Seventeenth Century*. Chapel Hill: University of North Carolina Press.

Food for Thought

Cook, Ramsay. 1995. '1492 and All That: Making a Garden out of a Wilderness', in Chad Gaffield and Pam Gaffield, eds, *Consuming Canada: Readings in Environmental History*. Toronto: Copp Clark, Ltd, 62–80.

Recommended Websites

Baccalieu Trail Archaeology
http://www.baccalieudigs.ca/

Investigating Ferryland
http://www.heritage.nf.ca/avalon/arch/default.html

Port-Royal National Historic Site
http://www.pc.gc.ca/lhn-nhs/ns/portroyal/index_e.asp

St Croix Island Settlement
http://collections.ic.gc.ca/saintcroixisland
http://www.pc.gc.ca/lhn-nhs/nb/stcroix

Chapter 5

Colonial Communities, 1632–1713

Following the Treaty of Saint-Germain-en-Laye in 1632, the French government returned to the task of rebuilding its North American colonies. Most of its attention was focused on the St Lawrence, but efforts in Acadia and Newfoundland bore fruit as well. By contrast, the English government showed little interest in sponsoring colonial endeavours of any kind in the Atlantic region north of New England, and in the later seventeenth century, some mercantile interests even argued that Newfoundland should be cleared of permanent settlers altogether. Nevertheless, the Atlantic colonies figured prominently in English negotiating strategies during their periodic wars with France—testimony not only to the significance of the fisheries but also to the Atlantic region's strategic location at the junction of competing territorial claims for imperial control in North America.

The Emergence of Acadia

France's new attitude towards Acadia became apparent when King Louis XIII's chief minister, Cardinal Richelieu, appointed Isaac de Razilly to take the surrender of Port-Royal in 1632 and commissioned him as the royal lieutenant-general in New France. He arrived with three ships and roughly 300 men, three Capuchin priests, and a few women and children. Most of the prospective settlers are thought to have come from Brittany and Anjou. Over the next three years Razilly, with his lieutenants Charles de Menou d'Aulnay and Nicholas Denys, laid the groundwork for a lasting Acadian colony which would serve as a French bulwark against New England.

Razilly established his main base at La Hève on the south shore, which was better suited to his military and commercial interests than Port-Royal. Meanwhile, Denys engaged in fishing, lumbering, and fur-trading, eventually concentrating his efforts at Canso, Saint-Pierre (St Peter's), and Nepisiquit on the Baie des Chaleurs. Razilly managed to maintain harmonious relations with Charles La Tour, who claimed title to Acadia himself and conducted major trading operations from his bases at Cape Sable and the mouth of the St John River. Essentially dividing the territory between them, Razilly and La Tour dealt separately with the Compagnie des Cent-Associés, the Paris-based seigneurs of New France.

Razilly's sudden death in early 1636 seems to have prompted many of his group to return to France. Fortunately for the colony, his successor, Charles de Menou d'Aulnay, was equally committed to the development of Acadia and arranged for the migration of settlers from his seigneury near Loudon in Poitou. Because he believed that agriculture should be the colony's mainstay, he moved most of the French settlers remaining at La Hève to the potentially more productive Port-

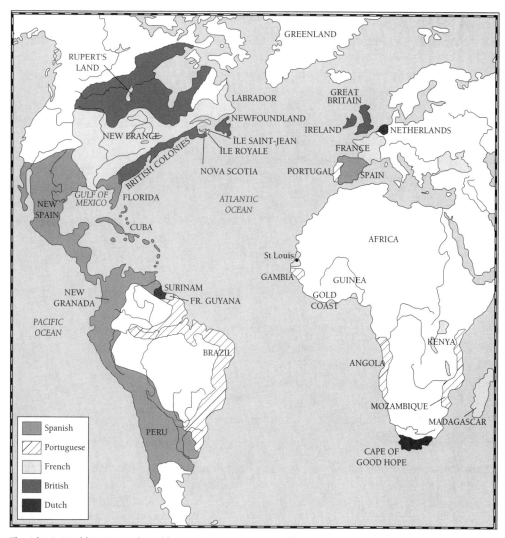

The Atlantic World in 1715. Adapted from www.wwnorton.com/college/english/worldlit2e/full/maps/atlantic.htm

Royal area. Families formed by marriages between the French and Mi'kmaq apparently remained at La Hève. By 1650, when d'Aulnay died, there were about 400 Europeans living in Acadia. Some returned to France, but most of them stayed to become the founding families of the French Acadie.

D'Aulnay's death marked the end of official French efforts to encourage immigration to the colony. It also brought to a close what has been described as 'a miniscule civil war between rival fur-trading seigneurs'.[1] Unlike Razilly, d'Aulnay was not prepared to accommodate La Tour's territorial claims, wanting to control all of Acadia and its trade. In 1640 commercial and political rivalry erupted into armed hostilities that culminated five years later in d'Aulnay's attack on La Tour's St John River fort, which was defended in La Tour's absence by his spirited and resourceful second wife, Françoise-Marie Jaquelin. She eventually surrendered and, so the story goes, was

Table 5.1	Timeline
1632	Isaac de Razilly appointed Governor of Acadia.
1634	The English government issues the Western Charter to regulate the Newfoundland fishery.
1637	Commercial monopoly of the Newfoundland fish trade granted to Sir David Kirke and his business associates.
1640	Hostilities begin between Charles de Menou d'Aulnay and Charles La Tour.
1645	D'Aulnay takes la Tour's fort on the St John River.
1650	Emmanuel Le Borgne seizes Port-Royal and attacks other settlements.
1654	English force led by Robert Sedgwick attacks Acadia and imprisons La Tour.
1662	France establishes a colony and military base at Plaisance.
1667	Acadia returned to France by the Treaty of Breda.
1670	Acadia declared a royal colony.
1689–97	War of the League of Augsburg.
1690	Sir William Phips plunders Port-Royal.
1696–7	Pierre Le Moyne d'Iberville attempts to drive the English out of Newfoundland.
1697	Treaty of Ryswick.
1699	'King William's Act' passed to govern the fishery and settlement at Newfoundland.
1702–13	War of the Spanish Succession.
1704, 1707	New Englanders attack Acadia.
1705, 1709	French attack English Newfoundland.
1710	English force captures Port-Royal.
1713	Treaty of Utrecht; France recognizes British sovereignty over mainland Acadia, Newfoundland, and Hudson Bay.

forced to watch the hanging of those of her men who had survived the battle. She died soon after, and La Tour went into exile in Quebec.

The dispute with La Tour had driven d'Aulnay deeply into debt. After his death his chief creditor, Emmanuel Le Borgne, seized Port-Royal and attacked other settlements in the region. Meanwhile, the equally debt-ridden La Tour attempted to consolidate his interests and reclaim his property. To this end, he married d'Aulnay's widow, Jeanne Motin, and resumed his position as governor—this time of all Acadia. The La Tours were joined in opposition to Le Borgne by Nicolas Denys, who by this time had substantial interests in the fishery and the fur trade between Canso and the Gaspé. Another civil war was averted in 1654 when an English force led by Robert Sedgwick plundered Port-Royal and other settlements. La Tour, taken prisoner, swore allegiance to England, sold his rights in Acadia to Sir Thomas Temple and William Crowne, paid off his debts, and retired to Cape Sable.

Oliver Cromwell's republican regime in England took the view that Acadia had reverted to its former identity as Nova Scotia or New Scotland and in 1656 ceded it to Temple and Crowne, the latter selling out in 1659. The French government took a very different view of the situation, and appointed Le Borgne governor of Acadia the next year. He and his son continued to attack English settlements, and the situation can only be described as confused and anarchic. For the Acadians, however, this was a period of consolidation when they learned to value pragmatism and to accept the necessity of living side-by-side with the English. Rival claims were eventually settled in 1667 by the Treaty of Breda, which returned Acadia to France. It was not until three years later that the English government forced a reluctant Temple to let the French assume control.

King Louis XIV of France began to intervene directly in matters relating to overseas colonization following his 1661 decision to take the reins of government into his own hands. As a result, most French colonies were put under the control of a powerful bureaucratic regime with a governor supported by a standing army; a legal system based on the Custom of Paris; a seigneurial system of land distribution that concentrated wealth in the hands of an aristocratic elite; a Roman Catholic church closely allied to the state; and a closed mercantile trading system designed to advance France's economic interests. Distance, administrative inefficiencies, and the King's preoccupation with European affairs meant that North American colonies could often avoid some of the strict regulations imposed upon them by officials based in France, but these factors were not enough to prevent the colonies from becoming pawns in the struggle for European ascendancy that Louis XIV's ambitions unleashed.

In 1670 Acadia was declared a royal colony like the others, with an administration subordinate to officials in Quebec. The St Lawrence–based colony of Canada received most of Louis XIV's attention and he had few resources, either financial or military, to spare for Acadia. Governor Hector d'Andigné de Grandfontaine established royal authority in the colony with only a handful of soldiers, and the 60 settlers he brought with him were joined by just 66 more (of whom only five were women) over the next 40 years. Without support from France, the 55 seigneuries failed to sustain social organization, and regulations forbidding trade with New England were openly flouted. The few priests in the area sometimes took on legal duties in the absence of judicial officers, and the settlers, especially those who moved beyond the confines of Port-Royal, learned to fend for themselves.

Despite the lack of imperial interest, a small colonial society managed to take root in Acadia. Colonial officials tried between 1670 and 1683 to establish their administrative base on the north side of the Bay of Fundy, first at Pentagouet, then at Jemseg and Beaubassin, but finally settled back in Port-Royal. With about 600 people in 1686, Port-Royal was the heart of French settlement. Other communities were developing in what is now Nova Scotia at Pubnico (Pobomcoup), Cape Negro (Cap Nègre), Musquodoboit Harbour (Mouscoudabouet), and St Peter's (Saint-Pierre). In the 1670s and 1680s, young families moved up the Bay of Fundy to Beaubassin and around the Minas Basin.

Geographical expansion reflected the spectacular population growth that characterized early French settlements. Well-adapted to their environment, people in Acadia were better nourished than most peasants in France and mercifully free of the plagues that periodically ravaged old-world communities. Few residents remained single, usually marrying in their early twenties. Although agriculture was central to their survival, fishing and fur-trading supplemented their well-rounded economy.

Roman Catholic clergy were present from the earliest days of French settlement and remained a significant force even after the British conquest of 1713. In the first half of the seventeenth century, Acadia was an open field for competing clerical orders. Récollet, Jesuit, and Capuchin priests conducted missions among the Native people, ministered to French settlers and sojourners, and clashed both with each other and with the secular authorities. The Capuchins were particularly active, sending at least 40 priests and 20 lay brothers to Acadia between 1632 and 1656. Most

DOCUMENT:
Building Dikes in Acadia, 1699

One of the most enduring features of colonial Acadia was dikeland agriculture. Instead of clearing the forests, the settlers reclaimed the rich alluvial soils flooded by the high tides of the Bay of Fundy. The practice began in the Port-Royal area in the 1630s, introduced by *saulniers* (salt marsh workers) from Poitou who knew how to drain and cultivate marshlands. As settlement spread so did the construction of dikes, creating a landscape that still distinguishes the Bay of Fundy region. The marshland farms were highly productive, allowing the settlers to grow wheat and barley, as well as fodder for livestock, and the salt produced in the drainage process was used to cure fish.

Dike-building represented a major engineering achievement. The Sieur de Dièreville, a French surgeon and writer who visited the colony in 1699, was clearly impressed by the labour-intensive process through which the marshland soil was reclaimed from the sea:

> To grow Wheat, the Marshes which are inundated by the Sea at high Tide, must be drained; these are called Lowlands & they are quite good, but what labour is needed to make them fit for cultivation! The ebb & flow of the Sea cannot easily be stopped, but the Acadians succeed in doing so by means of great Dikes called Aboteaux, & it is done in this way; five or six rows of large logs are driven whole into the ground at the points where the Tide enters the Marsh, & between each row other logs are laid, one on top of the other, & all the spaces between them are so carefully filled with well-pounded clay, that the water can no longer get through. In the centre of this construction, a Sluice is contrived in such a manner that the water on the Marshes flows out of its own accord, while that of the Sea is prevented from coming in. An undertaking of this nature, which can only be carried on at certain Seasons when the Tides do not rise so high, costs a great deal, & takes many days, but the abundant crop that is harvested in the second year, after the soil has been washed [of the salt] by Rain water compensates for all the expense. As these lands are owned by several Men, the work upon them is done in common.[2]

Acadians repairing dikes. Courtesy Nova Scotia Musuem #871202.

These ink drawings of missionaries teaching Christianity to the Mi'kmaq were used to illustrate Chrestien LeClercq's *New Relation of Gaspésia*, published in Paris in 1691.

priests spent only a few years in Acadia, but they achieved their goals. French settlers remained committed to Roman Catholicism, and many Mi'kmaq and Wolastoqiyik gradually reconciled their beliefs with those of the persistent Christians in their midst.

In 1676 Father Louis Petit was appointed vicar-general of Acadia, under the jurisdiction of the Bishop of Quebec. Bishop Saint-Vallier, who visited his Acadian province in the spring of 1686, subsequently appointed priests to outlying communities. From 1701 to 1710, a sister of the Congregation of the Holy Cross conducted a school for young girls at Port-Royal. Legal and clerical records show that most people followed clerical injunctions relating to marriage and sexual conduct. In a highly controversial case at Beaubassin in 1688, the local priest responded to a paternity suit by insisting that not only the reputed father but also 19 members of his family should be expelled from the community and their confiscated goods given to the girl's father.

Because Acadians generally did not settle on Native hunting and fishing grounds, and provided valued opportunities to trade, their relations with the Mi'kmaq and Wolastoqiyik were on the whole amicable. On occasion, marriages between Native women and French immigrants played a significant role in cementing military alliances. In 1670, for example, Bernard-Anselme d'Abbadie de Saint-Castin accompanied Governor Grandfontaine to Pentagouet (in present-day Maine) and married the daughter of a Pentagouet chief. He then devoted himself to extending French influence among the Abenaki in that area. Faced with the expansion of New England settlers up the Atlantic seaboard, the Abenaki welcomed the support provided by Saint-Castin and valued his advice. As war engulfed the region in the closing decades of the seventeenth century, the Abenaki, Penobscot, and Passamaquoddy joined the Wolastoqiyik and Mi'kmaq in an alliance—later known as the Wabanaki ('Dawnland') Confederacy—to confront the aggressive New Englanders and their Iroquois allies.

Cultural exchange between Natives and French immigrants, initiated by trade and military alliances, was extensive and long-lasting. Acadians adopted those elements of local cultures that they found most useful, including canoes, moccasins, and knowledge of local herbs and vegetables, while European metal products, foods, clothing, religious rituals, and military support became standard features of Aboriginal society. According to Naomi Griffiths, Natives in the eyes of Acadians 'were permanent neighbours, neither the middlemen in commercial enterprise nor a hostile force'.[3] This symbiotic relationship was highly unusual in the story of European settlement in North America.

A more ambiguous relationship developed between the Acadians and the English colonists in Massachusetts. Regarding Acadia as within their sphere of influence, New Englanders were hostile to the French presence and they periodically attacked Acadian settlements. At the same time they fished along the Acadian coastline and traded with Acadian settlers, who exchanged furs and surplus agricultural produce for a variety of manufactured goods and foodstuffs. Both La Tour and d'Aulnay had conducted extensive business in Boston, and this axis of trade continued after 1670, despite royal injunctions against it. Since few French merchants were interested in Acadia—there had been some heavy losses in the past—and because administrators lacked the resources to control the trade, the colony emerged as an economic satellite of New England. In the Acadian phrase, the English became 'our friends the enemy'.

By the turn of the eighteenth century the settled population of Acadia was approaching 1,500 and, with a balanced population of men and women, was doubling every generation. Most of the inhabitants were related to each other, giving a society of varied origins the close-knit character of an extended family. A common language and religion further cemented an interdependence that was also encouraged by the political vacuum in the region. With a government that was always distant, often ineffectual, sometimes English, sometimes French, the Acadians became singularly self-reliant and pragmatic. Periodic attacks on their communities—mostly conducted by the English but also in 1674 by the Dutch—drove home the reality of their precarious political situation. Learning to live both with their neighbours and with whatever regime was in power, the Acadians kept their own counsel. Frustrated French administrators accused them of being 'republican', and lacking in deference and respect.

The English Shore

Acadia was a permanent French colony, and was viewed as such in Paris. The English attitude towards Newfoundland was not as clear-cut. Officials in London were not opposed to settlement but were preoccupied by the economic and naval value of the migratory fishery and provided neither local administration nor a military presence. As a means of formalizing the rules and customs governing the English inshore fishery, Parliament issued a Western Charter in 1634. It detailed how masters could claim fishing rooms and empowered the fishing admirals (masters of migratory vessels who acquired authority by being the first to arrive in a given harbour) to settle disputes; it banned taverns, the dumping of ballast in harbours, the 'rinding' of trees, stealing, Sabbath-breaking, and the destruction of fishing stages and cookrooms. In the absence of penalty clauses—except for capital offences, which were to be tried in England—it proved to be a weak legal document, and its provisions were often ignored.

In 1637 King Charles I made a 'Grant of Newfoundland' to Sir David Kirke and some aristocratic associates and acquiesced in Kirke's appropriation of the Ferryland plantation the following year. Known as the Company of Adventurers to Newfoundland, the patentees had not been granted property, but a commercial monopoly: the right to 'the sole trade of Newfoundland, the Fishing excepted', with the power to tax French and Dutch vessels. The goal was to give English West Country merchants a monopoly of the fishery, while the patentees would monopolize the sack trade in association with a London business run by Kirke's brothers. David Kirke set himself up as a fish merchant in Ferryland and developed a profitable transatlantic trade in fish and wine. As governor, he held courts and administered the southern Avalon Peninsula in a rough-and-ready way.

Kirke's career in Newfoundland ended in 1651 with the victory of Parliament in the English Civil War and the subsequent establishment of a republic. Since he was a royalist, his estates were sequestrated. Moreover, it seems that he had manipulated his operations to benefit his brothers rather than the other patentees. Recalled to face a suit brought by the Calverts, Kirke died in prison in 1654. The Ferryland plantation survived under the management of his widow, Lady Sara Kirke, while her sons developed their own plantations at Ferryland and Renews. In effect, the Kirkes functioned as a provincial gentry under the new governor, a merchant from Maine named John Treworgie, who served in Newfoundland from 1651 to 1660.

The West Country merchants who controlled the migratory fishery were concerned about the activities of Kirke and Treworgie, but they faced other challenges as well. Among them was an

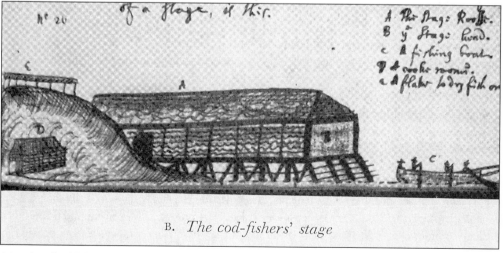

B. *The cod-fishers' stage*

A Newfoundland fishing room, *c.* 1663, sketched by the surgeon James Yonge at either Renews or Fermeuse. The key reads: 'A The Stage Roofe. B Ye Stage head. C A fishing boat. D A cooke room. E A flake to dry fish over'. From F.N.L. Poynter, ed., *The Journal of James Yonge, 1647–1721, Plymouth Surgeon*, (London: Green and Co., 1963).

David and Sara Kirke

David Kirke was the tough, adventurous son of an English wine merchant. When war broke out between England and France in 1627, Kirke led a privateering expedition against the French in Canada. Largely a family affair, this effort was partly financed by his father and included David's four brothers. With the help of Innu allies, the Kirkes eventually managed to take Quebec from Champlain in 1629 and stayed there until 1632, when the Treaty of Saint-Germain-en-Laye obliged them to return it to France. Knighted for his achievements, David Kirke turned his attention to Newfoundland.

Kirke and his partners were interested in the 'sack' trade—the term derived from *vina de sacca*, wine for export—in which fish was collected at Newfoundland, freighted to southern Europe, and exchanged for wines and other Mediterranean commodities that were then sold in England. The need for a steady and adequate supply of fish persuaded Kirke and his wife, Sara, to take over the Ferryland plantation, where in 1650, they were joined by Lady Kirke's sister, Lady Frances Hopkins, and her children. Because the Hopkins family had sheltered Charles I while he was under house arrest in 1648, they were suspect to Oliver Cromwell's new parliamentary regime.

By 1654 the sisters were both widows, and despite their royalist affiliations, they survived the English Civil War and interregnum with their properties intact. They did not go back to England but remained in Newfoundland to manage their substantial plantations—independent, and in local terms, wealthy. Although Frances had a short-lived second marriage to an Acadian merchant, Alexandre Le Borgne de Belle-Isle, Sara did not remarry. Peter Pope suggests that, as heirs to large plantations, these women 'had the least to gain and the most to lose from a new alliance' that would give control of the family wealth to a new husband. Both women died in Newfoundland in the early 1680s.[4]

extensive bye-boat fishery, carried on by independent fishermen who bought passage to and from England annually and leased fishing rooms. Bye-boat keepers worked closely with planters, whose presence also concerned some of the merchants. In the mid-seventeenth century, there were between 1,000 and 2,000 people who had some sort of permanent attachment to Newfoundland, living in about 30 settlements along the English Shore, all linked to West Country ports. Around this core group of planters moved a much larger, shifting, seasonal, and overwhelmingly male population that during the summer helped to produce salt fish and cod oil for export.

After the restoration of the monarchy in 1660, a West Country lobby argued that the growth of a settled population on the island, small as it was, threatened the viability of the migratory fishery because planters pre-empted the best fishing places and destroyed fishing stages. In addition, it was argued, settlement was not desirable since Newfoundland was 'productive of no commodities as other Plantations, [n]or affords anything of food to keep men alive'. The government responded with an addition to the Western Charter in 1661 purporting to forbid bye-boat fishing and, concerned by a decline in the migratory fishery, adopted an anti-settlement policy that was enshrined in a new charter issued in 1671. The naval commodore was instructed to encourage planters to leave the island.

By contrast, France placed a far higher value on the Newfoundland fisheries than on Acadia or even Canada. Determined to protect their interests in Newfoundland, the French established a colony and fort at Plaisance, on the island's southeast coast, in 1662. Theoretically subordinate to Quebec (like Acadia), Plaisance was designed to act as a base for the French fishing fleet, to monitor English activity on the Avalon Peninsula, and to protect the approaches to the Gulf. The community became home to a governor and other administrators, a military force, Roman Catholic priests, and, on its beach properties, bona fide settlers. By the end of the seventeenth century the resident population had reached approximately 200, swelled in season by *engagés*, and the crews of trading and fishing ships coming from France. As in Acadia, there was a flourishing clandestine trade with New England.

Delayed by the Anglo–Dutch war of 1672–4, during which the Dutch attacked both Ferryland and St John's, the English government did not try to enforce its anti-settler policy until 1675. The naval commodore then sent to implement the order reported that the policy was both impractical and mistaken: 'if the habitants are taken off and the French left solely in possession . . . they will in a short time invest themselves of the whole at least of Ferryland and St John's, where harbours are almost naturally fortified, to the disadvantage of the trade, if not the loss of all.'[5] Moreover, the planters were in reality an asset to the migratory fleet; they protected equipment, cut timber, made oars and boats, and provided hospitality. The government sensibly reconsidered its position, cancelled its instructions, and adopted a compromise: settlement in Newfoundland would be accepted and tolerated, but not encouraged. Eventually enshrined in the 1699 statute known as King William's Act, this policy remained on the books until 1824. There is an old and hardy myth that the British government opposed settlement in Newfoundland and made it illegal. In fact, until the 1660s the government supported settlement. Thereafter, British policy reflected the assumption that Newfoundland was an industry, not a colony.

The Impact of War, 1689–1713

When war was declared between England and France in 1689, Acadia and Newfoundland were seriously affected. The origins of the conflict (King William's War, or the War of the League of Augsburg) were European, but North Americans—both Natives and newcomers—could not avoid involvement. The Comte de Frontenac, Governor of New France, organized mid-winter raids along the New England frontier, while French privateers attacked English shipping. Alarmed by the prospect of a hostile alliance between the Aboriginal peoples and the French, the New Englanders struck back. In 1690 a force commanded by Sir William Phips attacked French posts along the coast and then plundered Port-Royal, taking the governor prisoner. Some inhabitants fled. The remaining men were ordered to assemble in the damaged church, where they were forced to swear allegiance to the English Crown. Phips also appointed a council of residents to act as a local government. Once Phips was gone, the residents publicly reaffirmed their allegiance to Louis XIV, but the French administration thought it prudent to leave the Phips-appointed council in place and itself moved north of the Bay of Fundy, locating at Jemseg, then Nashwaak, and finally at the mouth of the St John River. For ordinary Acadians, Maurice Basque argues, the imperative was to survive amidst ambiguity, and to that end the best strategy was 'a form of neutrality in which they could continue to trade with the English while avoiding conflicts with their Native neighbours and maintaining communication with the French administration of the colony'.[6]

Neutrality was no longer an option for the region's Aboriginal inhabitants. During King William's War, the Mi'kmaq, Wolastoqiyik, Penobscot, Passamaquoddy, and Abenaki—the Wabanaki Confederacy—threw in their lot with the French, attacking New England settlers and forts on Abenaki land. William Wicken points out that their motivation was twofold. Not only did they want to defend their territory against New England expansionism, but they also had a long-standing conflict with the Iroquois (Haudenosaunee) who were now allied with the English.[7] In retaliation for the damaging attacks on New England by the French and their Native allies, Benjamin Church and a force of New Englanders burned and pillaged the Beaubassin settlements in 1696 and extracted yet another pointless oath of allegiance from the Acadians.

The Massachusetts General Court forbade trade with Acadia, but there was no way to enforce the prohibition. As a result trade between New England and Acadia continued throughout the war. Wheat, fur, and feathers (the latter essential for mattresses) were traded for Indian corn, tobacco, molasses, sugar, spices, lace, ribbon, and fabrics. This was not the first time that economic and political policies were at odds in the Atlantic region nor would it be the last.

From the beginning of the war, there had been French raids on the English Shore and English raids on Plaisance, but as the war dragged on, the French decided to drive the English out of Newfoundland once and for all. In the fall of 1696, forces led by Jacques-François Mombeton de Brouillon, the governor of Plaisance, and the Canadian-born Pierre Le Moyne d'Iberville, fresh from campaigns in Acadia, converged on the defenceless communities along the English Shore. Had they co-operated effectively and received greater support, the French might have achieved more than they did.

D'Iberville arrived in Plaisance in September 1696 to find that de Brouillon had already departed to attack English settlements south of St John's. At Ferryland de Brouillon's force had inflicted devastation: 'the enemy dealt very hardly with us,' John Clappe complained, 'burnt all our houses, goods, fish, oil, train-fats, stages, nets and fishing craft . . . and sent us away with our wives, children and servants.'[8] D'Iberville led his men (including Canadian and Acadian militia, Mi'kmaq, and Abenaki) overland from Plaisance to meet de Brouillon at Renews. With the Canadians in the vanguard, they proceeded north (quarelling most of the time), captured St John's, and pillaged it. To encourage the surrender of the miserable inhabitants taking refuge in 'Fort William'—there was no military garrison—' the French took one William Drew, an Inhabitant a Prisoner and cutt all around his scalp and then by the strength of hand strip his skin from the forehead to the crowne and so sent him into the fortification, assuring the inhabitants that they would serve them all in like manner if they did not surrender.'[9]

De Brouillon returned to Plaisance while d'Iberville conducted a vicious winter war (in bitter weather conditions) against the English settlements in Conception and Trinity bays, most of which he pillaged and burned. Although his efforts to capture the inhabitants who had taken refuge on Carbonear Island failed and he was unable to press on to Bonavista, he had conducted a brilliant, if brutal campaign. In all, the French destroyed 36 settlements, killed approximately 200 people, took 700 prisoners, and captured 300 fishing vessels. Sir David Kirke's three surviving sons died as prisoners of war at Plaisance. One result of the campaign was that the planter gentry of the southern Avalon was effectively eliminated. It was, in effect, an English *dérangement*.

If the French had capitalized on this exercise in brutality, Newfoundland would have become a wholly French island, with important strategic consequences, but France lacked the resources necessary to do so. D'Iberville retreated to Plaisance and was then dispatched to campaign against the English in Hudson Bay. Newfoundland's English population had suffered a severe blow, but planters were back on the English Shore in 1698, now protected, in theory at least, by a garrison in St John's.

The Treaty of Ryswick officially ended the war in 1697, but in effect it only called a truce. In North America each side was awarded what it had held in 1689 and began preparing for the next round, which came in 1702 with the War of the Spanish Succession, also known as Queen Anne's War (after the reigning British monarch). It was during Queen Anne's reign that the term 'Great Britain' came into common usage as a result of the terms of union of 1 May 1707 which declared that 'the two kingdoms of Scotland and England shall . . . be united into one kingdom by the name of Great Britain'.

In the War of the Spanish Succession, Canada and Acadia again became bases for attacks on New England, which led to a trade embargo and retaliatory raids. In the summer of 1704 Benjamin Church led an attack against Acadia in response to the 'Deerfield Massacre' of the previous year, in which 50 New Englanders had been killed and 112 taken prisoner to Montreal, many of them women and children. Church and his men attacked all the major Acadian settlements except Port-Royal, which was defended by its fort and garrison. Leaving a trail of broken dikes, burned homes, slaughtered cattle, and devastated crops at Chignecto, Cobequid, Pisiquid, and Minas, the New Englanders also took some 50 Acadian captives to Boston. They were returned in 1706.

New England mobilized a force of 1,600 men to attack Port-Royal again the next year, but the new governor, Daniel d'Auger de Subercase, repulsed the attackers with the help of a hastily assembled Acadian militia. Although his situation was precarious, both militarily and economically, Subercase managed to hang on. Port-Royal became the base for privateers from the French West Indies, who attacked trading vessels from Massachusetts, securing much-needed foodstuffs and manufactured goods. In 1709 the privateers seized 35 vessels and took about 300 prisoners, fuelling the New Englanders' resolve to rid their frontiers of the French.

The following year proved to be a decisive one in the history of Acadia. Supported by a detachment of British marines and a company of grenadiers, General Francis Nicholson, a seasoned colonial administrator, led a force of 1,500 colonial troops and Iroquois allies in a bruising campaign against Port-Royal. After holding out for a week, Subercase and his small, demoralized garrison of 200 soldiers were forced to surrender. Articles of capitulation were signed on 2 October 1710 and Port-Royal, which had been passed back and forth between England and France several times over the previous century, was handed over for what turned out to be the last time.

Antoine Tecouenemac and the Conquest of Port-Royal

At the time of the British capture of Port-Royal in October 1710, Antoine Tecouenemac was 16 years old, living in a territory he understood as the land of the Mi'kmaq, or Mi'kma'ki. We know some of the details of his life because missionary Antoine Gaulin conducted a census of seven Mi'kmaq villages in Acadia two years before the siege. Although Gaulin may have been interested in how many able-bodied Mi'kmaq might be recruited to defend the colony (240 men over the age of 15, he concluded), his census had little impact on French military strategy in the region. Few Mi'kmaq bothered to answer Governor Subercase's plea for assistance.

Historian William Wicken draws on his knowledge of the seasonal rhythms of the Mi'kmaq to suggest why this might be so. Antoine, his parents, and his four siblings lived in the Cape Sable area of southwestern Nova Scotia and were loosely associated with nearly 100 other Mi'kmaq in the region. During the winter months the family moved inland to hunt moose, caribou, and beaver, and during the summer they frequented coastal areas. In the spring and fall they lived along rivers where migrating eels were plentiful and, when smoked, became an important source of food for the winter months. Wicken notes that few Mi'kmaq men would have had time for warfare in early October when the fall eel harvest was in progress.

Although largely oblivious to the capture of Port-Royal, Antoine and his family gradually felt its impact. The ongoing rivalry between the British and the French for control over Mi'kma'ki and the expansion of English settlement created an unstable situation on the northeastern frontier of North America that led to war from 1722 to 1725 between the Wabanaki Confederacy and the British. We do not know what role the Tecouenemac family played in the conflict—if, for example, they were among the nearly 60 Mi'kmaq and Wolastoqiyik who attacked Port-Royal in July 1724—but Antoine, his father, Paul, and his brother Philippe were among the 50 Mi'kmaq who signed a treaty ending the war, which explicitly acknowledged British jurisdiction over Europeans in the colony of Nova Scotia. As Wicken notes, in signing this treaty in 1726, they signified their conscious understanding of how their world had changed since 1710.[10]

In Newfoundland, settlers along the English Shore again suffered raids from Plaisance, which also served as a base for privateers. In 1705 Subercase and Montigny led a repeat performance of the 1697 raid, taking 1,200 prisoners and wreaking destruction as far north as Bonavista. In 1709 French forces took the fort at St John's, burned most of the town, and forced the inhabitants to pay a huge ransom. Again, the French found it impossible to secure their advantage: they withdrew to Plaisance, where they were blockaded by British naval vessels and suffered severe privation.

The Treaty of Utrecht

The Treaty of Utrecht, which ended the War of the Spanish Succession, is sometimes known as 'the Peace of Utrecht' because it consisted not of a single document but of a complicated series of agreements signed in 1713 and 1714 involving Britain, France, Spain, the Netherlands, and other European countries. At the heart of the settlement, which marked the end of Louis XIV's ambitions, was the concept of a European balance of power. This goal was most obvious in the provisions which effectively prohibited the union of the Crowns of France and Spain.

As for North America, the British were less concerned about balance, and aimed to severely contain French power. This they succeeded in doing. In the north, Britain refused to accept that the land between Hudson Bay and Hudson Strait (or the Labrador peninsula) was part of New France and insisted that the French abandon any claim whatsoever to the territory, known as Rupert's Land, which was dominated by the London-based Hudson's Bay Company. Unwillingly, France eventually agreed to 'restore' the territory between Hudson Bay and Hudson Strait to Britain. The question of how and where the boundary line should be drawn was left for future negotiation.

Acadia was partitioned. Britain acquired mainland Acadia and took over Port-Royal, soon to be renamed Annapolis Royal, after the Queen. Once again, however, a boundary was not agreed at Utrecht, which was to be a cause of friction and uncertainty for the next 50 years. France retained Île Royale (Cape Breton Island) and Île Saint-Jean (Prince Edward Island), hoping that bases on these islands would protect the route to Canada and serve as footholds for future attempts to assert French influence in the region. Moreover, they were adjacent to rich fishing grounds.

Since the French placed great value on the northwest Atlantic fisheries, their recognition of British sovereignty over the island of Newfoundland and the agreement to abandon Plaisance were major concessions. French negotiators managed to extract permission for their migratory fishermen to use in season the Petit Nord, defined as extending from Cape Bonavista to Point Riche. Because the exact nature of this fishing right was not defined, it became a source of dissension for almost 200 years.

French-Canadian historians sometimes refer to the Treaty of Utrecht as 'le début de la fin'. Certainly, the years of warfare since 1689 had led to significant restrictions on French power and influence, with Britain emerging as the dominant European power in northeastern North America. Despite the success of colonial settlement on the Avalon Peninsula and around the Bay of Fundy, Europeans remained in the minority. Most of the region was under the control of Aboriginal peoples, who were torn between the demands of the British and the French, neither of whom respected indigenous claims to the land and its resources. With so much in contention and no one power in control, another round in the long Anglo–French struggle seemed likely.

Conclusion

In retrospect, the Treaty of Utrecht marked the beginning of British dominance over France in North America, but this was hardly evident in 1713. The rivalry between Britain and France remained unresolved, and the two powers were left uneasily and resentfully to share northeastern America. For the residents of the Atlantic region, who had received a severe mauling during the wars beginning in 1689, the future was uncertain. French settlers in Acadia had the choice of swearing allegiance to a Protestant monarch hostile to France or moving to French-controlled territory. For English settlers in Newfoundland and New England, the prospect of the French re-establishing themselves on Île Royale and Île Saint-Jean was troubling because it would leave them vulnerable to attack in any future war between Great Britain and France. Meanwhile, the Mi'kmaq, Wolastoqiyik, and Passamaquoddy found that their land had been given away to European powers without their knowledge, let alone their consent. The Treaty of Utrecht, in short, left much to be contested.

Further Readings

Bailey, A.G. 1969. *The Conflict of European and Eastern Algonkian Cultures, 1504–1700*, 2nd edn. Toronto: University of Toronto Press.

Bannister, Jerry. 2003. *The Rule of the Admirals: Laws, Custom, and Naval Government, 1699–1832*. Toronto: University of Toronto Press.

Griffiths, Naomi E.S. 2005. *From Migrant to Acadian: A North American Border People, 1604–1755*. Montreal and Kingston: McGill-Queen's University Press.

Handcock, Gordon. 1989. *'Soe longe as there comes noe women': Origins of English Settlement in Newfoundland*. St John's: Breakwater Press.

Landry, Nicholas. 2008. *Plaisance, Terre-Neuve, 1650–1713: Une colonie française en Amérique*. Sillery: Septentrion.

Newfoundland Studies (Special Issue) 19, 1 (Spring 2003).

Pope, Peter E. 2004. *Fish into Wine: The Newfoundland Plantation in the Seventeenth Century*. Chapel Hill: University of North Carolina Press.

———. 2008. 'Newfoundland and Labrador, 1497–1607', in Newfoundland Historical Society, *A Short History of Newfoundland and Labrador*. St John's: Boulder Publications.

Reid, John G. 1981. *Acadia, Maine, and New Scotland: Marginal Colonies in the Seventeenth Century*. Toronto: University of Toronto Press.

———. 2008. *Essays on Northeastern North America, Seventeenth and Eighteenth Centuries*. Toronto: University of Toronto Press.

——— et al. 2004. *The Conquest of Acadia, 1710: Imperial, Colonial and Aboriginal Constructions*. Toronto: University of Toronto Press.

Food for Thought

Basque, Maurice. 2004. 'Family and Political Culture in Pre-Conquest Acadia', in John G. Reid et al., *The 'Conquest' of Acadia, 1710: Imperial, Colonial and Aboriginal Constructions*. Toronto: University of Toronto Press.

Recommended Websites

History of Plaisance
http://www.heritage.nf.ca/exploration/placentia_text.html

European Migratory Fishery
http://www.heritage.nf.ca/exploration/efishery.html

The Acadian Story
http://www2.umoncton.ca/cfdocs/etudacad/1755

Chapter 6

Renegotiating the Atlantic Region, 1713–63

Fifty years separate the treaties of Utrecht (1713) and Paris (1763). The first confirmed Great Britain's acquisition of territory in the Atlantic region; the second confirmed Britain's ascendancy. In the interim, the British and French continued to jockey for control, encouraged by ambitious colonial officials in Quebec and Boston. Caught between the two powers, Aboriginal peoples and Acadians suffered severely. As the equilibrium in the region gradually tipped toward the British, the area variously known as Mi'kma'ki, Acadia, or Nova Scotia took on global significance, becoming, John Reid argues, 'a virtual laboratory for cultural and political realignments in the Atlantic world'.[1]

Major European Settlements in Nova Scotia, Île Royale, and Île Saint-Jean, 1755. Adapted from Daigle, ed., *Acadia of the Maritimes, 33; Historical Atlas of Canada,* I (Toronto: University of Toronto Press, 1987), plate 30.

Across the Atlantic, 1689–1815

The 'long' eighteenth century from 1689 to 1815 witnessed some of the most remarkable developments in human history. In Europe the rise of nation-states led to imperial rivalries that were global in their reach. Wars for imperial domination were fought in the Americas, Africa, and Asia as well as in Europe. The final showdown between Great Britain and France was a prolonged affair that was finally laid to rest in 1815 with Britain the victor. As was the case with Poland and Vietnam in the twentieth century, what is now Atlantic Canada was caught in the crossfire when it emerged as an unstable borderland in the ongoing global conflict.

The expansion of Europe set people on the move in unprecedented numbers. Enslaved Africans, convicts, indentured servants, free labourers, adventurers, and ne'er-do-wells migrated to the frontiers of empire along with merchants eager to profit from access to new resources. Where Aboriginal peoples could be subdued, enslaved, displaced, or killed, intrepid settlers from Great Britain and continental Europe staked a claim to 'vacant' lands, which they put into agricultural production and resource extraction. With them, migrating peoples brought animals, plants, and diseases that forever altered the ecology of the areas where they settled. The Atlantic region of North America was the first frontier to be colonized by Europeans, and the on-again, off-again warfare imposed major adjustments on Aboriginal and settler societies alike.

By the eighteenth century, improvements in ocean transportation and print communication quickened the pace of change and bound colonial possessions ever closer economically and culturally to their 'mother countries' in Europe. In this period books and pamphlets poured off printing presses in Europe and increasingly also in North America, testimony to the intellectual ferment that was transforming everything Europeans thought about their world. The publication of the 35-volume French *Encyclopédie* between 1751 and 1772 signalled, much as Wikipedia does today, the emergence of a new way of mobilizing and accessing knowledge.

For many eighteenth-century intellectuals, reason rather than received knowledge was perceived as the best approach to understanding the world. Many members of the rising middle class of merchants and professionals agreed with them, gravitating to liberal notions of individualism, rule of law, free trade, separation of church and state, and representative political institutions. More egalitarian ideas, including the abolition of slavery, women's rights, and the political entitlement of all peoples were also in the air.

Under assault from new ideas and practices, old regimes based on authoritarian rule, state-supported churches, and hereditary privilege began to crumble. The American Revolutionary War, which erupted in 1775, produced one of the world's first great republican regimes. In France, republicanism triumphed briefly during a bloody revolution beginning in 1789 but was brought to heel by Napoleon Bonaparte, who, in turn, was defeated in 1815 by an alliance of European powers determined to put an end to French efforts to establish European and world dominance.

By the early nineteenth century military, aristocratic, and ecclesiastical powers had mobilized in defence of order, authority, and subordination but the political firmament had been forever altered. Power was increasingly defined as deriving from citizens (or at least some of them), not from on high. Political parties, once brief alliances for specific ends, now began to organize around principles that were loosely defined as 'conservative' or 'liberal'.

As colonies of Great Britain and close neighbours of the United States, the areas that became Nova Scotia, New Brunswick, Prince Edward Island, and Newfoundland were caught up in the political debates and institutional developments that animated the Atlantic world in this period. They were also recipients of waves of immigrants from England, Scotland, and Ireland that gradually anglicized what was once a region dominated by Aboriginal and then French inhabitants. Indeed, the Atlantic provinces as we know them today were forged in the dynamic events of this extraordinary period in their history, which set the contours for the region's development to the present day.

Administrative Challenges

The acquisition of Nova Scotia in 1713 presented the British with an imperial dilemma. How were they to deal with a colony with disputed borders, settlers who were primarily French Roman Catholics, and Native peoples allied with the enemy? These difficulties were compounded by the continued French presence on Île Royale, where an imposing military base at Louisbourg was soon under construction. Designed to contain British power in North America, safeguard the approaches to the St Lawrence, support the migratory fishery, and advance French commercial interests in the North Atlantic, the fortress of Louisbourg made a major statement about French intentions in the region. From the 1720s to the 1740s, Louisbourg absorbed between 10 and 20 per cent of France's colonial budget.

France also asserted its position through diplomacy. Since Nova Scotia's boundaries were ill-defined, France insisted that the area north of the Bay of Fundy (present-day New Brunswick) and even Canso (on the eastern end of the Nova Scotia peninsula) were still its possessions. In Newfoundland, France claimed that its fishing rights on the French (or Treaty) Shore were exclusive, rejecting the British government's argument that its nationals had every right to fish there so long as they did not interfere with French operations.

British officials, with a small garrison, established their capital at Annapolis Royal (the former Port-Royal.) It was a small enclave within a territory inhabited by 2,000 Acadians and 3,500 Mi'kmaq. Since both groups were unwilling to sever their ties with France, negotiations to secure an unqualified oath of allegiance to the British Crown failed. With the British hold on the territory apparently tenuous, few immigrants—British or otherwise—were interested in settling there. Nor was any thought given to introducing an elected assembly of the kind that was by now common in Britain's other North American colonies. Instead, a governor (or, more often, his delegate) and an appointed council were charged with legal and administrative issues.

In Newfoundland, despite a growing resident population, the British had no intention of establishing a regular colonial administration of any kind. Local problems, however, were sufficiently serious to warrant something more than the often-ignored provisions of King William's Act, which empowered the fishing admirals to decide local disputes and sent warship commanders to act as appeal judges each summer. This administrative structure, such as it was, disappeared altogether in winter. In 1718 a known murderer in Torbay remained free because no one had the legal authority to arrest him. Clearly something had to be done to ensure law and order.

Eventually it was decided that the commodore of the annual naval squadron would double as governor and commander-in-chief. The first migratory naval governor was Captain Henry Osborne,

Table 6.1	Timeline
1713	Treaty of Utrecht signed.
1720	French begin construction of Fortress Louisbourg; Saint-Pierre establishes a colony on Île Saint-Jean.
1722–5	Wabanaki–New England War.
1726	British sign treaties with Mi'kmaq, Maliseet, and Passamaquoddy; French send a military detachment to Île Saint-Jean.
1729	Captain Henry Osborne appointed naval governor of Newfoundland.
1744–8	War of the Austrian Succession.
1745	Louisbourg captured.
1746	D'Anville Expedition.
1747	Battle of Grand Pré.
1748	Treaty of Aix-la-Chapelle.
1749	Founding of Halifax by the British.
1750–53	'Foreign Protestants' arrive in Halifax.
1750	Construction of Fort Beauséjour and Fort Lawrence.
1752	Treaty of Peace and Friendship with the Mi'kmaq.
1753	Lunenburg founded.
1755	Fort Beauséjour falls to the British.
1755–62	Expulsion of the Acadians.
1756–63	Seven Years' War.
1760–1	Mi'kmaq, Maliseet, and Passamaquoddy sign peace treaties with the British.
1762	French attack on St John's.
1763	Treaty of Paris; Royal Proclamation.

who in 1729 appointed magistrates and constables along the coast from Bonavista to Placentia. In summer these new authorities were supplemented by naval officers acting as surrogate magistrates, and the fishing admirals in time disappeared as an independent force. Thus was born what has been called by historian Jerry Bannister a 'naval state'.[2] If the island did not fit the usual model of colonial development, neither was it—as sometimes has been assumed—a violent, anarchic frontier.

French Designs

Determined to challenge British ascendancy in the region, the French established their head-quarters at the ice-free port of Havre L'Anglois, on the south shore of Île Royale. Construction of the fortified town of Louisbourg began in 1720. It cost a fortune, fell both times it was attacked, and proved ineffective in protecting the St Lawrence, but in other respects Louisbourg succeeded admirably. It quickly became a major fishing port and commercial entrepôt, with a thriving trade that soon equalled Canada's in value. At the same time, French officials used Louisbourg as a base to maintain communication with the Acadians and the Mi'kmaq, in the hope of undermining the British position in Nova Scotia.

By 1744, with a population approaching 3,000, Louisbourg was the largest and most cosmopolitan community in the Atlantic region. Its residents included evacuees from Plaisance, French and Basque fishermen, German and Swiss soldiers, a few Irish, Scots, and Spanish sojourners, and both Native and black servants and slaves. The latter catered to the town's administrative and commercial elite, most of them from France, who lived in comfort if not opulence. Eager to maintain their standard of living when they returned home, many officials bilked the colonial treasury and traded discreetly with the English colonies. The troops, required to work long hours maintaining the fortifications, were only too aware that they were being cheated. In the winter of 1744–5 tensions reached such a pitch that they took over the town, demanding better food, more firewood, and adequate uniforms.

The Treaty of Utrecht had given Acadians a choice: stay where they were and accept British rule, or move away. French authorities hoped that they would choose the latter option, settle on Île Royale, and produce foodstuffs for the residents of Louisbourg. Most Acadians preferred to remain in British territory. Having established highly productive agricultural communities by 1713, they were reluctant to leave them. Pragmatic as ever, the majority saw little advantage in trying to farm on the thin soils of Île Royale. Only 60 Acadian families moved to the area in the two decades following the conquest.[3] Most of them settled in outlying communities, such as Port Toulouse (St Peter's), Rivière de Miré (Mira), Baie-des-Espagnols (Sydney), and Port Dauphin (St Ann's), where they farmed, fished, built boats, and mined coal.

Because Île Royale failed to develop a significant agricultural base and depended on imported foodstuffs, its security was threatened. Cod fishing, both sedentary and migratory, remained the chief economic activity, producing most of the island's exports to France and, importantly, to the West Indies, where slave plantations were becoming significant markets for salt fish.

Although Île Saint-Jean offered plenty of agricultural potential, it attracted little interest. Its forest-covered soils proved far less attractive to Acadians than their dikeland farms, and French authorities initially left development there to private interests. In 1719 the Comte de Saint-Pierre was granted the right to the cod fishery on Saint-Jean, Miscou, and the Îles de la Madeleine in return for sponsoring settlement. The following year his Compagnie de l'Île Saint-Jean sent out more than 250 colonists, who established themselves at coastal locations such as Port LaJoie (near present-day Charlottetown) and Havre Saint-Pierre.

The venture was well conceived and designed to be permanent. Twenty married couples arrived in 1720, and the company recruited potential brides for their unmarried workers and even a midwife. To encourage family formation indentured servants were promised that they would be released from their contracts if they married on Île Saint-Jean. Despite this careful planning, the company failed, its efforts dogged by competition from interlopers, crop failures, and ultimately bankruptcy. The settlers moved away, some of them to Île Royale.

In 1726 France installed a detachment of 30 naval fusiliers in the dilapidated buildings formerly occupied by Saint-Pierre's company. This was done to maintain French sovereignty over the island rather than to signal that the state planned to step in to encourage development as it had done in Île Royale. During the 1730s Jean-Pierre Roma, an energetic Parisian merchant, established fishing operations on the island. Building roads to connect his base at Trois-Rivières (now Brudenell Point) with Havre Saint-Pierre and Port LaJoie, he hoped to develop the colony into an important trading centre. He might well have succeeded if the War of the Austrian Succession had not intervened.

Slavery in Louisbourg

Europeans did not introduce slavery to the Americas—many Aboriginal societies used enslaved labour—but Europeans built whole economies in the Americas on the African slave trade. By 1750 over 3.8 million Africans had been shipped against their will to the Americas. Enslavement soon became equated with skin colour, and racial stereotyping quickly followed.

Slavery existed in both the British and French colonies. Male slaves worked as common labourers in the fishery, in the military, and in trade, artisan, and service occupations, while female slaves were employed primarily as domestic servants. Kenneth Donovan has determined that at least 216 slaves lived on Île Royale between 1713 and 1760.[4] Over 90 per cent were black, reflecting the close trading ties with the West Indies, where sugar, tobacco, indigo, and coffee plantations relied on African slave labour. The other slaves were Aboriginal, called *Panis* or *sauvages*. Most Panis came from the colony of Canada, where they outnumbered those of African origin.

In the French empire slavery was regulated, in theory at least, by the Code Noir, which was introduced in the West Indies in 1685. It obliged slave owners to house, feed, and clothe their slaves properly, to care for the aged and infirm, to encourage marriage, and to provide instruction in Roman Catholicism. Masters could whip their slaves, but not imprison or execute them without recourse to the courts. Women—about one-third of the enslaved population on Île Royale—were not to be sexually exploited, and children were not to be sold separately from a parent before reaching adolescence. Since the Code Noir was not registered in Île Royale, it is unlikely that its provisions were widely known. Only six slaves in the colony were freed in this period, and they had little recourse for help when subjected to physical, psychological, or sexual abuse.

Nevertheless, a few slaves at Louisbourg triumphed over their difficult circumstances. Marie Marguerite Rose, for example, obtained her freedom after nearly two decades in the service of the family of a Louisbourg officer, Jean Chrysostome Loppinot. On 27 November 1755 she married a man of Aboriginal descent, Jean Baptiste Laurent. They lived next door to Marguerite's former owners and set up a tavern. That 'Madam Rose negress' was able to open a business and secure credit in her own name for supplies of meat and rum suggests that there was a degree of 'limited opportunity' available to slaves in Louisbourg.

Imperial Rivalries and Local Strategies

The imperial contest between Great Britain and France was fuelled by the ideological conflict between Protestants and Roman Catholics, which penetrated every corner of colonial society. Under the provisions of the Treaty of Utrecht, Roman Catholic priests were permitted to minister to both the Aboriginal peoples and the Acadians in the region. French officials viewed the Acadian and Aboriginal inhabitants of Nova Scotia as their main bulwark against the British, and, using priests as agents, kept a watchful eye on these potential sources of wartime support.

The continued interest on the part of the French state in the northeastern frontier of North America made it difficult for the Acadians to be absorbed into the British Empire. Although most Acadians would have preferred to live under a French Roman Catholic sovereign, they were not prepared to jeopardize their security by challenging the new regime. A few ambitious families married their daughters to British officers, but most Acadians were wary of aligning themselves too closely with the British. Culture and tradition might predispose them to support the French, but their historical experience seemed to demonstrate that neutrality was the best option. Who could tell which power would win the imperial struggle and gain permanent sovereignty over Acadian lands?

For 30 years, the Acadian strategy of playing both sides paid off. The expansion of North Atlantic trade, much of it focused on New England and Île Royale, offered unprecedented opportunities for the Acadians to increase their wealth and well-being. Indeed, Naomi Griffiths has described the years between 1713 and 1744 as a 'golden age' in Acadian life,[5] largely because it was a rare period of peace. Family life flourished and, by the mid-eighteenth century, there were over 9,000 Acadians in Nova Scotia and 3,000 more on Île Saint-Jean and Île Royale.

Peaceful coexistence also extended to the relationship between the French and the Aboriginal peoples. It was French policy in North America to nurture alliances with local inhabitants through subsidized trade, annual gift-giving, and missionary influence. In the Atlantic region, two priests in particular were effective as missionaries and *agents-provocateurs*: Pierre-Antoine-Simon Maillard and Jean-Louis Le Loutre. By the 1750s Abbé Maillard's base at Chapel Island on Île Royale had

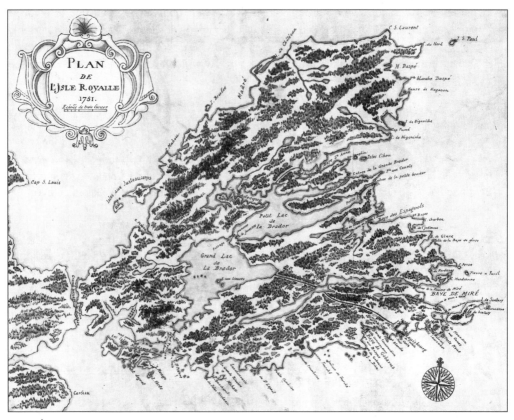

Map of Île Royale by Louis Franquet, 1751. This carefully labelled plan shows French settlement on the island before its final capture by the British in 1758. LAC, NMC-148.

become the site for an annual Mi'kmaq celebration combining worship, gift-giving, and trade. Le Loutre ministered to mainland Mi'kmaq from his base at Shubenacadie (some 50 kilometres north of Halifax) until 1750, when, because of his political activities, he was forced to move to the Isthmus of Chignecto.

After more than a century of French presence, the Mi'kmaq, Wolastoqiyik, and Passamaquoddy had little interest in an alliance with the British, whose language and religion were foreign. With Anglo-American settlement moving up the coast, France offering better terms of trade, and British authorities demanding an oath of allegiance, the Aboriginal peoples in the region soon made their position clear. During the summer of 1715, Mi'kmaq mariners seized Massachusetts fishing vessels off Cape Sable, declaring that 'the Lands are [ours] and [we] can make War and peace when [we] please.'[6] Governor Richard Philipps, who arrived in 1720, managed to extract a promise of friendship from the Wolastoqiyik, but the Mi'kmaq remained hostile, driving New England fishermen out of Canso in 1720 and capturing 36 trading vessels off Nova Scotia two years later.

The New Englanders were quick to retaliate, setting off an 'Indian War' along the New England–Nova Scotia frontier. In the summer of 1724, Mi'kmaq and Wolastoqiyik warriors attacked Annapolis Royal, burning part of the town and killing several British soldiers. A treaty concluded in Boston in December 1725 and ratified at Annapolis Royal in June 1726 finally ended hostilities. The text indicated that the Natives allied in the Wabanaki Confederacy were obliged to recognize British sovereignty. For their part, the British promised that the Natives would not 'be molested in their Persons, Hunting [,] Fishing and Shooting & planting. . . nor in any other [of] their Lawfull occasions. . .'. Since formal treaties were a British innovation, only time would tell whether they were worth the paper on which they were written.

DOCUMENT:
The Treaties of 1725–6

In the summer of 1725, delegates from New England and the Wabanaki Confederacy met in Boston to negotiate an end to the war that had started three years earlier. The Mi'kmaq and Wolastoqiyik were represented by four Penobscot Abenaki. On 15 December 1725 an agreement was reached, with the stipulation that each group would be required to ratify the treaty. Mi'kmaq, Wolastoqiyik, and Passamaquoddy did so at Annapolis Royal on 4 June 1726. The first part of the treaty consisted of the articles of peace and agreement on the rules that the Native peoples would be obliged to follow in their relations with the British colonies of Massachusetts, New Hampshire, and Nova Scotia. The second part of the treaty outlined Britain's obligations and was signed by Captain John Doucett, Lieutenant-Governor of Annapolis Royal. The treaties read in part:

Article of Peace and Agreement: Annapolis Royal, 1726

Whereas His Majesty King George by the Concession of the Most Christian King made att the Treaty of Utrecht is become ye Rightfull Possessor of the Province of Nova Scotia or Acadia According to its ancient Boundaries, wee the Said Chiefs & Representatives of ye Penobscott, Norridgewalk, St. Johns, Cape Sables, & of the Other Indian Tribes Belonging to & Inhabiting within This His Majesties Province of Nova Scotia Or Acadia & New England do for our Selves & the said Tribes Wee represent acknowledge His Said Majesty King George's Jurisdiction & Dominion Over The Territories of the Said Province of Nova Scotia or Acadia & make our Submission to His said Majesty in as Ample a Manner as wee have formerly done to the Most Christian King.

That the Indians shall not molest any of His Majesty's Subjects or their Dependants in their Settlements already made or now fully to be made or in their carrying on their Trade or any other affairs within the said Province.

That if there Happens any Robbery or outrage Committed by any of our Indians the Tribe or Tribes they belong to shall Cause satisfaction to be made to ye partys Injured.

That the Indians shall not help to convey away any Soldiers belonging to His Majesty's forts, but on the contrary shall bring back any soldier they shall find endeavouring to run away.

That in case of any misunderstanding, Quarrel or Injury between the English and the Indians no private revenge shall be taken, but Application shall be made for redress according to His Majesty's Laws.

That if there [be] any Prisoners amongst any of our aforesaid Tribes, wee faithfully promise that the said prisoners shall be releas'd & Carefully Conducted & delivered up to this Government or that of New England.[7]

Reciprocal Promises Made by Captain John Doucett, 1726

Whereas the Chiefs of the Penobscott, Norridgewalk, St. Johns, Cape Sable Indians and of the other Indian Tribes & their Representatives Belonging to and Inhabiting within this his Majesty's Province of Nova Scotia Conforme to the Articles Stipulated by their Delegates . . . at Boston in New England The Fifteenth day of December one thousand Seven hundred & twenty five have come to this His Majesty's Fort of Annapolis Royal and Ratifyed said Articles and made their submission to his Majesty King George . . . and Acknowledged his said Majesty's Just title to this his said province of Nova Scotia or Acadia & promised to Live peaceably with all his Majestys Subjects & their Dependants & to performe what Further is Contained in the Severall articles of their Instruments. I do therefore in His Majesty's name for and in Behalf of this His said Government of Nova Scotia or Acadia Promise the Said Chiefs & their Respective Tribes all marks of Favour, Protection & Friendship.

And I do Further promise & in the absence of the honabl the Lt Govr of the Province in behalf of the this said Government, That the Said Indians shall not be Molested in their Persons, Hunting Fishing and Shooting & planting on their planting Ground nor in any other their Lawfull occasions, By his Majesty's Subjects or Their Descendants in the Exercise of their Religion Provided the Missionarys Residing amongst them have Leave from the Government for So Doing.

That if any Indians are Injured By any of his Majesty's Subjects or their Dependants They shall have Satisfaction and Reparation made to them According to His Majesty's Laws whereof the Indians shall have Benefit Equall with his Majesty's other Subjects.

> That upon the Indians Bringing back any Soldier Endeavouring to run away from any of His Majesty's Forts or Garrisons, the Said Indians for this good Office Shall be handsomely rewarded.
>
> That as a Mark and token of a true Observation & Faithfull Performance of all and Every Article promised on his Majesty's part by the Government I have by and with the Advice of the Council for the said Government Releas'd and Sett att Liberty the Said Indian Prisoners.[8]

The War of the Austrian Succession, 1744–8

The test of Acadian neutrality and Aboriginal alliances came in 1744, with the outbreak of the War of the Austrian Succession. News that war had been declared reached Louisbourg three weeks before it arrived in Annapolis Royal and Boston. Taking advantage of this intelligence, Governor Jean Baptiste-Louis Le Prévost Duquesnel authorized privateers to attack New England shipping and dispatched a force against Canso. The 87 soldiers stationed there were caught off guard and surrendered almost immediately in May 1744.

Duquesnel then moved against Annapolis Royal, sending an advance force of some 300 Mi'kmaq and a few Acadians, mobilized by Le Loutre, to lay siege to the poorly defended capital. Fortunately for the British, a Massachusetts force intervened. Le Loutre's army took flight, believing that the New Englanders were accompanied by a contingent of Mohawks, reputed to be formidable enemies. Later in the summer, Captain François Du Pont Duvivier attacked Annapolis Royal with the help of 160 Mi'kmaq and 70 Wolastoqiyik. Lieutenant-Governor Paul Mascarene might well have been forced to surrender, but once again reinforcements arrived from Boston and assistance from France failed to materialize.

Alarmed by developments on their northeastern frontier, the New Englanders moved quickly against Louisbourg. In the spring of 1745 a volunteer militia of 4,300 men, led by William Pepperrell and supported by a naval squadron of more than 100 British and New England vessels under the command of British Commodore Peter Warren, laid siege to the fortress. Dragging their cannon over difficult terrain from their landing site at Gabarus Bay, the New Englanders pounded their objective for seven weeks. Governor Louis Du Pont Duchambon, his town in ruins and its inhabitants facing extreme deprivation, surrendered on 17 June. New Englanders also destroyed French installations on Île Saint-Jean, including Roma's base at Trois-Rivières. In June 1746 the French tried to recapture Louisbourg, but the large expedition led by the Duc d'Anville—54 ships carrying 7,000 men—was dogged by bad weather, poor management, and debilitating diseases. D'Anville died and his successor tried to commit suicide. By October the tattered remnants of the squadron had retreated to France without firing a shot against the enemy.

Its navy devastated, France could no longer support military campaigns in North America. Thus a force of 680 men under the Sieur de Ramezay, sent from Quebec to participate in the hapless Louisbourg expedition, was left to its own devices. Learning that Governor Shirley of Massachusetts had sent 500 colonial militiamen to keep the Acadians under surveillance, de

Ramezay dispatched Captain Louis Coulon de Villiers and 300 Canadiens on a classic winter guerrilla campaign. They made their way through heavy snow to Grand Pré, where the New Englanders were quartered in Acadian homes. Using information provided by sympathetic Acadians, the French surrounded the houses where the New Englanders were sleeping, killed 70, and forced the rest to surrender.

The 'Massacre of Grand Pré', as the English called it, made the Acadian strategy of neutrality irrelevant. The British would remember the few 'treacherous informers' and 'traitors' who had helped de Villiers, not the majority who had tried to maintain a desperate impartiality. British administrators were now convinced that Acadians could be pressed into supplying both French and Natives with billets, intelligence, and provisions. Whether their compliance was voluntary or extracted under duress was immaterial.

An Uneasy Peace, 1749–55

The Treaty of Aix-la-Chapelle in 1748 temporarily averted reprisals. Britain and France agreed to return what each had captured from the other. When they learned that Louisbourg was included in the deal, the New Englanders were outraged. Nevertheless, each side understood that the treaty represented a truce rather than a final settlement.

To counter the threat posed by Louisbourg, the British government decided to build a fortified base on the south shore of the Nova Scotia peninsula. In June 1749 Edward Cornwallis led an expedition of more than 2,500 British soldiers, settlers, and labourers to the shores of Chebucto Bay. The founding of Halifax was Britain's first serious attempt to colonize the territories acquired under the Treaty of Utrecht. As such it marked a turning point in the history of the Atlantic region, signalling a new determination on the part of the British to control Nova Scotia.

British efforts to assert dominance in the region included an immigration policy designed to swamp the resident population with loyal settlers. Between 1750 and 1753, nearly 2,500 German- and French-speaking Protestants (many of them from the Palatinate, Switzerland, and Montbéliard) arrived in Nova Scotia. Some of these 'foreign Protestants', many of them recruited by Rotterdam merchant John Dick, stayed in Halifax, but the majority settled along the south shore of the colony where, in 1753, they became the founders of the new town of Lunenburg. With the threats posed by hostile French and Aboriginal forces uppermost in their minds, British authorities designed Lunenburg as a compact community that would be more easily defended in the event of attack than scattered farm settlements. The rigid grid of streets marching up the steep slope from the harbour still testifies to the classic principles that governed town planning in the eighteenth century. Despite several difficult years, the Lunenburg settlers soon became productive farmers and eventually became skilled at fishing and shipbuilding.

Many of the disbanded soldiers and sailors who helped to build Halifax quickly escaped to Boston, but merchants and artisans, eager to profit from the money being invested in the colony, stayed, at least for a time. Merchants and office seekers from New England also sought opportunities in the new military base. Jersey-born merchant Joshua Mauger emerged as the most powerful figure in the capital, making his fortune from participating in the West Indies trade, smuggling with Louisbourg, and selling rum. In the early 1760s he returned to Great Britain, where, as a member of Parliament, he played an important role in determining colonial policy.

These British initiatives posed a threat not only to the French but also to the Native people in the region. Following the Treaty of Aix-la-Chapelle, the British insisted that all First Nations who had fought on the French side must sign separate peace treaties. The Wolastoqiyik and Passamaquoddy seemed prepared to reconfirm the treaty of 1726, but the Mi'kmaq remained defiant. They attacked the British at sea and harassed the settlers at Halifax, which had been established on a favourite Mi'kmaq summer encampment site.

It is difficult to determine the extent of Le Loutre's influence in perpetrating these assaults, but his intensions were clear. On 29 July 1749, he reported to his superiors in France that: 'As we cannot openly oppose the English ventures, I think we cannot do better than to incite the Indians to continue warring on the English; my plan is to persuade the Indians to send word that they will not permit new settlements to be made in Acadia. . . . I shall do my best to make it look to the English as if this plan comes from the Indians and that I have no part in it.'[9]

Cornwallis responded to the Mi'kmaq attacks not by declaring war—to do that, he reasoned, 'would be . . . to own them a free and Independent people'—but by ordering British subjects to 'take or destroy the savages commonly called Micmacks wherever they are found', offering a reward 'to be paid upon producing such savage taken or his scalp (as is the custom of America)'. Not surprisingly, the Mi'kmaq resistance continued, encouraged by Le Loutre and Maillard, who had been instructed to do everything possible to impede British expansion. Authorities at Louisbourg and Quebec strengthened their military presence and, not to be outdone by Cornwallis, offered bounties for British prisoners and scalps.

As tensions mounted, the Acadians were caught in the middle, pressed by both British and French to take sides. Shortly after his arrival, Cornwallis summoned Acadian representatives to Halifax and demanded that their people take an unqualified oath of allegiance. They refused, fearing reprisals from either the French or the Mi'kmaq, if not both. It was becoming impossible to remain neutral.

In 1750 the French built Fort Beauséjour north of the Missaguash River on the Chignecto Isthmus and urged Acadians to move to French-controlled territory, where they could establish farms to supply food to Île Royale, augment the colonial militia, and bolster French territorial claims. Acadians who refused to relocate were instructed on pain of death not to sell their produce to the British or to assist them in any way. In his usual ruthless way, Le Loutre considered employing pressure tactics to force Acadian compliance, including withdrawing their priests, abducting their wives and children, and destroying their property. The golden age of Acadia had come to an abrupt end.

In response to France's audacity in occupying disputed territory, inciting the Mi'kmaq to war, and mobilizing some of the Acadians into a fifth column, Cornwallis ordered the construction of Fort Edward at Pisiquid (Windsor) to keep an eye on the populous Minas settlements and dispatched Lieutenant-Colonel Charles Lawrence to build a fort across the river from Beauséjour. Despite stiff opposition from French forces, Fort Lawrence was completed in 1750, but the French still had the upper hand. Acadians and Le Loutre's Mi'kmaq allies began to move in significant numbers to the Chignecto area and to nearby Île Saint-Jean. In 1752 Cornwallis's successor, Peregrine Thompson Hopson, concluded a treaty of peace and friendship with the Mi'kmaq to the east of Halifax, but raids, skirmishes, and reprisals continued both in Nova Scotia and elsewhere. In 1753 Le Loutre paid 1,800 livres for 18 British scalps, an indication of the inflated value now placed on these grisly trophies.

Following clashes with the French and their Native allies on the Ohio frontier in 1754, the British and aggrieved New Englanders decided to launch a four-pronged attack against the outer defences of New France: Fort Duquesne in the Ohio Valley, Fort Niagara in the Great Lakes region, Fort Frédéric on Lake Champlain, and Fort Beauséjour in Nova Scotia. The offensive proved ineffective on all fronts save one. A colonial militia force of 2,500 men commanded by Colonel Robert Monckton captured Beauséjour on 12 June 1755 after a brief siege. With only 160 regular soldiers and 300 militia from Canada and Acadia, the French commander's position was hopeless.

For the British, the discovery that many of the French militiamen were Acadians marked a turning point. They had made plans to remove Acadians from the Chignecto region following the capture of Fort Beauséjour. Now the fate of the entire Acadian population, no matter how an individual had positioned themselves with respect to the British presence, hung in the balance.[10]

Le Grand Dérangement

In July 1755 Governor Charles Lawrence offered Acadian delegates one last chance to take an unqualified oath of allegiance. When they refused, Lawrence and his council decided to solve the problem of the 'neutral French' once and for all. Military commanders at Chignecto, Pisiquid, and Annapolis Royal were instructed to seize Acadian men and boys, along with their boats, so that they could not escape. The Acadians were to be deported to the other British colonies in North America, taking only what they could carry.

Awaiting the arrival of transports from Boston, Acadians watched in horror as soldiers burned their homes, barns, churches, and crops and seized their cattle to pay the costs of what was by any measure an expensive operation. The sorrows of the deportation did not end there. Since authorities in the receiving colonies had not been informed in advance, they offered little assistance, and some even refused to accept their quotas of deportees. By the time the expulsions ended in 1762, nearly 11,000 out of approximately 14,000 Acadians had been deported. Others managed to hide until hostilities ended. Some 2,000 made their way to Quebec. Many deportees died of disease and misadventure. Of the 3,100 Acadians shipped from Île St-Jean in 1758, for example, 679 drowned at sea and another 970 died from various causes before reaching their destinations.[11]

Even the French in Newfoundland were not spared. In August 1755 a British naval expedition had appeared off the southwestern coast. Commanded by Captain John Rous, who later played a role in the main deportation, it captured several French Basque ships and sent their crews north to Port au Choix to find passage home.

Acadian Population in 1763	
Massachusetts	1,050
Connecticut	650
New York	250
Maryland	810
Pennsylvania	400
South Carolina	300
Georgia	200
Nova Scotia	1,250
St John River	100
Louisiana	300
England	850
France	3,500
Québec	2,000
St John's Island	300
Baie des Chaleurs	700
Total	**12,600**

Source: Adapted from R. Cole Harris, ed., *Historical Atlas of Canada*, vol. 1 (Toronto: University of Toronto Press, 1987), Plate 30.

Joseph Broussard

The Acadians did not submit meekly to their fate. One of the most notorious resisters was Joseph Broussard, known later in life as Beausoleil.

Born in Port-Royal in 1702, Broussard courted controversy from an early age. In 1724 he was charged with assisting the First Nations' attack on Annapolis Royal and plotting with the French and the Mi'kmaq to challenge British authority in the region. Two years later, though married, he became involved in a contentious paternity case. Joseph and his brother Alexandre were also involved in land disputes with their neighbours.

Around 1740 the Broussards moved across the Bay of Fundy to the village of Beausoleil on the Petitcodiac River (near present-day Moncton). Joseph Broussard assisted the French in their attack on Grand Pré in 1747 and was declared, along with 11 others, an outlaw with a price of 50 pounds on his head by Massachusetts governor William Shirley. During the siege of Fort Beauséjour in 1755, Broussard led a militia force against the British outside the fortress. Captured and imprisoned in Fort Lawrence, Broussard with 86 fellow captives made a daring escape through a tunnel that they dug beneath the prison walls.

The Broussard brothers, their seven sons, and a young Canadian officer, Charles Deschamps de Boishébert, organized Acadians, Mi'kmaq, and Wolastoqiyik into an effective guerrilla unit that inflicted misery on British and colonial troops trying to establish control over the region. After the capture of Louisbourg and Quebec, Broussard and his comrades, now denied access to supplies of ammunition and food, were forced to surrender. Broussard was imprisoned, first in the fort at Piziquid (Windsor) and then on St Georges' Island in Halifax Harbour.

When the war ended, Broussard and his fellow Acadians hired ships to take them to Saint-Domingue (Haiti) and from there they moved to Louisiana in 1765. Shortly after his arrival, Joseph Broussard succumbed to the fevers common in southern climates and was buried in the present-day town of Broussard, which was named in honour of the man who had become a hero to the Acadians.[12]

The shore facilities and houses at five harbours between St George's Bay and Port aux Basques were burned and their 67 residents dumped on Île Royale, where they faced a second deportation.

The Acadian diaspora had a remarkable reach. It took some to Louisiana, where their descendants, the Cajuns, still live; to Canada, where they quickly integrated into the colonial population; to the Îles de la Madeleine, St-Pierre, the West Indies, Great Britain, France, and even the Falkland Islands. Those who went to France felt like strangers and asked to be returned to North America. When the war ended, some of them got their wish. In 1764 Acadians who agreed to take an oath of allegiance were permitted to settle in their former homeland but not, for the most part, in the areas where they had lived. New immigrants, many of them from New England, had already taken up their farms.

Brutal as it was, the expulsion of the Acadians had the military effect that Lawrence had intended. The food supply problem reached crisis proportions in Louisbourg, where the authorities were besieged by destitute Aboriginal allies and Acadian refugees. Even before warfare formally resumed in 1756, the French had lost the first round. 'Maybe more than any other single factor,' Stephen E. Patterson suggests, 'the supply problem spelled doom to French power in the region.'[13]

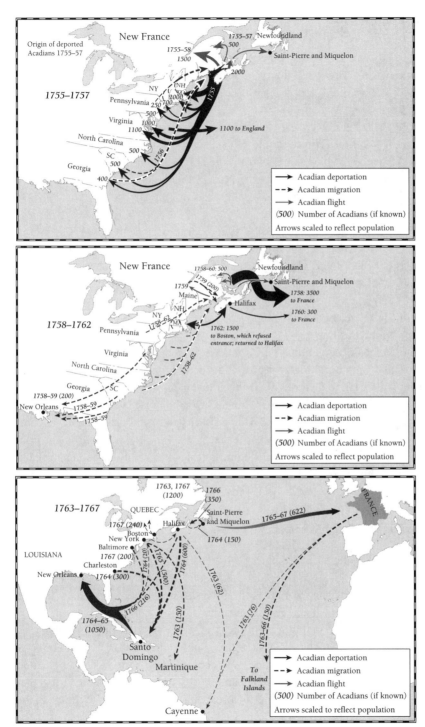

Acadian migrations, 1755–85. Adapted from R. Cole Harris, ed., *Historical Atlas of Canada, Vol.1, From the Beginning to 1800* (Toronto: University of Toronto Prtess, 1987), plate 30. Available at www.umaine.edu/canam/ham/acadiansettlement.htm

Newfoundland, 1713–55

Newfoundland escaped much of the drama that engulfed the Maritime region between the Treaty of Utrecht and the Seven Years' War. No military campaigns were conducted on the island, and as a result a settler society began to develop once again, untroubled by the kind of devastation wrought during earlier wars.

Until the late 1720s, the fisheries were generally poor, prompting the English to enter the off-shore bank fishery for the first time. Thereafter the banks became an increasingly important part of the overall fishery. The inshore failures may explain the fairly slow movement of the English fishery along the south coast, now abandoned by the French. Expansion on the northeast coast, into Bonavista and Notre Dame bays, was more vigorous, possibly because of the opportunities to diversify into furring, sealing, and salmon fishing.

Economic activity picked up in all the bays as fish catches improved from the 1730s onward. The number of winter inhabitants reached over 7,000 in the 1750s (the summer population was more than twice as large). Of these, just under half were immigrants from southeast Ireland. Before the 1720s Newfoundland's inhabitants had come almost exclusively from the hinterlands of the English West Country ports involved in the fishery. The arrival of the Irish reflected not only domestic economic problems but also the fact that West Country vessels habitually stopped at Waterford for provisions and fishing crews.

This change in the population was noted with some concern by the British authorities, but there was little they could do about it. Indeed, it was in this period that the views held by the authorities and the merchants began to diverge. While the government still saw Newfoundland as a fishery and a nursery for mariners, merchants increasingly saw it as a place to make money—not just by fishing on their own account, but by supplying residents and bye-boatmen and purchasing their catches. A quasi-colonial society began to emerge, without any encouragement from the British government. Largely male (women made up less than a third of the population) and transient, this society was composed of British merchants at the apex, planters in the middle, and servants at the bottom. A middle class, in the usual sense of the term, was lacking.

The Seven Years' War, 1756–63

The Seven Years' War had important consequences for the whole Atlantic region. Even before hostilities officially opened in 1756, it was clear that the Atlantic colonies would become a major theatre of war. Louisbourg and Halifax, as well as the fisheries, were important prizes and the instability of the border between British and French territory invited a military resolution.

Although the British were slow to mobilize their forces in North America, once in action they proved effective. Their first important victory was the capture of Louisbourg in 1758. Rebuilt by the French following the War of the Austrian Succession, Louisbourg had a civilian population of about 4,000 and was defended by French soldiers and sailors and a colonial militia, together numbering about 8,500. Recognizing the challenge before them, the British mobilized one of the largest military forces ever to campaign in North America: 27,000 soldiers and sailors under the command of Major General Jeffrey Amherst and Admiral Edward Boscawen. Early in June 1758 the energy of nearly 40,000 people was concentrated on the mighty fortress, testimony, John Johnson reminds us, of the 'importance the two imperial powers placed on Louisbourg'.[14]

'Britain's Glory or the Reduction of Cape Breton, By the Gallant Admiral Boscawen & General Amherst', engraving, 1758. News of the capture of Louisbourg was greeted with great rejoicing in Britain, where this engraving offered a visual representation of the bombardment of the fortified town. From Charles P. De Volpi, *Nova Scotia, A Pictoral Record* (Longman Canada, 1974), Plate 6.

Despite a spirited defence Governor Drucour had little hope of fending off his attackers, who blockaded the port. With supplies of food and ammunition running short, and the town in ruins from a stiff bombardment, he agreed to terms of surrender on 26 July 1758. The military and civilian populations were shipped to France, thus, in effect, more than doubling the number of people deported by the British from the Atlantic region. Aboriginal defenders had fled with Father Maillard before the surrender. To prevent Louisbourg from ever again becoming a centre of French power, the British demolished the fortifications.

Amherst consolidated his victory by sending troops to Île Saint-Jean, the Gaspé, the Miramichi, and the St John River Valley to round up Acadians for deportation and destroy both their settlements and those of their Native allies. To assist in these mopping-up operations, the British employed detachments of Rangers—special forces of colonial militia known for their ruthlessness. Even Amherst was shocked when he learned of the bloody campaign conducted along the St John River by Rangers under Moses Hazen. 'I gave a Commission of Captain to Lieutenant Hazen as I thought he deserved it,' he wrote. 'I am sorry to say what I have since heard of that affair has sullied his merit with me, as I shall always disapprove of killing women and helpless children.'[15] A similarly brutal policy was carried out in the Baie des Chaleurs, and Gaspésie by General James Wolfe, who had played a conspicuous role in the Louisbourg campaign. Wolfe was subsequently chosen to command the army that captured Quebec in September 1759, dying in the battle that marked the end of the French Empire in North America.

As French power collapsed, the Mi'kmaq, Wolastoqiyik, and Passamaquoddy made their accommodation with the British. During 1760–1, all bands sent delegates to Halifax to sign formal treaties of 'peace and friendship' with the governor and council, acknowledging 'the jurisdiction and Dominion of His Majesty George the Second over the Territories of Nova Scotia or Accadia' and agreeing to submit 'to His Majesty in the most perfect, ample, and solemn manner'. These treaties promised government-operated trading posts, but did not reserve lands for hunting and fishing. Governor Jonathan Belcher was instructed by the British government to draw up a proclamation forbidding encroachment on Aboriginal lands, which he obediently did, but he refused to publicize it because, as he told his superiors, 'If the proclamation had been issued at large, the Indians might have been incited . . . to have extravagant and unwarranted demands, to the disquiet and perplexity of the New Settlements in the province.'[16]

The final chapter in the Seven Years' War took place in Newfoundland. Following the surrender of Montreal in 1760, the French devised a bizarre plan to disrupt the English bank fisheries by capturing St John's and impressing French and Irish fishermen to help them retake Île Royale. In 1762 six vessels bearing 750 soldiers under the command of Charles-Henry d'Arsac de Ternay set sail from France. They occupied St John's, Harbour Grace, Carbonear, and Trinity, and destroyed fishing premises and fishing vessels along the coast. A hastily assembled British force, recruited from New York and Nova Scotia and led by Colonel William Amherst, recaptured St John's, the engagement being remembered as the Battle of Signal Hill. It was the last Anglo–French battle to occur in the Atlantic region.

Peace and Reconstruction

In the Treaty of Paris, which formally ended the war in 1763, France gave up its North American empire to Great Britain. A major sticking point in the negotiations was French insistence on access to the Newfoundland fisheries. The final agreement renewed the French right to fish on the Treaty Shore and ceded Saint-Pierre and Miquelon to France. The islands were to serve as an unfortified shelter for French migratory fishermen and a minimal replacement for Île Royale, which French negotiators had fought hard to keep.

On 7 October 1763 the British government issued a proclamation outlining, in broad strokes, what it intended to do with its newly-acquired territories. In the Atlantic region, Île Royale (renamed Cape Breton) and Île Saint-Jean (anglicized to the Island of St John) became part of Nova Scotia, while Anticosti Island, the Îles de la Madeleine, and 'the Coast of Labrador' were placed 'under the care and inspection' of the governor of Newfoundland, who had a naval squadron at his disposal.

The proclamation also set out the Crown's policy regarding Aboriginal peoples. No European settlement would be permitted west of the Appalachian Mountains. Elsewhere, Native peoples were not to be 'molested or disturbed' in the areas set aside for their hunting. All lands in the settled colonies not 'ceded or purchased by Us' were to be 'reserved to the said Indians', and no 'private person' was authorized to buy Native land. Conceived with the western frontier in mind, these policies were deliberately ignored by administrators in Nova Scotia, who were slow to establish reserves and only minimally involved in Native land transactions. Whether this aspect of the Royal Proclamation applied in Newfoundland and Labrador is unclear.

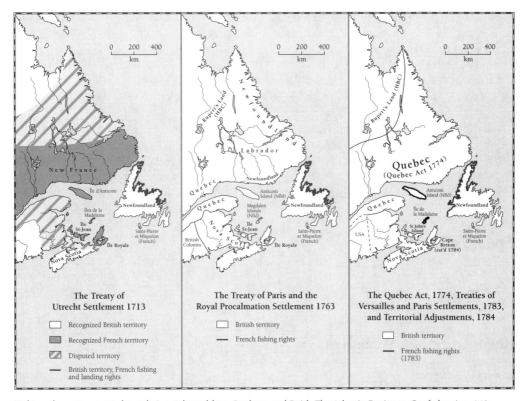

Eighteenth-century treaty boundaries. Adapted from Buchner and Reid, *The Atlantic Region to Confederation*, 143.

Conclusion

Fifty years of rivalry between Great Britain and France ended in 1763 when, for the first time, all of what is now Atlantic Canada came under a single jurisdiction, to which Aboriginal peoples and returning Acadians had no option but to submit. The French presence was reduced to a seasonal fishery on the Newfoundland Treaty Shore and a base at Saint-Pierre and Miquelon. In this situation, the British government was eager to see the region—apart from Newfoundland and Labrador—settled, preferably by English-speaking Protestants.

Further Readings

Faragher, John Mack. 2005. *A Great and Noble Scheme: The Tragic Story of the Expulsion of the French Acadians from Their American Homeland.* New York: W.W. Norton.

Janzen, Olaf. 2008. 'The "Long" Eighteenth Century, 1697–1815', in Newfoundland Historical Society, *A Short History of Newfoundland and Labrador.* Portugal Cove–St Philip's: Bolder Publications, 50–76.

Jobb, Dean. 2005. *The Acadians: A People's Story of Exile and Triumph*. Mississauga: Wiley and Sons.

Johnston, A.J.B. 1984. *Religion in Life at Louisbourg*. Montreal: McGill-Queen's University Press.

———. 2001. *Control and Order in French Colonial Louisbourg, 1713–1758*. East Lansing: Michigan State University Press.

———. 2007. *Endgame 1758: The Promise, the Glory, and the Despair of Louisbourg's Last Decade*. Lincoln: University of Nebraska Press.

Laxer, James. 2006. *The Acadians in Search of a Homeland*. Toronto: Doubleday Canada.

LeBlanc, Ronnie-Gilles, dir. 2005. *Du Grand Dérangement à la Déportation: Nouvelles perspectives historiques*. Moncton: Chaire d'études acadiennes, Université de Moncton.

Moore, Christopher. 1982. *Louisbourg Portraits: Life in an Eighteenth-Century Garrison Town*. Toronto: Macmillan.

Newfoundland Studies (Special Issue) 17, 2 (Fall 2001).

Wicken, William C. 2002. *Mi'kmaq Treaties on Trial: History, Land, and Donald Marshall Junior*. Toronto: University of Toronto Press.

Food for Thought

Wicken, William C. 1994. 'The Mi'kmaq and Wuastukwiuk Treaties', *University of New Brunswick Law Journal* 43: 241–53.

Recommended Websites

Acadian Deportation
http://www2.umoncton.ca/cfdocs/etudacad/1755

The Fortress of Louisbourg
http://epe.lac-bac.gc.ca/100/205/301/ic/cdc/louisbourg/default.htm

The English Fishery and Trade in the 18th Century
http://www.heritage.nf.ca/exploration/18fishery.html

Chapter 7

Community Formation, 1749–1815

Between the founding of Halifax in 1749 and the end of the Napoleonic wars in 1815, the Atlantic region was reorganized and essentially remade. The expulsion of the Acadians, the destruction of their farms and communities, and the razing of the great fortress of Louisbourg struck major blows to the region's economy, but these drastic actions ensured that British culture would prevail in the post-war reconstruction. Many communities in the region trace their origins to the second half of the eighteenth century, when nearly 75,000 people, mostly of British and Irish origin, arrived in the Atlantic colonies.

Between 1760 and 1775, Nova Scotia became home to about 8,000 New Englanders and smaller numbers of immigrants from Great Britain, but the most dramatic influx of population occurred following the American Revolutionary War (1775–83). As many as 50,000 people, known as Loyalists, fled the newly independent United States to live in what was left of 'British' North America, most of them settling in Nova Scotia, which was reduced in size in 1784 by the creation of two new colonies—New Brunswick and Cape Breton—to accommodate the refugees. With the arrival of the Loyalists, the uneasy equilibrium between Aboriginal peoples and the British in the Maritimes was swept away by the sheer force of numbers. Newfoundland, meanwhile, also increased in population and, during the French and Napoleonic Wars (1793–1815), became a settler society much like the others in the Atlantic region.[1]

Immigration and Settlement

In this period a great wave of immigration transformed Atlantic Canada. The early immigrants, such as the settlers brought to Halifax and Lunenburg between 1749 and 1753, were recruited by the British authorities, but in time others began to arrive independently. Some were refugees from the political and economic revolutions sweeping the Atlantic world; others were attracted by the region's potential to profit from resource development and warfare. A majority of the new settlers came from other parts of North America, and shared with immigrants from Great Britain and Europe a determination to improve their lot in an unstable and rapidly changing world.

The expulsion of the Acadians and the capture of Louisbourg opened Nova Scotia to settlement, but wartime conditions made it difficult for authorities to recruit immigrants from overseas. Although its proximity and rapidly growing population made New England a promising source of immigrants, people there were reluctant to move to a colony where their 'rights as Englishmen' were in question. This obstacle was overcome when the Board of Trade, which was responsible for colonial policy, obliged a reluctant Governor Charles Lawrence to call

Table 7.1	Timeline
1756–63	Seven Years' War.
1758–9	Governor Lawrence's Proclamations.
1759	New England Planters begin moving to Nova Scotia.
1763	Treaty of Paris; Royal Proclamation.
1764–8	Hugh Palliser serves as governor of Newfoundland.
1764	Samuel Holland surveys St John's Island; Acadians permitted to resettle in the Maritimes.
1767	St John's Island granted to British proprietors.
1769	St John's Island granted colonial status.
1770	George Cartwright builds a trading and fishing base in Labrador.
1771	Moravians establish mission station at Nain, Labrador.
1772–4	Yorkshire settlers arrive in Nova Scotia.
1772	The *Hector* arrives in Pictou.
1774–1809	Labrador under the jurisdiction of Quebec/Lower Canada.
1775–83	American Revolutionary War.
1783	Treaty of Paris.
1784	New Brunswick and Cape Breton Island established as separate colonies.
1789	French Revolution begins.
1791	Supreme Court established in Newfoundland.
1792	More than 1,200 Black Loyalists depart for Sierra Leone.
1793–1815	French Revolutionary and Napoleonic Wars.
1799	St John's Island renamed Prince Edward Island.
1812	War of 1812 begins.
1814	End of the War of 1812.
1815	End of the Napoleonic wars.

Nova Scotia's first elected assembly in 1758 and issue a proclamation, widely circulated in New England, inviting prospective immigrants to Nova Scotia. A second proclamation issued early in 1759 outlined the rights that settlers would enjoy: two elected assembly representatives for each settled township; a judicial system similar to the one in 'Massachusetts, Connecticut, and the other Northern Colonies'; and freedom of worship for Protestant dissenters, with Calvinists, Lutherans, and Quakers specifically mentioned as having 'liberty of conscience' and the right to be 'excluded from any Rates or Taxes to be made and levied for the Support of the Established Church of England'. Settlers were to receive land grants—100 free acres (40 hectares) for each head of household, with an additional 50 for each family member and servant—that would be exempt from taxes for 10 years. Assistance was even provided to help some of the immigrants move to their new homes.

    Their concerns addressed, nearly 8,000 New Englanders settled in Nova Scotia between 1759 and 1767. Known as 'Planters', they created a new New England on the south shore of Nova Scotia, in the Annapolis Valley, and in parts of the north shore of the Bay of Fundy. In 1762 James

Mapping the Region

To support their imperial objectives, the British sponsored extensive exploration and mapping. During the Seven Years' War, Captain James Cook, better known for his work in the Pacific, charted part of the Gulf of St Lawrence and helped to prepare the map that enabled General James Wolfe to reach Quebec in 1759. After the war, Cook became the naval surveyor for Newfoundland, and between 1763 and 1767 charted the island's south and west coasts and the Strait of Belle Isle, where the French were becoming increasingly aggressive in asserting their fishing rights. A century later Cook's charts were still in use, as were those of his successor, Michael Lane, who completed the work.

Cook's equivalent in Nova Scotia was Joseph F.W. DesBarres, who painstakingly charted the waters around the Nova Scotia peninsula, Cape Breton, and St John's Island between 1764 and 1773. His maps and drawings were published in his magnificent four-volume atlas, *The Atlantic Neptune* (1774–84), which was recognized in its day as a major cartographic achievement.

During the same period, the army officer Samuel Holland carried out extensive surveys in the Atlantic region. His report on St John's Island laid out counties, parishes, and townships; fixed the site of the projected capital, which he named Charlottetown in honour of King George III's Queen; and gave a detailed account of the island's resources and climate. Holland then moved on to the Îles de la Madeleine and Cape Breton, where he drew attention to the latter's deposits of coal, building stone, and gypsum. In the early 1770s he helped to map the coast from the St John River to New York and conducted hydraulic surveys in Nova Scotia.

Labrador also became better known to the British in the second half of the eighteenth century. Lane charted the south coast, and, beginning in 1765, the north coast was gradually explored by the Moravian missionaries. The interior of Labrador remained largely unknown to Europeans. The same was true of Newfoundland until concern about the dwindling numbers of Beothuk led to exploration of the Exploits River and Red Indian Lake, beginning in 1768 with an expedition led by Lieutenant John Cartwright. Local Mi'kmaq, who began moving to the island in increasing numbers after 1763, also ranged throughout the interior. It was the Mi'kmaq who informed Cook about the island's river systems, which he included on his 1770 general map.

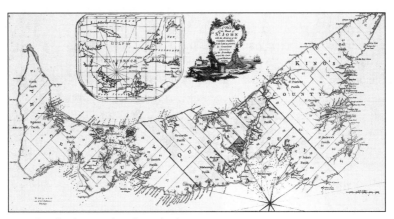

Samuel Holland's map of St John's Island. LAC, NMC-23350.

Simonds, James White, and William Hazen—New England merchants associated with Joshua Mauger—established trading operations in the region, eventually locating their headquarters at Portland Point, near the mouth of the St John River. They developed a flourishing trade with the local Native people and brought in labour to exploit the area's resources of fish, timber, and limestone. When, further up the river, a group of farmers from Essex County, Massachusetts, squatted on land reserved by the crown and occupied by Acadians and Wolastoqiyik, Mauger intervened to ensure that the newcomers prevailed. The grateful settlers named their community Maugerville. In 1765, 20 pacifist German Protestant families from Pennsylvania settled on the Petitcodiac River, where they became the founders of Hopewell, Hillsborough, and Moncton.

The largest group yet to settle in the Maritimes, the New England Planters added a distinctly 'Yankee' flavour to the region. They drew freely on the resources of their homeland, recruiting ministers for their Congregational churches, trading fish and farm produce in Boston and other New England ports, and returning 'home' periodically to visit family and friends. Although most Planters came with little capital, they were among the most fortunate of immigrants, making impressive progress in standards of living and institutional development in only one generation.

After the Seven Years' War, Acadians were again permitted to settle in the Atlantic region, becoming 'planters' in their own right. They carved out communities in a number of locations, especially Argyle and Clare in southwestern Nova Scotia, Île Madame and Cheticamp in Cape Breton, the northeastern shore of what would later become New Brunswick, and the western end of St John's Island. The Îles de la Madeleine, though settled by Acadians, were administered by Quebec after 1774 and granted in 1787 as a seigneury to Captain Isaac Coffin. Scratching a hardscrabble existence from the inferior soil typical of the lands granted them, the Acadians soon turned to fishing and became an indispensable labour force for the Jersey-based fishing companies that set up operations in the Gaspé and Cape Breton following the British conquest. By 1800 the Atlantic region counted at least 8,000 francophones, and this number would continue to grow impressively with each generation.

In an attempt to populate the region on the cheap and at the same time promote a land-based social hierarchy, British authorities made large land grants to 'proprietors' on condition that they recruit Protestant settlers, improve their properties, and pay quitrents (taxes) to sustain the colonial administration. In a 17-day period in 1765, more than one million hectares of mainland Nova Scotia were handed over to speculators. Two years later, in an even more spectacular display of largesse, 64 of the 67 lots on St John's Island that Samuel Holland had surveyed in 1764 were granted to favourites of the King and court.

Most of the proprietors failed to meet the conditions of their grants, but a few tried. Alexander McNutt, who had planned to settle thousands of Ulster Protestants from Ireland and from New Hampshire on his enormous grants, managed to bring a few hundred to communities such as Londonderry (Colchester County) and New Dublin (Lunenburg County). Near Windsor, Nova Scotia, two would-be aristocrats, Henry Denny Denson and J.F.W. DesBarres, employed tenant and enslaved labour to work their estates. Located on the Minas Basin, Windsor was fast becoming not only the country seat of the Halifax elite but also a commercial centre of some importance, and in 1767 it hosted the region's first agricultural fair.

The Philadelphia plantation, granted in 1765 to 14 proprietors in what is now Pictou County, attracted a few settlers from Pennsylvania, but the majority of its inhabitants arrived on board the

Hector in 1773—the beginning of what was to become a substantial wave of immigration from Scotland. Always alert to lucrative trading opportunities, Scottish merchants were drawn to the region specifically for its timber and fish. In 1765 William Davidson and his associates received a grant of 100,000 acres (40,500 hectares) on the Miramichi, where they developed a salmon fishery and eventually diversified into timber and shipbuilding.

Between 1772 and 1776 roughly 1,000 people from Yorkshire, many of them Methodists, settled in the Chignecto area and elsewhere in Nova Scotia. Pushed out of England by high rents, land enclosure, and their own ambitions, they arrived with commercial and farming skills of a high order. Many of them had sufficient capital to purchase their farms outright, and they quickly brought them into efficient production.

Most of the unsettled proprietorial grants in Nova Scotia eventually reverted to the Crown, but this was not the case on St John's Island (renamed after Prince Edward in 1799). By having the island proclaimed a separate colony in 1769 and controlling its administration, the proprietors succeeded in frustrating all attempts to settle 'the land question' in favour of freehold tenure. In this way the colony became saddled with a proprietorial land system that was increasingly out of step with land-granting policies in other areas of North America.

Despite this handicap, the island managed to attract settlers. Many of the early immigrants were Scots, whose homeland was suffering such severe political and economic upheaval that emigration seemed an attractive option even if it meant leasing rather than owning land. The first settlers, some 80 Scots recruited by Captain Robert Stewart for Lot 18, arrived on the *Arabella* in 1770. They were soon followed by a group of indentured servants under contract to grow flax on the estates of Sir James Montgomery, Roman Catholic Highlanders under the direction of John MacDonald of Glenaladale, Protestants from Ulster, and Quakers from London. By 1775 the 300 Acadian and Mi'kmaq residents of the island were outnumbered four to one by the 1,200 immigrants from Great Britain.

The year-round population of Newfoundland grew as well, to about 10,000 in the 1770s, but in the same way as earlier in the century: slowly, informally, and without official encouragement. Sir Hugh Palliser, governor from 1764 to 1768, did what he could to encourage a seasonal, migratory fishery, but this was no longer possible on the island, where the industry was becoming increasingly residential. He therefore focused his attention on southern Labrador. His policy was unrealistic even here, given that commercial success on that coast depended on the year-round exploitation of the available resources: cod, salmon, fur, and seals. Another problem was a state of virtual warfare between fishermen and the Inuit who travelled to the southern coast and the Strait of Belle Isle to trade whalebone and to scavenge from fishing camps.

Eager to pacify the area, Palliser welcomed a proposal from the highly disciplined Protestant sect commonly called the Moravians—officially the Unitas Fratrum (United Brethren)—to establish a mission in Labrador. In 1771 the first Moravian mission station, complete with a trading store, was built at Nain. Okak followed in 1776 and Hopedale in 1782. The mission's presence eventually helped to persuade the Inuit to stay in the north—as did the growing number of Europeans in the south, and the increasing mortality from European diseases among the Inuit living there.

Palliser was also concerned about ending clashes between the Beothuk and English fishermen on Newfoundland's northeast coast. He therefore commissioned Lieutenant John Cartwright to explore the Exploits River Valley in 1768, but he failed to make contact with the Natives. On the

Mikak

Born in Labrador around 1740, Mikak was a member of an Inuit band that frequented the south Labrador coast, trading with Europeans and often scavenging from their establishments. Conflict and violence were commonplace.

In 1767 trouble developed between Mikak's band and Europeans at Cape Charles. Marines from the blockhouse in Chateau Bay retaliated, and at least 24 men were killed in the ensuing skirmish, among them Mikak's husband. Taken captive—along with two other women and six children, including her son, Tutauk—Mikak spent the winter at Chateau Bay, where she and the second in command, Francis Lucas, each learned some words of the other's language.

In the summer of 1768 Lucas took his captives to St John's. Governor Palliser, impressed by Mikak, arranged for Lucas to escort her to England with Tutauk and a boy named Karpik. In London Mikak was visited by the Moravian Jens Haven, whom she had met in 1765, and was lionized at court. The Dowager Princess of Wales gave her presents, including a fine dress, and John Russell, a fashionable artist, painted her portrait. She returned to Labrador in 1769.

Mikak was now a person of status among her own people which, together with her knowledge of English, made her a potentially important intermediary for Europeans. In 1770, for example, both Lucas and the Moravians sought her assistance, but the Moravians reached her first. With her new husband, Tuglavina, Mikak agreed to help them find a suitable site for their mission. Lucas looked for Mikak in vain, and was lost at sea later that year.

The Moravians established Nain in 1771. Deciding not to live there, Mikak and Tuglavina drifted away from the mission and its influence. They separated in 1776, and she had a succession of other husbands. At one time she showed an interest in baptism, but in 1783 she left for south Labrador. In 1795 she became ill and returned to Nain, where she spent the last

10 days of her life. Tuglavina, now a convert, died there three years later.

Mikak's son Tutauk, who called himself Jonathan Palliser, moved back south. When a Methodist missionary met him in Hamilton Inlet in 1824, one of his wives was wearing Mikak's English dress. His descendants still live in Labrador.[2]

John Russell, 'Esquimaux Lady', oil on canvas, 1769. Mikak is clothed in a dress given to her by the Dowager Princess of Wales. Mikak was returned to Labrador in 1769, and later helped the Moravian mission become established there. Völkerkundliche Sammlung der Universität Göttingen, Germany.

south coast, naval ships actively tried to prevent large groups of Mi'kmaq from travelling to St-Pierre, now the only centre of French Catholicism in the area, also to prevent interference with the fisheries. As a result, the Mi'kmaq settled in St George's Bay on the west coast.

Among the British and French-Canadian entrepreneurs who had their eyes on Labrador in this period was Captain George Cartwright, John Cartwright's brother, who in 1770 established a fishing and trading base at Cape Charles, later moving to Sandwich Bay. A man of great energy, Cartwright published a lively account of his experiences in 1792. Although Labrador was placed under the jurisdiction of Quebec in 1774, the governor of Newfoundland continued to supervise the mission stations and the fisheries in the area, which was formally restored to the jurisdiction of Newfoundland in 1809.

The American Revolution

The Seven Years' War turned out to be only an interlude in the warfare that engulfed North America in the eighteenth century. By the early 1770s growing tensions over British taxation, trade, and military policies were moving the New England colonies towards armed conflict with their 'mother' country. Colonial defiance led the British, in 1774, to curtail the trade conducted by Massachusetts, close the port of Boston, and send in troops. In September of that year, delegates from all but five of Britain's North American colonies (Newfoundland, St John's Island, Nova Scotia, Quebec, and Georgia) met in Philadelphia to coordinate a response. The First Continental Congress demanded the repeal of what came to be known as the Coercive Acts. When Britain refused to back down, the colonial militia was placed on alert. The first shots were fired at Lexington, Massachusetts, in April 1775. Within weeks a second Continental Congress had commissioned George Washington to raise an army for the defence of 'American liberty'. After driving the British out of Boston, they planned to march on Quebec. The invasion of Quebec failed, but the colonial resolve remained strong. On 4 July 1776, the rebellious colonies declared their independence from Great Britain.

Historians have spent considerable energy exploring why the North Atlantic colonies failed to join the rebellion. In the case of Newfoundland, the reasons are fairly clear. Without formal political institutions, Newfoundlanders had no way of entering into an alliance with the rebelling colonies even had they wanted to, which they did not. Moreover, any sympathy that they might have had for the American cause was quickly blunted when, in retaliation against British regulations forbidding New Englanders from fishing in Newfoundland waters, the Americans put a ban on trade with the island. This move caused widespread hardship for Newfoundlanders, who had come to depend on New England for foodstuffs and shipping in the West Indies trade. Throughout the Revolutionary War, American predators at sea made all fishing hazardous, especially offshore. Migratory activity decreased, the resident population fell, and food shortages were frequent. In the winter of 1779–80 James Balfour, a Church of England missionary in Conception Bay, reported 'raging Famine, Nakedness & Sickness in these Parts. None can express the heart felt woe of Women & Children mourning for want of Food.'[3]

In Nova Scotia and St John's Island, as in Newfoundland, political and economic development was insufficiently advanced to make independence an appealing option. People who had received land from the Crown on exceptionally favourable terms were reluctant to support the rebels for fear that, as seemed likely at the outset of the war, the British would prevail. Even if there was sympathy for the rebel cause in certain areas, the British military presence in colonial capitals and coastal waters was a powerful deterrent to armed resistance.

The reach of Halifax was clearly demonstrated in the fall of 1776, when Jonathan Eddy and John Allen, both from the Cumberland area, led a force of 180 men, including Wolastoqiyik and Acadians, against the garrison at Fort Cumberland (formerly Fort Beauséjour). The attack was easily repulsed, but British authorities were obliged to remain vigilant. In July 1776 Mi'kmaq and Wolastoqiyik chiefs had attended a meeting in Massachusetts at which they agreed to support the Patriot cause. They became even bolder when the French formally entered the war on the side of the United States early in 1778. Mi'kmaq attacks on settlers in the Miramichi area and a Wolastoqiyik threat to Fort Howe, at the mouth of the St John River, underscored the continuing vulnerability of the British in the region. Michael Francklin, Superintendent for Indian Affairs for Nova Scotia, tried to address Native grievances by bringing in a French-speaking priest and agreeing to issue grants for lands promised in 1768. Although representatives of the Mi'kmaq and Wolastoqiyik signed a treaty with the British at Fort Howe on 24 September 1778, some chiefs remained committed to the American cause when France decided to join the war against Great Britain in 1778. The British finally decided to seek assistance from their Aboriginal allies outside of the region. In June 1780 'three hundred fighting men besides six hundred women and children' were assembled to meet with delegates from 'the Ottawas, Hurons, Algonkins, Abenakis and other nations from Canada', who promised to wage war against any Natives aligned with the Americans.[4] This intimidation tactic seemed to work, but British authorities were under no illusions about which side the aggrieved Natives would take if George Washington decided to send his forces into the region. While he considered such a move, British naval control over North Atlantic waters made a successful invasion of the area unlikely.

Notwithstanding the presence of the British fleet, raids by New England privateers were a fact of life even as far north as Labrador, where George Cartwright's trading posts in Sandwich Bay were plundered in 1778. In the autumn of 1775 the Continental Congress licensed New England ship captains to plunder, burn, or sell at auction British vessels bringing munitions and supplies to British forces in Boston. With a share of the spoils going to those prepared to take such risks, privateering attracted investment like flies to honey. The number of schooners cruising the Atlantic coast increased from about 20 to 4,000 during the course of the war, and soon any vessel sailing under the British flag was a target. So, too, were coastal communities in the colonies still under British control. Most raids were selective, leaving all but the targeted victims unmolested, but they did little to endear the rebels to the pioneer settlers. In November 1775 Yankees even attacked Charlottetown, seizing provisions and carrying away the colony's acting governor, Phillips Callbeck.

After the British defeat at Saratoga in 1777, the fighting moved away from the region and Nova Scotians settled down to profiting from the increased military presence and the influx of Loyalist refugees. Colonials also got involved in their own privateering ventures, with vessels from the Planter community of Liverpool being particularly successful. Meanwhile, a religious revival, led by the charismatic itinerant preacher Henry Alline, gained momentum in the colony. Many former New Englanders, who had more difficulty than other settlers in deciding where their loyalties lay, responded enthusiastically to Alline's message that good Christians should pursue spiritual salvation rather than fight military battles. Alline's ministry was short—he died in 1784—but he laid the foundations of an evangelical tradition that is still strong in many areas of Nova Scotia and New Brunswick.

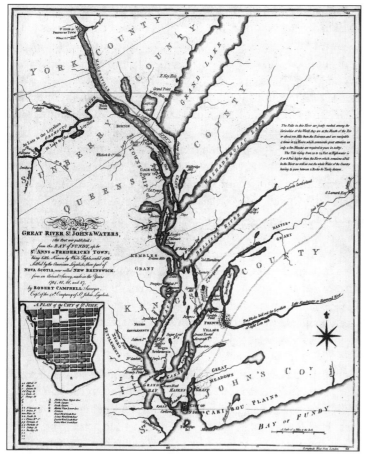

Robert Campbell, 'A Map of the Great River St John and Waters', engraved by S.I. Neele. The land along the St John River attracted the majority of Loyalists who settled in the colony of New Brunswick following the American Revolutionary War.

With the triumph of the Patriots at Yorktown, Virginia, in the fall of 1781, the British were forced to concede defeat at the hands of their former colonies. In the Treaty of Paris (1783) ending the war, Britain recognized the independence of the United States of America, leaving the Atlantic colonies, Quebec, and the Hudson's Bay Company territory—all originally claimed by the French—to form what was left of 'British' North America. In a significant concession, Americans were allowed to continue fishing in the Gulf of St Lawrence, on the banks, and along the Newfoundland coast outside the French Treaty Shore. They also had the 'liberty' to dry fish on the unsettled coasts of Nova Scotia, the Îles de la Madeleine, and Labrador.

In a separate treaty with Britain, France obtained concessions in Newfoundland. The boundaries of the Treaty Shore were moved to Cape St John and Cape Ray, away from the areas where the English now fished, and an appended declaration, while avoiding the word 'exclusive', in effect defined the shore as a French fishing zone. In addition, Saint-Pierre and Miquelon were returned to France without the deeply resented conditions of 1763. However, a vaguely worded undertaking that the islands would never become 'an object of jealousy' between Britain and France invited continuing dispute.

The Loyalists and Post-war Reconstruction

The American Revolution was a defining moment in the history of the Atlantic region. Not only did it create a new boundary separating the colonies from New England, but it also more than doubled their population. The first of at least 35,000 Loyalists began moving to Nova Scotia even before hostilities were officially declared, but most of them arrived between 1782 and 1784 on ships from New York, where they had gathered under British protection in the final stages of the war. Although they had few good words for 'Nova Scarcity', the Loyalists were luckier than many refugees. The British government supplied provisions and temporary shelter, compensated some of them for their losses, and provided most with free land.

Nearly 15,000 Loyalists landed at the mouth of the St John River, engulfing the tiny population already living there and founding the city of Saint John. Further up the river, Wolastoqiyik and Acadians were pushed off their land, the former into reserves, most of the latter to Madawaska. Even more Loyalists—approximately 19,000—went to peninsular Nova Scotia. Half of them settled in Shelburne, which for a time became the largest city in British North America. When the area failed to develop into the prosperous trading centre they had expected, most of the Loyalists drifted away. Some moved back to the United States when they judged it safe to do so. Others went to Quebec and still others to Halifax, Saint John, and the dozens of smaller communities established by other Loyalists, including Aylesford, Digby, Gagetown, Guysborough, Rawden, Ship Harbour, St Andrews, and Sussex Vale.

Relatively few Loyalists settled on Cape Breton, even though Sydney was founded as a Loyalist town. In 1784 the island was made a separate colony, largely on the strength of Abraham Cuyler's abortive scheme to attract 5,000 Loyalists from Quebec. Interest in St John's Island was low as well: only some 800 Loyalists were prepared to begin new lives as tenant farmers on land granted to proprietors. And no one was interested in what Newfoundland had to offer.

New Brunswick attracted a significant number of elite Loyalists. Determined to rebuild their fortunes in the frontier colony, which they expected to dominate, they hoped to make New Brunswick 'the envy of the American states', a model of order and hierarchy in contrast to the democratic anarchy that they felt would surely engulf their neighbours to the south. Concluding that the busy mercantile town of Saint John was both too crass and too close to the American border, they chose Fredericton as the capital of the colony of New Brunswick when it was established in 1784, hoping that it would become 'a stable agricultural society led by a landholding gentry'.[5] Not surprisingly, the pretensions of the Loyalist elite were not well received by the mass of the refugees. When 55 prominent Loyalists 'of the most respectable Characters', as they themselves declared, petitioned for estates of 5,000 acres (2,023 hectares)—nearly 10 times the average grant—the wishes of the majority prevailed and the request was denied. In the 1785 election the inhabitants of Saint John violently protested the condescension of the government based in Fredericton.

Loyalists were also politically active in Nova Scotia, where the New Hampshire-born Sir John Wentworth was appointed lieutenant-governor in 1792. Revelling in the court-like atmosphere of Halifax social life, the Loyalist elite were enchanted by the presence of the King's son, Prince Edward Augustus, and his beautiful mistress, Madame de St Laurent, who resided in the town between 1794 and 1799. Outside provincial capitals the pioneer experience had a levelling effect, and Loyalist roots counted for little in a region where, after 1783, nearly everyone claimed to have supported the British cause.

The Loyalists represented a thick slice of North American society and greatly increased the region's cultural diversity. As well as elites with aristocratic ideals, the mix included military veterans of all ranks, farmers and tradesmen, and a wide range of ethnic groups, including African Americans, many of them former slaves who had been encouraged to leave their masters by promises of freedom

DOCUMENT:
Edward Winslow's Plan for a 'Gentlemanlike' Colony, 1783

When the American Revolution began in 1775, 29-year-old Edward Winslow was a young man with great prospects. He was a Harvard graduate, descendant of one of the founders of Massachusetts Bay colony, and the only son of a prominent New England family with valuable estates in the Plymouth area. In the tensions leading to the war, Edward supported the British cause, and during the war he was based in New York as muster master general of the colonial troops that fought with the British. The success of the Patriots left Edward and his family nearly destitute. Without the resources to establish themselves in England, Edward, his mistress, Mary Simmonds, their three children, and their servants moved to Nova Scotia early in 1783.

From the St John River on 7 July 1783, Winslow wrote the following letter to his friend Ward Chipman in New York. The letter reveals much about the attitudes of elite Loyalists faced with beginning life over again on the colonial frontier. Not surprisingly, Winslow and Chipman were strong advocates of a separate colony north of the Bay of Fundy where they might seek the government positions denied them in Halifax.

We have just begun our operations in the land way—the people who have arrived here are prodigiously pleased with the country—& I shall certainly soon be possess.d of a good farm, and if we've our half pay I will be more than comfortable.—I have left those sweet little ones in as comfortable a place, as is in this province made so by my own exertions—I found a house & hired it for £6 a year & I've taken a lease for two years—I added two rooms—& a chimney & have now a spare bed-room at your service 'tis just on the bank of a most beautiful river immediately opposite the town of Annapolis.—I have left Thomson's William (now Q.r M.r) to superintend & Mother Silk & little George, we have plenty of poultry a good garden & such a variety of fish as you never saw & I have built a tolerable boat. So much for the family.

. . . I am determined at all events to distinguish myself by proposing a plan which affords the grandest field for speculation that ever offered.—take the general map of this province (even as it's now bounded) observe how detached this part is from the rest—how vastly extensive it is—notice the rivers—harbours &c. consider the numberless inconveniences that must arise—from [its] remoteness from the metropolis [Halifax] & the difficulty of communication.—Think what multitudes have & will come here—and then judge whether it must not from the nature of things—immediately become a separate government, & if it does it shall be the most Gentlemanlike one on earth. Suppose you & he go to England after being provided with the necessary facts—can you be better employed than in a solicitation of this kind—properly authorized. You know how Industrious I can be if I please—& you may rest assured that I will pursue this project with unremitted attention.—the people on the other side are already jealous—even the Gov.r fears it evidently—we have therefore [been] perfectly snug. . . .[6]

if they fought in British regiments. More than 3,000 black Loyalists moved to Nova Scotia, but they soon realized that freedom did not bring equality. Given smaller and less fertile grants than white Loyalists, they were often targets for hostility and violence during the tension-ridden early years of settlement. Nearly 1,200 black Loyalists left the region in 1792 for the new colony of Sierra Leone, though the 2,000 slaves in the Loyalist migration were denied that option. Following the abolition of the slave trade in 1807, slave-holding gradually disappeared in the Atlantic region, and in 1833 it was abolished throughout the British Empire by an act of Parliament.

In the wake of the American Revolution the British government was eager to strengthen the authority of the Crown and to create a rigid class system in the colonies. The Church of England, the established church in Great Britain, was selected to play an important role in achieving these goals. In 1787 Charles Inglis, the Loyalist former rector of Trinity Church in New York, was consecrated the first bishop of Nova Scotia, with jurisdiction over all the British North American colonies, including Newfoundland and Bermuda. The Society for the Propagation of the Gospel, the Church of England's missionary arm, helped to pay the salaries of clergymen and the cost of building churches. To help sustain the class structure, Inglis supported the founding of King's College in Windsor in 1788 as an exclusive institution for the sons of the Church of England elite, as well as the Provincial Academy of Arts and Sciences in Fredericton, which received its charter as the College of New Brunswick in 1800. Inglis and his clergy strenuously opposed evangelical enthusiasm and the 'levelling' tendencies it seemed to encourage. Despite all its efforts, the Church of England in the

Thomas Peters

Born in Africa, Thomas Peters was brought as a slave to Louisiana around 1760. After repeated attempts to escape his enslavement, Peters was sold by his owner to William Campbell in South Carolina. The American Revolutionary War provided a unique opportunity for Peters to secure his freedom. Along with thousands of other slaves, he took advantage of the British promise of emancipation for those who deserted their Patriot masters to join the British cause. Displaying leadership potential, the British promoted him to the rank of sergeant in the Black Pioneers, a military unit composed of former slaves.

At the conclusion of hostilities, Peters was among the more than 3,000 black Loyalists who migrated to Nova Scotia. He led a contingent of about 200 Black Pioneers, who settled in Brindley Town, near Digby. When he and his compatriots were denied the three years of provisions accorded to white Loyalists, offered smaller grants of land, and forced to work on construction projects rather than on their own farms, Peters petitioned the Governor of New Brunswick, Thomas Carleton, for land, but this request was refused. Since other black Loyalists also had their petitions for land dismissed and experienced other forms of discrimination from the white majority, they collectively protested their treatment in a petition to the British government.

Peters traveled to Great Britain in 1790 to continue his crusade for land and fair treatment. While in London, he became involved with abolitionists Grenville Sharp and Thomas Clarkson in a project to resettle emancipated slaves in Sierra Leone. The British government provided the funding for this venture and, in early 1792, 1,200 black Loyalists from Nova Scotia and New Brunswick, including Peters and his family, moved to Sierra Leone. Unfortunately, Peters had little time to help develop the new colony. In the summer of 1792, he died of fever.[7]

Maritimes steadily lost adherents to the Baptists and Methodists, whose ministers promised ordinary people personal salvation and spiritual equality.

In Newfoundland the American Revolution forced changes in customary trade patterns. Merchants began to send their own ships to the West Indies, sometimes using Bermuda shipowners as middlemen. Although it was still possible to import food from the United States after the war, so long as it was transported in British ships, Newfoundland importers increasingly looked to other sources of supply, especially in the Maritimes and the Canadas. A shipbuilding industry grew on the island, and a Newfoundland-based fleet, managed largely by merchants newly arrived from Greenock, Scotland, traded to the mainland and Caribbean. The winter population soon recovered to pre-war levels and began to grow steadily, with residents taking an increasing proportion of the total cod catch as migratory activity declined.

The naval state remained in place on the island, with the court system becoming more elaborate over time. A government house was built in the early 1780s, a supreme court was established in 1791, and civilians began to join naval officers as surrogate magistrates. It was a practical and reasonably effective system of government. The navy even contributed to religious life, since its chaplains were active on shore as well as on board their vessels, at least among Protestants. A proclamation of 1784 established religious freedom in Newfoundland. In the same year Father James O'Donnell arrived as prefect apostolic (he would become bishop in 1796) to organize the few Roman Catholic priests available to minister to the increasing numbers of Irish. As in the Maritimes, the Church of England clergy in Newfoundland were supported by the Society for the Propagation of the Gospel. Most immigrants from England belonged to the established church, but Protestant dissenters were gaining ground. From 1766 the Reverend Laurence Coughlan preached Methodism on the north shore of Conception Bay with considerable success, and in St John's dissenters attended John Jones's Congregational 'Dissenting Church of Christ'.

Between 1783 and 1803 nearly 17,000 Highland Scots immigrated to the Maritimes, most of them settling on the islands of St John's and Cape Breton and in eastern Nova Scotia. One of the most ambitious settlement schemes was sponsored by the Earl of Selkirk, who in 1803 brought 800 Highlanders to the Orwell–Point Prim area of Prince Edward Island. On the Miramichi, Fraser and Thom, a Scottish timber and shipbuilding company, recruited Scottish labourers. Highlanders tended to be Gaelic-speaking Roman Catholics, whereas Lowland Scots were more likely to be English-speaking Presbyterians and to place strong emphasis on education. Two immigrant Presbyterian ministers, James MacGregor and Thomas McCulloch, helped to make Pictou, Nova Scotia, a religious and educational centre.

Like Scotland, Ireland was experiencing major social and economic upheavals. In the wake of Irish unrest during the French Revolutionary War, the British passed the Act of Union in 1801 incorporating Ireland into Great Britain. Repressive measures against Roman Catholics imposed under British rule, along with periodic famines among a poor tenant population overly dependent on the potato for survival, contributed significantly to the stream of immigrants to the Atlantic region. While Irish Protestants quickly assimilated into the dominant culture, Roman Catholics remained distinct, separated by religion, history, and in many cases their Gaelic language. Irish Catholics swelled the population of southeastern Newfoundland outports, became tenant farmers on Prince Edward Island estates, harvested New Brunswick forests, and worked as domestic servants. In the major port cities such as St John's, Halifax, and Saint John, the Irish quickly came

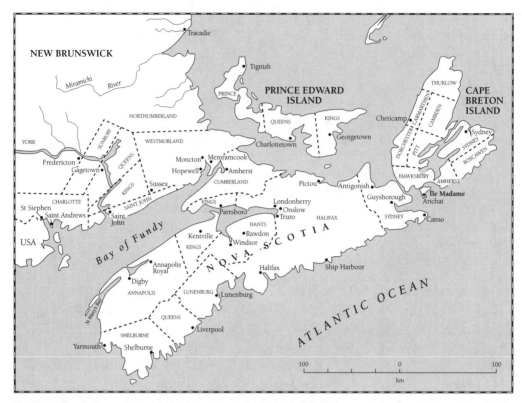

The Maritime colonies, *c.* 1800. Adapted from *Historical Atlas of Canada*, I (Toronto: University of Toronto Press, 1987), plates 25 and 32.

to constitute a significant portion of the population, and the desperate condition of many among them inspired their philanthropic compatriots to found a Charitable Irish Society in Halifax in 1776 and similar organizations in Saint John and St John's in 1806.

For the Mi'kmaq and Wolastoqiyik these migrations represented yet another threat to their survival as more territory fell into private hands and competition for fish and game increased. Recognizing their vulnerability, Aboriginal leaders petitioned for land and sometimes received it, but much of it was stolen back by squatters who knew that the authorities would not take action against them. In 1783 the Mi'kmaq chief John Julien obtained a licence of occupation for 20,000 acres (8,100 hectares) on the Miramichi River, but half of it was gone by 1807, when the government finally got around to establishing the Eel Ground Reserve. In Prince Edward Island the Mi'kmaq eventually received permission from proprietor James Montgomery to live on the barren and rocky Lennox Island, but no formal reserves were established.

The French and Napoleonic Wars

Following the outbreak of the French Revolution in 1789, Britain became engaged in the prolonged French and Napoleonic Wars that inevitably spilled over into North America. The final round of the Anglo–French struggle began in 1793 and would not end until 1815. Like its predecessors this lengthy conflict between Great Britain and France had a profound and lasting impact on the Atlantic region. British demand for fish, foodstuffs, and timber skyrocketed and, with alternative sources of supply cut off, the Atlantic colonies found ready markets for their resources. The Navigation Acts and the whole framework of mercantilist regulation that gave colonial producers preference in British markets over their foreign competitors further stimulated production. With the demand high and money pouring in to pay for defence against a possible French attack, colonials found themselves in a privileged and profitable position.

The most critical resource for an empire at war in the eighteenth century was wood, and for many years the British had reserved great stands of timber in North America to supply the Royal Navy. After 1800 these forest reserves came under intense development. Between 1805 and 1812 the exports of fir and pine timber from New Brunswick, Britain's pre-eminent 'timber colony'[8] increased more than twentyfold. Businessmen, many of them based in Greenock, brought their capital, labour, and technology to the shores of the Miramichi and St John rivers, and shipbuilding soon emerged as a sideline of the timber trade. By 1815 New Brunswick's economy was dominated by forest-based industries.

Attempts by the United States to remain neutral and trade with both sides were met by Great Britain's insistence on a strict definition of the rights of neutral countries, one that could be backed up with sea power. President Thomas Jefferson responded in 1807 with an embargo on British trade. While this hurt American exporters, it also wrought havoc with the British war effort. Britain retaliated by declaring Halifax, Shelburne, Saint John, and St Andrews to be 'free ports'—a clever manoeuvre that effectively undermined the embargo.

Annoyed by the restrictions, New England shippers took advantage of the free ports to sell their cargos and buy colonial produce and British manufactured goods. The policy not only served its purpose of keeping the British army and navy supplied, but it also helped to make the designated ports important commercial centres in the expanding regional economy. During the war vessels from the Maritimes also began competing successfully with New Englanders in the carrying trade to the West Indies, where the sugar plantations worked by vast numbers of slaves represented a lucrative market. Halifax in particular emerged as a significant entrepôt for produce shipped under convoy to the Caribbean.

Tensions over the rights of neutral shipping on the high seas and Native policy on the North American frontier finally prompted the United States to declare war against Great Britain in 1812 and launch attacks against Upper and Lower Canada (present-day Ontario and Quebec). Buffered by New England, whose leaders refused to participate in the war, the Atlantic region was spared military invasion and became the centre of a vigorous clandestine trade between the two belligerents. In addition, the British naval and military presence generated unprecedented market opportunities and increased the supply of hard currency. The war also inspired moments of great excitement. In June 1813 Haligonians were treated to the spectacle of HMS *Shannon* arriving with the infamous USS *Chesapeake* in tow after a brief engagement off Boston harbour. The following year, a British army under Sir John Sherbrooke occupied part of the coast of present-day Maine, providing more opportunities for commercial profit.

The War of 1812 expanded the potential for privateering, an activity that had a long history in the region. During the conflict with the Americans, 37 vessels from the Atlantic colonies captured 207 of the enemy's merchant ships. While historians still debate the military significance

Impressment during the French and Napoleonic Wars

Trade was not the only issue that created tensions between Great Britain and the United States in this period. Determined to maintain its supremacy at sea, the Royal Navy became notorious during the French and Napoleonic Wars for sending press gangs into seaport towns at home and abroad and boarding vessels at sea to impress sailors into service. Many actual and potential British seafarers attempted to avoid harsh naval discipline and low pay for more lucrative positions on American merchant ships. To catch deserters, the Royal Navy stopped American merchant ships and seized British-born seamen. Some of the unlucky captives were genuine deserters, but the very act of having their ships stopped and searched by armed British naval officers wounded American pride. Between 1793 and 1811, the British impressed from American vessels more than 12,000 alleged deserters, creating enormous resentment in the fledgling republic. American outrage reached new heights in 1807 when the British warship *Leopard* opened fire on the USS *Chesapeake*, killing or wounding 24 men and taking four alleged deserters.

Colonists in the Atlantic region also felt the effects of these high-handed tactics. Captains of merchant and fishing vessels in Atlantic coastal communities from Liverpool to Harbour Grace were leery of seeing a Royal Navy ship on the horizon, fearful lest their crews would be abducted. Occasionally, naval captains tried to fill their depleted complements—vessels under complement would be confined to port—by sending press gangs on shore. As major naval ports, Halifax and St John's were especially vulnerable to onshore recruitment. Volunteers were preferred—and at the end of the fishing season some men signed on—but as many as half of the crews on naval vessels were unwilling recruits.

In Halifax the civilian government was able to restrain the activities of press gangs but the 'naval state' of Newfoundland was different. Palliser's Act of 1775 formally sanctioned the use of press gangs in Newfoundland, ensuring that it continued to play its customary role as a 'nursery of seamen'. In 1794, the residents of St John's were so incensed by a press gang that they attacked it, killing one of its leaders, Richard Lawry. Two men were hanged for the crime, but the incident had the effect of changing impressment policy. After 1794, press gangs largely confined their activities to the waters surrounding Newfoundland rather than onshore. Impressment nevertheless remained a distressing feature of life in Newfoundland and in much of the rest of the Atlantic region until the end of the Napoleonic Wars, reaching its peak during the War of 1812.[9]

of privateering, there can be no doubt that it helped to line the pockets of ambitious merchants who bought the captured vessels in 'prize courts' and sold their contents at immense profit. The *Liverpool Packet*, the most successful of the privateer vessels, is reputed to have captured enemy prizes worth $1.5 million and greatly advanced the fortunes of its owner, Enos Collins. The communities where captures were auctioned, such as Halifax and St John's, also reaped financial rewards. On one memorable occasion, residents of St John's witnessed the spectacle of 30 American prize ships roped together in the harbour.

By 1815 St John's possessed a mercantile society, a newspaper, a constabulary, and a fire brigade, and had clearly emerged as the capital of Newfoundland, now a colony in all but name and constitutional status. The long period of warfare all but killed the English migratory fishery, and the bye-boatmen completely disappeared. As a result, the resident fishery expanded and the

The HMS *Shannon* leading its prize, the USS *Chesapeake*, into Halifax harbour, 6 June 1813. The inscription on this print by Captain R.H. King, RN, reads in part: 'As the ships entered the harbour, the men of war manned their yards in honour of the conquerors; the inhabitants crowded to the shore and lined the wharfs and buildings of the town. As they sailed past the assembled crowds, one burst of loud congratulations rose upon the air; but while the *Chesapeake* returned the cheering, an affecting silence distinguished the *Shannon*.' NSARM.

permanent population increased to more than 20,000. The settlers were not prosperous, but they were adept at exploiting the island's potential. Locally grown potatoes joined fish as a staple of settler diets, and in the 1790s, for the first time, schooners from Conception Bay and other areas began to exploit the spring seal fishery. It rapidly became an important feature of the local economy, and in good years a lucrative one. During the War of 1812, Newfoundland fish producers enjoyed a monopoly in Spain and Portugal, while continuing to supply the Italian and West Indian markets. Fish prices climbed to unprecedented levels, producing a few fortunes and attracting a wave of migrants, mainly from Ireland.

Conclusion

As the French and Napoleonic wars came to a weary end, the demand for colonial products declined and prices fell, but the contours of the Atlantic regional economy had been set. Newfoundland had found its niche in the rich fisheries off its shores; New Brunswick in the timber trade and shipbuilding; Prince Edward Island in wheat, root crops, and cattle. Nova Scotia had not only developed the most diversified economy (based on farm, fish, and forest resources) but was also carving a place for itself in the carrying trade to the West Indies and beyond. Meanwhile, in every colony, British settlers and culture prevailed.

Further Readings

Bitterman, Rusty. 2006. *Rural Protest on Prince Edward Island from British Colonization to the Escheat Movement*. Toronto: University of Toronto Press.

Bumsted, J.M. 1987. *Land, Settlement and Politics on Eighteenth-Century Prince Edward Island*. Montreal: McGill-Queen's University Press.

Cadigan, Sean T. 1995. *Hope and Deception in Conception Bay: Merchant-Settler Relations in Newfoundland, 1785–1855*. Toronto: University of Toronto Press.

Daigle, Jean, ed. 1995. *Acadia of the Maritimes: Thematic Studies*. Moncton, NB: Chaire d'études acadiennes, Université de Moncton.

Gwyn, Julian. 1998. *Excessive Expectations: Maritime Commerce and the Economic Development of Nova Scotia, 1740–1870*. Montreal: McGill-Queen's University Press.

———. 2003. *Frigates and Foremasts: The North American Squadron in Nova Scotia Waters, 1745–1815*. Vancouver, UBC Press.

Hornsby, Stephen J. 2005. *British Atlantic, American Frontier: Spaces of Power in Early Modern British America*. Hanover: University Press of New England.

Kert, Margaret. 1997. *Prize and Prejudice: Privateering and Naval Prize in Atlantic Canada in the War of 1812*. St John's: International Maritime Economic History Association.

MacKinnon, Neil. 1989. *This Unfriendly Soil: The Loyalist Experience in Nova Scotia, 1783–1791*. Montreal: McGill-Queen's University Press.

Mancke, Elizabeth. *The Fault Lines of Empire: Political Differentiation in Massachusetts and Nova Scotia, ca. 1760–1830*. London: Routledge.

Walker, James. 1976, reprinted 1992. *The Black Loyalists: The Search for a Promised Land in Nova Scotia and Sierra Leone, 1783–1870*. Toronto: University of Toronto Press.

Wright, Esther Clark. 1955. *The Loyalists of New Brunswick*. Wolfville, NS: Wright.

Food for Thought

Reid, John. 2004. 'Pax Britannica or Pax Indigena? Planter Nova Scotia (1760–1782) and competing Strategies of Pacification', *Canadian Historical Review* 85, 4 (December 2004): 669–93.

Ryan, Shannon. 1983. 'Fishery to Colony. A Newfoundland Watershed, 1793–1815', *Acadiensis* XII, 2 (Spring): 34–52.

Recommended Websites

Atlantic Canada Virtual Archives
http://atlanticportal.hil.unb.ca/acva

Island to Island: British Immigration to Prince Edward Island, 1763–1870
http://www.gov.pe.ca/cca/index.php3?number=1020743&lang=E

Newfoundland Government, 1730–1815
http://www.heritage.nf.ca/law/gov_1815.html

Nova Scotians in the Age of Slavery and Abolition
http://www.gov.ns.ca/nsarm/virtual/africanns/

Remembering Black Loyalists, Black Loyalist Communities
http://museum.gov.ns.ca/blackloyalists/

Chapter 8

Maturing Colonial Societies, 1815–60

Let the Frenchman delight in his vine-covered vales,
Let the Greek toast his old classic ground;
Here's the land where the bracing Northwester prevails,
And where jolly Blue Noses abound.[1]

As Joseph Howe's ode to 'The Blue Noses' suggests, colonials in the Atlantic region in the first half of the nineteenth century were beginning to express a new confidence in themselves. Expansion in farming, fishing, forestry, and shipbuilding nurtured a prosperous mercantile sector, while communities large and small sprouted newspapers, churches, schools, and even colleges. When Great Britain dismantled the mercantile system in the 1840s, the Atlantic colonies quickly adjusted to an era of free trade. They were also among the first in the British Empire to embrace a limited form of political autonomy, known as 'responsible government'. For some at least, this period would appear in retrospect as a golden age, when opportunities beckoned and anything seemed possible.

The Industrial Age

In the early nineteenth century, the Atlantic colonies and the entire world felt the effects of the 'great transformation' associated with the Industrial Revolution. Fundamental changes in technology and the organization of production not only encouraged new economic arrangements but also laid the groundwork for deep political, social, and intellectual changes that few could escape.[2]

The Industrial Revolution was sparked by technological advances in power generation. As the world's first industrial nation, Great Britain pioneered the application of steam power to machines and machines to production in agriculture, manufacturing, and transportation. The United States was quick to follow the lead of its former mother country, and in the second half of the nineteenth century became an industrial giant in its own right.

Under the industrial system, machines were developed to perform a wide range of tasks hitherto done by hand and made possible an explosion in output. Mechanization transformed work processes, encouraging the division of labour into repetitive tasks and centralizing production in factories controlled by the few capitalists who could finance such extensive operations. Under the factory system, labourers lost control over their work to supervisors, while factory owners, if they were successful, became wealthy.

As they grew in numbers and wealth, capitalists became adept at convincing governments to pass legislation to protect their new interests. The communal management of land in the countryside, the guild control of industry in the towns, and the privilege of monopoly were all eventually pushed aside to facilitate the industrial system. In Europe and the Americas, authoritarian governments and imperial regimes were toppled, or at least lost much of their power, as nation-states increasingly came under the influence of the new middle class who championed political structures that they could dominate. Uprisings in 1830 and again in 1848, many of them fuelled by nationalist and liberal sentiments, rocked European capitals and produced echoes around the world. Some people had more radical notions about how the benefits of the industrial age should be managed. In the *Communist Manifesto*, published in 1848, Friedrich Engels and Karl Marx urged the workers of the world to unite to throw off the chains of the capitalist system in which only a few people benefited. Charles Dickens and Victor Hugo, meanwhile, described the victims of the new world order in novels that had a wide and sympathetic readership.

Industrial capitalism changed everything. It introduced a new ethic of materialism that challenged traditional spiritual values, encouraged the growth of cities at the expense of the countryside, and created a new class structure based on relationship to production rather than heredity. It redistributed wealth geographically as well as socially and drove a wedge between the public world of work and the private realm of family. Even more fundamentally, it altered the relationships among men, women, and children and the relationship of human beings to their natural environment.

Industrialization also encouraged a new level of self-reliance among individuals, high and low, who were trying to adjust to the challenges and opportunities unleashed by the winds of change. In an effort to exert their interests outside of the formal political arena, people formed voluntary associations to achieve goals as diverse as tariff reform, temperance, literacy, abolition of slavery, elimination of poverty, prevention of cruelty, overseas missions, and the ascendancy of one group over another. Voluntarism in industrializing countries laid the foundation for a vigorous 'civil society', where new ideas and practices could be discussed and promoted. Reform became the watchword of the industrial age, which encouraged innovation and improvement in all aspects of society.

Even before factory smokestacks began dotting the landscape in the Atlantic region, revolutionary changes were everywhere in evidence. Colonials read about the new machines in their newspapers, purchased the products of Britain's factories with their hard-earned cash, and sent an increasing volume of their own raw resources to sustain Britain's expanding industrial economy. They also experimented with their own mechanical innovations and enthusiastically embraced the voluntary principle, sprouting colonial versions of many of the associations originating in Great Britain and the United States.

The triumph of industrial capitalism in Great Britain prompted changes in the nature of British imperialism. The economic orthodoxy at home was free trade, frugal spending, and low taxes. What has been called the informal empire of trade and investment steadily expanded, but this did not mean that any British government wanted to abandon the formal empire. 'The question was', writes Ronald Hyam, 'not whether to get rid of colonies, but how to organise them so as to make the best use of them with a minimum of effort and expense.'[3] One result of this attitude was the repeal of the protectionist Navigation Acts in 1849; another was the grant of responsible government to the colonies of settlement, which gave them internal self-government and full responsibility for their own finances.

Although the so-called 'Little England' view of empire was always contested, it informed the policies that took effect in the 1840s in the wake of the Irish Famine. The need for cheap foodstuffs to feed millions of starving Irish peasants led Great Britain to adopt free trade in 1846 and to dismantle the Navigation Acts three years later. Not entirely coincidentally, British resistance to colonial self-government was abandoned at the same time. By the mid-nineteenth century, the Atlantic colonies were challenged to forge their own destinies in the unstable and often unfriendly world of industrial capitalism.

People and Place

The international boundary between New Brunswick and the United States remained a source of tension in this period. Although the St Croix River and 'highlands' south of the St Lawrence River were established as the border following the American Revolution, no one was certain which river was the St Croix and the highlands proved difficult to find. A boundary commission eventually agreed on the location of the St Croix River in 1798, when the site of Champlain's ill-fated settlement on an island in the river's mouth was discovered, but the territory on the upper St John River remained in dispute. By the late 1830s tensions in the Aroostook–Madawaska region reached a fever pitch, prompting Great Britain and the United States to seek a diplomatic resolution. The boundary question was finally resolved in 1842 by the Webster–Ashburton Treaty, named after the principal negotiators. Although the treaty ended the uncertainty over the boundary, it disappointed New Brunswickers because it left a hump of American-controlled territory between their colony and the Eastern Townships in the United Province of Canada (United Canadas).

The flood tide of largely British immigration, most of it to the Maritimes, continued from 1815 until the 1840s. Thereafter population growth depended on natural increase, which in the 1850s and 1860s reached impressive levels. By 1861 there were nearly 800,000 people living in the Atlantic region, up from 200,000 in 1815. Census figures record a mature and relatively stable pre-industrial society: the ratio of men to women was nearly equal, more than half the inhabitants were under the age of 18, and in all of the four colonies 80 per cent or more of the population was native-born. Families were large, averaging seven children, although this statistic masked great differences in family size across class and culture. Like other areas of the Western world, the Atlantic region in the second half of the nineteenth century began to reflect the impact of new values that favoured later marriages and smaller families, especially among members of the urban middle class.

As in the eighteenth century, economic and political pressures in Great Britain encouraged emigration in this period. Irish (both Protestant and Catholic), Scots, English, and a few Welsh immigrants filled up unsettled areas in the Maritimes. Emigrants from southeast Ireland moved in large numbers to Newfoundland's Avalon Peninsula, and the population began to spread along the south and northeast coasts. Following the War of 1812, 2,000 African Americans, offered their freedom if they deserted their owners to join the British cause, also moved to the Maritimes, most of them settling in Preston and Hammonds Plains in Nova Scotia and Loch Lomond in New Brunswick.

Table 8.1	Timeline
1814–15	African-American refugees arrive in Nova Scotia and New Brunswick.
1818	John Young writes *Letters to Agricola*.
1820	Cape Breton re-annexed to Nova Scotia; Bank of New Brunswick founded.
1821–3	Thomas McCulloch writes *The Stepsure Letters*.
1822	William Cormack walks across Newfoundland.
1824	Newfoundland is granted colonial status; Julia Catherine Beckwith publishes *St Ursula's Convent*.
1825	Great Miramichi fire.
1826	General Mining Association receives a monopoly of Nova Scotia's mineral wealth.
1829	Death of Shawnadithit; Catholic emancipation.
1832	Representative government adopted in Newfoundland.
1833	British Parliament passes the Act to Abolish Slavery in the British Empire, to take effect in 1834.
1839	The region's first railway line opens between Albion Mines and Pictou.
1840	Samuel Cunard inaugurates the first transatlantic steamship service.
1841	Webster–Ashburton Treaty.
1845	Great Irish famine begins.
1846	Great Britain adopts free trade.
1848	Nova Scotia becomes the first British colony to be granted responsible government.
1849	Telegraph service comes to Nova Scotia and New Brunswick.
1852	Public schools established in Prince Edward Island.
1854	African United Baptist Association founded in Nova Scotia.
1854–66	Reciprocity Treaty with the United States.
1855	New Brunswick briefly adopts prohibition.
1858	General Mining Association's monopoly abolished.

Settlers came to the region seeking land and opportunity. Some found one or both, but others had a more difficult time. The African American refugees, like the black Loyalists before them, faced bureaucratic delays in securing land, and their grants were invariably small and located in less desirable areas. Although no strangers to hard work, many settlers from Great Britain were ill-equipped to survive on what was at best marginal land. In many remote settlements only an overgrown graveyard testifies to the hardship and heartbreak that characterized the immigrant experience.

The most tragic episode by far was the arrival of thousands of destitute Irish fleeing the Great Famine that began with the failure of the potato crop in 1845. The Atlantic region received only a small percentage of the more than 300,000 Irish who came to British North America between 1846 and 1851, and many of them quickly moved on, but they nevertheless represented a challenge to the port authorities whose job it was to process them. As many as 30,000 destitute and often disease-ridden refugees entered through Partridge Island, the quarantine station at the mouth of the St John River, while others fetched up in Chatham, Charlottetown, Halifax, St Andrews, and other ports connected to the North Atlantic carrying trade. Most of the good agricultural land in the Maritimes had been long taken up and the destitute Irish had to be content to work as labourers or eke out a living in marginal and often remote farming frontiers.

Clearing the land was a daunting task for most immigrants. Slashing and burning their way through the forests that impeded their progress, they often set runaway fires that devastated huge areas. Walter Johnstone, a Scottish visitor to Prince Edward Island, remarked in 1820 that the burnt woods around the settlements formed 'a scene the most ruinous, confused and disgusting the eye can possibly look upon'.[4] In 1825 a fire on the Miramichi consumed more than two million hectares of forests and took the lives of 160 people. Animals also felt the impact of the immigrants and their profligate ways. In New Brunswick moose had virtually disappeared by the 1820s, and the great auk, a large flightless bird that Cartier had observed in vast numbers on the Funk Islands off Newfoundland in the sixteenth century, had already become extinct by 1800.

A Dark Age for Aboriginal Peoples

With the increase of European settlement, Aboriginal peoples reached new levels of desperation. Their numbers remained low in the first half of the nineteenth century as settler hostility, disease, and poor living conditions took their toll. By 1850 there were no more than 3,000 Mi'kmaq, Wolastoqiyik, and Passamaquoddy living in the Maritimes. Reduced in numbers and in morale, they often found it impossible to prevent encroachment on reserve lands.

In the 1830s the Colonial Office began delegating responsibility for Indian policy to the colonies. New Brunswick and Nova Scotia appointed men of considerable integrity—Joseph Howe and Abraham Gesner in Nova Scotia and Moses Perley in New Brunswick—as Indian Commissioners, but the story remained the same. In the late 1840s Gesner made a telling comment on the unjust exchange between Native and newcomer: 'in return for the lands for which they were the rightful owners, they have received loathsome diseases, alcoholic drink, the destruction of their game, and threatened extermination.'[5]

Gesner's comment reflected a shift in attitude, at least at the official level, towards Aboriginal peoples. No longer a threat to European dominance, they became the subject of political, philanthropic, and ethnographic interest. In 1856 the Prince Edward Island government finally appointed an Indian commissioner, and with the assistance of the London-based Aborigines' Protection Society it would purchase Lennox Island as a reserve in 1870. Although his evangelizing efforts had little impact, the Baptist missionary Silas Rand helped to preserve Mi'kmaq culture by collecting oral history and compiling a Mi'kmaq dictionary. Native crafts—quill boxes, woven baskets, brooms, and birchbark canoes, in particular—were widely sought by collectors.

Despite predictions to the contrary, the resilient Mi'kmaq, Wolastoqiyik, and Passamaquoddy managed to survive the European presence. The fate of the Beothuk, in contrast, was tragic. Cut off from marine resources by the spread of European fishing and settlement along Newfoundland's northeast coast, they retreated to the interior, where their health declined along with their living conditions. Efforts to make contact with them, now that their survival was in doubt, sometimes led to disastrous consequences. In 1819, for example, a woman named Demasduit was captured at Red Indian Lake. Her husband was killed in the encounter, and her child was left behind to die. Two years later Demasduit (known to her captors as Mary March) died of tuberculosis. In 1829 Shawnadithit, the last known Beothuk, suffered the same fate. In the final year of her life she lived

DOCUMENT:
Chief Joseph Malli Goes to London, 1842

In 1842 Joseph Malli, Chief of the Mi'kmaq on the Restigouche River in New Brunswick, trav-elled to England in an effort to persuade the British government to stop incoming settlers from stealing Native property. His statement said in part:

> When the Superiority over the Territories in which we were born passed out of the hands of the French into those of the British, We—the Mic-Macs of the Restigouche River—were in possession of a Tract of Country, the quiet and undistinguished holding of which was secured to us by a written Deed.—The care of that Deed We entrusted to our Christian Priest.—He lost it. About 50 years ago a white man of the name of Mann came to us,—and asked our leave to build a Hut for him to sleep in when he came to fish—We said 'No! If we allow you to build the Hut, you will keep Pigs and Sheep—We Indians have many Dogs—the Dogs will worry the Pigs & Sheep and bad consequences will spring up'.—Mann did build his Hut, and we did not use force to expel him from our Reserve.—After some time Mann claimed a large Tract of our Reserve as his own.—We went and complained to the Governor.—The Governor sent three Commissioners [from Québec] to enquire into that Claim. I calculate that it must have been about eighteen years ago, in 1824, that these Commissioners were sent. . . . no portion of our own Lands have been restored to us, nor has any other land been allotted to us.—We remain without redress.[6]

in St John's under the care of William Cormack, president of the recently established 'Boeothick Institution', helping him to develop a Beothuk vocabulary and drawing pictures depicting the culture of her people as she had known it.

The Labrador Middle Ground

Labrador's story was quite different in this period. There the Innu and Inuit outnumbered the resident European population, which was small and widely scattered. By the 1860s there was a British 'settler' population of some 1,600 living along the coast from Blanc Sablon to Hamilton Inlet. Most of these people were the children or grandchildren of Native women and British fur traders and fishers who had arrived after 1830. In mid-century a clerical visitor remarked that 'all the females are either Esquimaux, or mountaineer Indians, or descended from them.' The settlers traded with Jersey and West Country firms established in south Labrador, with visiting traders, or with posts in Hamilton Inlet and Lake Melville operated by Quebec merchants. In 1837 these posts were purchased by the Hudson's Bay Company and linked through a chain of posts in the interior to Ungava Bay to tap the Innu fur trade.

Continuing to lead a migratory life, the Innu came to the North Shore, Ungava Bay, or the Labrador coast to trade, and increasingly, to meet Roman Catholic priests. The Oblates of Mary Immaculate arrived in Canada in the 1840s, and established a mission to the Innu, initially based on the Quebec North Shore.

North of Cape Harrison, the most significant European presence was that of the Moravians, with their mission stations and trading stores at Nain (1771), Okak (1776), Hopedale (1782), and Hebron (1830). After a religious revival in 1804–5 many Inuit were baptized and reorganized their lives to spend much of the time between Christmas and Easter near the missionaries. Besides stores and religious observances, the mission provided schools—where children were taught in Inuktitut—and rudimentary medical care. The Hudson's Bay Company broke the Moravian trade monopoly after 1850, and during the early 1860s the isolation of northern Labrador was further disturbed by the arrival each summer of migratory fishing schooners ('floaters') from Newfoundland.

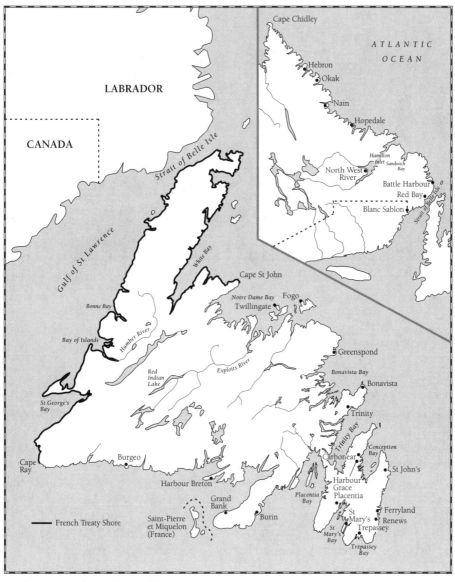

Newfoundland and Labrador, *c.* 1840.

Courtney Bay, New Brunswick, *c.* 1860. Many of the region's sailing ships were launched from this port, near East Saint John. Among them was the *Marco Polo*, famed for the speed with which it delivered its passengers and cargo to the Australian gold fields in the early 1850s. PANB George Taylor fonds, p5-360.

Colonial Economies

In the first half of the nineteenth century European society in the Atlantic region was buoyed by an increasingly productive commercial economy. A post-war recession caused hardship for rich and poor alike, but by the 1820s conditions began to improve. The colonial staples—fish, foodstuffs, and timber—found markets in an expanding global economy, and shipbuilding, financed by British and colonial capitalists, emerged as a major industry.

The success of the shipping and shipbuilding industries in Atlantic Canada between 1850 and 1878 has become the stuff of legend and a source of local pride. In this period the Maritimes and Newfoundland accounted for as much as 72 per cent of the tonnage registered in British North America, which boasted the fourth largest merchant marine in the world, after Great Britain, the United States, and Norway. Ships such as the *Marco Polo*, built in Saint John in 1851, broke world speed records on the Australian run and made the region's shipbuilding skills famous.

Although Saint John was the largest shipbuilding centre, other communities, such as St Martins, Yarmouth, Windsor, and Pictou, became well known for their output of wooden vessels.

Saint John, Charlottetown, Halifax, and St John's also emerged as major trade entrepôts. By the 1860s Maritime vessels, operated in large part by foreign crews, could be found in ports all over the world, carrying cargoes at competitive prices. In the 1880s, shipping barons in the Maritimes decided to invest their fortunes in railway and manufacturing ventures rather than in a steel- and steam-driven merchant marine, a decision that led to a rapid decline in shipbuilding and the carrying trade.[7]

The region's mineral resources also came under more intense exploitation in this period. Under a monopoly granted by the British Crown in 1826, the General Mining Association began developing Nova Scotia's coal resources in Cape Breton and Pictou County. The company brought in skilled miners and introduced modern technology, including steam-driven machinery and vessels. After its monopoly was abolished in 1858, investment in coal mining increased dramatically, stimulated by rising demand in the rapidly industrializing United States.

In Albert County, New Brunswick, more than 230,000 tons of Albertite (a sort of solidified asphalt yielding oil and gas) were produced between 1850 and 1880. Gypsum and stone for building and grinding found markets, both locally and in the United States. The discovery of gold on Nova Scotia's south and eastern shores stimulated a brief flurry of activity in the 1860s. By this time the iron works at Londonderry was turning out $40,000 of products annually. The founding of banking institutions, beginning with the Bank of New Brunswick in 1820 and the Halifax Banking Company in 1825, testified to the growth of the Maritime economy.

Newfoundland's resources attracted growing interest. In 1822 Cormack walked across the island—the first European known to have done so. In 1839–40 the government sponsored the first geological surveys, conducted by James Jukes. Copper was discovered in Notre Dame Bay in the late 1850s and copper mining commenced at Tilt Cove in 1864. In the same year, the government established a permanent Geological Survey that, under its first director, Alexander Murray, and his assistant, James P. Howley, undertook systematic exploration of the island. Their optimistic reports had an important influence on public policy, raising the possibility that Newfoundland might become something more than a producer of salt fish and seal oil.

Although constrained by their colonial location, the region's mercantile elite were anything but narrow in their ambitions. Samuel Cunard, who invested in the New Brunswick timber trade and owned estates in Prince Edward Island, inaugurated transatlantic steamship service between Great Britain and North America in 1840. Beginning with a clock-making business in St John's, Benjamin Bowring became the head of a highly successful mercantile house with links to Liverpool. The most successful entrepreneur of all in this period was Enos Collins, who, having made a fortune in trade and privateering during the French and Napoleonic Wars, went on to build a business empire based on trade and banking in Halifax.

The region's economic growth was tied to the fortunes of the Empire, but there were no special privileges after 1849, when Great Britain abandoned the last vestiges of colonial preference in trade and shipping. Although the dismantling of the old mercantile system helped to make the 1840s a 'decade of tribulation',[8] the transition proved less problematic than many had feared. Part of the reason was that Britain negotiated reciprocity (free trade) in primary products—fish, farm produce, minerals, and timber—with the United States in 1854. The Reciprocity Treaty remained in place until 1866 and, together with the high demand generated by the American Civil War (1861–5), stimulated colonial production and the carrying trade.

The Farmer's Bank of Rustico. In the early 1860s, Father George-Antoine Belcourt helped his fellow Prince Edward Island Acadians to establish a school and a banking co-operative to meet the challenges of the new industrial order. PEIPARO, Acc. 2320/20.4.

The Newfoundland economy was altogether more precarious. Nevertheless, merchants invested in larger wooden vessels—brigs and brigantines especially—mainly to exploit more effectively the seal fishery off the island's northeast coast. Although sealskins were taken, the main object of the hunt was the seal fat; rendered into oil, it was widely used during the nineteenth century for lighting and lubricants.

By mid-century the Industrial Revolution was beginning to transform production processes. The steam-driven machinery, the factory system, and the conflicts between capital and labour that were the hallmarks of the industrial age required difficult adjustments for people accustomed to artisan production, kinship loyalties, and noblesse oblige. Saint John, flush with capital from the timber trade and the shipbuilding industry, emerged as the major industrial centre, with foundry, footwear, and clothing industries all surpassing shipbuilding in value by the 1860s. Halifax also developed an industrial base, specializing in food-processing industries such as brewing, distilling, and sugar-refining.

Most people lived at one remove from industrial discipline, their lives dominated by the seasonal rhythms of domestic production based on farming, fishing, and forestry—or in many cases all three. Most families continued to make their own cloth and clothing, to produce and preserve their own

Sealing in Newfoundland

Seals were important to Native peoples, providing meat, oil, and skins for clothing and other purposes. Although European migratory fishers were not originally much interested in seals, migrating seals were caught in nets along the Strait of Belle Isle, the Quebec North Shore, and the northeast coast of Newfoundland. A growing demand for seal oil in the eighteenth century gave rise to a sealing industry, which became concentrated in Newfoundland and to a lesser extent in the Îles de la Madeleine and Cape Breton.

In 1802 the magistrate at Bonavista reported that 'This adventurous and perilous pursuit' was now carried on in two ways: 'during the winter months by nets, and from March to June in ice-skiffs and decked boats, or schooners'. Netting seals was a northern practice that continued well into the twentieth century, and seals are still hunted from small boats close to shore. The use of sailing vessels to 'go to the ice' in the spring to find whelping seals started in 1793, allowing St John's and other southerly ports to become involved in the industry. The spring sealing fleet reached a peak of nearly 400 vessels in the late 1850s, carrying about 14,000 men, and seal products—oil and skins—represented one-third of the value of Newfoundland's exports.

Over-exploitation of the seal herds led to a decline in the industry, from 546,000 skins in the early 1840s to 400,000 in the late 1850s. During the following decade, outfitters turned to steam-powered vessels—'wooden walls'—to increase both yields and profits, a process that centralized the industry in St John's and Conception Bay and also reduced the number of schooners and men involved.

Although sealing became steadily less important to the Newfoundland economy, it retained a considerable cultural significance. An outport man summed it up early in the twentieth century: 'Ye know, sir, that when we gets to be young men in this country they don't think much of a chap unless he's bin to de ice. It's a sort o' test of hardiness. . . . It's jest dog's work while it lasts, but somehow there's an excitement in it. . . . We sealers say, too, that man'll go for a swile where gold won't drag'un.'[9]

food, and to craft their own houses, barns, ploughs, carriages, horseshoes, furniture, soap, and candles. Milling was the most common industry in rural areas of the Maritimes. By 1871 Prince Edward Island alone boasted 500 carding, fulling, grist, dressing, saw, and shingle mills. Surplus produce was bartered for the imported items—flour, molasses, sugar, tea, cloth, and metal utensils of various kinds—that stocked the shelves of local merchants. In turn, the merchants sold the products of farm and fishery in colonial towns and cities; to the men engaged in the region's fishing, shipping, and timber trades; or to markets in Europe, the United States, and the West Indies. In many communities, especially those centred on the fisheries, survival depended on a credit system in which merchants advanced supplies and paid for local products in goods rather than cash. This 'truck system' encouraged dependence, but, as Sean Cadigan points out in his study of merchant–settler relationships in Conception Bay, it also enabled producers to participate, however minimally, in the market economy.[10]

Despite the growing complexity of the region's economy, poverty and destitution were common. The demand for foodstuffs outstripped the supply, and even farming families often had difficulty making ends meet. When crops or fisheries failed, as they sometimes did in all areas of the Atlantic region, disaster threatened. The potato blight hit the colonies in the late 1840s, creating

The Reverend Mr Richard Preston, ink drawing by Dr J.P. Gilpin, *c.* 1850. An African American who fled to Nova Scotia following the war of 1812, Preston studied for the ministry in Great Britain and helped to establish the African United Baptist Association in 1854. History Collection, Nova Scotia Museum, Halifax, NSM, p176.25 copy neg. N-4442.

hardship almost as severe as in Ireland and prompting at least one group of settlers in St Ann's, Cape Breton (under their puritanical leader the Reverend Norman McLeod), to search for greener pastures in Waipu, New Zealand. Others shipped off to the United States, where jobs in the expanding industrial and service sectors and free homesteads on the western frontier offered hope for a better life.

By the 1830s most of the good farmland in the Maritimes had been taken up, and free land was largely a thing of the past. Not only recent immigrants but growing numbers of descendants of earlier settlers were therefore obliged to purchase property or take up marginal lands that yielded a meagre subsistence. Some of the poor squatted on Crown and Native reserves; others drifted to urban centres to find work.

Given the small size and poor quality of their original grants, it is hardly surprising that blacks in Nova Scotia began moving to Halifax, where wage-paying jobs were more plentiful. They kept to themselves in an area on the Bedford Basin that soon became known as Africville. Shunned by their white neighbours, the residents of Africville found comfort in their own religious institutions. The spectacular growth of Baptist churches under the leadership of Richard Preston led to the establishment in 1854 of the African United Baptist Association, which was to become a lynchpin in the black community's struggle to seek justice in a society riddled with racial prejudice.

Societies in Transition

Christian churches became firmly rooted throughout the colonies in this period and played a major role in community life. At a time when the family economy was the main source of security, churches often stepped in when the family could no longer find the wherewithal for survival. Church leaders also offered spiritual counsel in an age when Providence was widely held to be the cause of human suffering.

Even before Roman Catholics were granted full civil rights in the British Empire in 1829, they had gained concessions in the Atlantic region. The laws that had prevented them from voting, acquiring land, and worshipping in public were abolished in the 1780s, and the ban on their holding public office was lifted first in Nova Scotia in 1823 for Lawrence Kavanagh, a Cape Breton merchant elected to the assembly. Although Newfoundland had its own Roman Catholic bishop as early as 1796, Maritime Catholics remained under the jurisdiction of Quebec until 1817, when

Edmund Burke was appointed bishop of Nova Scotia. Twelve years later, his jurisdiction was divided and separate bishops were appointed for New Brunswick and Prince Edward Island. These administrative changes marked the beginning of a new era in which a reinvigorated Catholic church ministered to a growing constituency. By the mid-nineteenth century, over 40 per cent of the populations of Newfoundland and Prince Edward Island, a third of New Brunswickers, and a quarter of Nova Scotians were Roman Catholics.

Evangelical churches—especially the Baptists and Methodists—generally took the lead in seeking converts and promoting moral rectitude, but all churches were swept up in the reforming spirit of the age. In the 1820s the temperance movement took root and became so popular that New Brunswick briefly experimented with legislated prohibition in 1855. Most denominations supported initiatives to found academies, Sunday schools, charity schools, orphanages, hospitals, and shelters. Eager to spread the gospel to lost souls near and far, evangelicals became prominent in both home and foreign missions. The Maritime Baptists sent Richard Burpee to India in 1845 and in the following year the Presbyterian Church of Nova Scotia sponsored John Geddie's mission to the New Hebrides. Major religious denominations either published or supported newspapers sympathetic to their views. In St John's, for instance, *The Public Ledger* represented a Protestant perspective, while *The Newfoundlander* and *The Patriot* reflected Roman Catholic viewpoints. The first French-language newspaper in the region, the *Moniteur Acadien*, founded by Israël J.-D. Landry in 1867 in Shediac, New Brunswick, was closely aligned with the Roman Catholic hierarchy.

Reformers argued that sectarian tensions could be alleviated by the creation of a system of public schools that were uniform, non-denominational, and state funded. In all the Atlantic colonies, their efforts were opposed not only by the Roman Catholic hierarchy but also by linguistic minorities such as the Acadians, who feared the homogenizing tendencies of a state-supported system. In 1852 Prince Edward Island became the first colony in the region to embrace a public school

The Roman Catholic Cathedral in St John's, Newfoundland, engraving by A. Ruger, 1878. To the right of this imposing building are the Presentation and Mercy convents, to the left St Bonaventure's College. Consecrated in 1855, it overlooks the harbour and represents Bishop Michael Fleming's determination 'to have a temple superior to any other in the island'. Courtesy John FitzGerald.

system, but controversy quickly erupted over Bible reading in the classroom. Protestants insisted that the practice was essential to instilling Christian values; Roman Catholics were staunchly opposed because independent Bible reading was associated particularly with Protestant denominations and could, it was feared, lead to proselytizing. They were ultimately placated by regulations that allowed students who found Bible reading offensive to be excused from attendance. In Newfoundland, efforts to introduce non-denominational public education in the 1830s were just as strongly opposed by the Church of England hierarchy as by its Roman Catholic counterpart. As a result, in 1842 the education grant was split between Protestants and Catholics.

Denominationalism prevailed in higher education throughout the region. The Church of England's exclusive control of King's College in Windsor and the College of New Brunswick in Fredericton inspired other denominations to establish their own institutions. In the mid-nineteenth century the foundations were laid for seven denominational colleges in the Maritimes: Acadia (Baptist); Mount Allison (Methodist); St Mary's, St Dunstan's, St Francis Xavier, Collège St-Joseph, and Mount Saint Vincent (all Roman Catholic). Dalhousie College, founded in 1818 as a non-denominational institution, became effectively Presbyterian when it finally began to offer classes in the 1860s. Prince of Wales College, established in Charlottetown in 1860, served a primarily Protestant student population.

Although clerics preached spiritual equality, church practices perpetuated worldly notions of hierarchy and prejudice. Many churches rented their pews, permitting the rich to sit closer to the pulpit. In some churches women were relegated to separate sections. People with black skin were almost always set apart. Protestants and Catholics each formed (or imported) their own organizations, of which the Protestant Orange Order was one of the most successful. Battles between Protestants and Catholics in the Maritimes became particularly violent during the late 1840s. On 12 July 1847, the 147th anniversary of the Battle of the Boyne, a confrontation between 300 Irish Catholics and an equal number of Protestants in Woodstock, New Brunswick, resulted in 10 deaths. Two years later, another bloody confrontation rocked the Catholic enclave of York Point in Saint John.

Violence was not confined to religious rivalries: it punctuated all aspects of colonial life. At election time, voting was conducted orally, with the result that polling stations often became scenes of violence and intimidation. Political tensions in Newfoundland were such that the conservative St John's newspaper editor Henry Winton had his ears cut off by masked opponents in 1835, and the Church of England archdeacon in the 1830s kept a pistol under his pillow. Mummering—a folk tradition associated with Christmas—became so menacing that in 1861 legislation made it illegal in St John's to appear in public wearing a mask or other disguise. In Prince Edward Island, tensions between tenants and their landlords (or their agents) often reached dangerous levels. Strikes by workers sometimes erupted in riots. Wife-beating was still legally sanctioned, and the foundation of discipline at home and at school was the adage 'spare the rod and spoil the child'. Cock fights and bear-baiting were popular pastimes.

Seaport towns were renowned for the violent and illegal activities that flourished along their waterfronts where an underworld of crimps (procurers of crewmen for sailing vessels), prostitutes, and unsavoury boardinghouse-keepers took advantage of the sailors in port. Like the British soldiers who were stationed in the region's major cities until mid-century, or the men confined to remote lumber camps throughout the long winters, sailors on board ship lived in an all-male environment, under repressive and often harsh conditions. Because colonial courts were likely to

A Communications Revolution

During the mid-nineteenth century, people throughout the world were engulfed by a revolution in communications and transportation. Steamships, railways, and telegraph lines represented a trio of new technologies that quickened the pace of life and brought people in the Atlantic colonies and elsewhere closer together.

Although these technologies were pioneered in Great Britain and the United States, the Atlantic colonies participated in their advancement. Halifax native Samuel Cunard was an early promoter of steamships and, in 1830, joined forces with merchants in Quebec City to run a mail service between the two port cities. This consortium also sponsored the *Royal William*, which in 1833 made one of the first Atlantic crossings under steam, taking 25 days to make the trip from Pictou, Nova Scotia, to Gravesend, England. In 1839 Cunard succeeded in capturing the contract for mail delivery between Great Britain and North America. The first scheduled steamer arrived in Halifax on 17 July 1840 with Cunard on board, and then sailed to Boston where the merchant prince of steam received an enthusiastic welcome.

By this time railways, the wonder of the age, were promising to overcome the limits of land-based travel and bring prosperity to those communities fortunate enough to be located near them. The General Mining Association opened the region's first rail line in 1839 to carry coal from Albion Mines (now Stellarton) to Pictou harbour. Four years earlier, in one of the first railway ventures anywhere in the world, capitalists in St Andrews and Quebec City hatched a plan to build a line to connect the two cities. The project drew angry protests from Washington, which saw the initiative as pre-empting the still-disputed territory between New Brunswick and Maine. By the time the boundary was settled, other ambitious cities, including Saint John and Portland, Maine, had staked a claim to be the terminus of continental railway lines. Construction on the St Andrews line finally began in 1847, but it was abandoned in the backwoods of New Brunswick when its promoters ran out of money in 1863.

The e-mail of the nineteenth century, the electric telegraph dramatically increased the speed of communication. Telegraphic communication developed quickly after it was successfully tested by the American inventor Samuel Morse in 1844. In 1848, Frederic Newton Gisborne, a Montreal-based promoter, convinced the Nova Scotia government to construct a telegraph line from Halifax to Amherst as part of his plan to improve telegraphic communications between the colonies. In his position as superintendent and chief operator of the Nova Scotia government telegraph lines, he urged the extension of the telegraph to St John's. With the blessing of the Newfoundland government, Gisborne completed a remarkable survey of a route along the island's south coast, travelling with Mi'kmaq and some white companions. In 1852 he connected New Brunswick and Prince Edward Island by the first undersea cable in North America. When his money ran out, he found financial backing from New York financier Cyrus W. Field to undertake an even more ambitious project: to lay a cable across the Atlantic.[11]

Field organized the New York, Newfoundland, and London Telegraph Company, which completed the line between St John's and Cape Ray in 1856. In the same year the company laid a submarine cable under the Cabot Strait. Although the first attempt, in 1858, to lay an Atlantic cable failed, it was successfully laid in 1866 between Valencia, Ireland, and Heart's Content, Newfoundland, by the *Great Eastern*, an enormous iron vessel designed by I.K. Brunel. Communication between the two continents thereafter became almost instantaneous—at least for those who could afford to pay for it.

side with captains, sailors were notorious for various forms of resistance ranging from absence without leave to desertion, insubordination, and even mutiny.

Middle-class citizens were concerned about violence and made concerted efforts to control it. City councils (in unincorporated areas, magistrates) appointed marshals and constables to keep the peace, swore in special deputies, and in extreme cases called on the military for help. By mid-century, full-time police forces began to emerge in the larger urban areas. Legislation, backed by force, was imposed to control workers who dared to use strikes or intimidation to improve their wages and working conditions. By encouraging self-discipline, public schooling, and church attendance, reformers hoped to create a society in which the values of peaceful coexistence and civic virtue would be internalized, and force would no longer be required to maintain social control.

Colonial life was not all conflict and drudgery. In rural areas 'bees' and 'frolics' brought people together in communal bonhomie, and everywhere Sundays offered relief from weekday routines. Significant events on the Christian calendar, such as Christmas, Easter, and saints' days, provided opportunities for holidays and celebrations. In cities and towns, regimental bands, choral recitals, and singing schools flourished. Organized sport was still in its infancy, but racing, yachting, rowing, curling, and cricket clubs were becoming popular in urban centres. Hockey, also called 'hurley' or 'shinny', made inroads in Nova Scotia, though one commentator in 1864 argued that such a rowdy and dangerous game 'ought to be sternly forbidden'.[12] In St John's an annual regatta on Quidi Vidi Lake, begun in 1826, became a highlight of the summer season.

Educated people in the Atlantic region were full participants in the intellectual awakening of the nineteenth century. In a matter of weeks, ideas percolating in Boston, New York, Edinburgh, and London became topics of debate among colonial newspaper editors, college professors, and members of the urban elite. Ambitious colonials travelled to Great Britain and the United States for their education and returned home to practise or teach what they had learned. In the 1830s Mechanics' Institutes, founded in Scotland to disseminate scientific education among the artisan class, took root in the colonies, offering a broad range of literary, dramatic, and artistic activities.

Literacy was highly prized. Newspaper editors emerged as influential political figures, often because they championed progressive causes. Others too took up writing, whether for literary glory or simply to make a living. Thomas McCulloch, the Presbyterian minister who founded Pictou Academy, wrote the *Stepsure Letters* (1821–3), one of the first works of fiction produced in British North America. In 1824 Julia Catherine Beckwith of Fredericton became the first native-born British North American novelist, with the publication of the little-read *St Ursula's Convent*, written when she was 17 years old. The Reverend R.T.S. Lowell's novel *The New Priest in Conception Bay* (1858)—the first to be set in a Newfoundland outport—captured a distinctive lifestyle and dialect. The most successful colonial writer was Judge Thomas Chandler Haliburton, who made an international reputation with his series recounting the adventures of the clock-peddling Yankee salesman Sam Slick. Before turning his hand to satire, Haliburton had written a two-volume history of Nova Scotia, published in 1829. By that time, the Reverend Lewis Anspach's *History of the Island of Newfoundland* (1819) and Peter Fischer's *First History of New Brunswick* (1825) had already appeared.

These pioneering works reflected a cultural maturity that also expressed itself in practical ways. In 1818 John Young, a Scottish merchant in Halifax writing under the name 'Agricola', published a series of letters encouraging scientific methods in agriculture. His efforts, together with financial assistance from the government, led to the establishment of numerous agricultural societies in Nova Scotia. This fashion spread throughout the region, and by 1842 a society was founded in Newfoundland to en-courage more effective use of the island's thin, acidic soils. Colonial inventors such as Charles Fenerty and Abraham Gesner were devising ways to make paper out of wood and kerosene from petroleum.

Political Awakenings

In the wake of the American Revolution, the British government had deliberately imposed on its re-maining North American colonies constitutions designed to limit the democratic tendencies of elect-ed assemblies. Power was weighted towards appointed elements—the governor, his council, and the judiciary. Assemblies—where they existed—were relatively powerless talking-shops, although their consent was needed to pass legislation relating to money bills. As a result deadlocks were common.

Cape Breton and Newfoundland were still without elected assemblies in the early nineteenth century. Although considered the birthright of all self-respecting Britons, representative government was denied to Cape Breton until the island colony was united with the mainland in 1820. Thereafter, with two seats in the Nova Scotia assembly, Cape Breton had representative government, at least in theory, but little political clout.

In Newfoundland the struggle for representative government was more protracted. After the end of the Napoleonic wars business and professional elites in St John's, led by Dr William Carson and Patrick Morris, began to demand formal recognition as a colony with representative government, security of land tenure, and the full range of British civil rights. Naval government no longer made sense, now that the English migratory fishery had died out and Newfoundland's economic and strategic importance to Britain had faded. Nevertheless, it took time and effort to change attitudes in London. Arguing that the migratory fishery and naval government had stunted Newfoundland's development, the reformers drew attention to injustices such as the case of two Conception Bay fish-ermen who, in 1820, were flogged for contempt by order of the surrogate magistrates and had their premises seized for debt. Finally, in 1824–5 circuit courts were instituted, King William's Act was re-pealed, and Newfoundland was declared a Crown colony. Sir Thomas Cochrane became the colony's first civil governor in 1825, and the naval state came to an end. After further agitation, representative government was established in 1832. Religious and ethnic divisions characterized Newfoundland politics in the early years of representative government, and electoral violence erupted in some districts. In an attempt to calm the situation and prevent legislative deadlocks, the Colonial Office instituted an experimental constitution that amalgamated the assembly and council in 1842, but it proved temporary, lasting only until 1848.

Meanwhile, the Maritime colonies were beginning to demand not just representative but 're-sponsible' government, in which the executive would be composed of members of the majority party in the assembly, to which it would be directly responsible. The most eloquent advocate of this reform was Nova Scotia's Joseph Howe, who in his famous letters to the Colonial Secretary, Lord John Russell, in 1840 insisted that 'every poor boy in Nova Scotia' should have 'the same rights to honours and emoluments as he would have if he lived in Great Britain or the United States'.

While Howe focused on the abuse of patronage, reformers in Prince Edward Island were animated by 'the land question'. By the late 1820s, more than half of the proprietors lived else-where, primarily in Great Britain. The absentee proprietors relied on agents to collect their rents and rarely set foot on the island. About one-third of the island's rural population consisted of

William Carson

Born in 1770 in Kirkcudbright, Scotland, Carson studied at the University of Edinburgh's Medical Faculty in the late 1780s. It seems that he did not graduate, but this did not prevent him from claiming that he had done so, from practising medicine, or from calling himself 'Dr'. He practised in Birmingham until 1808, when he left for St John's, Newfoundland. His reasons for emigrating are not known, but Newfoundland was prospering at that time, and he may have seen opportunities for himself and his family.

Carson had not been politically active in Britain, but once in St John's he started a career of almost ceaseless agitation. He was clearly influenced by British Whigs, such as Charles James Fox and Charles Grey, who stood for constitutional rights and reform, and against 'secret influences'. Thus Carson's first political pamphlets, published in 1812 and 1813, called for a civil governor and a legislative assembly to replace the naval state, which he viewed as autocratic and anachronistic.

Carson also promoted an interpretation of Newfoundland's past, drawn ultimately from John Reeves's 1793 *History*, which was to become the accepted orthodoxy. Residents had been oppressed by the infamous West Country merchants who opposed settlement, denied Newfoundlanders their just rights as British subjects, and deliberately retarded the economic development of the country—why else was there so little agriculture? Naval governors were generally ignorant and guilty of illegal and arbitrary behaviour, while the naval surrogates lacked any sense of 'the most common principles of law and justice'. Not surprisingly, local authorities were outraged. Governor John Duckworth wanted to sue Carson for libel, but eventually settled for removing him as surgeon to the St John's Loyal Volunteers and refusing to pay his salary.

Initially Carson had few active supporters, but the severe economic depression which descended at the end of the Napoleonic Wars in 1815 created a climate in which a reform movement could develop. In 1820 he was joined by the Irish merchant Patrick Morris, and together they agitated for official colonial status, which arrived in 1824. Three years later, Carson was appointed district surgeon, Governor Cochrane hoping 'to keep the Doctor quiet'. The appointment did no such thing, and Carson played a prominent role in a renewed campaign for the grant of a legislature, which the British government eventually conceded in 1832.

Carson was defeated in the ensuing election, but found a seat in the assembly in December 1833, thanks to the active support of the Roman Catholic bishop, Michael Fleming. For some time Carson had been cultivating support among the Irish Catholics of St John's, though he himself was a Presbyterian, which opened him to vicious attacks from the Protestant press, to which he replied in kind in the *Newfoundland Patriot*, a newspaper with which he was closely connected.

In 1834 Carson lost his position as district surgeon and had to resume his private medical practice, but he remained politically active, mounting a fierce and prolonged attack on the conservative and obtuse chief justice, Henry John Boulton. The campaign—Boulton finally left in 1838—continued even while Carson served as a controversial speaker of the House of Assembly from 1837 to 1842. He died in 1843 at the age of 73. Though cantankerous and difficult, Carson undoubtedly had the best interests of his adopted country at heart. He played a key role in Newfoundland's political and constitutional development, while making significant contributions to health care and to the development of agriculture.[13]

small freeholders, owing about one-fifth of the available land in the 1.4 million-acre colony. The contrast between tenant and freeholder accentuated the predicament of the latter and made them ready followers of William Cooper, who campaigned in an 1831 by-election on the issue 'Our country's freedom and farmers' rights'. He won the contest handily and soon emerged as the articulate spokesman for escheat of all proprietary holdings. As the movement gained momentum, tenants refused to pay their rents and resisted the efforts of landlords to use legal procedures to collect arrears.

The Escheat party won an overwhelming election victory in 1838, but the Colonial Office, reeling from agrarian radicalism that erupted in Upper and Lower Canada in 1837, refused to accept any legislation that undermined existing property rights. As Rusty Bittermann and Margaret McCallum argue, the temporary defeat of the movement did not end the struggle against proprietorship. Instead, it 'amplified, focused, and honed the conceptions and aspirations of much of the rural population, giving them a vision of a more just society and a historical, constitutional, and moral analysis that justified their efforts to realize that vision on Prince Edward Island'.[14]

In New Brunswick, the central issue in political debates was the revenue from the selling, leasing, and licensing of Crown lands. Charles Simonds, a powerful Saint John timber baron and leader of the reform cause, managed to extract two important concessions from the Colonial Office in 1837: control over Crown land revenues (as long as the salaries of appointed administrators were guaranteed) and consultation with elected representatives in the appointment of the governor's executive councillors.

Great Britain finally abandoned its resistance to responsible government in settler colonies after the adoption of free trade in 1846 made it unnecessary to maintain a closed economic system. In 1847 Nova Scotia's lieutenant-governor, Sir John Harvey, was instructed to choose advisers from the party that had a majority in the assembly. Reformers were victorious in an election held later that year, and on 2 February 1848 a Liberal government under the leadership of James Boyle Uniacke became the first 'responsible' administration in the British Empire. By 1855 all the remaining Atlantic colonies had followed Nova Scotia's lead. This milestone in the region's political history did not mean that the colonies were fully independent: the Colonial Office still kept a watchful eye over defence, external affairs, legal matters, and constitutional amendment.

Although the colonial franchise was quite wide, extending to men of modest means, political power was concentrated in the hands of the commercial and professional elites. Most of these men were conservative in their political outlook and wanted little to do with the liberal and radical ideas that by mid-century were being debated in Great Britain and the United States. Women, no matter what their property status, were disqualified from voting, along with Native people, landless labourers, wards of the state, and relief recipients. As for Labrador, it was entirely ignored in the debate over political rights, as were the inhabitants of Newfoundland's French Treaty Shore.

Despite—or perhaps because of—the closed circle in which it operated, responsible government in the early years was a messy and muddled affair. Administrations were often unstable, with 'loose fish' crossing the floor when they differed from their party on issues great or small. Bureaucratic processes were embryonic, patronage appointments commonplace, and alliances reflected religious affiliations—all to the detriment of good government. Governors continued to meddle even though (like the British monarch) they were supposed to stand apart from the daily routine of political life and follow the recommendations of their executive advisers.

Historian Ian McKay has argued that the achievement of responsible government in British North America was an early step in what he calls the 'project of liberal rule'. Although he emphasized individualism, rule of law, property rights, and civil liberties as key components of this ideology, McKay maintained that liberalism is 'something more akin to a secular religion or a totalizing philosophy than to a manipulated set of political ideas'.[15] It gradually defined the values of all political parties in the colonies, even those labelled 'conservative'.

There is no doubt that the ideals of freedom from traditional restraints galvanized many people to action, but historians disagree about the extent to which the liberal order prevailed in Canada either in the mid-nineteenth century or later. Jerry Bannister has noted that older aristocratic-loyalist notions have remained an essential feature of the Canadian story (a monarch is still the head of state, for example), and others have argued that communal values as expressed in families and among minorities complicated the embrace of liberalism. Nonetheless, those pushed to the side by the proponents of liberalism appealed to some of the tenets of the same ideology in their struggle to improve their living conditions and to assert their citizenship rights.[16]

Conclusion

Despite the ambiguities and difficulties, the rituals of responsible government and a limited notion of political liberalism gradually took root in the Atlantic colonies. By the 1860s political parties had emerged in all the colonies, borrowing the names (and often the programs) of their Liberal and Conservative counterparts in Great Britain, and colonial leaders had begun to move beyond religious and ethnic allegiances to define new community goals. With political visions increasingly defined by industrial progress, public works, and material well-being, politicians even found themselves discussing a plan for colonial union.

Further Readings

Acheson, T.W. 1985. *Saint John: The Making of a Colonial Urban Community*. Toronto: University of Toronto Press.

Buckner, P.A. 1985. *The Transition to Responsible Government: British Policy in British North America, 1815–1850*. Westport, CT: Greenwood.

Greene, John P. 1999. *Between Damnation and Starvation: Priests and Merchants in Newfoundland Politics, 1745–1855*. Montreal: McGill-Queen's University Press.

Hiller, James K. 2008. 'The Nineteenth Century, 1815–1914', Newfoundland Historical Society, *A Short History of Newfoundland and Labrador*. St John's: Boulder Publications.

Hornsby, Stephen. 1992. *Nineteenth-Century Cape Breton: A Historical Geography*. Montreal: McGill-Queen's University Press.

Keough, Willeen G. 2006. *The Slender Thread: Irish Women on the Southern Avalon, 1750–1860*. New York: Columbia University Press.

McCann, Phillip. 1994. *Schooling in a Fishing Society: Education and Economic Conditions in Newfoundland and Labrador 1836–1986*. St John's: ISER.

Murphy, Terrence, and Cyril J. Byrne, eds. 1987. *Religion and Identity: The Experience of Irish and Scots Catholics in Atlantic Canada*. St John's: Jesperson Press.

Ryan, Shannon. 1994. *The Ice Hunters: A History of Newfoundland Sealing to 1914*. St John's: Breakwater Press.

Sager, Eric W., with Gerald E. Panting. 1990. *Maritime Capital: The Shipping Industry in Atlantic Canada, 1820–1914*. Montreal: McGill-Queen's University Press.

Samson, Daniel. 2008. *The Spirit of Industry and Improvement: Liberal Government and Rural-Industrial Society, Nova Scotia, 1790–1862*. Montreal: McGill-Queen's University Press.

See, Scott W. 1993. *Riots in New Brunswick: Orange Nativism and Social Violence in the 1840s*. Toronto: University of Toronto Press.

Whitfield, Harvey Amani. 2006. *Blacks on the Border: The Black Refugees in British North American, 1815–1860*. Burlington: University of Vermont Press.

Wynne, Graeme. 1981. *Timber Colony: A Historical Geography of Early Nineteenth Century New Brunswick*. Toronto: University of Toronto Press.

Food for Thought

Campbell, Gail. 1990. 'The Most Restrictive Franchise in British North America? A Case Study', *Canadian Historical Review* 71, 2 (June): 159–88.

Recommended Websites

The Newfoundland Seal Fishery
http://www.heritage.nf.ca/society/seal.html

The Highland Scots
www.chebucto.ns.ca/Heritage/FSCNS/Scots_NS

The Labrador Inuit through Moravian Eyes
http://link.library.utoronto.ca/inuitmoravian

Part II

The Atlantic Region Since 1867

In the mid-nineteenth century, Britain's North American colonies struggled to find their place in a world being transformed by new industrial processes and new ideas about how the world and its people were created and meant to live. Industrial development, liberalism, and materialism ultimately informed the world view of most people in the Atlantic region, who shared and incorporated as their own a broad North Atlantic culture.

While Newfoundland resisted joining the Dominion of Canada in 1867, the Maritime colonies became part of the new political arrangement. They nevertheless all felt the impact of the larger economic, social, and intellectual forces that shaped global developments in this period. Capitalist cycles of boom and bust, two world wars, and a dreadful influenza pandemic in 1918 recognized no political boundaries. Despite valiant efforts to make adjustments to the challenges facing them, people in the Atlantic region fell behind most other areas of the North Atlantic world in the race for industrial development and increasingly looked elsewhere for opportunities.

When Newfoundland entered Confederation in 1949, it shared with its Maritime neighbours the distinction of being among the poorest provinces in Canada. Conditions improved in the region during the second half of the twentieth century, but new communication technologies symbolized by computers and neo-liberal values privileging the market as the arbiter in all things brought more challenges to small states everywhere in 'the global village'.

Chapter 9

Confronting Confederation, 1860–73

Between 1867 and 1873 the three Maritime colonies were swept into a new political arrangement with the colony of Canada, while Newfoundland remained independent. Nevertheless, all the Atlantic colonies faced the same economic and social challenges in the middle decades of the nineteenth century. The new world order characterized by faster communications, liberal political regimes, and galloping industrialization demanded new values and smart strategies. If they could not keep up with the pace of change, the Atlantic colonies faced marginalization in a world where literacy, railroads, and factories stood supreme as the symbols of progress.

Across the Atlantic in the Age of Industry

Following Great Britain's adoption of free trade and the acceptance of limited colonial self-government in the mid-nineteenth century, Atlantic colonists were preoccupied with how to position themselves in the new industrial order. Initially, the times were relatively good for undertaking bold initiatives. The British economy boomed for two decades after 1845, fuelled by expanding trade, the discovery of gold in California, Australia, British Columbia, and New Zealand, and the expansion of credit through banking and insurance companies, most of them connected to the great financial houses in London. The Crimean War in Europe (1854–6) and the Civil War in the United States (1861–5) further increased demand for colonial agricultural produce, coal, fish, and timber. As Great Britain consolidated its informal empire based on industrial supremacy, banking institutions, and free trade, the Atlantic colonies were well positioned on the edge of the North American continent to go along for the ride.

The 1860s was a critical decade for the Atlantic world. In 1861 the United States erupted in a bloody civil war that pitted the industrialized North against the slave-owning, agrarian South. Although the war brought an end to slavery as an institution, it failed to eradicate the racism that remained rampant in the United States and elsewhere in the post-war period. Meanwhile, nationalist movements achieved considerable success on both sides of the Atlantic. German and Italian states moved decisively along the road to nationhood, while the efforts of French Emperor Napoleon III to establish an imperial regime in Mexico ended with the execution of the leader of his puppet government, Archduke Maximilian, by a Mexican firing squad in 1867. Imperial regimes everywhere were on the defensive. Even Great Britain had its hands full with Irish patriots both home and in North America, who were determined to dissolve the hated union imposed upon their island in 1801.

The new industrial order demanded dramatic action. All four Atlantic colonies, whether in or out of Confederation, pursued industrial strategies with more or less enthusiasm and all four fell behind in the race for economic ascendancy. Failing to develop a metropolis that could compete with Montreal, Toronto, Boston, and New York, the Atlantic region became a source of willing workers who flocked to the other frontiers of opportunity. Out-migration reached significant proportions in the 1880s and continued until the 1930s Depression closed the doors of employment opportunity everywhere in North America. People in the Atlantic region were no strangers to hard times, which had engulfed the region from 1866 to 1896 and again in the 1920s. Nor were people in the region immune to European conflicts that took a huge toll on lives in both the First and Second World Wars.

Big Dreams

The American Civil War, which raged from 1861 to 1865, convinced many colonial politicians that republicanism had its flaws and that the colonies were better off under the British flag and parliamentary system, but staying the course seemed no longer an option. When the North emerged triumphant in 1865, some of its leaders made menacing noises about taking over all of North America. How could the small British colonies defend themselves against such a threat? The only way to do so, some argued, would be to beat the Americans at their own game. With the help of Great Britain, the colonies working together could perhaps build a transcontinental nation to rival their giant neighbour to the south.

Like their European counterparts, supporters of British North American unity were inspired by dreams of economic development. This was especially the case in the United Province of Canada (after 1867, Ontario and Quebec), where industrial development and escape from a crippling railway debt were predicated on acquiring Rupert's Land—the vast territory controlled by the Hudson's Bay Company. The major impediment to the United Canadas' dreams of a Western empire was the political deadlock between its two parts that had been cobbled together in 1840: a largely French-speaking and Catholic population in Canada East (formerly Lower Canada) and an English-speaking and Protestant population in Canada West (formerly Upper Canada).

Table 9.1	Timeline
1860	Prince Edward Island Land Commission appointed.
1861–5	American Civil War.
1861	Trent Affair.
1862	Collapse of negotiations with the Canadians on plans to build an Intercolonial Railroad.
1864	Charlottetown and Quebec Conferences on Confederation; Tenant League founded.
1865	Pro-Confederation government defeated in New Brunswick.
1866	Fenian raid on New Brunswick; pro-Confederation government elected in New Brunswick; London Conference on Confederation.
1867	Confederation of New Brunswick, Nova Scotia, Ontario, and Quebec; secession movement begins in Nova Scotia.
1869	Anti-Confederates in Nova Scotia accept better terms; Newfoundland decisively rejects Confederation.
1871	Treaty of Washington.
1873	Prince Edward Island joins Confederation.

Following the collapse of yet another coalition government in the spring of 1864, a constitutional committee was established to seek a solution to the colony's political problems. Chaired by George Brown, editor of the *The Globe* and leader of the Reform party in Canada West, it recommended a federal union of all the British North American colonies. To see the project through to fruition, a 'Great Coalition' was established, headed by Brown, the leaders of the Conservative-*Bleu* Party (John A. Macdonald from Canada West and George-Étienne Cartier from Canada East), and Alexander Galt, an early proponent of Confederation and spokesperson for the powerful business community of Montreal. It was a formidable alliance.

The Atlantic Colonies at the Crossroads

The Atlantic colonies initially had little interest in British North American union. Instead, they continued to focus their attention on the larger British Empire connected by the sea—that is, until railways began to dominate the agenda. Political and economic leaders in both Nova Scotia and New Brunswick saw their own colony taking advantage of its location to become the gateway to the continent. This goal seemed even more appealing when the fallout from the American Civil War made it clear that if war broke out between Great Britain and the United States, an ice-free port on the east coast would be essential to the security of the United Canadas, and that an all-British railway route linking the colonies together would have both military and economic benefits.

The American Civil War, from the Confederate attack on Fort Sumter in April 1861 to Abraham Lincoln's assassination by John Wilkes Booth four years later, preoccupied people in the Atlantic region more than dreary Confederation discussions.[1] Close and longstanding economic, social, and kinship ties—according to the 1870 US Census Maritimers and Newfoundlanders together formed the fourth-largest ethnic group in the republic—made the nearby conflict a matter of personal interest for many colonials, and incidents involving blockade running in waters off Nova Scotia and New Brunswick kept colonial tongues wagging. As British possessions, the colonies were officially neutral, but there were supporters for both sides. Several thousand Maritimers, many of them working in the United States when war was declared, enlisted in the Union or Confederate armies. One of them, Sara Emma Edmmonds, posed as a man so that she could join the Union Army, where she saw combat and worked as a nurse, spy, and general's aid.

The Confederacy hoped that Great Britain, which had a stake in the cotton and tobacco industries of the South, would formally support their cause. In November 1861 war seemed imminent when a Northern warship seized the *Trent*, a British steamer, on the high seas and arrested two Confederate agents. Although the two captives were eventually released, tensions remained high, and Great Britain sent 15,000 troops to supplement the 3,000 soldiers already stationed in the colonies. Arriving in winter, they were obliged to march overland to Quebec City from New Brunswick—convincing proof of the need for a railway connecting the Maritimes to the United Canadas.

Nova Scotia's Joseph Howe was an indefatigable promoter of railways. When he assumed the premiership of Nova Scotia in August 1860, he made railway building one of his top priorities. His favourite project was a line linking Halifax to the St Lawrence, generally referred to as the Intercolonial Railway. As early as 1849, Howe had proposed such a line at a Halifax conference convened to address the implications of Great Britain's adoption of free trade on the Atlantic colonies. Howe's railway projects, which managed only to link Halifax with Windsor and Pictou, fell far short of his larger goal and were the main reason that the provincial debt reached a total of $4.5 million in 1863. By that time there seemed little hope that the Intercolonial would proceed. The collapse, in 1862, of railway talks with representatives from the United Canadas seemed to be the final nail in the coffin. British capitalists had little enthusiasm for a railway project that required negotiations with a rabble of dysfunctional colonies, most of them teetering on the brink of bankruptcy.

Howe's government was defeated by the Conservatives in 1863. Under Charles Tupper, who assumed the premiership in 1864, the Conservatives continued to support public works and other progressive programs such as publicly funded schools. A medical doctor, Tupper had represented Cumberland County since 1855. With substantial investments in his constituency's coal mines and a keen sense of its strategic location with regard to any railway built between Nova Scotia and points further west, Tupper was a great booster of enterprise both public and private. The Intercolonial held the promise for Nova Scotians of new markets in New Brunswick and the United Canadas, but the colony lacked the financial resources to proceed. Under Tupper's government, the provincial debt ballooned to $8 million by 1866. How long would Barings' Bank in London be willing to underwrite the colony's debt?

New Brunswickers were also caught up in the railway mania. Although the St Andrews and Quebec Railway Company ran out of money before achieving its objective, the idea of the Intercolonial Railway continued to inspire support among New Brunswick's political and business leaders. So, too, did the idea of a link to Maine. The era of Reciprocity created a keen interest in north–south lines of communication, and a promoter from Maine, Joseph Alfred Poor, seemed poised to help make the idea a reality. When Poor declared bankruptcy in 1855, New Brunswick pressed ahead with a line linking Shediac to Saint John and continued making plans to extend its European and North American railway into the United States.

In 1861 Reform Premier Charles Fisher, an active supporter of railway construction, was brought down by a conflict-of-interest scandal relating to the purchase of Crown Lands. His successor, Leonard Tilley, was keen on the Intercolonial, but with a $5-million railway debt and annual revenues of only $600,000, New Brunswick could not move forward on its own. Without the support of the Canadians and financial assistance from Great Britain, neither of which was forthcoming, the project would never succeed.

Prince Edward Island was slow to jump on the railway-building bandwagon. As a result, its public debt in the 1860s remained under control. Islanders found export markets for their farm and fishery products in the United States under Reciprocity and, like other Maritimers, boasted a healthy shipbuilding industry. Even the persistent land question seemed to be on the verge of resolution. Under the voluntary Land Purchase Act of 1853, Premier George Coles began using provincial funds to buy out some of the proprietors so that tenants could become landowners. Although the landlords and the Colonial Office resisted his efforts, by 1860 nearly 40 per cent of the island's residents were freeholders.

The increased accessibility of land under freehold tenure inevitably highlighted the hardships of those who continued to pay rents. In 1860 Conservative Premier Edward Palmer, himself a landlord, created the Prince Edward Island Land Commission to inquire into the issue. Nova Scotia's Joseph Howe, along with Halifax lawyer J.W. Ritchie and New Brunswick Liberal politician John Hamilton Gray, submitted a report that was sympathetic to tenant demands. It recommended that the tenants be given the right to purchase land from their landlords and to have arrears in payments prior to 1 May 1858 forgiven. In cases where tenants and landlords could not agree on a fair price for the land, it would be established by arbitration. The landlords were livid and the Colonial Office became nervous. Although Palmer's government passed legislation to implement the commission's recommendations, royal assent was withheld on a 'technicality'.

DOCUMENT:
The Prince Edward Island Land Commission

In their report, submitted in 1861, the Prince Edward Island Land Commissioners included evidence from the hearings they had held throughout the colony. The document is thus an excellent source of information about the tensions between landlords and tenants on the Island. The following testimony by Nicolas Conroy, a Liberal member of the Island's assembly, describes how new landlords such as Samuel Cunard became more efficient than their predecessors in enforcing rent payments. Together with his son Edward, Cunard owned more than 190,000 acres (80,000 hectares), much of it acquired in the late 1830s.

In 1835, when I first settled in Tignish, no proprietors were recognized in Lots One and Two. There had been some competitors for proprietorship, but previous to that period, though the people were asked, and even pressed to pay rent, still they always refused. I was present when the first recognition of a proprietor took place on Lot Two. . . . Mr Peters, now Judge Peters, who was at the time agent for Mr Cunard, . . . desired me as I knew the people to accompany him . . . I did so. When we arrived, many of the inhabitants were assembled. Mr Peters told them, Mr Cunard was the proprietor of the Lot, and wished them to attorn to him as their landlord; but they refused, just as they had refused to attorn to Mr Hill, some years previous. They were free, and desired to remain so if possible. Mr Peters then spoke to them of the wealth and power of Mr Cunard in Halifax. He said he was an influential gentleman in that City, and to hold out against him would be preposterous. The better way was, to pay rents; he would protect them; and they would have an honorable gentleman for their landlord. After much coaxing, and half threatening they signed a paper which he wished them to subscribe. Some time after this Mr Peters and Mr Palmer came to some arrangement respecting Lot One. They accordingly sent word to the people, saying that they were coming to get them to take leases. The people met them, but unanimously refused to have anything to do with them. Messrs Peters and Palmer remained a week, and were on the eve of leaving, when, unfortunately, the people began to misunderstand each other—one thought the other was going to get his farm, and so forth, and the result was, all made a rush to the proprietor to attorn. I was present, I saw the rejoicing proprietors on that occasion. . . . The leases were for a term of 999 years, and at 1s sterling an acre. In addition to this, they signed notes of hand for £10, to be paid up the 25th March, then last past. Your Honors will remember that another year's rent was then nearly due, so that by the coming 25th of March, which was about one month hence, they were involved in £15 arrears. Now, some who signed those notes of hand, were very poor, and for them to make good their notes, was impossible. In the meantime, the proprietors pressed and threatened them, so that the greater number left their farms from sheer inability to pay these arrears. This I would call a real grievance.[2]

The rejection of the commissioners' award fuelled the resolve of the aggrieved tenants and their supporters to put an end to the colony's feudal landholding system once and for all. In 1864 a Tenant League was formed to support a tenant takeover of rented land, with rates of compensation for land-lords to be set by the townships. Members vowed to withhold rent payments, and when soldiers tried to serve writs on those in arrears, violence inevitably ensued. With chaos looming, finding the re-sources to solve the land question became the central focus of Prince Edward Island administrators.

In Newfoundland, where Liberals were mainly Roman Catholic and Conservatives overwhelmingly Protestant, denominational tensions continued to characterize political life in the years following the adoption of responsible government in 1855. There were also tensions within the Liberal camp. After the 1861 election, a major riot in St John's involving rival Liberal factions resulted in troops firing on the crowd, killing three people and wounding 20. This event prompted compromise. Religious leaders voluntarily withdrew from overt political activity, and the political elites gradually shaped an unwritten agreement whereby public patronage, and seats in the legislature and on the executive council, would be awarded to each denomination in proportion to its size. Premier Hugh Hoyles signalled the new at-titude by offering cabinet seats to a number of Roman Catholics. This denominational compromise was an important step, allowing the evolution of political parties based on factors other than religion.

Table 9.2 Population of Eastern British North America, 1851–71			
	1851	1861	1871
Ontario	952,004	1,396,091	1,620,851
Quebec	890,261	1,111,566	1,191,516
Nova Scotia	276,854	330,857	387,800
New Brunswick	193,800	252,047	285,594
Prince Edward Island	62,678*	80,857	94,021
Newfoundland†	–	122,638	146,536

* figure is from 1848
† Figures are from 1857 and 1869

Sources: 'Series A 2-14. Population of Canada by province, census dates, 1851 to 1976', in *Historical Statistics of Canada*, 2nd edn, ed. F.H. Leacy (Ottawa: Minister of Supply and Services, 1983) and James Hiller, 'Confederation Defeated: The Newfoundland Election of 1869', in James Hiller and Peter Neary, eds, *Newfoundland in the Nineteenth and Twentieth Centuries: Essays in Interpretation* (Toronto: University of Toronto Press, 1980).

British Financiers and Canadian Confederation

It has been long conceded that railway interests played a major role in promoting Confedera-tion, but a recent study by Andrew Smith documents the extent to which London's financial district facilitated the process. Indeed, Smith argues that 'Without the support of a small but influential group of investors, Confederation would not have occurred in 1867, if at all.'[3]

In the early 1860s, crises in British North American investments, both in private ventures and in colonial administrations, threatened the survival of some of London's most important financial institutions, including Barings' Bank and Glyn, Mills, and Company. In particular, the financial troubles of the Grand Trunk Railway Company compromised major investment houses and made the extension of the line from Quebec City to the ice-free ports of the Maritimes unlikely. At the same time, the American Civil War underscored the need for an all-British winter route to the United Canadas. Financiers, always on the lookout for bigger projects, promoted the improbable scheme of recouping the Grand Trunk's fortunes by extending rails across the continent to the Pacific. Such a line would not only secure an alternative route to Asia, they argued, but also open up Rupert's Land, which was still under the monopoly control of the Hudson's Bay Company, to settlement and development.

At the suggestion of Joseph Howe, who was in London in December 1861 drumming up support for the Intercolonial Railway, men with financial interests in the colonies formed the British North American Association (BNAA) in January 1862. Its first objective was to lobby the British government in support of both the long-awaited Halifax–Quebec railway and the union of the colonies under one administration, which would make negotiations relating to development projects less complicated. The more conservative among them also saw union of the colonies as a means of implementing stiffer voting regulations that would make it easier to eclipse opposition to government spending from penny-pinching petty producers in agriculture, forestry, and fisheries. In short order, the new lobby group had the ear of the Duke of Newcastle, Colonial Secretary from 1859 to 1864, who became an ardent supporter of Confederation.

Many London financiers and businessmen thought that a strong empire was good for trade and investment, and believed that a united British North America under a strong central government was the best approach to linking individual colonies to the British Crown and ensuring the success of empire around the world. Significantly, the first clause in the British North America Act of 1867 declared that 'the present and future prosperity of British North America will be promoted by a federal union under the crown of Great Britain.'

It is a common misconception that Canada achieved independence in 1867; this was not so. Foreign affairs, military policy, and constitutional amendments still required British approval, and the Privy Council in London remained the final court of appeal in legal matters. Only with the passage of the Statute of Westminster in 1931 did Canada and other British Dominions achieve political independence. By that time, New York had replaced London as the major source of investment capital for Canada and much of the developing world.

The Road to Confederation

Nova Scotia's Conservative Premier Charles Tupper inadvertently started the Confederation ball rolling by promoting the idea of Maritime Union. Discouraged both by the collapse of the negotiations with the Canadians on the Intercolonial project and by the general parochialism of colonial politics, he reasoned that the Maritime colonies would have more clout with British investors if they pooled their resources. Early in 1864 Maritime Union was debated in the Nova Scotia assembly, whose members agreed to send delegates to a conference on the subject. New Brunswick supported this initiative; Prince Edward Island ignored it.

The idea of Maritime Union would almost certainly have remained dormant if politicians in the United Canadas had not been seeking solutions to the political deadlock in their own legislature. On hearing of the developments in the 'Lower provinces', the Canadians sought permission to attend the proposed Maritime Union conference, held in Charlottetown in early September 1864. The location insured the involvement of Islanders and was more convenient than other Maritime capitals for the Canadian delegates who arrived by boat. The meeting quickly expanded to include discussion of the Canadian proposal for a federation of all the British North America colonies. A month later, the delegates reassembled in Quebec to hammer out a detailed agreement. Joined by two representatives from Newfoundland (invited as an afterthought), the delegates produced 69 resolutions, which became the basis of the British North America Act.

Since legislative union was unacceptable to most of the delegates, the Confederation agreement envisaged a federal system with two levels of jurisdiction: national and provincial. Members of the federal House of Commons were to be elected on the basis of population, giving the two sections of the United Canadas, with their far greater numbers, overwhelming control. The appointed Senate was designed to provide a regional counter-balance, but was dominated by the Canadians because the Atlantic delegates failed to insist on equal provincial representation, settling instead for equal *regional* representation—the Maritimes, Quebec, and Ontario—with four additional seats to be allocated to Newfoundland if it decided to participate. Coupled with the agreement that senators would be appointed for life by the federal government, this structure ensured that, as Phillip Buckner puts it, 'the Senate would have no moral authority to challenge the governing party in the House of Commons' and at the same time 'limited its effectiveness as the guardian of regional interests'.[4]

The federal government was assigned the most significant powers, including control over interprovincial trade and transportation; foreign policy and defence; criminal law; currency and banking; and Indian Affairs (Aboriginal people, not surprisingly, had no say in this decision). The federal

The delegates to the Charlottetown Conference, September 1864. LAC, C-733.

government also controlled all the major sources of taxation. The provinces had jurisdiction over commerce within their borders, natural resources, civil law, municipal administration, education, and social services. Agriculture, immigration, and fisheries would be joint responsibilities.

It is highly unlikely that internal pressures alone would have produced a Confederation agreement. External forces were also important, especially the threat posed by the United States. As the Civil War came to an end, Secretary of State William Seward began making noises to the effect that it was the 'manifest destiny' of the United States to control the whole continent. The purchase of Alaska from Russia in 1867 became the first step in the American thrust northward. The situation of the British North American colonies was further complicated by the Fenian Brotherhood, Irish nationalists whose leaders concocted a scheme to invade British North America from American soil—a clever way, they thought, of provoking a war between Britain and the United States that might give Ireland a better chance of achieving independence.

Neither the colonies nor Britain wanted a war with the United States. Indeed, the Colonial Office saw British North American union as a way of reducing military commitments in North America. (By 1871 British troops had been withdrawn entirely except from Halifax, where they would remain until the first decade of the twentieth century.) To compound what was developing into a full-scale military crisis, Washington served notice in 1864 that it would terminate the Reciprocity Treaty in 1866, causing consternation among those who relied on American markets. Confederation suddenly looked more interesting.

Selling Confederation

Since none of the leaders who attended the 1864 conferences had a mandate to negotiate political union, they were obliged either to call elections or to have the Confederation agreement endorsed by their legislatures. The Quebec resolutions passed easily through the legislature of the United Canadas, but the Atlantic colonies were less enthusiastic. In St John's Premier Hoyles found little support for Confederation either in his party or in Newfoundland at large. He therefore postponed a decision on the matter. Only 5 per cent of the island's trade was with British North America, and talk of railway building and military preparedness intensified well-founded fears that Newfoundland would be saddled with taxes from which it would receive little benefit. Among those of Irish descent, Confederation conjured up memories of the hated union of Great Britain and Ireland and invoked fears that newly won rights with respect to schools and political patronage would be jeopardized.

In Prince Edward Island, Conservative Premier John Hamilton Gray also shelved the issue. His own party was divided on the Quebec resolutions, and few Islanders saw much advantage in a union that gave their colony only five seats in the Commons and did nothing to resolve the 'land question'. So contentious was the issue in Nova Scotia, where Joseph Howe became the spokesman for the anti-Confederate cause, that Tupper was forced to delay introducing the Quebec resolutions into the legislature.

New Brunswick's Premier Tilley took a more direct route. In March 1865 he led his badly divided party to a resounding electoral defeat at the hands of anti-Confederates led by Albert J. Smith. Strong forces intervened, some intentionally, others fortuitously, to put the Confederation movement back on track. Smith's anti-Confederate government broke into warring factions, and

Joseph Howe on Confederation

In the winter of 1865, the Halifax *Chronicle* anonymously published Joseph Howe's 'Bother-ation Letters', attacking the Quebec scheme for British North American union. Claiming that the Confederation proposal was 'neither fish, flesh, nor good red herring', Howe outlined in these letters the reasons why the terms of union as embodied in the Quebec resolutions were inimical to the Maritime colonies. He summarized his objections in a letter to Earl Russell on 19 January 1865:

1. That by adopting the principle of Representation by population, the Maritime Provinces will be forever swamped by the Canadians.
2. That, if the Canadas, always in trouble of some sort, and two or three times in open rebellion, should repeat such eccentricities, we should be compromised, and our connexion with the Mother Country endangered.
3. Because the plan of double Legislatures, tried in Scotland and Ireland and swept away, is cumbersome and expensive, and cannot be carried out without raising our ad valorum duty, which is now only 10 percent to 20.
4. That, when we raise our duties to this point, for the benefit of 3,000,000 Canadians, we burthen our trade with the Mother country and with our British brethren in 50 other Colonies scattered all over the world.
5. That when the tariff is thus raised but £250,000 currency will be left for defence, a sum utterly inadequate for any such purpose while nothing is gained by weakening the unity of command and control now promised by Her Majesty's Government.[5]

Lieutenant-Governor Arthur Hamilton Gordon, in a high-handed manoeuvre that defied the principle of responsible government, forced another election in May 1866. This time Tilley, promising major revisions to the Quebec agreement, won a convincing victory. Support from Roman Catholic bishops and timber merchants, a timely invasion by the Fenians, and money from the Canadians and their Grand Trunk railway allies all helped to effect this reversal of fortunes. It would not be the last time that patronage rather than policy was used to legitimize Confederation in the Atlantic region.

In April 1866 Tupper made his move. With the assistance of Lieutenant-Governor William Fenwick Williams, a native of Nova Scotia and a decorated military officer, Tupper twisted enough arms to ensure passage of a resolution in the Nova Scotia legislature authorizing continued discussion of British North American union. Significantly, Tupper's resolution made no reference to the Quebec 'scheme', which had been thoroughly discredited by the anti-Confederate forces in the colony.

The final negotiations were conducted in London in the fall of 1866. Although no substantive changes were made to the constitutional arrangements forged in Quebec in 1864, Tupper managed to secure a clause in the British North America Act providing for the 'immediate' construction of the Intercolonial Railway 'by the Government of Canada'. The Maritime delegation also ceded to the federal government exclusive control over the fisheries—the original agreement had provided for joint jurisdiction as with agriculture and immigration—and export duties on coal.

Samuel Leonard Tilley

Samuel Leonard Tilley LAC PA-012632

With the exception of John A. Macdonald, no one played a more prominent role in the early years of Confederation than Samuel Leonard Tilley, commonly known as Leonard. He was born in Gagetown, New Brunswick, in 1818, a descendant of Loyalists on both sides of his family. At the age of 13, he began an apprenticeship with a pharmacist in Saint John, and in 1838 he and his cousin, Thomas Peters, opened their own 'Cheap Drug Store'. A year later Tilley was so deeply moved by a sermon that religious conviction thereafter governed his life. He taught Sunday school, served as a warden in the Church of England, and embraced the temperance movement. In 1854 he reached the highest office of the Sons of Temperance when he was named Most Worthy Patriarch.

Elected to the New Brunswick assembly in 1850, Tilley became a major player in the movement for responsible government, which was fully achieved in 1854. As provincial secretary he was a moving spirit behind the 1855 Prohibition Bill, but opposition to it was so great that he was defeated in the election of 1856 and the measure was rescinded. Regaining his seat in 1857 along with his position as provincial secretary, he became premier of the colony in 1861. With Joseph Howe, Tilley worked tirelessly to secure British and Canadian backing for the Intercolonial Railway. When the Canadians withdrew from the deal in 1862, he refused to give up the dream and pushed an enabling bill through the assembly.

By the summer of 1864 Tilley was convinced of the need 'to bind together the Atlantic and Pacific by a continuous chain of settlements and a line of communications for that [was] the destiny of this country, and the race which inhabited it'.[6] He fought two bitter elections in New Brunswick over the Confederation issue and was appointed Minister of Customs in John A. Macdonald's first cabinet.

An early proponent of tariff protection for New Brunswick's infant industries, Tilley twice drew the wrath of commercial interests in the Maritimes with his initiatives. The tariff structure that he introduced in December 1867 helped to fuel the secession movement in Nova Scotia, and it was Tilley who made the initial overture to Howe about accepting 'better terms' rather than abandoning Confederation. As Minister of Finance, Tilley introduced the 1879 tariff legislation that became the keystone to Macdonald's National Policy. High tariff walls to protect Canadian industry was a measure that would define the nation's economic strategy until the Canada–US Free Trade Agreement went into effect on 1 January 1989.

Despite a strong lobby from Halifax's Archbishop T.L. Connelly for a clause providing legal support for separate schools in the Maritimes, the delegates could not be moved, with the result that separate schools were constitutionally recognized only in Ontario and Quebec.

Notwithstanding his failure to get major concessions from the Canadians, Tupper remained optimistic about the potential of Confederation to stimulate industrial development in Nova Scotia. In justifying the transfer to the federal government of the power to levy coal duties, he told the members of the Nova Scotia assembly in the spring of 1867 that 'the possession of coal mines, together with other natural resources must, in the course of time, make Nova Scotia the great emporium for manufactures in British America.' He went on to explain that 'in taking out of the power of any Legislature to double the amount of royalty, we were giving a guarantee to capitalists who might come and invest their money in these coal mines.'[7] In short, if Tupper had his way, Nova Scotia would be open for business.

With little debate, the British North America Act passed in the British Parliament in March 1867, and on 1 July 1867 Ontario, Quebec, New Brunswick, and Nova Scotia came together to form the Dominion of Canada. The *Morning Chronicle*, a Liberal newspaper in Halifax, appeared with a black border of mourning to mark the occasion, while the New Glasgow *Eastern Chronicle* carried a mock birth notice: 'On Monday last, at 12:05 a.m. (premature) the Dominion of Canada—illegitimate. This prodigy is known as the infant monster Confederation. . . .'

Nova Scotia's Secessionist Movement

Nova Scotians had good reason to feel they had been hoodwinked into joining the new union. Neither voters nor their elected representatives had given their approval to the proposals that ultimately became the basis for Confederation. Even worse, they felt that they had been literally 'railroaded' into a bad bargain. Commercial elements in the colony were particularly wary of a political structure initiated by 'Upper Canadians' who might pursue trade and tariff policies that would cripple their prospects.

In the elections held in September 1867, Nova Scotia voters finally had their say and they made their views clear. Thirty-six of 38 seats in the provincial assembly were won by candidates running on anti-Confederate tickets—political parties in the province were entirely disrupted by the issue. Only Tupper survived the federal contest that elected 18 anti-Confederates to the 19 seats available to Nova Scotia in the House of Commons.

Nova Scotia separatists were so determined to smash the union that some of them even saw joining the United States as preferable to Confederation. In 1869 an Annexation League was formed to promote this alternative. Support for annexation was especially strong in southwestern Nova Scotia, which was virtually a suburb of Boston, and in Cape Breton, where coal interests were keen to restore access to American markets. At a meeting held in the summer of 1869, the annexationists drew up a manifesto, which they circulated around the province:

> Our only hope of commercial prosperity, material development and permanent peace lies in closer relations with the United States. Therefore be it resolved that every legitimate means should be used by members of this convention to sever our connection with Canada and to bring about a union on fair and equitable terms with the American Republic.[8]

Nova Scotia's opposition to Confederation represented more than wounded local pride. As constituted in 1867, the Dominion of Canada was little more than the United Canadas writ large, and was designed to serve the needs of the larger colony. The capital of the new nation was Ottawa, the former capital of the United Canadas, and the civil service was Canadian in structure and personnel. With their small populations compared to Quebec and Ontario, the Maritime provinces could never dominate either the House of Commons or the cabinet table. The financial arrangements established by the British North America Act were particularly disadvantageous to small provinces. By absorbing the revenues from customs duties, Ottawa took away the chief source of funds for colonial administrations and offered the less populous colonies a per capita grant formula that would prove inadequate to fund their provincial responsibilities.

Nova Scotians were not opposed to becoming part of a larger political entity: imperial union, with colonial representation in London, was Howe's preferred option, while Maritime Union and annexation to the United States also had their supporters. What rankled was the obvious Canadian bias in the constitutional arrangements of 1867. This is not to say that the Maritime colonies would have fared better outside the Dominion of Canada—the fate of the Newfoundland government in the 1930s is often cited as proof that Confederation at least allowed the Maritimes a 'shabby dignity' in hard times.[9] Nevertheless, most of the predictions of the anti-Confederates proved correct in that

the Maritimes did indeed have difficulty making their way in the new political structure.

In 1868 Howe led a delegation to London seeking repeal of the hated union, but the British had no interest in granting his request. Faced with growing support for annexation at home, Howe—ever loyal to Britain—agreed in 1869 to an accommodation with Ottawa that gave seats in the federal cabinet to two anti-Confederates and promised the province a 10-year bridging subsidy of about $800,000, with additional compensation for those public buildings that were transferred to federal control. Largely because of the lingering separatist sentiment in Nova Scotia, Prime Minister John A. Macdonald immediately authorized construction of the Intercolonial Railway.

Macdonald also tried to represent Nova Scotia's interests as a member of the British delegation that met with American representatives to settle a variety of issues left over from the Civil War. At the top of his agenda was

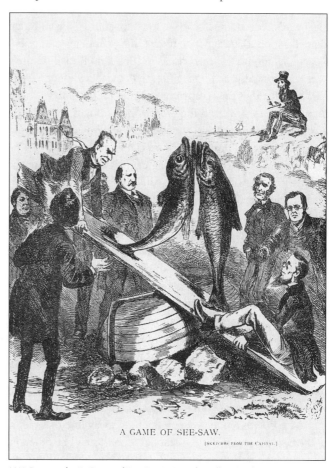

A GAME OF SEE-SAW.
[SKETCHES FROM THE CAPITAL.]

J.W. Bengough, 'A Game of See-Saw', *Canadian Illustrated News*, 4 May 1872. In the 1872 election, Maritime opposition to Confederation was sufficiently muted to give the federal Conservatives a large majority of seats. One reason, this cartoon suggests, was Macdonald's success in gaining entry to American markets for Canadian fish. Courtesy of Chinook Multimedia, Edmonton.

a new reciprocity treaty. Although protectionists in the United States were too strong to permit such a concession, Macdonald managed to ensure that the Treaty of Washington, signed in 1871, provided free entry for Canadian fish into the American market and compensation, to be determined by arbitration, for American access to Canadian inshore waters—terms that also applied to Newfoundland.

While Nova Scotians—and Canadians generally—had hoped for more from the Washington negotiations, they accepted what was on offer. Only two Nova Scotia MPs voted against the treaty, and in the federal election of 1872 two-thirds of the MPs from Nova Scotia supported Macdonald. Nevertheless, the province's continuing financial problems and the difficulties faced by both the primary and the commercial sectors guaranteed that anti-Confederation sentiment could easily be rekindled in the future.

Courting the Islands

Meanwhile, Macdonald made efforts to entice Newfoundland and Prince Edward Island into Confederation. Determined to unite Canada from sea-to-sea, he had already managed to incorporate Rupert's Land into the new nation in 1869, and British Columbia would follow two years later.

Despite widespread opposition to the idea, Confederation remained on the political agenda of Newfoundland's Conservative premier, Frederic Carter, who perhaps doubted the colony's ability to prosper on its own. In the months preceding the 1869 election, he persuaded the assembly to accept draft union terms that were more generous than those proposed in the Quebec resolutions. Canada was prepared to offer a special annual grant of $175,000 in exchange for the surrender of the island's Crown lands, an agreement that no export tax would be levied on its fish, and a promise that Newfoundlanders would not be drafted into the Canadian militia.

With no overwhelming debt and little tangible advantage to be gained from union, voters were not impressed. Anti-Confederate forces, led by the eloquent and persuasive merchant Charles Fox Bennett, won two-thirds of the seats in the assembly, and the margin of victory was enough that Confederation would not re-emerge as a viable political issue until the 1940s. Most Newfoundlanders apparently believed that their country had the resources to support an independent future.[10]

Prince Edward Islanders, by contrast, eventually warmed to Macdonald's blandishments. The main issue in their 1867 election was not Confederation but the funding of denominational schools. Supported by a majority of the Roman Catholic voters, the Liberals defeated the Conservatives. Once in office, however, they proved equally unwilling to embrace denominational funding. Consequently, they lost much of their support and in turn suffered defeat in the 1870 election. The triumphant Conservatives under James Pope, a leading businessman and supporter of Confederation, formed the new government in alliance with the Roman Catholic independents who had broken away from the Liberals.

An apostle of progress, Pope built a railway line that wound a serpentine route through many of the island's communities. Islanders soon found, as others had before them, that railway building was hard on the pocketbook. Meanwhile, the land question remained unresolved. Although the Tenant League had collapsed in the autumn of 1865 (when confronted by two companies of British troops called in from Halifax) historian Ian Robertson argues that it succeeded in convincing many landlords that the system was impossible to sustain.[11] In May 1865 Samuel Cunard and Laurence Sullivan, who together owned 20 per cent of the land in the colony, announced that they

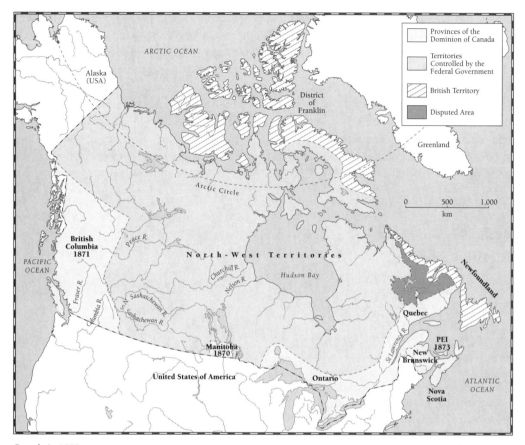

Canada in 1873.

would be selling, not leasing, their land, and others began to follow their lead. Only the lack of funding made a general policy to manage the transition from leasehold to freehold elusive.

Pope argued that the answer was to let Ottawa come to the rescue. Although he lost the 1872 election, his successor, Robert Haythorne, continued building railway lines and chalking up debts. To alleviate a financial burden that was rapidly becoming untenable, Haythorne's government negotiated a Confederation agreement and took it to the electorate in March 1873. Pope then returned to power—not because he opposed Confederation but because he promised to drive a harder bargain with Ottawa. In the end he succeeded in securing most of the concessions that Islanders had wanted in 1864 and more besides. Prime Minister Macdonald agreed not only to assume the railway debt and help to buy out the remaining proprietors but also to establish year-round communications with the mainland and give Islanders the six Commons seats that they demanded.

Conclusion

The debate over Confederation in the Atlantic region was defined to a striking degree by economic considerations. At the risk of oversimplification, it might be said that anti-Confederates tended to look east and south—to the North Atlantic, Britain, the oceanic trades, and the promising American market—whereas supporters of Confederation looked west, seeing the future in economic integration with the central provinces and expansion to the Pacific. Both groups recognized the need to adjust to a world in which Britain had abandoned imperial protectionism for free trade, reduced its defence commitments, and accepted colonial demands for responsible government, and in which the Americans had retreated behind a wall of protectionism. These changes were compounded by the spread of new technologies, based on coal, iron, and steel, that threatened traditional industries based on wood and wind. In a time of flux, it seemed to many people in the Maritimes that political consolidation made sense. Newfoundlanders took much longer to accept that their future was as a North American, not a North Atlantic, country.

Further Readings

Bitterman, Rusty, and Margaret McCallum. 2008. *Lady Landlords of Prince Edward Island*. Toronto: University of Toronto Press.

Bolger, Francis W.P. 1964. *Prince Edward Island and Confederation, 1863–1973*. Charlottetown: St Dunstan's.

Hiller, James K. 1993. 'Newfoundland Confronts Canada, 1867–1949', in E.R. Forbes and D.A. Muise, eds, *The Atlantic Provinces in Confederation*. Fredericton/Toronto: Acadiensis Press/University of Toronto Press.

Marquis, Greg. 1998. *In Armageddon's Shadow: The Civil War and Canada's Maritime Provinces*. Montreal; McGill-Queen's University Press.

Martin, Ged, ed. 1990. *The Causes of Canadian Confederation*. Fredericton: Acadiensis Press.

Pryke, Kenneth G. 1978. *Nova Scotia and Confederation, 1864–74*. Toronto: University of Toronto Press.

Robertson, Ian Ross. 1996. *The Tenant League of Prince Edward Island, 1864–1867: Leasehold Tenure in the New World*. Toronto: University of Toronto Press.

Smith, Andrew. 2008. *British Businessmen and Canadian Confederation: Constitution Making in an Age of Anglo-Globalization*. Montreal: McGill-Queen's University Press.

Food for Thought

Buckner, Phillip A. 1990. 'The Maritimes and Confederation: A Reassessment', in Martin, Ged, ed., *The Causes of Canadian Confederation*. Fredericton: Acadiensis Press.

Recommended Websites

Confederation
http://www.collectionscanada.gc.ca/confederation/index-e.html

Newfoundland and Canada, 1864–1948
http://www.heritage.nf.ca/law/confed.html

Chapter 10

The Industrial Challenge, 1873–1901

The three Maritime provinces and Newfoundland had chosen separate political destinies, but in the last three decades of the nineteenth century they followed parallel paths. While the Maritimes worked out their position within a federal state dominated by Ontario and Quebec, Newfoundland was obliged to deal with an imperial government that hoped the colony would soon see the error of its ways and join Canada. Relations with central governments, whether in Ottawa or London, were characterized by ambivalence and frustration.

In this period Maritimers faced a difficult transition from the traditional staple export trades to a more diversified economy characterized by industrialization and continental integration. The Canadian government under the leadership of Prime Minister John A. Macdonald embarked on an ambitious 'National Policy' that included building a transcontinental railway, development of the western territories, and a high tariff against imported manufactured goods to give infant Canadian industries a chance to grow in the face of stiff US competition. Although this framework initially seemed to work for the Maritimes, it eventually served to concentrate development in the St Lawrence heartland. Newfoundlanders also attempted industrialization and diversification, but with limited success. The adjustment was made all the more difficult by an extended economic recession from 1866 to 1896.

As they struggled to adjust to the larger forces swirling around them, most Maritimers gradually became conscious of being Canadians, but they also, like Newfoundlanders, were proud of their association with the ever-expanding British Empire. Imperial ties helped to balance the growing economic and cultural impact of the United States. Located at the crossroads of British, Canadian, and American influences, individuals and governments in the Atlantic region faced the difficult task of finding their place in the fast-paced new world order.

Primary Industries in Transition

Industrializing processes forced changes in all sectors of the economy. Of the primary industries, agriculture—central to the Maritimes' economy—did better than most. Output increased, if modestly. Falling prices forced some farmers into subsistence agriculture, often in combination with other occupations such as lumbering and fishing. Others turned to livestock and dairy farming to supply a growing urban market or focused on specialties for export. Orchards proliferated, especially in Nova Scotia's Annapolis Valley, while potatoes became an important crop in Prince Edward Island and New Brunswick. By the 1890s fox farming was increasing in popularity, especially in Prince Edward Island. Except for apple growers exporting to Great Britain, agricultural producers had difficulty finding foreign markets after the end of reciprocity in 1866. Newfoundland, where there were few commercial farms, relied heavily on imported livestock and foodstuffs, and St-Pierre provided a market for Cape Breton produce.

The forest industry, the traditional engine of the New Brunswick economy, was badly damaged by the decline in British demand for both lumber and wooden ships. During the 1870s Saint John lost 29 per cent of its population as the unemployed and those with high ambitions drifted to opportunities in the United States. A disastrous fire on 20 June 1877, causing losses estimated at $27 million, was a further blow. Nevertheless, logging and sawmilling remained important industries, and in the 1890s Saint John was Canada's leading lumber producer. Maritime lumbermen extended their activity to Newfoundland, first assaulting the pine forests of the Humber River valley and later establishing sawmills in the watersheds of rivers along the island's east coast.

All three Maritime provinces suffered as shipbuilding gradually declined into insignificance and the world's carrying trade became dominated by other sea-going nations. With iron (later steel) hulls and steam taking over the marine world, wooden sailing ships were increasingly confined to the coastal trades, fishing, and some long-distance freight routes. Shipbuilders in the Maritimes might well have attempted to build iron or steel vessels and maintain a competitive merchant marine, but the smart money tended toward consumer goods and heavy industries associated with railways. Although locally built cargo schooners remained in use until the 1940s, small-vessel fleets gradually contracted everywhere except in Newfoundland, where expansion continued until 1919.

Table 10.1	Timeline
1875	Caraquet riots.
1876	Intercolonial Railway completed.
1877	Saint John fire.
1879	Protective tariff imposed under National Policy; Provincial Workmen's Association established.
1881	First Acadian National Convention.
1882	Nova Scotia Steel and Coal Company founded at New Glasgow.
1885	Treaty of Washington concessions regarding fisheries expire.
1886	Secession motion in Nova Scotia.
1890	Newfoundland attempts to negotiate reciprocity.
1891	Intercolonial Railway reaches Sydney and Yarmouth.
1892	St John's fire; Dr Wilfred Grenfell arrives in Labrador.
1893	Nova Scotia legislature rejects women's suffrage; Dominion Coal Company established at Glace Bay.
1894	Newfoundland bank crash.
1897	Newfoundland Railway completed.
1900	Dominion Iron and Steel Company begins building steel mill at Sydney; Nova Scotia Steel and Coal Co. at Sydney Mines; Prince Edward Island becomes the first province in Canada to adopt prohibition.
1901	Bank of Nova Scotia moves headquarters to Toronto.

A famous photograph of a small boy with two prize codfish at Battle Harbour, Labrador, c. 1900. The Rooms Provincial Archives, VA 21-18, Big cod fish from the trap, Battle Harbour, Labrador, 1900/R.E.H. [Robert Edwards Holloway], Holloway family fonds.

The swarm of small Newfoundland schooners reflected that colony's continued reliance on the cod and seal fisheries, as well as the absence of reasonable road and rail connections until the turn of the twentieth century. In the 1880s the fisheries represented 67 per cent of goods production, compared to 13 per cent in the Maritimes, and employed 85 per cent of the workforce. The Newfoundland economy was therefore especially vulnerable to falling international prices for salt cod and seal oil. There was little fisheries diversification, apart from the development of an offshore bank fishery in the 1880s. This development was a response to government restrictions on the sale of bait to foreign offshore fleets, particularly the French banking fleet, whose product competed with Newfoundland exports. Lobster canning, an industry started by Maritimers, became increasingly important. However, salt cod remained the staple, tied to increasingly congested markets in southern Europe and the Caribbean.

Nova Scotians, by contrast, had expanded the range of their fisheries by mid-century to include Labrador, the Gulf of St Lawrence, and the offshore banks. Federal bounties helped to stimulate this expansion until 1886, when the concessions granting easy access to US fish markets (under the Treaty of Washington) expired. In response, many Nova Scotian skippers and crew moved to Gloucester and other New England ports. The demand for salt fish also fell in this period. Among the businesses that went bankrupt as a result was Charles Robin and Company, the largest inshore cod firm in the Maritimes. Although salt fish production declined, bank fishing continued to be an important industry, centred in Lunenburg and adjacent ports. Inshore fishers came to rely less on codfish and more on salmon, sardines, oysters, and lobsters. The 1880s and 1890s brought a lobster canning boom throughout the region. Maritimers were well placed to meet the demand for fish, both fresh and frozen, from the United States and central Canada, primarily because of improvements in railway connections and refrigeration technology.

An Industrial Revolution in the Maritimes

Coal, abundant in Cape Breton, northeastern Nova Scotia, and to a lesser extent in southern New Brunswick, was the key component in the efforts of Maritime elites to join the Industrial Revolution. When the Reciprocity Treaty expired in 1866, the United States slapped prohibitive duties on Nova Scotia coal. Maritime coal producers then turned their attention to markets in central Canada. The success of this strategy depended on the completion of a railway to the St Lawrence and the imposition of a protective tariff to keep out cheaper imports. When the Intercolonial Railway linked Halifax and Saint John to Lévis in 1876, Maritime producers finally had their long-desired access to central Canadian markets. Extensions to Sydney and Yarmouth were in place by 1891.

The National Policy budget of 1879, which imposed high tariffs on imported manufactured goods, set off a binge of investment in secondary industries in the Maritimes. There were two zones of development: in the south the ports of Halifax, Saint John, and Yarmouth, where imported staples such as cotton, spices, and sugar were processed for sale elsewhere; and in the north the corridor defined by the Intercolonial Railway, where manufacturing was based on coal, iron, and steel. By 1885 Nova Scotia and New Brunswick supported eight cotton mills, three sugar refineries, two confectionaries, two rope works, and a glass factory.

Alexander 'Boss' Gibson

Born in 1819 near St Andrews, New Brunswick, Alexander Gibson was the son of hard-working pioneer farmers. Young Alexander had a rudimentary education and then began work in the lumber business in which he prospered. By the time he was 30 years old, he was an expert in the management of water-powered sawmills and the new technology of gang saws. A tall, powerful, and highly ambitious man (though shy, according to some sources), Gibson soon became a force to be reckoned with in his native province.

In the 1850s, in partnership with an American lumberman, he worked sawmills on the Lepreau River and in the early 1860s he acquired mills and timber rights from the Scottish firm of Gilmour, Rankin and Company on the Nashwaak River near Fredericton. Eventually controlling about 300,000 acres (120,000 hectares) of forest, Gibson shipped deals (sawn spruce and pine) to Saint John and onward to Britain and the United States. He added other enterprises, such as a tannery and leather factory, and a shipyard.

Like many other entrepreneurs of his time, Gibson became involved in railway promotion. He was a director of the Fredericton Railway Company and later president of the New Brunswick Railway Company, which built a narrow-gauge railway, known as 'the Gibson line', on the east bank of the St John River. The interchange with river traffic was located at the village of Gibson (at the mouth of the Nashwaak), where there was a roundhouse, machine shops, and a freight yard. He was also instrumental in building a railway line from Gibson to Chatham.

Gibson's most ambitious (and quixotic) project was the building of a large cotton mill on the Nashwaak at Marysville, a community he named after his wife and their eldest daughter, who died in 1867. From the outset, Marysville had been a company town, the creation of 'Boss' Gibson, who in the 1860s and 1870s, at his own expense, built school, a store, a fine Methodist church—Gibson paid the minister and the organist, and forbade the sale of alcohol—and 'a palatial residence' for his family on 'Nob Hill'. The cotton mill, which began production in 1885, was a magnificent structure, designed by a Boston firm to house 1,100 looms and 60,000 spindles. Around the mill, Gibson built 53 two-storey brick tenements to house his workers. Now at the height of his career, Gibson employed up to 2,000 people in his various enterprises.

By the 1890s, Gibson's lumber and leather companies were encountering difficulties, and there were problems with his railway interests. Cotton proved to be a highly competitive business, increasingly subject to central Canadian intervention. As Murray Young has written, 'the Gibson enterprise was an old-fashioned family concern dependent on the banks for its working capital, with a patriarchal head who was contemptuous of banking rules and regulations and given to arbitrary decisions'. By the early twentieth century the firm was deeply in debt. In a 1907 settlement, Gibson retained only a pension and the lifetime use of his house. He died in 1913 at the age of 94. His cotton mill continued production, passing through various owners, until the 1970s. Now part of Fredericton, Marysville is a national historic site and a monument to the early age of industrialization in the Maritimes.[1]

The National Policy also imposed a duty on imported coal: initially 50 cents a ton, rising to 60 cents the following year. The Maritimes accounted for most of the coal produced in Canada, and shipments to the Quebec market increased dramatically, but the region's producers were not able to supply much more than 10 per cent of the total demand. High-quality anthracite coal for domestic use came largely from the United States, as did the bituminous coal used by industries west of Montreal.

The development of a flourishing iron and steel industry seemed to confirm Nova Scotia's industrial pre-eminence. In the last decades of the nineteenth century two companies were established in the province that soon emerged as corporate giants. Founded in Pictou County in 1882, Nova Scotia Steel and Coal became, for a time, Canada's leading producer of iron and steel products. Using iron ore from Bell Island, Newfoundland, the company integrated its operations at Sydney Mines in 1900. A second corporate success story began in 1893 with the creation of the Dominion Coal Company, spearheaded by Boston financier Henry M. Whitney. Six years later the company was granted a 99-year lease on all unassigned coal resources in Cape Breton in return for a royalty. Armed with this assurance, Whitney incorporated the Dominion Iron and Steel Company and began construction of a primary steel mill at Sydney in 1900. Small rolling mills

Workers at the Intercolonial Railway shop in Moncton. Completed from Halifax to Lévis in 1876, the Intercolonial helped to make Moncton, the railway's eastern headquarters, a major distribution and manufacturing centre. Moncton Museum Collection.

were established in Halifax and Saint John, as well as in Amherst, where in 1893 J. Rhodes, Curry, and Co. built the first railway cars to be manufactured in Canada.

The Intercolonial Railway and other lines that were built in this period were the key to economic development in many Maritime communities. Strategically located towns such as Moncton, Truro, Windsor, and Yarmouth produced textiles, foundry goods, furniture, and processed foods that found markets near and far. On the surface at least, the Maritimes appeared to be making a successful transition to an industrial economy.

Yet as Table 10.2 shows, the gross value of production in the manufacturing sector increased only by 32 per cent between 1880 and 1900—about the same as forestry—and as a percentage of the total actually declined by 3 per cent. In 1901 manufacturing employed only 28 per cent of the workforce (47 per cent were in primary production and 25 per cent in services). Maritime factories tended to be smaller and less efficient than those in central Canada, which meant lower pay for workers and lower profits for owners. Handicapped by a relatively small local market, managerial inexperience, and a long recession, they fought an uphill battle against central Canadian competitors.

Increasingly reluctant to invest in regional enterprises, Maritime banks looked for safer and more profitable places to do business. A clear sign of this shift was the Bank of Nova Scotia's decision to move its headquarters to Toronto in 1901. Meanwhile, to 'rationalize' production and protect their profits, central Canadian interests moved into the Maritimes. Dominion Cotton Mills and the Canadian Coloured Cotton Company, both of Montreal, took over the region's cotton mills, while Diamond Glass, also of Montreal, bought and eventually closed the three glassworks at Trenton. It was the same story in coal, sugar, and cordage. By 1895 only spices, confectionary—most notably Ganongs in St Stephens and Moirs in Halifax—and manufacturing related to iron, steel, and local staples remained under regional control.[2] Small manufacturers as well as traditional trades were vulnerable to the marketing, through branch businesses, of goods

Table 10.2	Timeline Gross Value of Production ($000), Maritimes					
	Agriculture	**Forestry**	**Mining**	**Fishery**	**Manufacturing**	**Total**
1880	41.9	13.3	3.1	14.9	42.6	115.9
1900	58.7	17.2	14.4	20.3	56.4	167.1
Change (%)	40.1	29.3	364.5	36.2	32.4	44.1

Percentage of Gross Value of Production, Maritimes					
	Agriculture	**Forestry**	**Mining**	**Fishery**	**Manufacturing**
1880	36	12	3	13	37
1900	51	10	9	12	34
Change	15	(–2)	6	(–1)	(–3)

Source: David G. Alexander, 'Economic Growth in the Atlantic Region, 1880–1940', in Alexander, *Atlantic Canada and Confederation. Essays in Canadian Political Economy*, Eric W. Sager, Lewis R. Fischer, Stuart O. Pierson, comps (Toronto: Memorial University and University of Toronto Press, 1983), 58–9.

produced elsewhere. With the completion of nationwide railway systems, mail-order companies such as the one run by Timothy Eaton in Toronto extended their reach to the most remote corners of the country.

Newfoundland's National Policy

Newfoundlanders were also caught up in dreams of new industries and diversification. Realizing that political independence had to be underpinned by a stronger economy, the government led by Sir William Whiteway in the late 1870s and early 1880s adopted a local version of the National Policy, trumpeted as the 'Policy of Progress'. The centrepiece was a railway across the island—the first track was laid in 1882—which, like the Canadian Pacific Railway (CPR), was designed to link the east and west coasts and stimulate the development of land-based industries. Tariff policy was adjusted to protect small manufacturers in St John's. Convinced by Geological Survey reports that the island contained valuable natural resources in abundance, railway enthusiasts predicted rapid growth in agriculture, forest industries, and mining.

Another dimension of this policy was a determined attempt to gain unrestricted access to the resources of the French Treaty Shore. Having long claimed an exclusive right to fish between Cape St John and Cape Ray, France maintained that settlement (and by implication economic development) in that region was illegal because it would interfere with the fishery. As a result, the growing numbers of settlers on the Shore were not represented in the legislature, had no local government, and were denied Crown land grants as well as mining and timber licences. Although the French Shore fishery was declining as the bank fishery based at St-Pierre expanded, France was reluctant to give up its privileges. For its part, the British government was wary of precipitating a diplomatic crisis. Whiteway succeeded in extending the authority of the colonial government to the Shore, but with some important limitations.

DOCUMENT:
The Royal Commission on Labour and Capital, 1889

The Industrial Revolution was built on the backs of workers who initially had little say in the conditions of their employment. In 1886 the Canadian government responded to concerns about the exploitative nature of industrial capitalism by establishing a Royal Commission on Labour and Capital. The commissioners heard nearly 1,800 witnesses, many of them from Nova Scotia and New Brunswick.

The following testimony by Joseph Larkins, a young factory worker in Halifax, was published in the commission's 1889 report. It reveals the tendency of entrepreneurs, pressured by stiff competition, to hire children under 16, paying them less than adults for doing the same work. Reformers demanded that legislation be passed to regulate the employment of children and to provide compensation for workers injured on the job.

Q. How old are you? A. I am 11 years.

Q. What is the matter with your hand? A. It got hurt in the machinery.

Q. How? A. It got caught in the rollers.

Q. What rollers? A. The rollers of a cracker machine—a biscuit machine.

Q. How long were you working in the biscuit factory? A. About seven weeks.

Q. Was it part of your work to look after the machinery? A. No; I was taken in as a packer and was then put to work on the machinery.

Q. How much wages did they give you? A. A dollar a week first, and then a dollar and a quarter.

Q. How much do they give you now? A. Nothing at all.

Q. How long is it since you were hurt? A. Nine weeks Thursday.

Q. And have they not given you anything? A. No; except for the week when I was hurt.

Q. Did you ask for employment? A. My mother asked for a job for me, and they said I could get a job biscuit packing; then they changed me to where the machinery was.

Q. How long were you working at the machinery before you were hurt? A. I could not say.

Q. What were you doing at the machinery? A. I was brushing the dough off according as it came through.

Q. Are other boys your age employed in the concern? A. I could not say. There was a boy about the same size.

Q. Did you lose any fingers? A. I lost one.

Q. Did you lose any of the joints in the others? A. I think I will lose a second finger.

Q. Who paid the doctor? A. I could not say.

Q. Who took you to the doctor? A. A man who was there. The doctor put seven or eight stitches in. . . .[3]

In the short term at least, the Policy of Progress failed to alter the island's economy in any significant way. Nevertheless, employment in primary industries fell by 20 per cent between 1874 and 1901, while employment in secondary and service industries increased. The economic imperialism of central Canada reached the island when, in 1890, the railway project was taken over by Montreal-based contractor Robert G. Reid, who had close links with the CPR and the Bank of Montreal. The latter became banker to the Newfoundland government after the crash of the colony's two private banks in 1894. Like the Maritime provinces, Newfoundland lost control of its financial institutions, and its currency became tied to the Canadian dollar. During the 1890s mainland steel companies took over the huge deposits of iron ore at Bell Island in Conception Bay, shipping it to their blast furnaces at Cape Breton.

Societies in Transition

In the last three decades of the nineteenth century, people throughout the Maritimes and Newfoundland were on the move from country to town and from the Atlantic region to other areas of North America. The lure of urban jobs in factories, service industries, and emerging professions such as medicine, teaching, and engineering drew young people like a magnet and was typical of wider North American trends. Since the Atlantic region lacked a major metropolis to absorb young talent, they became part of what was described by contemporaries as 'the exodus'. New England was the main attraction, but there were few parts of North America where Maritime and Newfoundland migrants could not be found.

Out-migration was both a result and a cause of the region's shaky economic performance. As early as the 1860s, the Maritimes began to suffer net migration loss, which reached a peak in the 1880s but continued at a significant rate until the 1930s. Between 1871 and 1881 the population grew by 13.5 per cent; thereafter growth dropped to 1.2 per cent between 1881 and 1891 and to 1.5 per cent between 1891 and 1901. After 1891 the population of Prince Edward Island began to decline in absolute terms. In all, some 250,000 people left the Maritimes between 1871 and 1901. Women were more likely to leave than men, the young more likely than the middle-aged, anglophones more likely than francophones, and people living in rural areas more likely than urban dwellers. In the view of historian Judith Fingard, the 'exodus of the last quarter of the nineteenth century may have resulted in the decapitation of Maritime society'.[4] The hemorrhage was not quite as severe in Newfoundland, but the trends were similar. In the 1880s the population grew by only 3 per cent, and for the first time more people left the colony than arrived from elsewhere. Most districts on the southeastern Avalon declined in absolute numbers.

The emphasis placed by scholars on out-migration has masked the attention paid by policymakers in this period to immigration. Immigration was a major priority in Ottawa, which assumed responsibility for funding the immigrant bureaucracy, including quarantine facilities in Halifax, Saint John, and Quebec City. New Brunswick was particularly aggressive in seeking immigrants. In anticipation of the completion of the Intercolonial Railway, which opened up new areas for settlement, the province implemented a generous land grants policy in 1872. Over 800 immigrants arrived that year, with numbers reaching a high of 3,714 in 1889, most from Great Britain. The Maritimes also became a receiving area for 'home children'—orphaned or destitute British children who were shipped to 'the colonies' to begin a new life, most of them as domestic servants or farm labourers.

The Mi'kmaq and Wolastoqiyik were subject to the same pressures as their non-Native neighbours, but for them the barriers to modernization were insurmountable. As cheap factory goods increasingly flooded the market, income from sales of crafts began to decline and, for all practical purposes, Native people were barred from industrial ventures by lack of capital, local prejudice, and the rigid provisions of the Indian Act.

Following Confederation, those living on reserves became 'Status Indians' under the jurisdiction of the federal government. The 1876 Indian Act consolidated policies across Canada on the Ontario model, with little concern for regional and cultural differences. Based on the premise that Aboriginal people were incapable of integrating into 'civilized' society, the Act insisted on their close supervision, making it difficult for them to change their sub-standard living conditions. They could neither vote nor drink alcohol, and they risked losing their status if they pursued higher education or took up a profession. Native women who married white men automatically lost their Indian status. Freezing the Mi'kmaq and Wolastoqiyik in patriarchal, pre-industrial social and economic arrangements, the Indian Act made integration into the larger Maritime society all but impossible.

Newfoundland had neither reserves nor any equivalent to the Indian Act. The approximately 200 Mi'kmaq living there—mainly in the Conne River area—made their living by working as guides, mail carriers, and trappers and by fishing, hunting caribou, and selling basketry. For most of the nineteenth century they had the island's interior largely to themselves, but the situation changed in the 1890s with the building of the railway, the subsequent development of forest industries, and the arrival of sport hunters.

In Labrador the Innu relied heavily on trapping furs, which they traded at North West River, Davis Inlet, and elsewhere. By the 1890s, however, white and mixed-blood settlers living in Hamilton Inlet were encroaching on their hunting territory, causing angry confrontations. Meanwhile, the Inuit population of about 1,000 was assumed to be on the way either to extinction or to absorption into white society. With up to 1,200 Newfoundland fishing schooners arriving each summer, diet, clothing, and housing all began to change, and fishing for cod and char became the mainstay of the local Inuit economy. As contact with whites increased, Inuit proved susceptible to diseases brought from elsewhere, such as measles and influenza. In 1893, several Inuit were put on display at the Columbian Exhibition in Chicago, where they were exposed to typhoid fever.

Political Machinations

Inadequate federal subsidies meant that all the Maritime provinces experienced severe financial problems. Prince Edward Island—which, unlike Nova Scotia and New Brunswick, lacked the resources to generate timber and mineral royalties—was particularly hard pressed. By 1900 the province relied on federal subsidies for 64.5 per cent of its provincial budget. The island government therefore had little choice but to retrench, going so far as to abolish the secret ballot (which was more expensive than open voting) and to introduce statutory road labour. At the same time, Islanders were preoccupied with the federal government's failure to provide the 'efficient and continuous communication' with the mainland promised by the Confederation agreement. Only in the mid-1880s, after making a direct appeal to the imperial government, did they get a better ferry (although there was considerable local support for a fixed link in the form of a tunnel).

In New Brunswick the economic recession of the mid-1880s exposed the weakness of the province's industrial base and underscored the steady decline of the once world-renowned shipbuilding industry. Discontent was manifested in a loose alliance of all political interests that coalesced under Andrew G. Blair in 1886 to become a powerful Liberal machine. Although Blair resorted to such popular cost-saving measures as abolishing the Legislative Council, he was at a loss to find a way to bring prosperity to his province. Ottawa, preoccupied with a second uprising in the Northwest and with completing the Canadian Pacific Railway, seemed deaf to demands that attention be paid to the Maritimes, especially in provinces that persisted in electing Liberal governments.

Frustration with Ottawa led Nova Scotia's Liberal Premier W.S. Fielding to introduce a motion in the Nova Scotia legislature in 1886 calling for Maritime union as a preliminary to secession from Canada. The responses from New Brunswick and Prince Edward Island proved lukewarm, and even Nova Scotia voters effectively repudiated Fielding's proposal in the 1887 federal election, when John A. Macdonald's Conservative government won a majority of seats provincially and nationally. As a fallback position, Fielding took up two new causes: provincial rights within Confederation and free trade with the United States. These policies were supported by a number of provinces with Liberal premiers, as well as the federal Liberal Party, now led by Wilfrid Laurier. Blair and Fielding attended the first interprovincial conference in 1887—a harbinger of what would prove to be long-standing tensions between federal and provincial jurisdictions in Canada.

The idea of reciprocity was also popular in Newfoundland, where fish exporters, facing heavy French and Norwegian competition in Europe, were looking for new markets. Asserting its rights within the Empire, the Newfoundland government asked for and received permission to open talks with the American government. When its representative, Robert Bond, and the American Secretary of State, James Blaine, concluded a draft reciprocity treaty, there was surprise in London, consternation in Ottawa, and outrage in Halifax. If Newfoundland was allowed to gain advantages outside Confederation that Nova Scotia could not obtain within it, secession might well become more than a threat. The treaty was swiftly killed by London.

Humiliated and angry, Newfoundland retaliated by imposing extra duties on imports from Canada and refusing to issue bait licences to fishermen from Nova Scotia. Canada countered with similar measures. The crisis eventually blew over and the two sides met in Halifax in 1892 to discuss their differences, but nothing was resolved. The Newfoundlanders were unwilling to talk about Confederation, and the Canadians maintained their objections to a separate Newfoundland reciprocity treaty. Since London and the courts had already ruled that Newfoundland could not discriminate against other British subjects, Canadians were confident that their interests would prevail.

Social Unrest

As in the past, political divisions prompted by economic concerns were complicated by issues of class, ethnicity, and religion. Labour unrest—a product of urbanization, industrialization, and new political ideas—became increasingly common. The centre of organized labour activity was the Nova Scotia coal fields, where increasingly repressive and unsafe corporate practices led to the formation of Canada's first industrial union, the Provincial Workmen's Association (PWA), in 1879. A relatively conservative organization, the PWA sought to advance the position of miners as skilled tradesmen and lobbied the provincial government on safety, workmen's compensation, and other issues with considerable success, but it did not challenge the industry's structure or promote collective bargaining. As a result, coal strikes were restricted to individual fields: Pictou in 1886–7, Springhill in 1890 and 1897, and Joggins in 1896. Nova Scotia's mines nevertheless saw some of the most protracted strikes in Canada in the late nineteenth century. Other sectors experienced strikes as well—for example, the Saint John and Halifax waterfronts—but the labour movement was too decentralized and scattered to have much overall impact.

If strikes reflected growing class divisions, prolonged debates over education revealed religious, ethnic, and linguistic cleavages. The basic question was how far public school systems should (or could) go to accommodate cultural diversity. The Newfoundland solution, finalized in 1873, was to cut the education budget in three and allow a denominational school system with separate Roman Catholic, Church of England, and Methodist schools. Over time, compromises emerged in Nova Scotia and Prince Edward Island whereby Roman Catholic schools were allowed to operate with provincial funding.

Such an accommodation was more difficult to achieve in New Brunswick. In the wake of the Common Schools Act of 1871, the provincial government insisted on a fully non-sectarian system in which all vestiges of religion were prohibited. Outraged, Catholics refused to pay school assessments and appealed to Ottawa for disallowance. The federal government declined to intervene on the grounds that education was a provincial responsibility, and the courts ruled the act to be

Robert Harris, *The Meeting of the School Trustees*, oil on canvas, 1885. Only seven years old when his family migrated from Wales to Prince Edward Island, Harris (1849–1919) became one of Canada's best-known artists. His fine portrait work won him a commission to paint the Fathers of Confederation, which he completed in 1884. Scenes similar to the one depicted here must have been played out in many communities following the introduction of publicly funded schooling. National Art Gallery of Canada, Ottawa, Purchased 1886, #6.

constitutional. Thus fortified, the provincial government went to the polls in 1874 and, emerging victorious, began legal actions against those refusing to pay school assessments.

Resistance was especially fierce among the Acadian population. Since only one Acadian child in six received any schooling and few attended for more than five or six years, there was little incentive to pay taxes to support schools of any kind, let alone schools that excluded Catholic teachings. Tensions culminated in the Caraquet riots of 1875, in which two people died. A compromise then emerged: where numbers warranted, Roman Catholics could be taught by members of religious orders and have religious instruction after school hours. For Acadians, though, the availability of French language instruction remained a serious problem since New Brunswick, like the other provinces, insisted on the use of English in schools.

The schools dispute served as a rallying point for the scattered but increasingly self-conscious Acadian community, which by the 1870s numbered about 90,000, half of them in New Brunswick. Longfellow's poem *Evangeline* (1847), a love story set against the background of the deportation, had begun to circulate in French translation during the 1860s. Adopted for use in the Collège St-Joseph at Memramcook (founded in 1864), the poem seemed to the growing Acadian elite to be 'the poetic distillation of their history, the true legend of their past'.[5] It became, in effect, a unifying narrative at a time when Acadians were trying to establish a collective identity. At the first Acadian national convention, held in 1881 at Memramcook, the majority of delegates decided to adopt the Feast of the Assumption (15 August) as the national holiday rather than that of St-Jean-Baptiste,

The original Acadian flag, 1884, conceived by Father Marcel-François Richard. Photo Léo Blanchard, Musée acadien, Université de Moncton.

thus choosing distinctiveness over closer ties with Quebec. The 1884 convention at Miscouche adopted an Acadian flag—the French tricolour (which at that time was also used in Quebec), with a yellow star signifying devotion both to the Virgin Mary and to the papacy—and 'Ave Maris Stella' became the national hymn. The Société Nationale l'Assomption, founded in 1881 (now the Société Nationale de l'Acadie), provided leadership and continuity by promoting Acadian interests. Several newspapers appeared, among them *L'Évangeline* in 1887, and in the 1890s new colleges were established at Pointe de l'Église in Nova Scotia and Caraquet in New Brunswick.

More reluctant than anglophones to leave the region, Acadians also had a high fertility rate; accordingly, their numbers increased both absolutely and as a percentage of the Maritime population. In New Brunswick, which lost 76,000 people to the United States during the last two decades of the nineteenth century, Acadians made up 24 per cent of the population by 1901, replacing the Irish as the largest Roman Catholic group. Not surprisingly, it was in this province that the issue of cultural uniformity—a sensitive issue throughout Canada—surfaced in the Maritimes. At a time when a revived cult of Loyalism, with its strongly imperial overtones, was spreading among Protestant New Brunswickers, Herman H. Pitts used a difficult schools dispute in Bathurst to launch a determined campaign in favour of 'equal rights'. The same euphemism was used in Ontario to identify a movement designed to end 'concessions' to Roman Catholics and francophones and to promote an evangelical

Acadian National Identity

Between 1881 and 1890 Acadians met in three large congresses in each of the Maritime provinces: Memramcook, New Brunswick; Miscouche, Prince Edward Island; and Church Point, Nova Scotia. The inspiration came from a meeting in Quebec City in 1880, when francophones from all over North America were invited to a convention held on Saint-Jean-Baptiste Day. There was a special committee for Acadians, which was well attended. Joseph-Octave Arsenault, a prominent political leader in Prince Edward Island, encouraged Island Acadians to attend the Saint-Jean-Baptiste convention, in part because they were experiencing massive out-migration prompted by a lack of available agricultural land. As this newspaper summary of his comments at a parish assembly in Egmont Bay indicates, Arsenault was aware of efforts underway in Quebec to open rural areas for group settlement and hoped that a similar approach might help to preserve the distinct Acadian 'national' identity from the homogenizing tendencies of industrial cities.

It is here, under national banners, that we the Acadian people will find the strength and resources to gain respect for our rights which have been ignored for too long, and to preserve the integrity of our national character and the language we love and that our mothers taught us; in short, everything that is of concern to our nation: religion, education, science, industry, and colonization. He made us realize that we could benefit from joining our Canadian brothers to form one national family. Above all, the Honourable Arsenault emphasized the question of colonization. Since this issue is on the programme of the convention, it would be very much in our interest to be represented, if only to discuss a subject that concerns us so much; our properties are already too small and we shall soon be forced to seek settlements elsewhere for our children, and that will certainly be in Canada.[6]

Protestant reform agenda that included non-sectarian schools, prohibition, sabbatarianism, political reform, and, eventually, limited female suffrage. A central (and divisive) figure during the 1890s, Pitts was ultimately rejected by an electorate that opted for accommodation over confrontation.

The Pitts crusade was an unattractive manifestation of the reform movement that swept the region in the late nineteenth century: a mix of (usually Protestant) religion, imperialism, and faith in progress. Rooted in cities and churches—including the Salvation Army, which arrived in the mid-1880s—it addressed many of the problems associated with industrial development. The temperance movement was already well established, and there had been widespread support in the Maritimes for the 1878 Scott Act, which permitted municipalities to bar the sale of alcohol. Newfoundland had similar legislation, and organizations such as the Sons of Temperance and the Women's Christian Temperance Union were active across the region.

Reformers were equally concerned with public health, urban renewal, the rights of women and children, social and economic justice, and moral uplift. Increasingly, they looked to the state to enact aspects of their program, a prospect not always welcomed by political leaders who understood the potentially divisive nature of some issues on the 'social gospel' agenda. In 1900 Prince Edward Island became the first province in Canada to legislate prohibition, but other provinces were slow to follow the island's lead.

Although married women gained rights relating to child custody, marital property, and the municipal franchise in the Maritimes, women's right to vote at the provincial level was denied. In 1893 the Nova Scotia legislature narrowly passed a motion for female suffrage, but it was quashed in committee by Attorney General J.W. Longley, who was appalled by the prospect of Nova Scotia's leading the nation in such a controversial measure. The Women's Christian Temperance Union presented a suffrage petition to the Newfoundland legislature in 1891, but motions in support were defeated in each of the following two sessions. Together, caution and lack of money dictated that such social intervention as did occur should be largely the work of the churches and voluntary organizations such as the YMCA and the YWCA, city missions, and children's aid societies.

A dramatic example of the social reform activism associated with the 'muscular Christianity' of the era was the work of the tireless Dr Wilfred Grenfell. In Newfoundland and Labrador he was a controversial figure who offended church leaders by attacking denominational education, the mercantile establishment by alleging exploitation, and some politicians by arguing that the government was corrupt and incompetent. Nevertheless, his ceaseless energy and activism helped to improve health care and stimulated the emergence of a public health movement that became primarily concerned with a tuberculosis epidemic then sweeping the colony. Similar anti-TB campaigns were also undertaken in the Maritimes, where death rates from the disease were lower but still significant.

Close economic and ethnic ties in the region helped to ensure that many people were swept up in the rising tide of imperial sentiment that characterized the closing decades of the nineteenth century. The New Brunswick-born George Parkin, in his own words 'the wandering evangelist of Empire', became in the 1880s a leader of the Imperial Federation Movement, designed to draw Great Britain and its colonies closer together. Portraits of Queen Victoria could be found in many homes, and her diamond jubilee was celebrated with enthusiasm in 1897. The same year marked the 400th anniversary of Cabot's voyage. With Maritimers claiming Cape Breton as the first land sighted and Newfoundlanders Cape Bonavista, commemorative ceremonies were held at both Halifax and St John's. In both cities traditions were invented and embellished, speakers in each

Wilfred T. Grenfell

Grenfell's name is still associated with northern Newfoundland and Labrador, the area to which he devoted his working life after his first visit in 1892, at the age of 27. An English evangelical Christian who had recently qualified as a doctor, Grenfell was employed by the Royal National Mission to Deep Sea Fishermen to investigate the condition of fishers engaged in the Labrador fishery.

Each spring hundreds of schooners sailed from the island of Newfoundland to the Labrador coast. Some fished as 'floaters', following the fish, salting their catch on board, and carrying it back to their home ports for drying. Others carried crews of 'stationers' who fished from fixed locations and dried their catches there. Grenfell found widespread poverty and a serious need for medical facilities, both for the fishermen and for the residents ('livyeres').

Over the following years he raised money to build hospitals and nursing stations that eventually extended from Newfoundland's Northern Peninsula to Lake Melville in Labrador, with a headquarters at St Anthony. More than this, Grenfell attempted to reshape the economy and society of the region, arguing that poverty, ignorance, and malnutrition were the causes of most disease. He encouraged the formation of co-operatives; promoted improvements in both hygiene and diet; started a sawmill and an industrial crafts program; tried to improve educational facilities; and, in the hope of providing a new source of food, clothing, and jobs, introduced reindeer (the experiment failed).

In many ways the Grenfell Mission was a colony within a colony. Its staff came from the United States, Britain, and Canada, as did the money that supported it. Grenfell himself had to spend much of the year on fundraising tours; though known as 'Grenfell of Labrador', he never spent a winter there. He was the dynamo, but the actual work of the mission was done by remarkably dedicated staff members and, in summer, unpaid volunteers.

Grenfell died in 1940. Although there can be no doubt that he and his mission did a great deal of good, the region's structural economic and social features proved intractable, at least during his lifetime.[7]

case celebrating Cabot as the founder not only of their respective countries but also of the British Empire, of which they were proud members.

Family in the Industrial Age

Notwithstanding the challenges, the closing decades of the nineteenth century were heady times for many people in the Atlantic region. Advances in communications, new ideas about the universe, new ways of making a living and enjoying leisure time, higher levels of literacy, and the growth of cities were only a few of the modernizing trends that affected everyday life. By making decisions about where to work, what to believe, how long to stay in school, if and whom to marry, and whether to protest injustices, people of all ranks and cultures participated in creating a new social order in the region. Not surprisingly, this new social order was similar in many ways to the one taking root elsewhere in the North Atlantic world. Long accustomed to being 'transatlantic

The McQueen Family Adjusts to the Modern Age

The family of Daniel and Catherine McQueen of Pictou County, Nova Scotia, illustrates the challenges and opportunities available to rural young people in the Industrial Age. Of Scottish heritage, the members of this mobile family valued education and were highly literate. In the more than 1,200 letters that the family wrote and preserved, historians are able to trace in remarkable detail their strategies for upward mobility and family well-being in the second half of the nineteenth century.

On 31 March 1849, Daniel McQueen (1819–94) married Catherine Olding (1823–1916), the daughter of one of Pictou County's leading families. A carpenter by trade, Daniel was determined to have Catherine live in the style to which she was accustomed. In 1852 he bought a farm for £260 near the mouth of the Sutherland River, where he built a fine new house for his already expanding family. Daniel also invested in industrial enterprises in coal-rich Pictou County, where mining communities mushroomed within a few kilometres of the McQueen's farm. When Daniel's investments ended in bankruptcy in 1878, the family thereafter depended primarily on the produce of their farm and the wages of their maturing children for survival.

Between 1850 and 1865, Catherine gave birth to eight children, all but one of whom survived to adulthood. The McQueen children were keenly aware of the opportunities opening up around them and, like many other young people in this period, saw education and geographic mobility as keys to their success. The only surviving son, George William, attended Dalhousie University and briefly taught school in Nova Scotia before moving to New York City in 1879. Although he found employment in a number of companies there, he failed to prosper and died alone in a rooming house in 1899 at the age of 41. Five of the six daughters became school teachers, working in various communities in Nova Scotia. The two youngest daughters also taught school in British Columbia, arriving shortly after the completion of the Canadian Pacific Railway in 1885. Lured west by higher salaries, they could make as much in one month in British Columbia as they could in one term of teaching in Nova Scotia. Four of the daughters eventually married, all to business and professional men. Jane, who as a child fell from a wagon and thereafter suffered from mental illness, never married. Nor did Jessie, who was obliged to abandon her teaching career in British Columbia to care for her sister and aging mother, a fate common to many unmarried daughters in this period.

In her book, *Sojourning Sisters*, Jean Barman explores in detail the lives of Jessie and her youngest sister, Annie. Their careers, she argues, testify to the role that these and other women like them played in 'Canadianizing' the west. In the case of Jessie and Annie, they brought to British Columbia their commitment to Presbyterian values, civic engagement, and formal education as well as an unshakable belief in the superiority of Anglo-Canadian values.[8]

subjects',[9] people in the Atlantic region brought back new ideas from their distant travels and helped to modernize other areas where they chose to live and work.

The family remained the fundamental economic and social unit in the late nineteenth century, but its general contours changed dramatically. As employment opportunities expanded, young people married later—on average age 25 or 26 for women and a couple of years later for men—and about 5 per cent never married at all. The later age of marriage and the increased use of birth control reduced the number of children in any given family. So concerned was the Canadian government about the tendency of women to bear fewer children that in 1892 it made the promotion of birth control and abortifacients an offence under the Criminal Code. The desire for social control also led same-sex relationships to be deemed unnatural and proscribed by law. For homosexuals this situation meant hiding sexual desires and often leading unhappy, unfulfilled lives.

Legal sanctions on birth control and same-sex relationships had little impact on the general trends. In colonial society married women of normal fertility could expect to have a child every two or three years, and completed families (families in which both parents lived for the mother's child-bearing years) were large, averaging seven or eight children. By the end of the nineteenth century, this figure was cut nearly in half. These averages mask considerable variation across class and culture. Acadians married earlier and had larger families, a practice encouraged by the Roman Catholic Church. Scots, especially those of Presbyterian persuasion, married later and had smaller families. Concerned with the possibility of complicated estate claims, middle-class couples were more likely than working-class couples, who relied on children for security in their old age, to limit the size of their family.

The gender roles in the family were also changing, and, again, the trends were most evident among the middle class. In rural pre-industrial societies, families were economic units, producing most of what they consumed. With the increase in availability of manufactured products, the introduction of public schooling, and the tendency toward smaller families, much of what was considered women's work moved outside the home. Middle-class men, however, expected their wives to stay at home to show that, as husbands, they were good providers. The careful delineation of separate spheres meant that men dominated the public sphere and its expanding opportunities, while women were relegated to the private spheres of motherhood, domesticity, and good works. To enforce this injunction, women were denied access to higher education, the professions, the boardrooms, and political office. No sanctions, of course, were placed on women working in factories or as domestics in homes that could afford to employ household help.

Exclusionary policies in this period were an extension of the subordinate position that women in settler societies had experienced since colonial times. Under the provisions of British common law, which prevailed in the Atlantic region, husband and wife were treated as one person, with the sole right over property and children vested in the male head of household. Divorces were exceedingly rare and difficult to obtain, especially for women who were at the mercy of a cruel, despotic, or deserting husband. Even in relatively harmonious families, it was difficult for a married woman to own property in her own right, and her husband could control any income she earned. In the latter half of the nineteenth century, values relating to women's rights and industrial development began to converge, but governments dragged their feet in granting political equality for women, and most women were unable to take advantage of new legislation that advanced married women's rights over property and children.

The Atlantic region was not unique in its treatment of women in marriage or in adopting the separate spheres ideology. Nor were women in the region slow to take up opportunities where they could be found. Women flocked to the new professions open to them, especially teaching, nursing, and clerical work. A study conducted in 1905 estimated that 75 per cent of the nurses working in Massachusetts came from Canada, most of them from the Maritimes. The same study noted that with incomes equal or better than those of the men they know, 'they refuse to exchange single competence for the double poverty that must result in marriage.' For this reason, they remained single, a situation that worried many traditionalists.[10]

A few women in the Atlantic region were at the forefront of efforts to break down barriers to their advancement in the public sphere. When Grace Annie Lockhart graduated from Mount Allison University in 1875, she became the first woman in the British Empire to receive a university degree, and Maritime Baptist women were the first in Canada to establish female missionary societies. While Acadia and Dalhousie quickly followed Mount Allison in opening their doors to women, Catholic colleges rejected co-education. Instead, the Roman Catholic Church encouraged separate educational facilities for women. The Congregation of Notre Dame, which established an academy for young women in Antigonish in 1883, began giving collegiate courses for women in affiliation with St Francis Xavier University (StFX) in 1894. Three years later four young women received Bachelor of Arts degrees from StFX, the first degrees granted to women by a Catholic university in North America.

Conclusion

As the long Depression lifted in the late 1890s, the region was in some ways much changed from what it had been 30 years earlier. Farms, forests, and the sea still underpinned life in the region, but a quarter of Maritimers now lived in towns; new industries had been established; mining and the service sector had expanded significantly; and the economy (in the Maritimes at least) no longer relied so extensively on the old staple trades. Political divisions and local rivalries remained deeply entrenched, but by the turn of the century transportation links were in place across the region: the Newfoundland railway was completed in 1897, and regular ferry service across the Cabot Strait began the next year. At the same time many people throughout the region shared common enthusiasms, whether for the Empire, for temperance, or for social reform. Despite bitter disputes over education, levels of literacy had improved, and a more sophisticated society was emerging. There were signs that not all was well—the control exercised by central Canadian banks and corporations was especially troubling—but as the twentieth century dawned there was some reason for optimism.

Further Readings

Alexander, David. 1983. *Atlantic Canada and Confederation: Essays in Canadian Political Economy*, comp. Eric W. Sager, Lewis R. Fischer, and Stuart O. Pierson. Toronto: University of Toronto Press.

Barman, Jean. 2003. *Sojourning Sisters: The Lives and Letters of Jessie and Annie McQueen*. Toronto: University of Toronto Press.

Beattie, Betsy. 2000. *Obligations and Opportunity: Single Maritime Women in Boston, 1870–1930*. Montreal: McGill-Queen's University Press.

Couturier, Jacques Paul, and Phyllis E. LeBlanc, dirs. 1996. *Économie et société en Acadie, 1850–1950*. Moncton: Éditions d'Acadie.

Fingard, Judith. 1989. *The Dark Side of Life in Victorian Halifax*. Porters Lake, NS: Pottersfield Press.

Forbes, E.R. 1989. *Challenging the Regional Stereotype: Essays on the 20th Century Maritimes*. Fredericton: Acadiensis Press.

Frank, David, and Gregory S. Kealey, eds. 1995. *Labour and Working-Class History in Atlantic*

Canada: A Reader. St John's: Institute of Social and Economic Research.

Guildford, Janet, and Suzanne Morton, eds. 1994. *Separate Spheres. Women's Worlds in the 19th Century Maritimes*. Fredericton: Acadiensis Press.

Inwood, Kris, ed. 1993. *Farm, Factory and Fortune: New Studies in the Economic History of the Maritime Provinces*. Fredericton: Acadiensis Press.

Porter, Marilyn. 1993. *Place and Persistence in the Lives of Newfoundland Women*. Aldershot: Avebury.

Sager, Eric W., and Gerald E. Panting. 1990. *Maritime Capital: The Shipping Industry in Atlantic Canada, 1820–1914*. Montreal: McGill-Queen's University Press.

Food for Thought

Acheson, T.W. 1972. 'The National Policy and the Industrialization of the Maritimes, 1880–1910', *Acadiensis* 1, 2 (Spring): 3–28.

Alexander, David. 1978. 'Economic Growth in the Atlantic Region, 1880 to 1940', *Acadiensis* VIII, 1 (Autumn): 47–76.

Recommended Websites

Cape Breton Miners Museum
http://www.minersmuseum.com/

Industrial Revolution
http://ca.encarta.msn.com

Labour History in New Brunswick
http://www.lhtnb.ca

The McQueen Family Letters, 1866–1934, Atlantic Canada Virtual Archives
http://atlanticportal.hil.unb.ca

Newfoundland and Labrador Heritage: Industrialization and Diversification
http://www.heritage.nf.ca/society/industry.html

Saint John: An Industrial City in Transition
http://website.nbm-mnb.ca/Transition/English/index.asp

Chapter 11

The Promise and Peril of a New Century, 1901–19

For almost two decades after 1900, most Maritimers and Newfoundlanders thought that they lived in an age of social and economic achievement and promise. It was only as the First World War drew to a close that the mood shifted. Expectations of growth and security vanished in the face of the Spanish influenza epidemic, a wave of strikes, and the onset of economic and financial difficulties. The twentieth century, as it turned out, brought disillusionment and uncertainty.

The Busy East

Optimism was not unfounded at the turn of the century. The populations of Nova Scotia and New Brunswick were growing, if modestly—only Prince Edward Island experienced a net loss—and between 1900 and 1920 the gross value of production expanded in every sector except the fisheries. Agriculture was stimulated by strong demand for potatoes and apples in central Canada and the rapidly growing West, as well as expanding urban markets in the Atlantic region itself; Britain was still importing apples and sawn lumber in large volumes; and demand for fashionable silver fox pelts sparked a boom for breeders on Prince Edward Island. Meanwhile, the annual output of coal increased from approximately 2.9 million short tons in the 1890s to 6.5 million in 1916–20. In this instance, the regional market was all-important, much of the coal being consumed by the expanding iron and steel industry.

The history of the fisheries in this period arguably represents a missed opportunity. By the turn of the century, the trend was clearly towards the production of fresh and frozen fish, and steam trawlers were making their appearance. New Englanders moved most of their vessels from the Grand Banks to grounds closer to shore and rapidly developed a large trawler fleet. By 1908 the French had between 10 and 15 trawlers on the banks (which put into Sydney for ice and coal) in addition to their fleet of over 200 sailing vessels. If fishermen in the Atlantic region hoped to compete for the common resource located on their very doorstep, they would have to modernize their practices.

Maritimers, especially Nova Scotians, proved cautious. While they were prepared to adopt the gasoline engine and the motor boat, invest in bait freezers (at Canso and Halifax, for example), and respond to the demand for fresh fish, there was strong opposition to trawlers from inshore fishermen and schooner owners who feared—with reason—damage to fish stocks and the dominance of large corporations. Accordingly, in 1915, trawlers were forbidden to fish within 12 nautical miles (22 kilometres) of the coast. As a result, the Canadian trawler fleet grew slowly in comparison to its competitors, and the Atlantic fishery stagnated. Salt fish production declined from an annual average of 693,000 hundred weight (35,206,025 kilograms) early in the century

Table 11.1	Timeline
1902	Sealers strike in St John's.
1904	The *entente cordiale* settles the Newfoundland French Shore dispute.
1906	Federal subsidies to provinces revised.
1907	Canada passes Lord's Day Act.
1908	William Coaker founds the Fishermen's Protective Union in Newfoundland; *Anne of Green Gables* published; automobiles prohibited on Prince Edward Island.
1909–11	Strikes in Nova Scotia's coal industry, including a 22-month strike by coal miners in Springhill.
1909	Formation through mergers of Dominion Steel Company; Glace Bay miners form local of United Mineworkers of America; the region's first pulp and paper mill opens at Grand Falls, Newfoundland; J.A.D. McCurdy becomes first person in the British Empire to fly an airplane.
1910	Prohibition legislated in Nova Scotia.
1911	International Court at The Hague rules on American fishing rights.
1912	Saint John adopts commission government.
1914	Outbreak of the Great War; Newfoundland sealing disasters.
1916	Newfoundland Regiment decimated at Beaumont Hamel on 1 July.
1917	Conscription imposed in Canada; explosion in Halifax Harbour.
1918	Prohibition across Canada; women's suffrage legislated in Canada and Nova Scotia; Great War ends on 11 November.
1918–19	Spanish influenza epidemic.
1919	Women's suffrage legislated in New Brunswick.

to 448,000 hundred weight (22,759,450 kilograms) by 1914, in spite of rising prices. The value of Nova Scotia's fresh fish exports increased by almost 50 per cent between 1901 and 1911, but the total could have been even higher.

In Newfoundland, as on the mainland, the fishery remained much as it had been. Merchants in St John's invested in steel-hulled steamers for sealing, passenger, and freight services and showed considerable interest in product diversification. They also experimented with steam trawling, but were at a comparative disadvantage given their small domestic market and Newfoundland's distance from potential markets in Canada, the United States, and Europe. Inherently conservative, the Newfoundland Board of Trade opposed government intervention in the fishing industry and, given the relative economic prosperity of this period, there was little incentive to undertake radical change. Had the Canadian and Newfoundland governments been willing and able to emulate the American and French governments by actively encouraging the fishery, the story might have been very different.

The steel and coal industries, by contrast, seemed to be fulfilling the promise of the National Policy. Nova Scotia now produced 44 per cent of Canadian pig iron and over 80 per cent of the coal mined in Canada. Many communities along the Intercolonial route were booming. Between 1901 and 1911 the population of Cape Breton County increased by 49 per cent, and 60 per cent of the region's industrial workforce was to be found between Moncton and Glace Bay. Little wonder that a new regional business magazine, founded in 1910, was called the *Busy East of Canada*.

In Newfoundland a short-lived sawmilling boom followed the completion of the trans-island railway, in which Maritime, American, and Scottish investors were prominent. But it soon became obvious that the colony's stands of good timber were limited and that its forests were best suited for the manufacture of wood pulp. That opportunity attracted the English newspaper tycoons Harold and Alfred Harmsworth, who reached an extraordinarily generous (and controversial) deal with the Newfoundland government in 1905. Their Anglo-Newfoundland Development Company was granted what amounted to a perpetual lease of timber lands in the Exploits River valley, with mineral and water power rights thrown in. Four years later the region's first pulp and paper mill opened at Grand Falls. As the supporters of the Policy of Progress had hoped, the colony had a new staple industry and the first settlement of any size in the island's interior. A century later, the mill has closed, and the Harmsworth deal remains a sensitive political issue.

There was also interest in the natural resources of Labrador. In the 1890s, a series of remarkable pioneering surveys conducted by A.P. Low for the Geological Survey of Canada confirmed the existence of huge iron ore deposits in the interior and the potential of the Grand (now the Churchill) Falls for hydroelectricity. These resources were too remote for development at that time. Instead, attention focused on exploiting the Labrador forests. A grant of timber concessions on the Hamilton (Churchill) River to a Nova Scotia company in 1902 raised once again the long-standing question of who owned the Labrador interior.

In 1898 the Canadian government, without consulting Newfoundland, legislated a new northern boundary for the province of Quebec. The line was drawn westwards from the Eastmain River on James Bay to Hamilton Inlet until it met the coastal strip, which in Canada's opinion was all that Newfoundland rightfully controlled. The governments of Quebec and Canada thereupon began protesting the timber licences, but the Newfoundland government refused to cancel them. By 1907 all parties had agreed to submit the question of where the boundary lay to the Judicial Committee of the Privy Council, the central question being what constituted 'the coast of Labrador'. The decision, eventually in Newfoundland's favour, was slow in coming.

In the Maritimes, there were signs that the gains made in the heavy industry sector in the early decades of the National Policy were eroding. Difficulties were intensified by the disappearance of the region's financial sector, severe competition from branch businesses, and further takeovers and mergers promoted by central Canadian interests. For example, in Amherst, one of Canada's busiest manufacturing towns, the firm of Rhodes, Curry was amalgamated with two Montreal businesses in 1909—in a deal masterminded by New Brunswick's Max Aitken—and eventually closed down. In 1901 Henry M. Whitney sold his share of the Cape Breton-based Dominion Coal and Dominion Iron and Steel to Montreal interests, and in 1909 the company was amalgamated with the Cumberland Coal and Rail Company at Springhill to form the Dominion Steel Corporation. With close links to the Bank of Commerce and the Bank of Montreal, Dominion Steel controlled most of the Nova Scotia coalfields. The company also had an eye on the Nova Scotia Steel and Coal Company but it eluded them, at least for the moment.

Holding at least 179 directorships among them, the directors of Dominion Steel were the high priests of the Gilded Age in Canada. They lived in opulence in Montreal and Toronto and built elegant summer homes in communities such as St Andrews. Sir William Van Horne's estate on Minister's Island, New Brunswick, included a model farm and a swimming pool filled by the ocean tides twice a day. As David Frank points out, these men integrated the Nova Scotia coal and steel industries into the national economy, but in so doing they contributed to the crises that those

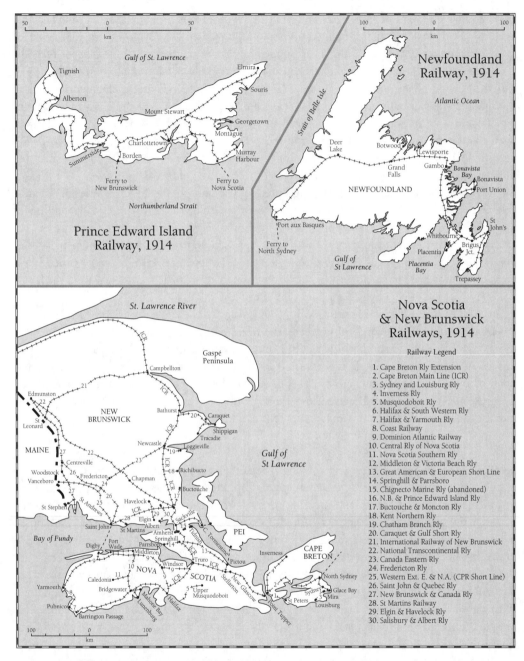

Railways in the Atlantic Region, 1914. Adapted from Shirley E. Woods, *Cinders and Saltwater: The Story of Atlantic Canada's Railways* (Halifax: Nimbus, 1992).

industries faced at the end of the First World War.[1] Political and economic fragmentation and the competition between towns and governments to attract investment meant that the region had no defence against either economic imperialism or dependency.

Labour Unrest and Social Reform

Industrial expansion was accompanied by labour unrest. Between 1901 and 1914 there were 411 strikes in the Maritimes—evidence of a workforce that was becoming increasingly class-conscious, unionized, influenced by syndicalism, and aware of the way competition between industrial giants was being waged on the back of labour. Workers faced employers who had no particular attachment or loyalty to the region and who were prepared to fight employees with any weapons at their disposal, safe in the knowledge that they could count on the support of all levels of government.

A particularly bitter dispute occurred in 1909, when Glace Bay miners, disillusioned with the Provincial Workman's Association (PWA), formed a local of the United Mineworkers of America (UMW) led by Scottish-born James B. McLachlan. Dominion Steel refused to recognize the union, brought in strike breakers (Newfoundlanders among them) protected by troops obligingly provided by the federal government, and gradually wore the strikers down. The same happened at Springhill, where miners held out for 22 months in 1909–11.

Newfoundland also experienced labour militancy. Between 1901 and 1914 there were 120 strikes in St John's, mostly by unskilled workers. Bell Island miners, longshoremen, fish curers, and fishing crews struck as well, and in 1902 3,000 sealers refused to board the steamers in St John's harbour until the owners agreed to improvements in pay and conditions. Remarkably, 42 per cent of those strikes were successful and 21 per cent ended in compromise.

William Ford Coaker

Born in St John's, Newfoundland, in 1871, William Coaker had a checkered career as an outport trader, telegraph operator, farmer, and minor office holder until, in 1908, he formed the Fishermen's Protective Union (FPU) at Herring Neck in Notre Dame Bay.

Its motto was *suum cuisque* ('to each his own') a demand that fishermen and other outport 'toilers' should receive fair treatment. Did a fisherman receive 'his own', asked Coaker, when

> . . . he boards a coastal or bay steamer, as a steerage passenger and has to sleep like a dog, eat like a pig, and be treated like a serf? . . . does he receive his own at the seal fishery where he has to live like a brute, work like a dog and be paid like a nigger? Do they receive their own when they pay taxes to keep up five splendid colleges in St John's . . . while thousands of fishermen's children are growing up illiterate? Do they receive their own when forced to supply funds to maintain a hospital at St. John's while fishermen, their wives and daughters are dying daily in the outports for want of hospitals?[2]

This was a powerful message. He may have been derided in St John's as 'the Moses of the North', but to his members (about 20,000 by 1914) the phrase had another meaning:

> We are coming Mr. Coaker, men from Green Bay's rocky shore,
> Men who stand the snow white billows down on stormy Labrador;

> We are ready and a-waiting, strong and solid, firm and bold,
> To be led by you like Moses led the Israelites of old.[3]

Strenuous opposition from the Roman Catholic Church meant that the FPU became an almost exclusively Protestant organization, largely confined to the island's northeast coast. Nevertheless, Coaker was determined to take the FPU into politics, its aims spelled out in the 'Bonavista Platform' of 1912 and publicized in the union's newspaper, *The Fishermen's Advocate*. The platform was bold, radical, and comprehensive, calling for sweeping changes in the fishing industry, administrative and constitutional reform, free and compulsory education, old age pensions, a minimum wage, and other legislation that would benefit outport residents. In the 1913 election, Coaker and seven other FPU candidates won seats in the assembly. At the same time, Coaker was president of the Fishermen's Union Trading Company, founded in 1911, which in 1918 relocated to the union's new town in Bonavista Bay, called Port Union.

In 1917 the Union party joined the wartime National Government, and Coaker became a minister without portfolio. He was immediately faced with the difficult and divisive issue of conscription, which was strenuously opposed by the union membership. He eventually decided to support conscription, as he did prohibition, moves which significantly damaged his standing and reputation among fishermen. The pre-war crusade was clearly over.

Coaker might have re-established his position had he been able to implement the fisheries reforms he had advocated for so long. But as minister of marine and fisheries between 1919 and 1923 his efforts failed, largely as a result of the post-war economic crisis and opposition from the fish trade (of which he, of course, was a part). He stayed out of politics between 1924 and 1928, became increasingly preoccupied with the union's various commercial enterprises, and resigned as president of the FPU. He played only a minor role in the second administration of Sir Richard Squires between 1928 and 1932, by which time he had become so disillusioned that he endorsed the idea of government by an appointed commission. Coaker spent an increasing amount of time at a property he owned in Jamaica—a far cry from Herring Neck—and died in 1938.

With trade unions established in St John's and Grand Falls, William Coaker decided to organize rural 'toilers', as he called them: fishermen, loggers, and sealers. The Fishermen's Protective Union (FPU) was launched in 1908. A populist who took his cue from Canadian farmers' movements, Coaker wanted economic, social, and political reforms that would ensure fair treatment for his members. The response was immediate and impressive except in predominantly Roman Catholic districts, which followed a conservative church hierarchy opposed to unions and class-based politics. The union also became a political party, winning eight seats in the 1913 election. Serving as the official opposition in all but name, the FPU promoted an ambitious reform program with goals that ranged from government control of fish grading and marketing to non-denominational night schools.

Labour organizers joined professionals, church leaders, and women's rights activists in an impressive coalition to demand a growing list of reforms. These 'progressive' thinkers believed that society could be improved by legislation and regulation in many areas of life, including the sale of alcohol, Sabbath observance, sexual practices, urban development, working conditions, public health, and the treatment of women, children, and animals. When provincial governments were slow to respond, social reformers established powerful voluntary organizations to lobby governments and find alternative ways of implementing their ideas.

The progressive forces scored some victories. The federal Lord's Day Act, passed in 1907, controlled what people could do on Sundays. In 1910, Nova Scotia (Halifax excepted) followed Prince Edward Island's lead a decade earlier by adopting prohibition. After much prodding, Nova Scotia Premier George Murray introduced legislation to improve working conditions, provide compensation to workers injured on the job, and establish the Nova Scotia Technical College, which opened in 1909. In the hope of promoting efficiency and honesty in public life, Saint John in 1912 became the first city in Canada to replace the old system of ward elections, which could be dominated by small cliques, with a commission-style council elected by all voters on a city-wide basis. A government-appointed commission was instituted in St John's in 1914. Although this reform in municipal government was designed to usher in an era in which appointed experts would determine best practices, commission governments, too, were often open to influence.

Politics in the Industrial Age

Reformers wanted a better society, but politicians were preoccupied by the challenge of finding money to pay for expanding government responsibilities. In 1906 Ottawa revised its subsidy policy, but the increases for the Maritimes were much lower than those granted to Quebec, Ontario, and British Columbia. Such discrimination reflected the region's diminished power and influence. In the redistributions of 1892 and 1903 the Maritimes lost eight seats in the House of Commons, and the reductions might have continued over the years had it not been for a 1915 agreement that no province could have fewer MPs than Senators. The meanness of this concession spoke volumes about the disadvantages faced by small provinces compared with giants like Ontario, Quebec, and Manitoba, each of which more than doubled its size in 1912 by absorbing huge, resource-rich sections of the Northwest Territories. In 1908 New Brunswick's Conservative Premier J.D. Hazen called for a 'United Acadia' to counter the region's declining power in Ottawa, but there was little response.

Even if Maritime politicians had managed to present a common front to Ottawa, it is unlikely that much could have been achieved. With the opening of the Prairies and continuing discontent in Quebec, the Cabinet's attention was invariably focused elsewhere. If anyone could have made a difference, it was Robert Borden, an earnest Halifax lawyer who became leader of the Conservative Party in 1907 and prime minister in 1911. Borden was sensitive to the problems facing the Maritimes and occasionally used his power to achieve results. He responded, for example, to Prince Edward Island's demand for better winter ferry service and supported African Canadians from the region in their efforts to participate more fully in the First World War, but with national and international issues always at the forefront, he had little time to address the systemic problems facing the region.

As the Maritime provinces were becoming marginalized in Ottawa, Newfoundland remained a very junior player in London. Although recognized as one of the dominions, it carried less weight than the others, and the imperial government had no compunction about overriding its decisions. A happy exception was the 1904 agreement, part of the Anglo–French entente cordiale that ended the French Shore dispute and was a genuine compromise between Britain, France, and the colony.

Admittedly, Britain had smoothed the way to compromise in 1902 by granting Newfoundland permission, over Prime Minister Wilfrid Laurier's objections, to attempt once again to negotiate reciprocity with the United States.

A draft treaty was arranged in 1902, but this time it was effectively killed in the US Senate. In response, the government of Sir Robert Bond in 1905 launched a campaign of harassment against American vessels engaged in the winter herring fishery in the Bay of Islands. London swiftly intervened, unilaterally imposing a modus vivendi pending arbitration on the interpretation of the 1818 fisheries convention (which applied to Canadian as well as to Newfoundland waters) and forbidding by imperial order-in-council the seizure or arrest of any American vessel. Colonial protests against this heavy-handed treatment were disregarded. The eventual arbitration at The Hague in 1911 largely upheld Britain's—that is, Canada's and Newfoundland's—arguments relating to American rights under the 1818 convention and made important recommendations concerning the delineation of the three-mile marine limit and the definition of bays.

These arcane diplomatic manoeuvrings had nothing to do with everyday concerns about economic development and social reform. Most Newfoundlanders found Bond's crusade irrelevant and they defeated his government in 1909 (after a tied election in 1908 and a subsequent political hiatus).

Cultural Currents

In this period, technological innovations continued to make headlines and transform ways of doing things. Typewriters and telephones were coming into practical use in business establishments, while motor cars and even airplanes promised to revolutionize transportation. For ordinary people the bicycle was the favoured new form of transportation, at least in the summer time. Better communications linked the region's creative writers to the larger English-speaking world where the demand for novels and poetry seemed insatiable.

Cape Breton made communication history in the early years of the twentieth century. In 1902 Guglielmo Marconi's Wireless Telegraph Company began operating the first transatlantic link from Glace Bay, Nova Scotia. The previous year, Marconi had used kites flying from Signal Hill in St John's to pick up the first wireless signal sent across the Atlantic. Cape Breton was also involved in transportation innovations. In February 1909 J.A.D. McCurdy and F.W. Baldwin, under the auspices of Alexander Graham Bell's Aerial Experiment Association, made the first controlled manned flight in the British Empire. With McCurdy at the controls, the *Silver Dart* soared over the ice of Lake Bras d'Or near Bell's home in Baddeck. By that time the invention of the telephone had made Bell a household name.

Improved communications helped to fuel the growth of sporting activities in the region. With reliable railway service, teams could compete on a regional basis in leagues designed to manage and promote competitive sports. By 1900 professional baseball teams, many of them on tour from the United States, drew large numbers of spectators. The Maritime Provinces Amateur Athletic Association (MPAAA) initially turned a blind eye as amateur teams, eager to best their opponents, stiffened their ranks with professional players. In 1907 the MPAAA took a more principled approach and put an end to the experiment with semi-professional baseball in the region. This prompted many teams to turn professional, beginning with the Socials and the Standards in Halifax in 1911. All efforts to put an end to the gambling and 'fixed' matches proved fruitless.

As in the late nineteenth century, many Maritimers continued to make their sporting reputations south of the border. Nat Butler, a Halifax native who began his bicycle racing career in Boston, broke all records at the Winter Velodrome in Paris in 1905. The region's best baseball players were quickly snapped up by American teams, and keeping up with the careers of men who once played in the region provided plenty of copy for local newspapers, which now included whole sections devoted to individual and team sports.

In 1908 Prince Edward Island's Lucy Maud Montgomery launched a spectacular international career with the publication of *Anne of Green Gables*. In these and subsequent works, she tapped into the growing demand for fiction that sentimentalized rural life and the values that readers believed it represented. In Newfoundland, Norman Duncan's stories sympathetically explored the lives of outport fishing families. Three literary periodicals began publication in St John's in the early years of the century, which was also a golden age for ballads and poetry—including the 'Ode to Newfoundland' (1902), which became the national anthem.

Journalists and boosters were also hard at work, often at the behest of the railroads and the emerging tourism industry. They scripted Evangeline's *Acadia*, conjuring an image of Nova Scotia

Lucy Maud Montgomery

Lucy Maud Montgomery (1874–1942) became one of North America's most popular authors following the publication of *Anne of Green Gables* in 1908. PEIPARO Acc. 3110/1.

Lucy Maud Montgomery is one of Atlantic Canada's best-known authors. Born in 1874 in Prince Edward Island, she lost her mother at an early age and was raised by her grandparents in Cavendish. She was educated at Prince of Wales College and spent a year at Dalhousie University. Although she began making money from the publication of poems and short stories in the expanding magazine market in the 1890s, her fame derived from the 1908 publication of *Anne of Green Gables*. The red-haired orphan girl sent to work on an Island farm quickly won the hearts of readers all over the world.

In 1911, following the death of her grandmother, for whom she was the primary care-giver, Montgomery married the Reverend Ewan Macdonald. The couple moved to Ontario, where Ewan ministered in a number of Presbyterian churches. Between raising two sons, coping with her husband's debilitating depressions, and attending to the endless round of public duties demanded of a minister's wife, Montgomery continued to write. She produced 22 novels, including seven sequels to *Anne*, as well as 450 poems and 500 short stories. One of her most enduring legacies is 'The Island Hymn', the unofficial anthem of Prince Edward Island. In addition, from 1889 to 1942 she kept a diary chronicling the more serious and darker aspects of her life. Selected diary entries have been published in five volumes that Montgomery fans have read no less avidly than her novels.[4]

Skating behind the college at Caraquet, New Brunswick. Hockey became an increasingly popular sport in the Maritimes in the second half of the nineteenth century. PANB, Père Joseph Courtois fonds, P38-109.

as 'a gently rolling and fertile land filled with Old World Charm'.[5] So widespread was Evangeline's appeal in this period that she became the subject of Canada's first feature film in 1913. In Prince Edward Island, the prohibition of automobiles in 1908 helped to preserve the pastoral image so important to the development of tourism, while fishing and hunting were heavily promoted elsewhere in the region. Overall, the literature helped change the image of rural people from that of backward bumpkins to that of picturesque, stalwart 'folk', living enviably simple lives. With an apparently straight face, the Reid Newfoundland Company assured potential tourists that 'no people in the world maintains a more comfortable and contented existence than the Newfoundland fisherman'.[6]

The reality was somewhat different. The loss of life in the Newfoundland seal fishery in the spring of 1914 was the highest in the history of that dangerous industry. Loaded with pelts taken in the Gulf, the SS *Southern Cross* sank with its crew of 174 men in a storm somewhere off Trepassey Bay. Meanwhile, out on the floes off the northeast coast, the crew of the SS *Newfoundland* was left on the ice for 53 hours during a blizzard. Seventy-eight men died of exposure or drowning, their bodies brought back to St John's 'stacked like cordwood'. In retrospect, these twin tragedies appear as local harbingers of the world crisis that was to erupt the following August.

The Great War

A European crisis in the summer of 1914 developed into a war between Germany and Austria-Hungary on one side and the so-called 'entente powers' of Great Britain, France, and Russia on the other. Britain declared war against Germany on 4 August, after the latter invaded Belgium. Canada and Newfoundland, as members of the British Empire, were automatically involved. Not that people in the Atlantic region objected. They remained imperial enthusiasts and at first responded willingly. Militia regiments were called out in the Maritimes and headquarters staff in Halifax began a recruitment campaign, first to bring the regiments up to strength, and then to provide additional overseas drafts. Involving clergy, teachers, and the press, the war effort soon became all-consuming.

Newfoundland had no militia and hence no militia department. The Newfoundland Regiment was raised—indeed, improvised—by the Patriotic Association of Newfoundland (NPA), founded in August 1914 by Governor Sir Walter Davidson in consultation with the prime minister, Sir Edward Morris. Composed mostly of prominent St John's men from a variety of political and religious backgrounds, the NPA functioned as the unofficial war ministry for three years, with a wide range of responsibilities. Its creation reflected a desire to place the war effort above political and denominational rivalries.

Voluntary enlistment rates in the Maritimes were higher than in Quebec and Saskatchewan, but lower than in other provinces. In Newfoundland the proportion of the population that volunteered was similar to that in the Maritimes, although an appallingly high number of medical rejections reduced the numbers of those who actually served. The native-born and those living in rural areas in both Canada and Newfoundland were least likely to volunteer, and the rate was reduced further in the Maritimes by the importance of war-related industries such as coal mining, steel production, and agriculture. Including those compelled to enlist under conscription, implemented in Canada in 1917 and Newfoundland in 1918, some 72,500 men from the Atlantic region joined the allied army. Others served at sea, in the air, or in the forestry corps. About 300 women from the Maritimes and 43 from Newfoundland went overseas as nurses. Among those travelling with the First Canadian Division in October 1914 was Pictou County's Margaret MacDonald, the matron in charge of 101 volunteer nurses who were the first women to become full-fledged members of the Canadian Expeditionary Force.

By 1916 the difficulty in filling the escalating demand for soldiers gave ethnic minorities, who were initially not welcome as recruits, a chance to enlist for overseas service. The Mi'kmaq were for the most part integrated into existing units, but most blacks were hived off into the No. 2 Construction Battalion under the command of white officers. Attached to the Canadian Forestry Corps, the battalion produced lumber for the trenches and coal mines. The efficiency of white soldiers, it was argued, would be reduced if they were forced to fight on the battlefields alongside black recruits.

Of those who went overseas, about 14 per cent of Canadians and 25 per cent of Newfoundlanders were killed. In town centres throughout the region, war memorials testify to the appalling death toll. A great blow was inflicted on the newly formed Newfoundland Regiment at Beaumont Hamel on 1 July 1916, the first day of the Battle of the Somme. The anniversary is still observed each year, and the battlefield is preserved as a memorial park.

Women throughout the region, schooled for generations to embrace volunteer work, 'did their bit' to support the war effort. In Newfoundland a Women's Patriotic Association (WPA) was formed at the outset of the war under the presidency of Lady Davidson. With branches throughout Newfoundland and Labrador, it attracted 15,000 members within a few months. By 1916 women and children of both sexes had produced, among other 'comforts', 62,685 pairs of socks (an astonishing number which achieved legendary status abroad). The WPA became involved with

The Newfoundland Regiment, D Company, on the march near St John's, 1915. PANL E-22-45.

the Red Cross and health care, as well as general welfare issues, and raised money for a range of causes. Women in the Maritimes were also heavily engaged in war-related activities, often working through the Red Cross and the St John Ambulance. In Halifax, a busy port throughout the war, women's volunteer services were stretched to the limit.

The demands on everyone in the Halifax area were dramatically increased on 6 December 1917 when the French munitions ship *Mont Blanc*, loaded with TNT, collided with the Belgian relief ship *Imo* in the city's harbour. The resulting explosion, the largest man-made blast before Hiroshima, levelled the city's North End, killing nearly 2,000 people, injuring 9,000, and leaving 22,000 without adequate shelter. Homes, factories, train stations, churches, and a great sweep of harbour facilities disappeared in the subsequent fires and tidal wave that engulfed the city. Already stretched to the limit by wartime demands, the citizens of Halifax were overwhelmed by the disaster.

As word of the tragedy spread, help poured in from across Canada and around the world. Massachusetts and Newfoundland were among the most generous 'foreign' contributors to the devastated city, testimony to the close family ties connecting these Atlantic coast communities. A Massachusetts–Halifax Relief Commission was established to collect donations in Massachusetts, and, in conjunction with the American Red Cross, it dispatched a train equipped with medical supplies to the crippled city. Sir John Eaton, president of the T. Eaton Company, well known in the region for its merchandise catalogues, arrived in Halifax with his own train, food, sleeping car, and medical unit. In Eaton's supply depot, his staff handed out building materials and other necessities free of charge to anyone with a requisition from a pastor or relief committee official. Nearly a month after the blast, the federal government established the Halifax Relief Commission to take charge of relief, medical care, and reconstruction. Some $30 million, over half of it from Ottawa, was provided to help Halifax and its sister city, Dartmouth, which had also suffered from the blast, to recover from the devastation.

The explosion exposed deeply rooted tensions in the city. Class divisions were heightened when the Halifax Relief Commission used its extraordinary powers to determine wages and working conditions for the projects it sponsored, blithely ignoring agreements with the organized building trades in the city. The Mi'kmaq living along the Dartmouth side of the harbour at Turtle Cove, which took the full brunt of the blast, were offered free land if they agreed to relocate, but the promise was conveniently forgotten. An opportunity to establish better public health facilities in the city was also squandered. In treating the victims of the blast, it became clear that the people in Halifax suffered from high rates of infant mortality and tuberculosis. When the Massachusetts–Halifax Relief Commission sent public health expert Victor G. Heisner to report on health services, local officials felt threatened and let their narrow vision of the issue blunt efforts to build the infrastructure that the city so badly needed.

The horror of the explosion brought the war closer to home and contributed significantly to a growing mood of disillusionment. The mounting death rate overseas, rampant inflation, food restrictions, and a series of tawdry scandals further dampened the enthusiasm that had characterized the war effort in the early days. When Prime Minister Robert Borden's Conservatives formed a Union government with the badly split Liberals in 1917 and imposed compulsory military service on men between the ages of 20 and 35, class and cultural divisions deepened. Even the granting of

After the Halifax Explosion, December 1917. This photograph of women travelling downtown from Africville reveals the extent of the devastation along the waterfront. City of Toronto Archives, Fonds 1244, Item 2451.

What about the Children?

Following the Halifax Explosion, people searched desperately for missing relatives. The most vulnerable were young children who became orphaned in the tragedy or simply got lost in the chaos. For weeks advertisements relating to foundlings filled Halifax newspapers. Three examples from 13 December speak poignantly to the plight of the very young.

The owner of the girl baby about 2 months old which was handed to a young lady on Gottingen Street, being previously picked up on Almon Street by a soldier, in a pasteboard box covered with an older child's check coat, can get same by applying at 1461 Shirley Street.

Missing. Donald Cameron. Answers to Donnie, 4 1/2 years, fair hair, dark grey eyes. Wore red sweater or night gown. Was moved on first ambulance from Roome Street on Thursday morning. Father anxious.

Would the soldier who rescued baby from unconscious woman's arms on Longard Road the morning of the explosion return baby to its parents, 9 Longard Road.

Recognizing the special difficulties facing children, authorities established a children's committee, chaired by Ernest Blois, the provincial superintendent of neglected and delinquent children. The committee handled 1,500 cases by the end of December. Of those under the committee's care, 200 needed hospital treatment, 8 were blind, and 48 suffered from other eye injuries. The committee worked tirelessly to process the children, find temporary shelter, match them with missing family members, and get 'possession of children unlawfully taken possession of by improper persons'.

Offers of help came from people all over North America willing to take the 70 orphaned children and the many more whose mothers and fathers, for various reasons, were unable to assume their parental duties. Prince Edward Island, home of the famous fictional orphan Anne Shirley, was particularly generous. On 14 December authorities in Charlottetown sent a telegram announcing: 'HAVE SIXTY PRIVATE HOMES FOR CHILDREN MOSTLY PROTESTANT/SOME FOR PERMANENT ADOPTION/REST WILLING TO HOME INDEFINITE TIME.' They also offered to send a committee to take charge of transporting their young charges to their new Island homes.[7]

---

suffrage to female relatives of men serving overseas prior to the December 1917 election—a move crudely calculated to win votes—initially spoiled what turned out to be a major step in women's political emancipation. Conscription was widely opposed in the Maritimes, and the majority of electors in both Prince Edward Island and Nova Scotia voted against the Union government. So, too, did most Acadians in all three Maritime provinces.

As the evidence of profiteering mounted and the gap between rich and poor grew, labour unrest increased and the incidence of strikes escalated. The Maritimes experienced more than 30 strikes in 1918 alone, and the Newfoundland Industrial Workers Association's 3,500 members successfully struck against the Reid Newfoundland Company in the spring of that year. Calls for the conscription of wealth as well as manpower grew louder. Farmers became disenchanted when the government refused to honour its promise to exempt their sons from the draft, and fishing crews could not afford the loss of young men. Although Acadians were not as uniformly

Beaumont Hamel

The Allied war plan for 1916 called for a major offensive by French and British troops in the region of the Somme. British troops—which included Canadians and Newfoundlanders—were in the majority, and preparations were complete by late June.

The offensive began at 7:30 a.m. on 1 July. In the Beaumont Hamel area, the plan called for a 5,000-metre advance led by the 86th and 87th Brigades, while the 88th (1st Essex and Newfoundland regiments) attacked other German positions. The plan proved to be irrelevant. Withering enemy fire caused the advance to falter, but the commanding general, mistaking German flares for a signal from the 87th Brigade that it had succeeded, ordered the 88th to advance.

The Newfoundlanders went into battle at 9:15 a.m. It was all over in 30 minutes. Unprotected by artillery, they advanced into heavy fire concentrated on the gaps in the British wire from which they emerged. 'The only visible sign that the men knew they were under this terrific fire,' wrote one observer, 'was that they all instinctively tucked their chins into an advanced shoulder as they had so often done when fighting their way home against a blizzard in some little outport in far off Newfoundland'.[8] Most were cut down before they reached the British front line.

The Regiment at the front on 30 June had consisted of 25 officers and 776 non-commissioned officers and other ranks. After the battle, 233 were listed as killed, 477 as wounded or missing. For a small country this was a devastating loss.

Beginning in 1917, 1 July was observed as Memorial Day, Newfoundland's own national day of remembrance. Although the Regiment fought other battles, Beaumont Hamel became iconic. As an expression of the sterling qualities and imperial loyalty of Newfoundlanders, the failed offensive was transmuted into an occasion for solemn patriotic pride. Memorial Day is still observed today, although now it coincides (perhaps uneasily) with the upbeat Canada Day celebrations.

opposed to the war as their counterparts in Quebec, they resented not only the anti-francophone tone of the conscription debate but also the heavy-handed tactics used against 'deserters'. In New Brunswick, one Acadian resister was seriously wounded and 26 others were taken to Saint John under military escort for resisting compulsory service.

The same factors led to a full-blown crisis in Newfoundland, where Morris manoeuvred the three political parties into a National Government and then promptly departed for London and a peerage, leaving his successors to bring in conscription. As unpopular in Newfoundland as in the Maritimes, conscription created tensions between urban and outport districts. A militia department replaced the Patriotic Association in 1917 and, as in Canada, income and profits taxes made their first appearance—as did prohibition, which was already more or less in place everywhere else in the region except Halifax. Ottawa imposed nationwide prohibition in 1918.

Social unrest and cultural tensions during the war emerged against a background of general economic prosperity. Although the fur-farming bubble burst, and the overseas markets for apples temporarily collapsed, the steel industry expanded as many factories converted to munitions manufacturing; fisheries and agriculture generally did well; and lumbermen supplied pit props to British coal mines. The gains were undermined to some extent by inflation, rising freight rates, and a shortage of shipping, but the region's economic performance during the war still provided grounds for optimism, which government propaganda did its best to encourage. These were, as Ian McKay notes, the 'last years of abundant hope'.[9]

Post-war Challenges

The end of the war was greeted with relief, if not jubilation. In any event, people were preoccupied with the Spanish influenza pandemic that was raging throughout the Atlantic region along with the rest of Canada, affecting approximately one in six people. The impact was particularly devastating in northern Labrador, where the infection was carried by the Moravian mission ship *Harmony*. As many as a third of the Inuit in the area of the mission died between November 1918 and January 1919. The worst affected settlement was Okak: of a population of 263, only 56 women and children survived. An observer described the appalling scene:

> When the *Harmony* left Okak, people were beginning to fall sick. . . . Crews went off to their sealing places only to fall sick and die. . . . the dogs played havoc with the corpses. At Sillutalik 36 persons died, but only 18 remained to be buried. The only visible remains of the others were a few bare skulls and a few shankbones lying around in the houses.[10]

The epidemic had a lasting impact on northern Labrador. Okak was abandoned, and the Moravians, recoiling from the tragedy and facing persistent economic difficulties, gradually reduced their activities and handed over their trading stores to the Hudson's Bay Company in 1926.

Veterans returned home to perfunctory welcoming ceremonies and inadequate government help with the challenges of reintegration into a society that had been subjected to severe strain. Their discontent merged with a militant class-consciousness sparked by wartime injustices and fanned by the success of the 1917 Bolshevik Revolution in Russia. There were riots in Sydney and Halifax, in which veterans played prominent roles, and in 1919–20 a wave of labour unrest swept the Maritimes resulting in 93 strikes, including general strikes at Amherst and on the Miramichi. The recession that arrived in 1920 blunted the effectiveness and much of the militancy of the labour movement. With companies experiencing severe difficulties amid the cutthroat competition of the post-war period, workers faced a drab future.

There was no strike wave in Newfoundland, where problems in the Italian market brought the wartime fishery boom to a sudden end in the fall of 1918. Overextended fish merchants, pressed by their bankers, faced heavy losses and the possibility of a general market collapse. The crisis was so acute, and the political situation so unstable in 1919, that attention was diverted from Newfoundland's humiliation at the Paris peace conference.

During the war the Dominion (as it officially called itself from 1918) had been represented in the Imperial War Cabinet and at the Imperial War Conference, but at Paris its fragile status was clearly exposed. Manoeuvring between the United States' objections to separate dominion representation and the justifiable expectations of the dominions themselves, the British government decided to sacrifice the claims of the least influential dominion in order to obtain representation for the others. Newfoundland found itself sidelined, excluded not only from the list of signatories of the Versailles

Treaty but also from the list of original members of the League of Nations. There could not have been a clearer demonstration of Newfoundland's subordinate place in the imperial hierarchy.

While Newfoundland politics after 1918 became personal and factionalized, Maritime voters increasingly threw their support to new political parties. The comfortable give-and-take of political power between Liberals and Conservatives came to an end in the wake of the war with the emergence of Farmer and Labour parties in New Brunswick and Nova Scotia and the Progressive Party at the federal level. Meanwhile, no one was certain what impact female suffrage would have on electoral politics. Women were granted the federal vote on the same basis as men in May 1918. Nova Scotia had already passed similar legislation the previous month and Prince Edward Island followed suit in 1922. New Brunswick granted women the right to vote in 1919 but withheld the right to hold elected office until 1934. Newfoundland finally adopted the British model in 1925, extending the franchise to women over the age of 25.[11]

Conclusion

The First World War destroyed the confidence and optimism that had prevailed in the early twentieth century. Pride in wartime achievements abroad was tempered by post-war frustrations and disappointments at home. Only time would tell if the political turmoil of 1919 was part of the new world order to which the Great War had played midwife or just a brief, if troubling, interlude in the region's long history. Two things were certain: the stakes in the industrial age were high and the competition was keen. Unless the Atlantic region could sustain economic growth and staunch the tide of out-migration, the prospects for the future would be bleak.

Further Readings

Bishop-Stirling, Terry, and Jeff A. Webb. 2008. 'The Twentieth Century', in Newfoundland Historical Society, *A Short History of Newfoundland and Labrador*. St John's: Boulder Publications.

Bogaard, Paul A., ed. 1990. *Profiles of Science and Society in the Maritimes prior to 1914*. Fredericton: Acadiensis Press.

Duley, Margot L. 1993. *Where Once Our Mothers Stood We Stand: Women's Suffrage in Newfoundland, 1890–1925*. Charlottetown: gynergy books.

Hiller, James, and Peter Neary, eds. 1994. *Twentieth Century Newfoundland: Explorations*. St John's: Breakwater Press.

Howell, Colin D. 1995. *Northern Sandlots: A Social History of Maritime Baseball*. Toronto: University of Toronto Press.

———, and Alan Ruffman, eds. 1994. *Ground Zero: A Reassessment of the 1917 Explosion in Halifax Harbour*. Halifax: Nimbus and Gorsebrook Research Institute.

Kitz, Janet F. 1989. *Shattered City: The Halifax Explosion and the Road to Recovery*. Halifax: Nimbus.

MacDonald, Edward. 2000. *If You're Stronghearted: Prince Edward Island in the Twentieth Century*. Charlottetown: Prince Edward Island Museum and Heritage Foundation.

McDonald, Ian D.H. 1987. *'To Each His Own.' William Coaker and the Fishermen's Protective Union in Newfoundland Politics, 1908–1925*. St John's: ISER.

Mann, Susan. 2005. *Margaret Macdonald: Imperial Daughter*. Montreal: McGill-Queen's University Press.

Noel, S.J.R. 1971. *Politics In Newfoundland*. Toronto: University of Toronto Press.

Roberston, Ian Ross. 2008. *Sir Andrew Macphail: The Life and Legacy of a Man of Letters*. Montreal: McGill-Queen's University Press.

Rubio, Mary Henley. 2009. *Lucy Maud Montgomery: The Gift of Wings*. Toronto: Doubleday Canada.

Theobald, Andrew. 2008. *The Bitter Harvests of War: New Brunswick and the Conscription Crisis of 1917*. New Brunswick Military Heritage Series, Vol. 11. Fredericton: Goose Lane.

Food for Thought

Forbes, E.R. 1989. 'Battles in Another War: Edith Archibald and the Halifax Feminist Movement', in E.R. Forbes, ed., *Challenging the Regional Stereotype: Essays on the 20th Century Maritimes*. Fredericton: Acadiensis Press.

Recommended Websites

Balls, Bats, and Boats: Sporting and Recreation in New Brunswick
http://website.nbm-mnb.ca/BBB/starte.asp

The First World War
http://www.vac-acc.gc.ca/remembers/sub.cfm?source=history/firstwar

Halifax Explosion
http://museum.gov.ns.ca/mma/AtoZ/HalExpl.html

Jack Turner's War [PEI soldier]
http://epe.lac-bac.gc.ca/100/205/301/ic/cdc/turner/default.htm

L.M. Montgomery Research Centre
http://www.lmmrc.ca

Newfoundland and the Great War
http://www.heritage.nf.ca/greatwar/articles/default.html

Chapter 12

Between the Wars, 1919–39

Between the end of the First World War and the beginning of the Second, the Atlantic region faced adverse economic conditions. Poverty, unemployment, and labour unrest were endemic throughout the period and out-migration continued at alarming levels until the onset of the Great Depression. Facing severe financial problems, all governments in the region were forced to turn to Ottawa or London for assistance. The fundamental reasons for the economic crisis were beyond the region's control. The boom and bust cycles of the global economy created a roller-coaster ride that culminated in the stock market crash of October 1929. Although the worst was over by 1933, except possibly in Newfoundland, recovery would be difficult and prolonged.

Economic Uncertainty

Some sectors of the economy coped with the roller-coaster ride better than others. Between 1920 and 1939, the gross value of production in the Maritimes actually increased by 17.3 per cent and more than doubled in Newfoundland, but the overall figures disguise uneven experiences. Agriculture in the Maritimes and the fishery in Newfoundland declined after 1929, while manufacturing took a hit from which it never recovered. In many other areas of North America, economic development was focused on the production of mass consumer goods such as cars, radios, and home appliances, but with industry increasingly concentrated and owned in central Canada, the Atlantic region failed to make the transition.

The fisheries that sustained many families, in whole or in part, continued to languish. In the Maritimes the production of salt fish, whether dried or green, collapsed. The extent of the decline was reflected in the size of the Lunenburg fleet of saltbankers, which dropped from about 140 to 20 vessels between 1919 and 1939. Given the uncertainty of international markets for salt fish in this period, it is little wonder that Maritime fishermen sought other ways of making a living. European markets for salt fish were slow to recover after the war, demand for Canadian fish in the Caribbean and South America weakened, and the competition from Norway and Iceland became aggressive. Newfoundland also emerged as a serious competitor, increasing its low-priced exports to the West Indies and Brazil when European markets became unstable.

To make matters worse, the United States raised its tariffs and revoked the permission it had given Canadians to land fish in American ports. As a result, 1921 was the worst year for the Atlantic fishery in four decades. There was some recovery thereafter, largely in the fresh fish sector, which was stimulated by the expanding demand of fish processing firms. By the mid-1920s Nova Scotia boasted 11 trawlers, and Halifax was beginning to emerge as the centre of a modern

Table 12.1	Timeline
1919–23	Intercolonial Railway integrated into Canadian National Railways.
1921	Scotia and Dominion Steel merge to form British Empire Steel Corp. (BESCO); launch of the *Bluenose*; W.F. Coaker's attempt to regulate the Newfoundland fishery fails.
1922	Cape Breton miners' strike; women in Prince Edward Island gain the right to vote.
1923	Cape Breton steelworkers' strike.
1925	Cape Breton miners' strike; Royal Commission on the Coal Mining Industry in Nova Scotia chaired by Sir Andrew Rae Duncan; newsprint mill opens at Corner Brook; women's suffrage legislated in Newfoundland.
1925–9	Prohibition ends in Newfoundland, Nova Scotia, and New Brunswick.
1926	Duncan Royal Commission on Maritime Claims; Moravians lease their trading stores in Labrador to Hudson's Bay Company.
1927	Maclean Royal Commission on the Fisheries of the Maritime Provinces; Labrador boundary defined by the Privy Council.
1929	Great Depression begins.
1933	Report of the Newfoundland (Amulree) Royal Commission.
1934	Responsible government suspended in Newfoundland.
1939	Second World War begins.

industrial fishery. Resistance to modernization of the fishery remained strong, however, and was reinforced when a 1927 royal commission on the fisheries (the Maclean Commission) recommended restrictions on steam trawling. By 1939 the trawler fleet was reduced to three. Together, uncertain markets and resistance to change stunted the overall development of the Maritime fisheries. Instead of pursuing technological innovation, the industry continued to rely on cheap labour, to the detriment of both the well-being of the workers and the value of the catch, which sank to approximately what it had been in 1880.

The Newfoundland government met the fisheries crisis with a dose of state intervention as prescribed by William Coaker, founder of the Fishermen's Protective Union and, after 1919, minister of fisheries. His aims were to regulate the marketing of salt fish and to end destructive competition between rival exporters. He failed for a variety of reasons. European markets were difficult and congested, prices were low, and exporters were under pressure from their bankers. Moreover, Coaker was regarded with suspicion by the 'long-coated chaps' of St John's because of his union affiliations and a perceived conflict of interest as president of the Union Trading Company, itself a major exporter. Merchants could not afford to hold fish until prices and markets improved—which is what Coaker's scheme essentially required—and the government lacked the financial resources to provide the trade with a cushion. As a result the 'Coaker regulations' had a short life. It was only in 1933, in the depths of the Depression, that a merchant-supported government finally created a Salt Codfish Board to control exports. Coaker now turned his attention to finding alternative employment for poverty-stricken fishing families and enthusiastically supported plans originally developed by the Reid Newfoundland Company to establish a second newsprint mill at Corner Brook, which began production in 1925—just as the post-war boom in paper prices ended.

Built by British interests, the Corner Brook mill was sold to International Power and Paper (IPP) in 1927, an American firm that was expanding in the Maritimes. IPP developed hydro power at Grand Falls in New Brunswick and built mills at Dalhousie and Bathurst. Other firms constructed pulp mills at Edmundston and Atholville in New Brunswick and at Liverpool, Nova Scotia. The pulp and paper mills partially made up for the decline in sawmilling, which faced a twofold challenge: the costs of lumber production were increasing as the more accessible stands of trees disappeared, and there was stiff competition from Pacific coast producers, who could now ship efficiently through the recently completed Panama Canal to the east coast and Britain.

Agriculture also faced challenges during this time. The apple industry recovered its coveted British market following the Great War and expanded production. In 1933 growers sold 82 per cent of their bumper crop of more than 8 million bushels (nearly half of the entire Canadian output) overseas. The competitive position of Maritime apples depended on price, not quality, with the result that growers concentrated on medium-quality cooking apples for their profits. By the 1930s apples from the United States, British Columbia, and New Zealand were making serious inroads, and consumers everywhere were turning to the larger dessert varieties. Maritime producers would have to plant new orchards, develop new packing techniques, and improve their marketing skills or be left behind.

The potato industry, which relied on markets in the United States and the Caribbean (mainly Cuba), expanded during the 1920s. Prince Edward Island seed potatoes found a ready market, and potato acreage expanded at the expense of other types of farming. Although some Maritime farmers focused on dairy, chicken, and beef production for local consumption, most did not specialize, and their operations gradually became unsustainable. As a percentage of total gross value of production in the Maritimes, agriculture fell from 34.3 per cent in 1920 to 27.8 per cent in 1939. Farm families needed other sources of income, and many farmers had to take seasonal jobs to make ends meet. During the 1930s, family farms became a refuge for those who lost their jobs in the urban centres, but the general trend was clear. Young people who could do so abandoned the rural life for jobs in cities, often outside the region. In the 1920s the Maritimes' population increased by less than 1 per cent, and both Nova Scotia and Prince Edward Island experienced absolute declines.

There was also trouble in the industrial belt that had grown along the Intercolonial route. Between 1919 and 1923, the regional railway was integrated into Canadian National Railways, a Crown corporation with scant sympathy for Atlantic problems and aspirations. Freight rates, now determined outside the region, quickly increased by 140 to 216 per cent, making it virtually impossible for Maritime producers to compete in the central Canadian market. With the end of railway expansion, the market for rails and railway equipment contracted sharply. The region's iron and steel industry had difficulty adapting because it was hampered by lack of capital and the difficulty of competing with central Canadian producers.

The result was a sudden downsizing. Between 1919 and 1921, the labour force employed in iron and steel declined by 85 per cent and in manufacturing generally by 40 per cent. This contraction in turn hurt the region's coal industry, since iron and steel had absorbed 25 per cent of its output. Nor was this the only problem that coal producers faced. The Quebec market had been lost during the war and would take time to regain. High freight rates and cheaper American imports effectively blocked sales west of Quebec, where hydro power and oil were gaining ground. For Maritime producers to compete, they would have to reduce their prices—but the costs of production in Cape Breton, where the shafts extended under the seabed, were higher than elsewhere because of the long distance to and from the coal face, and because of the need for expensive ventilation and drainage systems.

Overall, the manufacturing sector was badly crippled in the early 1920s as plants closed or were consolidated into central Canadian companies. The net value of production declined from $325 million in 1920 to a low point of $192.5 million in 1924, and employment fell significantly below the levels of the 1890s. As S.A. Saunders pointed out as early as 1939, the Maritimes failed to make the transition from heavy industry geared to railway and nation-building to light industry producing consumer goods.[1] The consequences would be felt for the remainder of the twentieth century.

A significant contribution to the regional economy in the interwar years was the illicit liquor trade that emerged as a by-product of prohibition, which remained in place in most Canadian provinces following the war and became federal law in the United States in 1920. With the fisheries languishing, many Maritimers were only too happy to make a living as rum-runners. Typically, liquor from Europe, the Caribbean, and Canada was delivered to Saint-Pierre and Miquelon. There Maritime vessels would pick it up and then legally carry it to 'rum row', just outside the American 12-mile limit, where they would wait for a fast motor launch sent by one of the American crime syndicates that made fortunes smuggling it into the country.

The tidy income made by bootleggers was not lost on provincial administrations looking to finance mother's allowances, old age pensions, and essential public works. One by one, governments in the Atlantic region abandoned prohibition and took control of liquor sales (and profits) themselves: Newfoundland in 1925, New Brunswick in 1927, and Nova Scotia in 1929. The US trade continued unabated until the American Congress finally gave up the fight and repealed prohibition in 1933. Only Prince Edward Island held out until after the Second World War, though the island supported plenty of bootleggers.

Maritimers Take a Stand

Maritimers were not passive in the face of these blows to their economic aspirations. In Nova Scotia, members of the newly formed Labour Party entered a loose alliance with alienated farmers to win 11 seats in the 1920 provincial election, making the Farmer–Labour coalition the official opposition to the reigning Liberals, who had held office since 1882. Later the same year the United Farmers did equally well in New Brunswick, where they already had 141 locals and ran a wide range of co-operatives. In Prince Edward Island fishermen became formally organized and, like the farmers, began to form co-operatives to compete with corporate interests.

Union membership had grown dramatically during the war. Although the post-war recession blunted labour militancy, Cape Breton remained a battlefield. In 1921 Nova Scotia Steel and Coal merged with Dominion Iron and Steel to form the British Empire Steel Corporation (BESCO), with headquarters in Montreal. The following year BESCO announced a 37.5 per cent wage cut for miners. Already hit by plant closures and reductions in hours, the UMW local in Cape Breton called for 'the complete overthrow of the capitalist system' and went on strike. Alarmed by this local eruption of Bolshevism, authorities called in soldiers and special police to crush labour activism. A year later the troops returned to put down a steelworkers' strike. An unprovoked mounted charge through the Whitney Pier district of Sydney led coal miners to walk out in sympathy, and union leaders 'Red' Dan Livingstone and J.B. McLachlan were arrested. On 11 June 1925, a protracted

Lawren S. Harris, 'Glace Bay'. A member of the Group of Seven, Harris visited Cape Breton in 1921. This stark image of a miner's family appeared on the cover of the July 1925 issue of the *Canadian Forum*, which included an article on the strike-bound island. LAC, C-110249.

and bitter strike by coal miners ended in the death of William Davis, a 37-year-old miner who was shot by the police. At a subsequent district convention, the day of his death was declared Davis Day—a date that is still commemorated in Cape Breton.

By the mid-1920s all workers in the coal and steel industries had suffered severe wage cuts, and BESCO was on the edge of bankruptcy. It was cold comfort for the miners that a 1925 provincial royal commission on the coal industry found the size of the original wage cut unjustified. Chaired by British lawyer-industrialist Sir Andrew Rae Duncan, the commission criticized the company for bad faith and intransigence, but since neither the commission nor the provincial government was prepared to consider genuinely radical solutions, the tensions continued.

The rise of western Canada and the dominance of Ontario and Quebec underlined the minority status and increasing political marginalization of the Maritime provinces. Federal leaders were inevitably more sympathetic to the demands of the more powerful regions, tending to view the Maritimes as backward and their leaders as chronic grumblers with no good reason for complaint. Unable and sometimes unwilling to counter hostile and unsympathetic federal policies and attitudes, Maritime Members of Parliament exerted little influence on national policy. In the 1921 federal election, voters in Nova Scotia and Prince Edward Island registered their hostility to the Conservatives under Borden's successor, Arthur Meighen, by awarding all their seats to the Liberals. Only New Brunswick showed some resistance to the trend, returning five Liberals, five Conservatives, and one Progressive to Ottawa. Although the Conservatives were defeated, it soon became clear that the Maritime vote counted for little. At the head of a minority Liberal government, the new prime minister, William Lyon Mackenzie King, was held hostage by the spectacular success of 65 Progressive Party candidates, most of them from constituencies in the badly alienated Prairie provinces and rural Ontario.

After more than a half-century of Confederation, Maritimers were no more reconciled to federal structures than they had been in 1867, and the list of grievances continued to grow. Federal subsidies to all three provinces were parsimonious in the light of the generous financial terms granted to Alberta and Saskatchewan when they achieved provincial status in 1905. And where was the compensation to other provinces for the huge chunks of Crown Land (formerly Hudson's Bay Company territory) awarded to Manitoba, Ontario, and Quebec in 1912? Ottawa showed no signs of moving on these issues. Nor was it prepared to act on freight rates—indeed, in 1922 it prepared to restore the advantageous Crow's Nest Pass rate, while allowing Intercolonial rates to increase dramatically.

An all-pervasive sense of injustice finally found political expression in the Maritime Rights movement. A genuinely regional phenomenon, Maritime Rights was dominated by professionals and businessmen—the Conservative Party and the Maritime Provinces Board of Trade both played conspicuous roles in the movement—but it received widespread support from people of all classes and cultures. Farmers were especially supportive. Although the western-controlled farmers' movement had its own regional agenda, the two groups shared a sense of indignation at the declining power of the country's rural areas. The Nova Scotia Conservatives, led by the industrialist E.N. Rhodes, fought the 1925 election under the banner of Maritime Rights, winning 40 out of 43 seats. The Conservative premiers of New Brunswick and Prince Edward Island, J.B.M. Baxter and J.D. Stewart, respectively, were quick to climb on the bandwagon, although the frugal Islanders (who believed in minimal government and usually ran a budget surplus) never adopted Maritime Rights with the same enthusiasm as other provinces.

Maritime Rights campaigners made sufficient noise for even the unsympathetic Mackenzie King to take notice. Needing support from the Maritime members in the House of Commons to sustain his minority government, he reluctantly appointed a royal commission on Maritime Claims, chaired by the same Sir Andrew Duncan who had investigated the problems in the coal industry. In a carefully worded report released in 1926, the commission

Let's Keep It At The Masthead!

This cartoon captured the spirit of the Maritime Rights movement that helped to define issues in both provincial and federal elections in Nova Scotia in 1925 and 1926. Donald McRitchie, 'Let's Keep it at the Masthead', *Halifax Herald*, 2 May 1925.

recommended increased subsidies, lower freight rates, development of the harbours at Saint John and Halifax, a subsidy for the steel industry, and improved ferry service to Prince Edward Island (Duncan had been convinced of the need for this item by his trip to Charlottetown). It avoided any discussion of tariffs or special grants to ensure that services in the Maritime provinces would not fall behind those in the rest of the country.

Well received in the Maritimes, the report met heavy opposition in Ottawa. The result was a compromise that, according to historian E.R. Forbes, 'changed Duncan's program for Maritime rehabilitation into a plan for Maritime pacification . . . to be achieved with the fewest possible concessions'.[2] And it worked. Though the federal government refused to budge on the subsidy issue, Maritime Rights leaders gratefully accepted the Maritime Freight Rates Act (1927), the Dominion Fuel Act (1927), port development for Saint John and Halifax, and a new ferry for Prince Edward Island. With that, the movement petered out.

Mona Wilson and Public Health

In the interwar years, governments in the Atlantic region were hard pressed to provide the level of health services that wealthier jurisdictions could afford. New Brunswick was the first province in Canada to establish a Department of Health in 1918, but most of the work of keeping people healthy tended to fall on nurses and voluntary associations such as the Red Cross. In Newfoundland, the staff of the Newfoundland Outport Nursing and Industrial Association (NONIA), formed in 1924, brought modern ideas about health and nutrition to outport communities and encouraged the production of handicrafts to help pay for nursing services.

In Prince Edward Island, the dynamic Mona Wilson played a remarkable role in advancing public health. Born in Toronto in 1894, she was educated at Johns Hopkins University and served overseas with the American Army Nursing Corps in the First World War. She joined the American Red Cross in 1919 and served in Vladivostock and the Balkans. After studying for her Public Health diploma at the University of Toronto, she became Chief Red Cross Public Health Nurse in Prince Edward Island in 1923.

Wilson and her small staff introduced a variety of programs to serve the island's health needs. They introduced school medical inspections; established dental clinics, tuberculosis clinics, and camps for physically handicapped children; organized province-wide smallpox and diphtheria vaccinations; and promoted eating fruits and vegetables, drinking milk, and maintaining scrupulous hygiene. Through the Junior Red Cross Clubs, children were taught that they should have a warm bath at least once a week, brush their teeth twice a day, cough or sneeze into a handkerchief, and sleep 10 hours a night with their window open.

When the province finally established a Department of Health in 1931, Wilson was appointed Provincial Director of Public Nursing. She held this position until her retirement in 1961, except during the Second World War, when she served as Red Cross Commissioner for Newfoundland. Wilson's contributions to Island life include the establishment of the Girl Guides, Zonta Club, and Business and Professional Women's Club. Found among her personal effects when she died in 1981 was a poem that she had kept since 1925. It summed up her approach to life:

Mona Wilson is shown here conducting a school health inspection at the Charlottetown Model School in 1926.

> be strong!
> we are not here to dream, to play, to drift;
> we have hard work to do and loads to lift.
> shun not the struggle; face it
> 'tis god's gift.[3]

Trouble in Newfoundland

The Dominion of Newfoundland had no federal government to blame for its problems, which mirrored those experienced by the Maritimes. The post-war recession meant major losses for fish exporters, and many businesses declared bankruptcy between 1921 and 1923. In addition, the war had changed the nature of Newfoundland politics. With the collapse of the National Government in 1919, the three parties dissolved into factions and party labels came to mean little. There was, however, a broad distinction between conservative, St John's-based politicians, and those who were more populist and outport-oriented. The 1919 election saw a victory for the second grouping, a coalition between William Coaker's Fishermen's Protective Union and Richard Squires's Liberal following. Like all interwar administrations, it found its freedom to address the economic crisis curtailed by a public debt that had grown substantially as a result of the war effort. As unemployment mounted and emigration increased to between 1,000 and 1,500 people annually, there were demonstrations in St John's and, in 1921, mob scenes in the House of Assembly.

The building of the Corner Brook paper mill was a major achievement, but the government had to take over the operation of the dilapidated railway—yet another financial burden. In 1923 the government collapsed amid charges that Squires had taken kickbacks from the mining companies on Bell Island and had turned the Board of Liquor Control into a covert bootlegging operation with the profits from 'private' sales going into his political account. The charges were largely substantiated by an independent inquiry. With Squires temporarily out of public life, the St John's-based Conservatives took over, promising clean, stable, businesslike government. They also belatedly enfranchised women in 1925.

A piece of good fortune for Newfoundland came in 1927, when the Judicial Committee of the Privy Council ruled that the western boundary between Newfoundland and Canada in the Labrador peninsula should, for the most part, follow the height of land. This bonanza meant little in the short term. When Newfoundland offered to sell the territory, neither Canada nor Quebec was interested in buying. For the moment Labrador remained a potential rather than an actual asset, its resources too remote for effective development. The Newfoundland government provided only minimal services, preferring to leave Labrador in the hands of the missions and the Hudson's Bay Company. But this was scarcely a lasting solution.

First Nations in Troubled Times

In the interwar years, the living conditions in most Aboriginal communities in the Maritimes continued to deteriorate, and the provisions of the Indian Act remained unyielding. Amendments to the Act in the twentieth century only made matters worse, permitting governments to relocate Natives from reserves near towns and cities with more than 8,000 residents and to expropriate reserve lands anywhere for roads, railroads, and other public purposes. These provisions were invoked in Nova Scotia to move Mi'kmaq from the Halifax and Sydney areas. Because they were distant from jobs and markets, the Mi'kmaq relied more than ever on subsistence activities of hunting, fishing, and peddling their crafts from door to door.

On numerous occasions the Mi'kmaq and Wolastoqiyik raised questions about land and their hunting and fishing rights and petitioned governments to pay attention to their plight, but to little avail. In 1899 Ottawa imposed an electoral system for choosing band chiefs and councils, but, other than disrupting traditional methods of choosing their male leaders, it had little impact. The granting of female suffrage at the federal level in 1918 was not extended to Aboriginal women in band elections. Local Indian Agents, always white and poorly paid, were appointed to serve as intermediaries between Ottawa and their Indian charges, but they were rarely effective.

Meanwhile, the courts were deaf to the rights of Native peoples under treaties signed in the eighteenth century. This was evident in 1928 when Chief Syliboy, a Mi'kmaq living in Cape Breton, was tried for possessing pelts in contravention of the Lands and Forests Act. In court, Syliboy argued that as a 'Registered Indian' he was exempt from the provisions of the Act and that he had 'by Treaty the right to hunt and trap at all times'.[4] Although he lost his case both before a magistrate and on appeal, Syliboy represented a new spirit among First Nations people in Canada, who were beginning to use the colonizer's institutions to make their case.

In 1935 the Department of Indian Affairs hired Dr Thomas Robertson to study the conditions on Maritime reserves. His report, which noted sub-standard housing, rampant tuberculosis, and poor nutrition on many reserves, warned that the federal government was facing a much higher outlay for assistance if Natives did not become self-supporting. 'The opinion of the man on the street,' he noted, 'is that the Indian is lazy, useless and himself responsible for his present conditions. However, a study of the record of each individual shows that the great majority of the Indians are good workers and that his present condition is due to matters over which he has no control.'[5]

In this period, Germain Laksi, born in Maine in 1854 to Mi'kmaq parents originally from Nova Scotia, played a major role in preserving the history of his people. Trained in herbal medicine, he played the role of Dr Jerry Lonecloud in American medicine shows and then settled in Halifax, where in 1910 he began helping Harry Piers, curator of the Provincial Museum of Nova Scotia, to collect Mi'kmaq artifacts. From 1923 to 1929, Halifax reporter Clara Dennis conducted a series of interviews with Laksi about his life and Mi'kmaq culture. Together, the interviews and artifacts survive as a rich historical legacy in the region.[6]

Literature and Tradition

Amid the difficulties of the 1920s, there was an upsurge of romantic interest in the region's heritage and folklore. The image of the mid-nineteenth century as a mythical Golden Age for the Maritimes became firmly embedded with the publication in 1924 of F.W. Wallace's *Wooden Ships and Iron Men*, which idealized the hardy mariners and fishing folk of the sea-bound coast. Billed as 'Canada's Ocean Playground' as early as 1929, Nova Scotia led the region in the invention of tradition. The *Bluenose*, designed as a banking schooner and a racer, was launched at Lunenburg in March 1921. Only once defeated in races for the International Fishermen's Trophy sponsored by the *Halifax Herald*, the schooner entered local mythology as an enormously potent symbol, and its image has been on the reverse of the Canadian dime since 1937. Around the same time Nova Scotia's cultural elite discovered Peggy's Cove, located conveniently near Halifax, which rapidly became 'the region's primary symbolic landscape' that epitomized the hardiness, simplicity, and virtues of the seafaring life, as well as the physical beauty of Nova Scotia's south shore.[7] As a result of the new interest in the pre-industrial past, folklore became a subject of systematic study. Helen Creighton embarked on a lifelong career collecting Maritime folk songs and stories. Gerald S. Doyle, Elisabeth Greenleaf, and Maud Karpeles similarly collected songs in Newfoundland.

However well the 'cult of the folk' sold to tourists, the folk themselves were less enthusiastic about becoming cultural artifacts. In 1927 Frank Parker Day, one of the Maritime literary group known as the 'song fishermen', published *Rockbound*, a thinly disguised fictional account of the people of Ironbound Island, an area off the south shore of Nova Scotia. The Ironbounders felt that Day had misrepresented and betrayed them, and in a letter to the *Lunenburg Progress-Enterprise* protested that they were not the 'ignorant, immoral and superstitious' people portrayed in the novel.[8]

Invented traditions were also a standard feature of the developing tourist industry, which received government assistance throughout the region, mainly in the form of new roads. Major hotels were built in Halifax, Saint John, Charlottetown, Digby, Pictou, and St John's. The Newfoundland government created a Tourist and Publicity Commission, which, apart from the usual emphasis on fin, fur, feather, and scenery, began to trumpet what is now known as heritage tourism. It was following the example of Nova Scotia, where in the 1930s motoring tourists were encouraged to visit the newly constructed Cabot Trail or to participate in Champlain's 'Order of Good Cheer' at the reconstructed Port-Royal. Under the Liberal premiership of Angus L. Macdonald, Nova Scotians were urged to remember their Scottish heritage, and in 1939 Cape Breton acquired its own Gaelic College at St Ann's. It was not long before 'tartanism', complete with bagpipes, kilts, and crests, trumped all other local identities in the province.

In this context, an art movement developed in the Maritimes which had an impact beyond the region's borders. It was orchestrated in large measure by US-born educator and arts activist Walter Abell, who was Professor of Fine Arts at Acadia University from 1928 to 1943. Supported by funds from the Carnegie Corporation, Abell taught courses and published widely on the importance of art; brought the region's artists together through the Maritime Arts Association established in 1935; and founded *Maritime Art*, the first fine arts magazine in Canada, in 1940. Armed with these impressive accomplishments, he proceeded to play a leading role in the creation of the Federation of Canadian Artists in 1941. Abell introduced new ideas about modern and socially relevant art that were finding favour in New York, which also inspired some of the region's most distinguished artists, including Miller Brittain, Ted Campbell, Julia Crawford, and Jack Humphrey, who were members of a vibrant artistic community in Saint John in the 1930s. Although Abell eventually found Canada too small a canvas for his ambitions, he left a legacy as a 'missionary for culture' that continued to percolate among artists who shared his vision of a more just and democratic society.[9]

The Great Depression

Conditions seemed to be improving in the late 1920s, but all hopes were dashed by the onset of the Great Depression. Prices fell, markets collapsed, and unemployment climbed even higher. The resulting social problems were accentuated by the fact that the safety valve of emigration was no longer readily available: the US border was closed to all newcomers looking for work, and Canada for the first time restricted the entry of immigrants from Newfoundland. In 1930 the Smoot–Hawley tariff closed the US market to most products, and by 1931 almost one in five Maritime wage earners (19 per cent) was unemployed. Although this figure was only slightly above the national average, the Maritime provinces had fewer resources than most other provinces with which to participate in Ottawa's cost-shared relief programs.

The strain on all levels of government was extreme. By 1931 Guysborough County in Nova Scotia was virtually bankrupt, and several counties in northern New Brunswick soon found themselves in the same position. Provincial governments were also in difficulty. Income per capita had fallen to 71 per cent of the Canadian average by 1933, revenues stagnated, and borrowing drove debt charges to impossible heights—more than 30 per cent of revenue in Nova Scotia and more than 50 per cent in New Brunswick, where the government was on the verge of bankruptcy by the end of the decade. In 1933, 12 per cent of Maritimers were on direct relief, which in most cases paid only a pittance and sometimes was cut off for the summer months. The Prince Edward Island rate of $1.93 per person per month (the same as in Newfoundland) was the second lowest in Canada.

Many people looked to charities, the churches, and the Red Cross for assistance. Fishermen and urban labourers were the worst hit. As for the elderly, strictly means-tested pensions (introduced in the Maritime provinces between 1933 and 1936 at rates 20 to 40 per cent lower than the national average) were a convenient way to reduce relief rolls. There was near-starvation in some areas and widespread malnutrition. But amid it all, Maritimers found the time, energy, and

Letters of Desperation
to R.B. Bennett

During the early years of the Depression, a number of desperate people in Canada wrote directly to Prime Minister R.B. Bennett, a multi-millionaire, for assistance. Many of the letters came from New Brunswickers who felt a special connection with the New Brunswick-born politician. Although Bennett occasionally responded positively to the call for help, one man's fortune could not begin to address the misery that so many people experienced in his native province.

Campbellton, NB, Nov. 29, 1932
Dear Friend
I am taking the pleasure in riting you a few lines to ask you if you would help me out in some way for I am sick and I can[t] work and the Doctor wount halp me in anny way witeout money[.] I toat you would halp me wite a treaman for I tink you are the ony one would halp me out for I vouted for you so trie to halp me out some way and I will never gor get you I amyours very truly. . . .

Townsend NB feb the 18th 1935
Dear sir I am dropping you a few lines to let you no that I voted for you and have a hard time to live so I am Cripple with that make it harder for me so if I woulden be Cripple I woulden Call on you for help I try to do the Bess I can and then vt for you again so if youhelp me I would be afful glad if you could if you please and exquse bad riting. . . .
[Reply $5.00]

Personal Napan Bay NB [1935]
Hon R.B. Bennett
Dear Sir
I wrote you once before begging a little help in my time of need, but evidentially you either never rec'd it or turned it down. Now I am writing to you again (if you will excuse pencil writing). Seeing by the papers where you spend so much on broadcasting and advertising, I thought perhaps you might help me out a little at this time. My husband is a smelt fisherman on the Miramichi and although some have done very good fishing this season his nets were not among the lucky number, and he lost three in the ice drift in Dec. Now during the past three years I have been sick a great deal, in hospital 3 times and had serious operations, these bills very large (to me) and are not nearly all paid. Now I need doctors care again and have no means to do so, therefore I am calling upon you for some help although entirely unknown to me. We have lived thru the last 5 years of depression, and have never asked for the dole.

If you can assit me in any way please do so at your earliest convenience, and please remember I would not wish my friends or any one else to know. If you have any thing to give please do so privately and you will probably never realize how much it means to me

Thanking you, I remain
Yours Truly. . . .

[Reply $10.00][10]

resources to send aid to the Prairies, where the wheat economy had collapsed as a result of falling world prices and a devastating drought.

The Depression precipitated the final scenes in the drama of Newfoundland under responsible government. In 1928 Squires had returned to power. His government was soon engulfed by the economic collapse. Four years later, revenue had fallen by 21 per cent; spending had risen by 7 per cent; the debt had increased by 23 per cent; and servicing it now absorbed more than 60 per cent of government revenue. These bald figures represented an escalating crisis: low prices, poor catches, rising urban unemployment, a quarter of the population on the dole (which was centrally administered), and the necessity of borrowing to maintain the basic operations of the state, even after swingeing cuts in public expenditure. When bank loans became ever more difficult to arrange, another futile attempt was made to sell Labrador, this time for $110 million, but there were no takers.

The atmosphere was especially tense in St John's, where the prime minister's opponents sensed blood and organized a march on the legislature on 5 April 1932. It turned into a violent riot, and Squires was lucky to escape unharmed. His party was virtually wiped out in the ensuing general election and the Conservatives took over once again. Having assessed the financial situation, they suggested what Squires had consistently refused: a partial default on debt payments. There seemed to be no other alternative.

Crowds outside the Colonial Building, St John's, 5 April 1932. Accusations of corruption levelled against the Prime Minister, Sir Richard Squires, precipitated this demonstration, which turned into a riot. A-19-23, The Rooms, Provincial Archives Division.

Newfoundland and Dominion Status

The concept of 'dominion status' in the British Empire evolved between the mid-nineteenth century, when responsible government was first established in the colonies of settlement, and 1931 when, by the Statute of Westminster, the British Parliament granted dominions the freedom to exercise their independence in domestic and foreign affairs. The term came to mean autonomy under the British imperial umbrella and applied to the self-governing countries of Canada, Australia, New Zealand, South Africa, Newfoundland, and the Irish Free State (from 1922).

Newfoundland proved to be a special case. Officially, it had the same status as its peers. Its prime ministers attended imperial conferences and, during the Great War, meetings of the Imperial War Cabinet and the Imperial War Conference. Its affairs were administered in London by the Dominions Office, even during the period (1934–49) when the country was governed by an appointed commission. However, unlike its theoretical equals, Newfoundland was not a signatory to the Versailles Treaty in 1919 and was not a member of the League of Nations. It allowed its external affairs to be handled by the imperial government and in 1931 decided (like Australia and New Zealand) not to accept immediately the Statute of Westminster, which recognized the self-governing territories as 'autonomous communities' within what was now called the British Commonwealth. A British official noted that Newfoundland was unique as a 'minor' type of dominion.[11] After 1934 Newfoundland can be best characterized as a dominion in suspension.

Alarm bells rang in London and Ottawa, where the possibility that a dominion might default on its debt was viewed with dismay. Newfoundland was given a proposition that it was not allowed to refuse: Canada and Britain would assist with the debt payments on condition that an imperial royal commission investigate the situation and advise on what to do in the longer term. Chaired by Lord Amulree, the commission reported in October 1933. It placed the primary blame for the debt crisis not on the Depression, structural economic problems, or the cost of the war and the railway but rather on 'persistent extravagance and neglect of proper financial principles', 'greed, graft and corruption', and general incompetence, along with various other shortcomings. Its central recommendation, fabricated by the Whitehall bureaucracy, was that the country's debt should be rescheduled and guaranteed by the British government. In return, Newfoundland would surrender responsible government and be administered by a British-appointed commission until such time as it was again 'self-supporting'.

Weary of persistent economic problems, disillusioned with the political elite, fearful of further violence and unrest, Newfoundlanders threw in the towel. There were very few dissenting voices. The legislature voted itself out of existence, and the Commission of Government took office in February 1934. Though welcomed at the time, the surrender of responsible government soon came to be (and is still) seen as a humiliation and the analysis in the Amulree report as unfair. Joining Canada might have proved less of an indignity, but there was little support for Confederation on the island and none at all in Ottawa.

Lady Hope Simpson's Impressions of Newfoundlanders, 1935

The Commission of Government took office in Newfoundland in early 1934. Sir John Hope Simpson was appointed commissioner for natural resources, serving until 1936. In 1935, he and his wife toured the south coast of the island on a coastal boat, the SS *Malakoff*. In a letter to her son, Lady Hope Simpson offered her impressions of the poverty she encountered.

. . . La Hune was our first port of call . . . It is a most miserable place—so poor—so wretched. The children ran away like little wild animals & hid at our approach. We went into some of the houses. The people hardly stirred when we came in . . . All looked dreadfully dirty, the men grey & unshaven, their clothing ragged & patched; the children many of them in a cotton nightgown with bare feet, the women often with nothing on under a cotton gown & the snow still lying down to the seashore in many places. . . .

They are a queer people. Wherever we go, we get a first impression of unfriendliness . . . But it has been our experience everywhere that all this apparent unfriendliness is a sort of smokescreen of shyness, almost indeed a custom of the country. Very quickly it goes down before an assault, and before we leave the people are responsive & friendly . . . .

The most marked case was yesterday at Isle aux Morts . . . On the wharf lounged about a dozen men, lying on a pile of planks. They let us approach without moving to greet us, as usual. . . . 'Well, how are things with you here?' 'Worse than ever before. Isn't that so, lads? Worse than ever before they are; and that's so.' 'But you've had good fishing this winter, haven't you?' 'Yes, that's so, plenty of fish there be.' 'Yes, plenty fish,' corroborated the crowd; then silence. We know what that means—low prices for their fish & high prices for their supplier & the merchant getting all the profits. The truck system is the ruin of the people. . . .

The school was truly a dreadful place, great holes in the floor & a broken roof. But the crowd pushed in after us, & I suggested that the children make room for the men & [John] talked to them, asking them questions & making notes of their difficulties & telling them what the government is doing & suggesting what they could do. . . .

It always comes as a surprise to me when these children talk English—they seem such little foreigners—so wild & furtive. One little figure specially stands out in my memory—a girl child of about six with straight fair hair & delicate features, standing on the edge of a wharf seeing us off from Grey River—barelegged & barefooted in a grimy white nightgown, snow on the hillside behind her. I wanted to go back & wrap her in my coat & carry her into her house.[12]

Responses to Hard Times

To help those most devastated by the economic crisis, two strategies were adopted across the region. The first was to provide unemployed people with land and encourage them to become self-sufficient farmers. This program was most popular in New Brunswick, where the government opened new areas for pioneer settlement and provided some minimal assistance. Acadians were particularly involved in the scheme, establishing a number of new settlements in the northern part of the province. In Nova Scotia some 600 vacant farms were made available, but most of the beneficiaries were unemployed miners and their families. Lacking the necessary agricultural skills, many of them soon drifted away. The results were similarly disappointing in Newfoundland, where the Commission government created eight land settlements and relocated approximately 365 families. The second, more famous and influential strategy was developed by the Extension Department of St Francis Xavier University under the direction of Father Moses Coady.

Moses Michael Coady

Born in 1882 into a large Irish Catholic family living in Cape Breton's Margaree Valley, Moses Coady was a late developer. He was unable to attend school regularly until he was a teenager, but then went on to the Provincial Normal School in Truro and in 1905 graduated from St Francis Xavier University (StFX) in Antigonish. His cousin, Father James ('Jimmy') Tompkins, 12 years his senior, persuaded him to enter the priesthood. Coady studied in Rome, was ordained in 1910, and then began teaching at StFX, where Tompkins had been appointed vice-president.

Tompkins was a liberal and progressive Catholic who believed that education was the key to economic and social revival in eastern Nova Scotia. Not surprisingly, his 'social gospel Catholicism' and his support in the early 1920s for a single non-denominational university in Nova Scotia outraged conservative Catholics. Tompkins soon found himself exiled to a rural parish. The move did not end his relentless social activism, though, and one result was the Royal Commission on the Fisheries chaired by Justice A.K. McLean.

Coady's appearance before the commission is considered a defining moment in his career. He had spent much of the decade organizing the Nova Scotia teachers' union and editing its *Bulletin*. Following Tompkins and others, he argued that the local economy could be revitalized by the education of ordinary people, who should be encouraged to take charge of their futures rather than succumbing to what he called a 'weird pessimism [that] benumbed everybody'.[13] Adult education, credit unions, and co-operatives, as Tompkins had long preached, were the key. Indeed, Coady argued that co-operatives were an acceptable, non-revolutionary middle way between socialism and capitalism.

One result of the Mclean Commission's report was the decision by StFX to establish a Department of Extension with the immensely energetic Coady as its director. Funded by the Carnegie Foundation and the federal Department of Fisheries, Coady and his colleagues formed study groups and promoted adult education, co-operatives, and credit unions. In 1929–30 Coady played a leading role in helping to organize the United Maritime Fishermen's Cooperative, designed to improve the living conditions of the families in the many communities dependent on the fisheries.

The 'Antigonish Movement' that emerged from Coady's department was controversial. While many Roman Catholics found Coady uncomfortably liberal, businessmen disliked his critique of capitalism as inherently exploitative. Protestants felt uneasy about the Catholic leadership of the movement, and Acadians were unhappy about the overwhelmingly Celtic nature of StFX. Nevertheless, the physically impressive Coady and his department became enormously influential throughout the Atlantic region and far beyond. It has been suggested that as a result he developed a degree of dogmatic arrogance, believing that he was doing God's work as God's agent, and that his 'blueprint for the masses' was therefore irrefutable.

The Second World War extinguished the fire in the Antigonish Movement, and during his final years—he died in 1959—Coady had to wrestle with the growing realization that his co-operative utopia would not be achieved and that, though much good had been done, neither he nor the Antigonish Movement had changed the world.

The Antigonish Movement, as it came to be known, focused on self-help through adult education and the establishment of co-operatives to do everything from marketing fish to building houses. Although co-ops were not new to the Maritimes, the Antigonish Movement provided a new impetus for them, especially in rural areas where the Roman Catholic church was strong. By the end of 1939, Antigonish claimed involvement in 2,390 study clubs and 140 credit unions throughout all three Maritime provinces.

The Newfoundland government established its own division of co-operatives in the mid-1930s, with Antigonish alumni as the director and field workers. There was considerable early success both in St John's and on the island's west coast. Less well-received was the commission's insistence that, to prevent beriberi, dole recipients should use brown rather than white flour—unemployed marchers in St John's in 1935 responded with a banner reading 'We work for our cash; we want money not cattle feed'.[14]

The Antigonish Movement was inherently conservative, and its leaders had no interest in socialism or radical politics. Indeed, it has been accused of being more romantic than realist and of failing to involve industrial and urban workers. Some people in the region were less willing to accept the status quo. Until it was banned by the federal government, there was support in the Maritimes for the Communist party, as well as the social-democratic Cooperative Commonwealth Federation (CCF), which won both provincial and federal seats in industrial Cape Breton within a decade of its founding in 1932. The upstart Reconstruction Party, which split from the Conservatives, attracted followers in eastern Nova Scotia in the 1935 federal election. Even the Ku Klux Klan reared its ugly head, making Roman Catholics, blacks, and other minorities scapegoats for these difficult times.

The emergence of new parties did not substantially transform Maritime politics, and there was no meaningful change in federal–provincial relations. In Nova Scotia a royal commission appointed by Macdonald's Liberal government recommended in 1934 that the federal government either base its subsidies to the provinces on their individual fiscal needs or take over the entire responsibility for certain services. Real change had to await the report of the Royal Commission on Dominion–Provincial Relations (the Rowell–Sirois Commission), which appeared in 1940. Also important was the increasing acceptance during the Second World War of Keynesian economic principles, such as the use of government spending to offset capitalist boom and bust cycles. In the meantime, provincial governments had no option but to borrow money to pay for relief works and essential services.

Widespread unemployment in the 1930s left unions on the defensive but also encouraged new departures. In the summer of 1932, dissidents from the United Mine Workers organized the Amalgamated Mine Workers of America (District 26), whose radical stance soon garnered the support of over half of the coal miners in Nova Scotia. The steelworkers, encouraged by the US-based Committee for Industrial Organization (CIO), also became more militant. In 1936 they supported, by an overwhelming 90 per cent, a new CIO-inspired union led by Sylbie Barrett. When the Dominion Steel and Coal Corporation refused to bargain with the upstart organization, it looked as if the labour troubles of the 1920s would be repeated.

Facing an election in 1937, Premier Macdonald was determined to avoid such a calamity. Unlike Ontario's Liberal Premier Mitch Hepburn, who fought tooth and nail to keep the CIO out of his province, Macdonald decided to institutionalize collective bargaining and thereby earn the support of workers. In this he was following the lead of US Democratic President Franklin D. Roosevelt, who had made an accommodation with labour in the 1936 Wagner Act. Early in 1937, the Nova Scotia legislature passed a Trade Union Act that compelled employers to recognize and bargain with the union chosen by a majority of their employees; prohibited 'yellow dog' contracts and the dismissal of employees for being involved in union organizing activities; and provided a check-off of union dues from employee paycheques. The Canadian Manufacturers' Association denounced the legislation as giving too much power to 'foreign agents and agitators' but they were whistling in the wind.

As a result of Macdonald's prescience, Nova Scotia led Canada in adopting legislation that would, after 1944, become nationwide. The impact of these legislative initiatives in both Canada and the United States was far-reaching. They encouraged the growth of unions and ushered in a new era of labour–employer relations, one that depended more on bureaucratic negotiations than on strikes to achieve better wages and working conditions. And, most importantly from the point of view of politicians who supported the new accommodation with labour, they blunted the thrust of radical alternatives to the liberal order that had taken root in North America.

In Newfoundland, the Commission government was a caretaker regime subject to the supervision of the Dominions Office and the British Treasury. London wanted to see progress, but at the same time insisted on economy and avoidance of controversy—there were to be no awkward questions raised in Parliament about Newfoundland. The Commission's achievements were real: it reorganized the civil service, reformed taxation, introduced improvements in health and education, and encouraged modernization in the fishing industry. It also created the Newfoundland Ranger Force, whose members were to be at once policemen, administrators, and the government's eyes and ears in rural districts, including Labrador. Valuable as such initiatives were, most Newfoundlanders could see little change in their economic circumstances, and the inflated expectations that had been associated with the Commission's inauguration were soon replaced by disillusion. The Commission was no more capable than its predecessors of balancing the budget, reducing the debt, or finding work for the unemployed. By the late 1930s it was widely unpopular.

In the Maritimes there was a slow recovery after 1933, fuelled in part by ambitious road-building programs. Exports of lumber and apples were protected by the 1932 Ottawa agreements on imperial trade, an achievement of New Brunswick–born Conservative Prime Minister R.B. Bennett. Thanks to government subventions and increased tariff protection, steel and coal production revived. The lobster and fresh fish industries expanded, as did dairy and poultry farming. In Newfoundland mining was the only sector to show any significant improvement, though newsprint, as in the Maritimes, maintained its position. Yet prices remained low and markets uncertain, and employers drove down wages as far as possible. In terms of national income per capita, the region continued to lag behind. In the late 1930s, average annual income in Newfoundland was approximately $150; in the Maritimes $248; and in Canada as a whole $360.

To counter the general misery and mean-spiritedness of the 1930s, many people found solace in the mass consumer culture that was transforming North American society. Radio, movies, mail-order catalogues, glossy magazines, cars, and modern conveniences exploded on the market in the 1920s with dramatic effect. Older values such as self-discipline, self-denial, duty, and religious observance began to give way to self-fulfilment and secular pleasures. Although Atlantic Canadians were on the periphery of this revolution, they were no less attracted to the new values than people elsewhere; all they lacked was the economic wherewithal to insist that they too have 'a chicken in every pot and a car in every garage', or at least indoor plumbing to replace the outdoor privy.

Conclusion

The interwar years left an indelible mark on the Atlantic region. In the era when other areas of North America were making the transition, however unevenly, to mass consumer society, the Maritimes and Newfoundland were left behind. Much would change with the outbreak of the Second World War, but the image of the Atlantic region as the 'sick man' of North America would continue to have an impact long after it was no longer true.

Further Readings

Brym, Robert J., and R. James Sacouman, eds. 1979. *Underdevelopment and Social Movements in Atlantic Canada*. Toronto: New Hogtown Press.

Fizzard, Garfield, ed. 2000. *Amulree's Legacy: Truth, Lies and Consequences*. St John's: Newfoundland Historical Society.

Forbes, E.R. 1970. *The Maritime Rights Movement: 1919–1927: A Study in Canadian Regionalism*. Montreal: McGill-Queen's University Press.

Frank, David. 1999. *J.B. McLachlan: A Biography*. Toronto: Lorimer.

Journal of Canadian Art History XXVII (2006, Special Issue).

MacEachern, Alan. 2001. *Natural Selections: National Parks in Atlantic Canada, 1935–1970*. Montreal: McGill-Queen's University Press.

McKay, Ian. 1994. *The Quest of the Folk: Antimodernism and Cultural Selection in Twentieth-Century Nova Scotia*. Montreal: McGill-Queen's University Press.

Morton, Suzanne. 1995. *Ideal Surroundings: Domestic Life in a Working-Class Suburb in the 1920s*. Toronto: University of Toronto Press.

Neal, Rusty. 1999. *Brotherhood Economics: Women and Cooperatives in Nova Scotia*. Sydney: University of Cape Breton Press.

Neary, Peter. 1988. *Newfoundland and the North Atlantic World, 1929–1949*. Montreal: McGill-Queen's University Press.

Taylor, M. Brook. 2006. *A Camera on the Banks: Frederick William Wallace and the Fishermen of Nova Scotia*. Fredericton: Goose Lane.

Food for Thought

McKay, Ian. 1992. 'Tartanism Triumphant: The Construction of Scottishness in Nova Scotia, 1933–1954', *Acadiensis* XXI, 2 (Spring): 5–47.

Recommended Websites

The Bluenose: A Canadian Icon
http://www.gov.ns.ca/nsarm/virtual/bluenose

The Coady International Institute
http://www.coady.stfx.ca/history.cfm

The Commission of Government
www.heritage.nf.ca/law/commission_gov.html

The Rise of Economic Democracy (Antigonish Movement)
http://www.uccb.ca/CED/ced/1/rise.html

Chapter 13

The Emergence of an Atlantic Region, 1939–49

The Second World War originated in the determination of Adolf Hitler's Nazi regime to forcefully undo what it saw as the humiliations imposed upon Germany by the Treaty of Versailles, which had ended the First World War. In an effort to establish Germany as the dominant European power, Hitler began acquiring bordering European states, annexing Austria and the former Czechoslovakia in 1938. Britain declared war against Germany on 3 September 1939, two days after the German invasion of Poland, whom Britain and France had pledged to support. Newfoundland automatically joined the war effort on the same day; Canada followed on 10 September.

The war brought prosperity to the Atlantic region, but it was artificial and uneven. Post-war readjustment was difficult and, as it had been 25 years before, in some ways disillusioning. The reforms undertaken during and after the war did little to change the structure of federal–provincial relationships, and no solutions were offered to the growing problems of regional disparity and dependency. In Newfoundland (and Labrador), though, the war precipitated fundamental political and constitutional change. The suspended dominion became a Canadian province in 1949, and the term 'Atlantic Provinces' came into use. Many citizens of the new province hoped and expected that joining Canada would solve major economic problems. Only time would tell whether they were right.

Across the Atlantic, 1939–49

The Second World War ushered in a new era for the Atlantic region, indeed, for people around the globe. Not only did the war slay the dragon of depression, but it also marked the transition of world dominance from Great Britain to the United States, which had enormous implications for people everywhere, especially for Canadians. Economic, military, and political ties between the United States and Canada were strengthened during the war and, in its aftermath, Canada became a willing American ally in the Cold War between the Soviet Union and the United States.

In 1945 Canada helped to establish the United Nations (UN), an international body headquartered in New York and designed to keep the peace. When the UN became hamstrung by posturing among the major nations in the Security Council, Canada participated in the 1949 creation of the North Atlantic Treaty Organization (NATO), a military pact to protect Western nations from Soviet aggression. It was in this context that Newfoundland and Labrador joined Confederation and that the governments of the four Atlantic provinces embarked on efforts to translate wartime prosperity, such as it was, to peacetime development.

The Military Occupation

For the duration of the war, the Atlantic region was essentially a military base extending from Labrador to the American border. As the part of North America nearest to the European theatre of war, the region provided an indispensable base for air and sea links to the United Kingdom. There was investment in military infrastructure, but the main permanent benefits of Canada's war effort went to Quebec and Ontario, where the industrial component was centralized. Ottawa had little interest in using the opportunities presented by the war to promote regional development. The role of the Maritimes and Newfoundland was simply to shield the industrial heartland and to provide the necessary conduit to Europe.

In the Maritimes approximately 47.5 per cent of the eligible male population joined the armed forces. More than 11,000 Newfoundlanders and Labradorians joined the British or Canadian forces and several thousand more crewed merchant vessels. Unemployment disappeared as men and women from across the region either migrated to industrial jobs in central Canada or found work closer to home. Many of the local jobs involved building and strengthening military bases, not only in the Maritimes but also in Newfoundland and in Labrador, where the Canadian government assumed the responsibility for defence.

The most important military centre on the east coast was Halifax, followed by Sydney. Each had a large and potentially vital harbour, as well as a base for each of the three armed forces: army, navy, and air force. All three services also had detachments at Saint John and Gaspé, while the Royal Canadian Navy had additional bases at Shelburne and Cornwallis; the Royal Canadian Air Force (RCAF) at Greenwood, North Sydney, Chatham, Moncton, Yarmouth, Shelburne, Debert, East Passage, Summerside, and Charlottetown; and the army at Debert, Edmundston, Sussex, Aldershot, and Little River.

The Canadian government had understood from the start that Newfoundland would have to be included in its defence planning, and RCAF planes began to patrol the waters around the island, using the seaplane base at Botwood, which had served civil aircraft on transatlantic flights since 1937.

Table 13.1	Timeline
1940	Unemployment insurance legislation passed in Canada.
1941	Anglo-American Leased Bases Agreement signed; Canadian High Commission established in St John's.
1942–4	U-boats sink vessels in Gulf and approaches, including the ferry *Caribou*.
1942	Newfoundland government takes over the north Labrador trade.
1944	Maritime provinces conduct inquiries on reconstruction; Canada adopts family allowance legislation.
1945	End of the Second World War; riots in Halifax, Sydney, and New Waterford; formation of National Sea Products Ltd.
1946–8	National Convention debates Newfoundland's future.
1947	Maritime coal miners' strike.
1948	Newfoundland voters choose Confederation with Canada.
1949	Newfoundland becomes a province; Hal Banks' union-breaking in Halifax.

By June 1940 Canadian troops and aircraft were stationed at Gander, where the 'Newfoundland Airport' had opened in early 1938, and before long both Botwood and Gander were placed under Canadian control, along with the Newfoundland Militia (renamed the Newfoundland Regiment in 1943). Starting in 1941, the Canadians built another air base (now St John's International Airport) at Torbay, a short distance north of St John's, and the next year began to construct naval facilities there on behalf of the Royal Navy. HMCS *Avalon*, with 3,600 personnel by 1943, became the Canadian navy's second largest base. The Canadian government also rapidly constructed a huge new airfield at Goose Bay, Labrador, which was operational by the end of 1941. In total, the infrastructure established in Newfoundland and Labrador cost roughly $65 million.

In September 1940, the British and American governments agreed in principle that in return for 50 aging destroyers and other military equipment, Britain would allow the United States to lease base sites in Newfoundland, Bermuda, and the Caribbean 'freely and without consideration' for 99 years. The Leased Bases Agreement, finalized in June 1941, was unpopular in Newfoundland since it gave the United States virtual sovereignty over its bases. Great Britain's wartime leader, Winston Churchill, felt it necessary to appeal to Newfoundlanders to accept the deal 'for the sake of the Empire, of liberty and of the welfare of all mankind'. The Commission government had little choice but to accept. The Americans built an army base at St John's, a naval and army base at Argentia, and an air base at Stephenville; leased part of St John's harbour; and stationed personnel at Gander, Goose Bay, and elsewhere. In 1943, at the height of the military occupation, there were 10,000 Americans and more than 6,000 Canadians stationed in Newfoundland and Labrador—tangible proof of the country's strategic importance.

Early in the war people in the Atlantic region had a real sense of being on the front line and vulnerable to German attack. Those fears eventually faded, even though German submarines

Internment Camps

Soon after the outbreak of war, Canada began to establish camps where enemy nationals and Canadian citizens who were considered security risks could be interned. Twenty-six camps were constructed, one of them at Ripples, 34 kilometres east of Fredericton.

From 1940–1 the camp housed over 700 German and Austrian male Jewish refugees, who were then given the opportunity to return to England and join the military or to obtain a sponsor to remain in Canada or the United States. One who decided to stay in Canada was Fritz (Frederich) Bender, an inventor who moved to Ottawa and continued his efforts to waterproof plywood, which led to the development of the Mosquito bomber.

Between 1941 and 1945, the camp held German and Italian seamen as well as some Canadians who had expressed opposition to the war—such as Camillien Houde, former mayor of Montreal. The internees worked in the forest, cutting the wood required to keep the 100 wood stoves in the camp burning, and as helpers in the camp's kitchen, hospital, library, canteen, and dormitory huts. The internees received 20 cents a day for their labour.

The Newfoundland government established a small internment camp in St John's, which housed German and Italian seamen and a few resident foreigners who had aroused suspicion. From 1941, Newfoundland internees were transferred to Canadian camps.

continued to bring danger into home waters. In time, the forces stationed in the region came to concentrate not so much on defending North America as on providing protection for the convoys of merchant vessels crossing the Atlantic; the coastal vessels sailing to and from Quebec, Corner Brook, and Bell Island; and the ferry service between North Sydney and Port aux Basques. In addition, Goose Bay and Gander were used as take-off points for the almost 12,000 aircraft ferried from North America to Britain during the course of the war. Other functions included the training of personnel and the repair and maintenance of ships and aircraft.

Protecting convoys from German U-boat attacks placed an immense strain on the Canadian navy and air force. Inevitably, rapid expansion meant that officers and crews often lacked training and experience, equipment was sometimes inadequate, and base facilities could be substandard. In particular, repair and refit capacity in the region was limited, in part because skilled tradesmen were in short supply and more directly because the federal government decided to locate the major repair centre at Montreal—despite the danger posed by U-boats in the St Lawrence and the fact that the river was impassable to ocean-going vessels for half the year. British and American authorities questioned the decision to no avail.

Bedford Basin, on the inner reaches of Halifax Harbour, offered shelter to merchant ships and their naval escorts assembling for the dangerous voyage across the North Atlantic during the Second World War. Department of National Defence, LAC, PA-112993.

Between May 1942 and November 1944, submarines sank 23 ships in the Gulf. In September and November 1942, four vessels were sunk at Bell Island with the loss of 69 lives, and in October the Newfoundland ferry *Caribou*, though escorted by a minesweeper, was torpedoed 40 miles off Port aux Basques with the loss of 137 passengers and crew. After a shaky start, Canadian aircraft and naval vessels contained the U-boat threat, won the Battle of the St Lawrence, and played a significant role in the Battle of the Atlantic. Stories of Germans landing in remote places along the region's long coastline circulated—an automatic weather station was in fact placed by the Germans on the north Labrador coast—but by 1944 the region was safe from direct enemy threats.

In July 1945 Halifax once again suffered a major explosion as a result of its role as a munitions storage site. Fire and explosions racked the city for 24 hours after the Bedford Magazine, on the Dartmouth side of the Bedford Basin, caught fire. When Halifax residents north of Quinpool Road were ordered to evacuate their homes, many refused and instead lined the slopes of the harbour to watch the fireworks.

The Economic Impact of War

Notwithstanding the bias toward central Canada, the war boosted the Atlantic region's economy. Steel production and processing at Sydney and Trenton revived and expanded, and shipyards were busy at Saint John, Halifax, Dartmouth, and Pictou. Newsprint production increased, and overall employment in manufacturing expanded by 25,000 (74 per cent). Even the cotton industry bounced back, and for a time wool producers enjoyed a steady demand for their product, which was used in military uniforms.

The Halifax docks generally functioned well, thanks to a reorganization of labour and the imposition of a minimum wage, which more than met the increase in the cost of living. There was a three-month strike in 1944, when the Dominion Steel and Coal Corporation (DOSCO)-owned Halifax Shipyards Limited unsuccessfully challenged the legality of the union dues check-off. War did nothing to resolve tensions in the coal industry, with its history of intense antagonism between workers and management. Vital as coal was to the war effort, production actually declined between 1941 and 1945, and there was serious labour unrest until 1943, when the federal government agreed to top up miners' wages. This decision reflected both poor government control of skilled labour and the inability (or unwillingness) of corporations and governments to find a permanent solution to the industry's problems. Allowing more than 1,000 miners to join the armed forces and the number of coalface workers to decline by 29 per cent proved to be unwise moves, as was the appointment of W.F. Carroll, a known anti-union Liberal, to chair a royal commission to investigate the industry in 1944.

As urban-based industries expanded to meet wartime needs, they drew labour away from the rural economy at the very time when demand for fish and farm products was increasing sharply. Between 1939 and 1945 the total farm income for the Maritimes rose by 98 per cent (from $25 million to $49 million). Apple growers faced disaster when the British market was abruptly closed at the beginning of the war so that capital and shipping could be diverted to the military effort. At the request of growers and shippers, the federal government stepped in to help, establishing marketing boards to dispose of some of the vast surplus and to process the rest as juice, sauce, and pie filling. As a result, processing accounted for nearly 80 per cent of the crop in 1942, up from

Clarie Gillis

Clarence 'Clarie' Gillis was born in 1895 in Londonderry, Nova Scotia. In 1904 his family moved to Glace Bay, where his father worked in the mines and became a close associate of the union activist J.B. McLachlan. Because of this union activity, the entire family was expelled from company housing and forced to spend a winter living in a tent. Blacklisted, the elder Gillis worked from 1910 to 1923 in the United States.

At the age of 14, with a grade 5 education, Clarie began his career as a miner in No. 2 colliery in Glace Bay. When war was declared, he volunteered for service overseas and was wounded three times. Back in Cape Breton, Gillis played an active role in the coal miners' struggle against British Empire Steel Corporation (BESCO), supported the co-operative movement, and helped establish a local branch of the Canadian Legion.

In 1927 Gillis was elected president of the Phalen Local—known as the 'Red Local'—of District 26 of the United Mine Workers of America (UMW). After a group broke away from District 26 in 1932 to form the Amalgamated Mine Workers of Nova Scotia, he served as its vice-president, but by 1938 he was back in the UMW and deeply involved with the recently founded Cooperative Commonwealth Federation (CCF). After decades of bitter internal struggle, Cape Breton miners were ready to bury their differences and put their weight behind a political party dedicated to serving the interests of working people.

District 26 was the first union to affiliate with the CCF at the national level, and in a provincial by-election in December 1939 a miner named Douglas Macdonald won the riding of Cape Breton Centre for the party—its first seat east of Ontario. In the federal election of the following year Clarie Gillis won Cape Breton South and became the first miner to sit in the Canadian House of Commons. He was to hold the seat until the Diefenbaker landslide of 1958.[1]

11.4 per cent in 1938, and growers continued to get good returns as they waited for overseas sales to resume once the war had ended.

The war helped to stimulate astonishing gains in the fisheries: the value of Maritime fish landings increased 230 per cent (from $8 million to $27 million), while the value of Newfoundland's salt fish exports quadrupled, from $4.1 million to $16.7 million, over the same period. In the Maritimes and Newfoundland alike, governments encouraged modernization, offering financial incentives for the construction both of larger vessels (including trawlers and draggers) and of freezing plants. The establishment of the giant National Sea Products Limited in 1945 marked the arrival of mechanized, industrial fishing. This trend was endorsed in an influential report written in 1944 by Stewart Bates for Nova Scotia's royal commission on reconstruction. Soon to become federal deputy minister of fisheries, Bates argued that the future lay with fresh fish, trawlers, centralization, consolidation, and the North American market. The Newfoundland government made almost identical recommendations the same year.

The militarization of the region also created economic spinoffs. Although rationing, shortages, and restrictive liquor laws limited what they could buy, people had money to spend. Men and women in the armed services received regular salaries, and the construction of military bases created many jobs—about 20,000 in Newfoundland and Labrador alone in 1942. In the Maritimes, base development in communities such as Summerside, Greenwood, and Chatham generated economic growth and work for people in the surrounding area. Some bases became nuclei for new or vastly expanded towns and displaced families and communities. Farms belonging to francophones in St George's Bay were expropriated to make way for the Stephenville base, while at Argentia two villages were closed down and their residents, and even cemeteries, moved a short distance away.

The construction of the Goose Bay airfield is considered, with reason, to be the watershed dividing the old Labrador from the new. Labradorians from all over the region, including some Inuit and Innu, came to build the base and establish the town of Happy Valley—originally called 'Refuge Cove' because there was no place to stay (workers had to live in tents and shacks). Another significant change came about in 1942, when the Hudson's Bay Company decided to abandon the trading posts it had leased from the Moravians in 1926. Now the Newfoundland government had no choice but to take over. Labrador could no longer be governed by proxy.

War and Society

The military presence was not an unmixed blessing for cities and towns still recovering from the Depression. The 65,000 residents of Halifax, Canada's main Atlantic port, were particularly hard pressed to make room for some 100,000 additional people, including military personnel, their families, and sundry camp followers, as well as industrial workers. With many unpaved streets and a dilapidated water system, Halifax was a dismal place for many of the new arrivals: rents were high, living conditions often disgraceful, and hospitals and schools overstretched. The city had never been particularly open at the best of times, and the Depression had taken its toll on amenities such as restaurants and theatres. Thus it was left to volunteers to set up hostels and canteens and to arrange concerts. Conditions were similar in Sydney and Saint John, which also were required to host expanding military and civilian populations. In St John's, relations between townspeople and the military were generally good, the Americans being especially popular. The Americans sent military dependents home, and the number of Canadian dependents was capped, which helped to alleviate the strain on housing and food supplies.

When the end of the war in Europe was announced on 8 May 1945, the city of Halifax erupted in two days of rioting and looting. The immediate cause may have been the authorities' decision to close all shops, cafés, and liquor stores, which led frustrated revellers to break in and help themselves, but the violence spread, and the total damages amounted to more than $5 million. In the federal inquiry that followed, Rear-Admiral L.W. Murray was relieved of his commission for failing to control the men under his command, and 211 people (civilians as well as military personnel) were indicted for offences. There were also riots in Sydney and New Waterford, where authorities followed the same practice as in Halifax.

With such events serving as examples to support their claims, some people claimed that the war had weakened traditional morality and encouraged 'licence'. The reality was that attitudes towards alcohol, sex, and religion had been changing for some time, and the war only accelerated the process. Bootleggers and prostitutes plied their trades more openly than before, and casual liaisons between servicemen and local women were not unusual. In an era when 'safe sex' was rarely discussed, the number of illegitimate children increased, and venereal disease became a growing cause for concern.

War brides arriving in Canada at Pier 21. Many of the nearly 48,000 war brides and their 22,000 children arrived in Canada through Pier 21. While they were destined for communities all across Canada, many of them found homes in the Maritimes. LAC, PA-47114.

The war also strained marriages and family life. Husbands who were absent for long periods of time might form new relationships, as might wives left at home. Wartime circumstances encouraged hasty marriages—in Newfoundland alone, more than 900 women married servicemen from either the United States or Canada, while many young men from the region found brides in Europe. As the war came to an end, there were demands in the Maritimes for easier and cheaper divorce, and in Newfoundland, where divorce was a taboo subject, the courts for the first time agreed to handle formal separations.

Post-war Reconstruction

As the war began to wind down, Ottawa asked each province to take stock of its future. Nova Scotia appointed a Royal Commission on Provincial Development chaired by Robert McGregor Dawson, a political scientist at the University of Toronto. New Brunswick enlisted Norman A.M. Mackenzie, president of the University of New Brunswick, to chair a commission, while Prince Edward Island chose Dr J.E. Lattimer, chair of the Department of Agricultural Economics at Macdonald College, McGill University, to head its inquiry. All three commissions recognized that the prosperity brought by the war was transient, that the unequal distribution of wartime benefits had aggravated regional disparities, and that the economy remained dangerously vulnerable. Nevertheless, there was hope that a post-war slump could be avoided and there was a growing consensus that state intervention would help to prevent a return to the desperate conditions that prevailed in the 1930s.

In 1940 the Rowell–Sirois Commission on Dominion–Provincial Relations had recommended equalization payments and national standards in basic services, reflecting a new approach both to federalism and to the poverty that co-existed with the wealth created by the industrial system. Since the beginning of the war Ottawa had been seriously considering a national policy that incorporated some welfare-state measures. Unemployment insurance was introduced in 1940 to cover industrial workers; in 1944, family allowances became the first in a series of universal programs; and in 1945 Mackenzie King proposed an ambitious federal reconstruction plan designed to address deficiencies in public works and social services.

Condemned by Ontario and Quebec as 'state socialism', this approach was also opposed by Angus L. Macdonald, who regained the premiership of Nova Scotia in 1945 after a wartime stint as minister of national defence for naval services. Macdonald had witnessed at close range the extent to which federal politics was dominated by central Canadian interests, and he had no wish to strengthen Ottawa's hand. As a result of provincial opposition the program was modified. In any event, it had never aimed to remedy uneven economic development or to give any special consideration to the Maritimes. The federal government had no desire to play the interventionist role and focused on cutting its losses. It closed down DOSCO's steel plate mill, for example, and paid farmers to uproot their apple trees when the British market remained closed to Canadian producers after the war.

Family Allowances and Public Schooling

After the establishment of public schooling in the mid-nineteenth century, education reformers in the Maritimes began demanding that attendance be compulsory. Poor families, who depended on the labour of their children to make ends meet, often found themselves in trouble with truant officers once compulsory schooling up to a certain age was made mandatory. Attitudes changed when the federal government tied payment of family allowances to school attendance for children up to the age 16. In Prince Edward Island François-E. Doiron, who monitored school attendance, noted in his 1946 report:

> The appointment of an Attendance Officer and the granting of Family Allowance, I believe, has been a forward step in education in this province. It is pleasing to note a very marked improvement in attendance in this inspectorate under the new system. In fact some of the schools are now overcrowded and hardly able to accommodate the increased number of pupils in attendance. It is true there are still some children of school age not going to school and trying to circumvent the work of the Attendance Officer, but as time goes on I believe the children will gradually become accustomed to attend regularly as they begin to realize that they cannot absent themselves from school with impunity as they have done in the past.[2]

The failure of governments to address regional needs in post-war reconstruction had disastrous results. By the late 1940s Pictou and Cape Breton counties had the highest unemployment rates in Canada, and employment in secondary manufacturing was fast declining. Out-migration again became the solution to economic problems. Unions, meanwhile, faced anti-communist hysteria and intimidation. Nowhere was this more obvious than on the Halifax waterfront, where in 1949 goon squads orchestrated by American labour leader Harold ('Hal') Banks used violence to break up the Communist-controlled Canadian Seamen's Union. The Canadian Fishermen and Fish Handlers' Union (CFFU), which launched a strike in December 1946, also faced intimidation tactics. The Nova Scotia government did not help matters—10 years after demonstrating a progressive approach to union matters, it introduced a Trade Union Act in early 1947 that weakened the position of organized workers.

For the three Liberal premiers in the Maritime provinces—Macdonald in Nova Scotia, J.B. McNair in New Brunswick, and 'Farmer' Walter Jones in Prince Edward Island—the post-war picture looked bleak. Their provinces lagged behind most of the rest of the country in health and educational services, and their roads could no longer accommodate the growing traffic. Other parts of North America were beginning to take electricity and running water for granted, but many people in the Maritimes still lived without either. New Brunswick had the dubious distinction of having the highest illiteracy rate in Canada and a social welfare policy that invited ridicule. In Prince Edward Island, 405 of the 473 schools had only one room and 69 of those were beyond repair. Elsewhere in Canada, the trend was toward large consolidated schools, but where would the Maritimes find the money to build them? As the North American economy began to improve, out-migration accelerated. There seemed to be no end to the dreary tale of economic decline.

While economic difficulties could not be ignored, other issues also began to dominate the political agenda. As a direct result of a war fought against the injustices of fascist regimes, issues of human rights and social justice became part of the post-war political agenda. Individual Canadian provinces began passing human rights legislation—Saskatchewan was the first in 1944—and the UN issued a Universal Declaration of Human Rights in 1948, which all members were urged to sign and implement. John Humphrey, born in Hampton, New Brunswick, played a leading role in crafting the stirring words of the declaration which claimed for all peoples basic human rights. These included the right to life, liberty, and security; the right to freedom of speech, thought, and assembly; and the right to a standard of living adequate for health and well-being, including 'food, clothing, housing and medical care and necessary social services, and the right to security in the event of unemployment, sickness, disability, widowhood, old age or other lack of livelihood'. Article 2 stated that 'Everyone is entitled to all the rights and freedoms set forth in this Declaration, without distinction of any kind, such as race, colour, sex, language, religion, political or other opinion, national or social origin, property, birth or other status.'[3]

The Maritimes and Newfoundland were slow to pass human rights legislation, but they could not ignore the issue for long. In 1945, the Nova Scotia Association for the Advancement of Coloured People (NSAACP) was organized, and the following year it raised money to help Viola Desmond, a beautician from Halifax, fight segregation in the province's movie theatres. The case against a New Glasgow theatre owner, who required Desmond to sit in the balcony because blacks were excluded elsewhere, was thrown out of court on a technicality, but the incident generated so much negative publicity that practices endorsing racial discrimination were gradually abandoned.

Newfoundland Joins Canada

The British government understood that Newfoundland's remarkable wartime prosperity was ephemeral and that its economy remained narrowly based and fundamentally unchanged. It also accepted that Commission government could not continue indefinitely, but feared—with reason—that if Newfoundland returned to responsible government there would be another financial crisis sooner or later and another application for British help. To insure against that possibility, a $100-million reconstruction scheme was developed by the Newfoundland government and approved by the Dominions Office. When the British Treasury denied funding, an approach was made to Ottawa, where the reaction was equally negative. Canadian officials did indicate, however, that they would favour bringing Newfoundland into Canada, preferably without a prior return to responsible government. Thus the reconstruction scheme was buried and the two governments quietly agreed, in late 1945, that their objective would be Confederation.

Ottawa was not enthusiastic about taking on what it saw as another 'Maritime' province, but it now recognized that Canada had vital long-term interests in Newfoundland and Labrador. The war had demonstrated how important that country was for defence and aviation; the economic potential of Labrador was well understood; and Ottawa feared that the large American presence on the island might draw Newfoundland into the orbit of the United States. Moreover, reports from the Canadian High Commission in St John's, established in 1941, suggested that Confederation might attract majority support.

In December 1945 the British government announced that citizens of Newfoundland and Labrador (the latter having the franchise for the first time) would elect a national convention to recommend the constitutional options to be placed on a referendum ballot. It was a calculated gamble, in that the British and Canadian governments could only hope that opinion in Newfoundland would come to favour Confederation.

The convention sat from September 1946 to January 1948. From the beginning it contained a vocal Confederate minority led by journalist, farmer, and broadcaster Joseph Smallwood and lawyer-turned-outport-businessman Gordon Bradley, who had been a member of the last Squires administration. Neither man was a member of the colonial elite, which was largely anti-Confederate. The convention's debates concerning the country's condition and prospects, broadcast by the government radio station, were closely followed. Delegations were sent to both London and Ottawa, where Smallwood and Bradley persuaded the federal government to formulate draft terms of union. Finally, after days of passionate discussion, Smallwood's motion to make Confederation an option was defeated, and the convention recommended that the referendum choice be between continuing with Commission government and returning to responsible government. However, the British government overruled the convention and placed all three options on the ballot. Anti-Confederates responded with outrage: where were British justice and fair play now?

As a result of this decision the anti-Confederates would have to mount an effective campaign to counter the Confederate crusade, but they were divided and lacked effective leadership. Smallwood and his allies stressed how Confederation would improve social security payments and services while reducing the cost of living. In his words, the referendum gave voters 'the best chance that they EVER HAD to make Newfoundland a better place for themselves and their families'. Who opposed these goals? 'Water Street [merchants] . . . the rich and wealthy . . . the few fortunate, well-fed, well-clothed, well-housed people amongst us.' Confederation was the cause of 'the toiling masses' who wanted 'a NEW Newfoundland'.[4]

The referendum, held on 3 June 1948, failed to settle the issue: responsible government received 44.6 per cent of the vote, Confederation 41.1, and Commission government 14.3. Thus a second, run-off vote was scheduled for 22 July. Although the Avalon Peninsula, including St John's, was strongly anti-Confederate, the Confederates were confident that victory was within reach. Stressing the economic benefits of Confederation, they also deliberately played the sectarian card. Members of every Orange lodge were reminded that many Roman Catholics—including members of religious orders, voting for the first time in history—opposed Confederation. Anti-Confederates were viciously accused of disloyalty to Britain, while Confederation was presented as 'British Union'.

In the end, Confederation emerged with a majority of 4.6 per cent over responsible government. The geographical voting pattern was largely unchanged. What gave the Confederates the edge was their success in attracting most of those who had supported Commission government in the first referendum—voters described by one member of the St John's elite as 'ignorant and avaricious outporters' who had 'handed over [Newfoundland] to Canada as a free gift'.[5] Although the victory was narrow in numerical terms, the fact that the Confederates took every district off the Avalon Peninsula and in Labrador meant that they had won the equivalent of an electoral landslide. Three factors in particular contributed to the final result: the significant social and economic changes that had taken place in Newfoundland and Labrador since the early 1930s, genuine uncertainty about the wisdom of returning to independence, and the desire to benefit from the social programs offered by post-war federalism. Newfoundlanders and Labradorians had great hopes and expectations for their future as a province.

During the negotiation of the final terms of union, there were difficulties over fisheries administration. That Newfoundland had to place its main industry under federal control caused some justifiable shaking of heads. Financial arrangements also caused some concern. The final deal included a special 12-year transitional grant and a federal

Joseph Smallwood as 'The Barrelman' on radio station VONF. Courtesy of the Atlantic Guardian, 1946, Archives and Manuscript Division, QEII Library, Memorial University, St John's.

The Radio and Confederation

Before he emerged as Newfoundland's Father of Confederation, 'Joe' Smallwood had become a household name throughout Newfoundland as the popular host of *The Barrelman*, a radio show intended to make Newfoundland better known to Newfoundlanders. The show's title referred to the lookout stationed on the 'barrel' or 'crowsnest' of a sealing vessel. During the Second World War radios became more widely available, and people listening to *The Barrelman* saw themselves reflected in Smallwood's folksy programs. Smallwood used the radio to great effect during the Confederation debates between 1946 and 1948 and in this passage notes the role that he believed it played in clinching the outcome of the referendum.

I had spent many years in broadcasting and I knew the magic of it. The sheer, sheer magic, especially in a place like Newfoundland with so many isolated people. Radio, I always contended, was invented by God especially for Newfoundland, and having done it for Newfoundland, He graciously allowed it to be used in other parts of the world. It was *meant* for Newfoundland. It was meant for remote and isolated people who never met, who never saw each other. Radio was a great unifying thing. I knew how to use it. I never let my mouth turn away from that microphone. Never. Many of the debaters at the Convention disdained the microphones. They wouldn't go near them with the result that my point of view was heard loud and clear in every home. The anti-Confederationists, disdaining radio as they did were not heard. The result was that when the referendum was held, Confederation passed by a narrow margin. I credit that margin to the use of radio.[6]

'Shall We Say Grace?' This cartoon from *The Confederate*, 20 May 1948, draws on memories of the Great Depression to emphasize the message that the wealthy elites supported a return to responsible government, which (allegedly) had only brought misery to the common people in the past.

undertaking, in Term 29, to establish within eight years a royal commission that would determine what additional assistance might be required to maintain adequate public services while keeping taxes comparable to Maritime rates. Although little was made of it at the time, it was significant that the benchmark for Newfoundland's success as Canada's tenth province under Term 29 was the standard of living in the Maritimes, not Canada as a whole. It is also significant that Native peoples disappeared from the text, the tacit decision being that they would be administered by the provincial government, with the federal government supplying the necessary funds.

By the end of 1948 the terms of union were settled, and Newfoundland became Canada's tenth province on 31 March 1949. Smallwood served as its first premier, and Bradley became its first representative in the federal cabinet. The ceremonies were subdued.

The entry of Newfoundland into Confederation was generally well received by people in the Maritime provinces. At Halifax's Mount Saint Vincent Ladies' College

The Aboriginal Peoples of Newfoundland and Labrador and the Terms of Union

The final draft of the terms of union between Newfoundland and Labrador and Canada made no mention of the new province's Native peoples, who were placed under provincial jurisdiction. How did this situation develop?

At the start of serious negotiations it was assumed on both sides that the federal government would, as elsewhere in Canada, take responsibility for Native people. The Canadian position changed in the fall of 1948 after a Newfoundland official suggested— during an unofficial discussion—that to apply the Indian Act to Native peoples in Labrador (Native people on the island of Newfoundland were not even mentioned) would be retrograde, and that it might be preferable for the provincial government to administer 'Indian affairs' with federal subsidies.

This proposition was eagerly adopted on the Canadian side, where there was no enthusiasm for taking responsibility for Native peoples—indeed, the federal government had recently tried to avoid taking responsibility for the Quebec Inuit. Another advantage was that it avoided the difficulties implicit in adapting the Indian Act to the different circumstances prevailing in Newfoundland and Labrador, where there was no equivalent to Canadian legislation, no treaties, no reserves, and where Native people were enfranchised. Moreover, this expedient seemed likely to save a considerable amount of money. Additional (and less convincing) justifications included the small number of Native people and the degree of racial mixing and absorption, which was exaggerated. The Newfoundland delegation accepted this position, and Native peoples disappeared from the terms of union.

It has been argued that the federal government in this way evaded its constitutional responsibilities to the Native peoples of Newfoundland and Labrador and that they have been significantly disadvantaged as a result. Certainly, they have not been treated on an equal footing with Native peoples elsewhere in Canada.[7]

the union prompted a pageant to welcome its Newfoundland students as Canadians. As the Antigonish *Casket* described it:

> The infant country was depicted through its long struggle for independence, with Great Britain, Canada and the United States always ready to hold out an invited hand. The hard choice being made, the new province was welcomed by Mother Canada who called in the nine provinces to extend individual welcomes, bring their gifts, and witness the crowning of Newfoundland as a tenth province.[8]

Others saw economic and political advantages to be gained by Newfoundland's entry into Confederation. One of the first and most ardent proponents of union was New Brunswick Senator and fishing magnate A. Neil McLean, who had invested in a modern fish-packing plant near Corner Brook and was eager to see a canal built across the Isthmus of Chignecto to facilitate communications within the region. Prince Edward Island Premier Walter Jones, who had spent considerable effort enhancing agricultural trade with the area, correctly predicted that greater volumes of Island beef and vegetables would soon reach kitchen tables in Newfoundland. Nova

Scotia Premier Angus L. Macdonald's enthusiasm was more muted, but even he saw the potential that the new province offered in providing justification for a causeway connecting Cape Breton to the Nova Scotia mainland. A few commentators saw the possibility of closer collaboration—perhaps union—among the four jurisdictions to mount a more effective campaign for better treatment from Ottawa, but none of the Maritime premiers (Liberals all) were prepared to go too far down that road, at least not then.

Conclusion

In 1949 a new region was born. Rather than being absorbed as a 'Maritime province', Newfoundland inspired new labels: 'Atlantic Provinces' and, by the 1960s, 'Atlantic Canada'. These were convenient terms for Ottawa to describe a space that had no effective regional identity and whose provinces often followed separate, at times conflicting, agendas. Although cushioned now by a kinder, gentler federalism, optimistic about the future, and part of a prosperous country, the region had to accept that 'Atlantic Canada' would function in a world where the centralization of political and economic power was irreversible.

Further Readings

Blake, Raymond B. 1994. *Canadians at Last: Canada Integrates Newfoundland as a Province.* Toronto: University of Toronto Press.

Christie, Carl. 1995. *Ocean Bridge: The History of RAF Ferry Command.* Toronto: University of Toronto Press.

Henderson, T. Stephen. 2007. *Angus L. Macdonald: A Provincial Liberal.* Toronto: University of Toronto Press.

Hiller, James K. 1998. *Confederation: Deciding Newfoundland's Future, 1934–1949.* St John's: Newfoundland Historical Society.

Jarratt, Melynda. 2008. *Captured Hearts: New Brunswick's War Brides.* Fredericton: Goose Lane and New Brunswick Military Heritage Project.

MacKenzie, David. 1986. *Inside the Atlantic Triangle: Canada and the Entrance of Newfoundland into Confederation, 1939–1949.* Toronto: University of Toronto Press.

Milner, Marc. 1985. *North Atlantic Run: The Royal Navy and the Battle for Convoys.* Toronto: University of Toronto Press.

———. 1994. *The U-Boat Hunters: The Royal Canadian Navy and the Offensive against Germany's Submarines.* Toronto: University of Toronto Press.

Neary, Peter. 1988. *Newfoundland and the North Atlantic World, 1929–1949.* Montreal: McGill-Queen's University Press.

Tennyson, Brian, and Roger Sarty. 1997. *The Maritime Defence of Canada.* Toronto: Canadian Institute for Strategic Studies.

Webb, Jeff A. 2008. *The Voice of Newfoundland. A Social History of the Broadcasting Corporation of Newfoundland, 1939-1949.* Toronto: University of Toronto Press.

Food for Thought

Tanner, Adrian. 1998. 'The Aboriginal Peoples of Newfoundland and Labrador and Confederation', *Newfoundland Studies* 14, 2 (Fall): 238–52.

Recommended Websites

Canadian War Brides
http://www.canadianwarbrides.com/

Newfoundland and Labrador Heritage
The Second World War, 1939–1945:
http://www.heritage.nf.ca/law/wwii.html

Newfoundland and Canada, 1864–1949:
http://www.heritage.nf.ca/law/confed.html

Pier 21
http://www.pier21.ca

The Second World War
http://www.vac-acc.gc.ca/remembers/sub.cfm?source=history/secondwar

Chapter 14

The Real Golden Age?
1949–75

The historian Eric Hobsbawm has argued that the three decades following the Second World War were a 'golden age' of 'extraordinary economic growth and social transformation, which probably changed human society more profoundly than any other period of comparable brevity'.[1] Scarred by two world wars and the Depression of the 1930s, almost everyone wanted to ensure that those experiences would never be repeated. At the same time, the Cold War underlined the opposition between two distinct routes to that end—capitalism and communism—and policy-makers on each side were eager to prove the merits of their own system. Governments at all levels played an important role in shaping a new world order that was designed to appeal to a broad spectrum of society.

In Canada, the federal government's commitment to economic planning, social welfare, and human rights created a receptive environment for efforts to pursue development in the Atlantic region. The result was economic and social transformation. Although this new golden age faded to bronze with the oil crisis of the 1970s, it left a legacy of interregional co-operation, institutional development, and claims to entitlement that still inform public policy.

The Atlantic Revolution

During the immediate post-war years, the trends long associated with the Atlantic region—low incomes, high unemployment rates, mass out-migration—continued unabated. Indeed, conditions became relatively worse as many other areas of North America experienced a period of unprecedented economic growth. In 1945 per capita income in the Maritimes was 24 per cent below the national average; by 1955 the difference had increased to 33 per cent. In that year Newfoundland, the nation's poorest province, recorded a per capita income 55 per cent below the national average.

Having promised Newfoundlanders that Confederation would usher in a new era, Premier Joseph Smallwood proved to be Atlantic Canada's most articulate and persistent spokesman for regional development. He recruited entrepreneurs from elsewhere and badgered what he called 'Uncle Ottawa' for financial aid. To improve his province's chances in that regard, he persuaded J.W. Pickersgill to run for the seat of Bonavista–Twillingate in 1953. As a former assistant both to Mackenzie King and to his successor, Louis St Laurent, the Manitoba-born Pickersgill was well placed to manipulate the levers of federal power, giving Newfoundland a powerful voice in Ottawa.

The Maritime premiers were also eager to obtain federal support for regional development. Following his election victory in New Brunswick in September 1952, Progressive Conservative

Table 14.1	Timeline
1951	Maritime Provinces Board of Trade establishes an office in Moncton
1954	Atlantic Provinces Economic Council founded; resettlement program begins in Newfoundland and Labrador.
1955	Canso Causeway opened; preliminary report of the Royal Commission on Canada's Economic Prospects.
1956	Ottawa passes equalization legislation; Conference of Atlantic Premiers.
1957	Industrial Estates Limited established in Nova Scotia.
1958	Ottawa approves Atlantic Provinces Adjustment Grants.
1959	Loggers' strike in Newfoundland.
1960	Aboriginal people in Canada granted the right to vote on the same terms as other Canadians.
1962	Atlantic Development Board established; Halifax City Council decides to relocate residents of Africville.
1964	Bryne Report advocates municipal reform in New Brunswick.
1967	Cape Breton Development Corporation created.
1968	BRINCO signs deal to sell transport Churchill Falls power to Hydro-Quebec through Quebec.
1969	New Brunswick declared a bilingual province; Prince Edward Island development plan signed; Black United Front founded; White Paper on Indian Policy; Department of Regional Economic Expansion created.
1970	Deutsch Report recommends Maritime Union; Report of the Royal Commission on the Status of Women.
1971	Council of Maritime Premiers founded.
1972	Parti Acadien founded.
1974–5	Strike by trawler crews in Newfoundland.

Premier Hugh John Flemming pursued an energetic program to develop 'power for industry' and was outraged when the St Laurent government refused assistance for the Beechwood power project on the St John River. Prince Edward Island's Liberal Premier Alexander Matheson was similarly offended when Ottawa insisted that his province return $1.4 million mistakenly paid out in per capita grants. In Nova Scotia, Premier Angus L. Macdonald, who had had his fill of federal politics during his wartime stint in Ottawa, was suspicious of federal schemes of any kind. His death in April 1954 opened the way for a more interventionist approach under Robert L. Stanfield, who led a Progressive Conservative government from 1956 to 1967.

Business interests played a critical role in defining the post-war version of regional protest. In 1951 the Maritime Provinces Board of Trade established an office in Moncton and began an aggressive campaign to encourage regional co-operation. The board sponsored a meeting with Atlantic premiers in 1953 and a year later helped create the Atlantic Provinces Economic Council, (APEC) designed to spearhead development efforts.

With economic development high on their agendas, government leaders were quick to respond to the demand for action. Ottawa's decision in 1955 to appoint the Royal Commission on Canada's Economic Prospects, chaired by Toronto accountant Walter Gordon, played into the regional agenda. In July 1956, when the Atlantic premiers met at the first of what would become regular conferences, Flemming presented a list of proposals that he hoped his fellow premiers would support: federal subsidies based on need; assistance for resource development; and fiscal, tariff, and transportation policies that would help to stimulate regional economic growth.

Blessed with treasury surpluses in the 1950s, the federal government looked for ways to accommodate what historian W.S. MacNutt described as an 'Atlantic Revolution'.[2] Equalization payments to the poorer provinces were instituted in 1956. The following year, Ottawa offered concessions on freight rates and power development and, at Pickersgill's insistence, seasonal fishery workers became eligible for unemployment insurance. Meanwhile, the preliminary report of the Gordon Commission, released in January 1957, singled out the Atlantic provinces as deserving 'positive and comprehensive' attention. A proposal to offer assistance in moving people from the region to growth centres elsewhere received well-deserved derision and was deleted from the final document.

The Progressive Conservatives adopt the Atlantic Resolutions

In his book *Gentlemen, Players and Politicians*, Progressive Conservative party organizer Dalton Camp described how the Atlantic Resolutions, which became the basis for the party's national platform in the June 1957 election, took shape. A meeting of the candidates from the Atlantic provinces, including two from Newfoundland, met in a Moncton hotel on 11 May. Along with New Brunswick organizer Kenneth Carson, Camp retreated to an upstairs room while candidates pondered their strategies downstairs. George Nowlan, the only Progressive Conservative to win a Nova Scotia seat in the 1953 election, Camp notes, 'commuted from the downstairs meeting to our upstairs room, offering encouragement, topping off our glasses, and refilling his own'. Camp continues:

> When we had had drafted a resolution to our common satisfaction, Nowlan would bear it downstairs, place it before candidates who cheerfully and promptly gave their consent. After the resolutions had been completed and approved, we drafted the preamble:

>> We, the Progressive Conservative Candidates from the 31 federal constituencies in the Atlantic provinces, believe the just demands of the Atlantic Community for recognition of their economic problems and special needs urgently require more united and forceful representation in the Parliament of Canada.

>> In keeping with the growing co-operative spirit of the people of the Atlantic community, which has already led to the creation of APEC and the Conference of Atlantic Premiers, we are resolved to stand together in support of these measures which will help to overcome the historic disabilities which have limited and even denied opportunity to this area. We believe our young people have the right to opportunity at home and we are convinced that only by united action by all individuals and all levels of government and the constructive efforts of private organizations, can this right be made real.

>> We believe that all those who live in this Atlantic community are entitled to the benefits of opportunity and security which shall be no more, but certainly no less, than all Canadians have the right to enjoy.

> Amendments and changes were few. Bill Browne, representing the unknown and isolated Tory party in Newfoundland, asked only that his province be specifically mentioned in the manifesto and this was cheerfully agreed. But apart from that the words remained largely as they were when George Nowlan brought them from our hotel room to the meeting below.[3]
>
> Dalton Camp continued to play a major role in the affairs of the Progressive Conservative Party and was central to convincing Robert Stanfield to challenge John Diefenbaker for national party leadership in 1967.

The Progressive Conservatives under John Diefenbaker also began to show greater sensitivity to regional concerns. During the 1957 election campaign, the party's candidates developed a series of 'Atlantic Resolutions' based on Flemming's proposals and the recommendations of the Gordon Commission. Diefenbaker squeaked through to victory and, for the first time in Canadian history, cabinet ministers from the Atlantic and Western provinces outnumbered those from Quebec and Ontario. Several policies dear to the hearts of Atlantic ministers were implemented before the next election in March 1958. With a $25-million Atlantic Provinces Adjustment Grant, a $29.5-million loan to the Beechwood power development, subventions for coal, and aid to thermal power development, 25 Progressive Conservatives from the region were smiling when the Diefenbaker government won by a landslide.

Only Newfoundland failed to give the Progressive Conservatives a majority of seats. Smallwood was not prepared to abandon the federal Liberals, and his influence remained dominant. Since 1949, he had generally stood at one remove from the 'Atlantic front' in the hope that his province's special status as the youngest member of Confederation would serve him better than the politics of regionalism. The strategy backfired. Smallwood had expected an annual grant of $15 million under Term 29, but in July 1958 the royal commission on the matter chaired by former New Brunswick premier John McNair recommended only $8 million. The Diefenbaker government not only accepted McNair's recommendation but also refused to make payments beyond 1962. A bitter confrontation erupted, and the province eventually settled with the Liberal government of Lester Pearson for $8 million in perpetuity. In 1996 Premier Brian Peckford negotiated a lump sum payment to cover a 20-year period. Whether payments will resume in 2016 is uncertain.

In the short term, the row over Term 29 was a useful diversion from Smallwood's belligerent suppression of a loggers' strike that occurred in central Newfoundland in 1959. The paper companies had deliberately tried to keep labour costs low by hiring subcontractors, who could be expected to underbid each other. Since the Newfoundland Lumbermens' Association had become ineffective, and its leader, Joe Thompson, wanted to retire, the loggers turned to the more aggressive International Woodworkers of America (IWA) and struck for better wages and working conditions. The Anglo-Newfoundland Development Company at Grand Falls resisted the union's demands, and the situation became increasingly tense. When Diefenbaker refused to send RCMP reinforcements as Smallwood requested, the premier dispatched members of the Newfoundland Constabulary—an urban police force—to keep the peace. A constable died in a confrontation with loggers at Badger. Smallwood and public opinion then turned against the IWA, the premier claiming that the IWA was riddled with communists, outsiders, and gangsters. The legislature decertified the IWA and created a new, conciliatory union. Although widely condemned for his actions, Smallwood survived. It was now clear, however, that if forced to choose, his government would side with corporate interests rather than with labour.

The Atlantic provinces benefited from a succession of minority governments in Ottawa between 1962 and 1968. In the dying days of the Diefenbaker administration, the Atlantic Development Board (ADB) was established to orchestrate investment in the region. When the Liberal Party under Lester Pearson formed a minority government after the 1963 election, it expanded the functions of the ADB and endowed it with funds. Other federal programs were tailored to meet the region's needs. After Pierre Elliott Trudeau became prime minister in 1968, his government replaced the ADB with the Department of Regional Economic Expansion (DREE), which applied regional development principles to the entire country.

Planning in the Provinces

Spurred by infusions of federal money, politicians and planners in the Atlantic provinces and Ottawa embarked on ambitious programs. Development agencies were created to attract industrial investment, and blueprints for social change multiplied impressively. Newfoundland had the farthest to go and went the fastest. Tapping into the cash surplus of $40.2 million bequeathed by the Commission government, Smallwood induced European firms to invest in 16 new industries between 1950 and 1956. All but one of the investors were German. Few of these industries survived for any length of time, and the program exhausted much of the surplus. It was perhaps unfortunate that Smallwood had decided to recruit—on C.D. Howe's recommendation—the Latvian economist Alfred Valdmanis as director of economic development. He spent money extravagantly and was eventually convicted in 1954 of fraud and extortion. However, not all the blame for the failure of the 'new industries' can be placed on Valdmanis's shoulders: he was, after all, doing what the provincial government wanted him to do.

The best prospects for resource development appeared to be in Labrador, with which Smallwood was increasingly obsessed. Western Labrador was opened to development in 1954 with the completion of the Quebec, North Shore, and Labrador Railway to Sept-Îles. The first mines were on the Quebec side of the border, but in the 1960s new mines and new towns—Labrador City in 1962 and Wabush in 1964—appeared on the Labrador side.

Robert Chambers, 'The Order of Good Cheer—circa 1960', *Atlantic Advocate*, September 1960. This cartoon reflects the optimism that circulated in the region as the 'Atlantic Revolution', led by the region's premiers, got under way. With permission from the Chambers family.

Smallwood was intent on exploiting the hydro potential of Labrador's Grand or Hamilton Falls (renamed Churchill Falls in 1965). In the early 1950s the province had leased the falls to the British Newfoundland Corporation (BRINCO), a consortium put together by the Rothschilds on Smallwood's initiative. Since Quebec refused to allow transmission lines to run across its territory to customers in Ontario and the United States, and the federal government would not intervene, BRINCO's subsidiary, the Hamilton Falls Power Company, was obliged from the outset to agree in principle to a long-term low-price deal with Hydro-Québec. In the protracted bargaining which eventually led to the 1968 power contract, Hydro-Québec was in a position to drive a hard bargain, and did so. BRINCO and HFPCo (from 1965 the Churchill Falls Labrador Co) were in financial difficulties, Hydro-Québec was the sole customer, and moreover, it was represented on HFPCo's board, having inherited the stake held before 1962 by a private Quebec power producer. Not only did Hydro-Québec obtain cheap power for 40 years, but it also insisted upon automatic renewal at the same mill rate for a further 25 years. A rate of 2.2 mills per kilowatt hour was cheap in 1968; today, it is 'an unbelievably low price' and a virtual giveaway if the renewal clause comes into operation in 2016.[4] Quebec has been reaping windfall profits from Churchill Falls since the mid-1970s, when energy prices began to rise steeply. Newfoundland's attempts to challenge the contract have failed, and it seems that Quebec will continue to collect a great deal of money from Churchill Falls until at least 2041. This debacle haunts the people of Newfoundland and Labrador to this day. Although Smallwood is often blamed for making the bad deal, it must be stressed that the provincial government was not directly involved in the negotiations and that Smallwood was presented with a fait accompli in 1968.

Smallwood was a leading proponent of another controversial policy. In 1954, as part of its diversification and modernization program, the government of Newfoundland began to encourage people living in small and remote outports to move to larger communities. A joint federal–provincial resettlement program followed in 1965. Approximately 30,000 people were relocated, and 250 communities disappeared between 1954 and 1970. By any standard, this was a spectacular exercise in social engineering and one that evidence suggests was supported more by outport women than by men. Those who moved enjoyed better public services, including education, medical care, electricity, and roads, but 'growth centres' often failed to provide the expected jobs and abandoning a deeply rooted way of life left many people with a profound sense of loss.

Smallwood was not alone among the Atlantic premiers in exercising state powers in controversial ways. In New Brunswick a young Louis J. Robichaud led his Liberal party to victory in June 1960 and appointed a cabinet in which the majority of members were francophones. Determined to improve conditions in the poor, rural municipalities where most Acadians lived, Robichaud established the Royal Commission on Municipal Finance and Taxation, chaired by Edward G. Byrne. Its 1964 report documented the inequalities that characterized New Brunswick municipalities and recommended sweeping changes. For Robichaud, this was a green light for massive reform in the province's municipal government.

For his 'Programme of Equal Opportunity' to succeed, Robichaud needed a civil service with the capacity to implement it. He therefore imported administrators from Saskatchewan, where the defeat of the CCF government in 1964 had freed up a significant pool of talent. The most important member of the so-called 'Saskatchewan mafia' was Donald Tansley, who became deputy minister of finance. Tansley's motto was 'Process Is the Policy', and he played a critical role in persuading Robichaud's cabinet to embrace new policies, including unionization of significant sectors of the civil service.[5]

Many anglophones complained that Robichaud's administration represented a 'French takeover', but they could not stop the transformation of New Brunswick's political landscape. The centralization of health and educational services, the establishment of a francophone university in Moncton in 1963, and the decision in 1969 to declare New Brunswick a bilingual province—the only one in Canada—underscored the growing power of the francophone minority. Robichaud lost the 1970 election to the Progressive Conservatives under Richard Hatfield, who wisely resisted pressure to turn back the clock. The new political and cultural realities were in New Brunswick to stay.

Prince Edward Island also joined the Atlantic Revolution. In 1969 Liberal Premier Alexander Campbell agreed to a 15-year Comprehensive Development Plan that promised an investment of $725 million ($255 million from Ottawa) to help restructure farming and fishing activities, improve infrastructure, and diversify the economy, most notably in the area of tourism. The agreement recognized that Prince Edward Islanders needed help if they were to maintain adequate services without sinking farther into debt. By 1971 the island had slipped below Newfoundland as the poorest province in Canada and its per capita debt was higher than that of any other Atlantic province. Even so, many Islanders were offended by the apparent arrogance of the planners. Del

Malcolm Rogers's house, moored off the beach at Dover, Bonavista Bay, waiting for high tide so it can be hauled ashore. It had been floated from Fox Island as part of Newfoundland's outport resettlement program in the 1960s. B. Brooks, LAC, PA-154123.

Gallagher, a New Brunswicker who spearheaded the development program, was particularly un-popular, and jokes about 'Gallagher's Island', in reference to a popular American television series, became commonplace.[6]

The Stanfield government in Nova Scotia signalled its interest in economic planning with the creation in 1957 of Industrial Estates Limited to promote investment. By the early 1960s two Swedish firms, Volvo and Stora Forest, had been persuaded to locate in Nova Scotia. Michelin Tire arrived in the 1970s and became one of the province's largest employers with plants in Bridgewater, Granton, and Waterville.

The crisis in the coal and steel industries spurred further government intervention. With oil and gas rapidly replacing coal as the fuels of choice and the demand for steel rails shrinking dra-matically, Nova Scotia's industrial base collapsed. Following the recommendations of the 1960 Royal Commission on Coal, chaired by Chief Justice Ivan Rand, the federal government embarked on a program to develop alternative industries on Cape Breton Island, where the hardship was most acute. Money was pumped into Cape Breton Highlands National Park and the rebuilding of the fortress of Louisbourg, but these initiatives absorbed only a fraction of the workers facing unemployment. Cape Bretoners left in droves for jobs on the mainland, their departure made easier by the completion of the Canso Causeway in 1955. To mitigate both human distress and unpleasant political repercussions, Ottawa created the Cape Breton Development Corporation in 1967, which purchased and operated the mines. The provincial government established the Sydney Steel Corporation, which bought the steel mill.

The push for economic development in Atlantic Canada had positive and negative aspects. With government assistance, Halifax, Port Hawkesbury, and Saint John emerged as superports and a few home-grown entrepreneurs emerged—K.C. Irving, the McCain brothers, Frank Sobey, Harry Steele, and R.A. Jodrey, in particular. At the same time, there was a price to pay for governments that jumped on the corporate bandwagon. To keep their investors happy, both Newfoundland and Nova Scotia passed restrictive labour legislation (Nova Scotia's became known as 'the Michelin bill'). K.C. Irving moved to Bermuda to avoid Canadian taxation even though his oil, transporta-tion, and media empire benefited greatly from government assistance.

Eager to support economic development, political leaders notoriously backed a series of 'white elephants'. Clairtone Sound and the Point Tupper Heavy Water plant were serious embarrassments for the Stanfield government. Hatfield's image was tarnished when the Bricklin gull-wing sports car on which he had pinned his industrial hopes proved unviable. Throughout the region, government-assisted food- and fish-processing operations appeared and disappeared with unnerving regularity. Smallwood, ever a gambler on the next big project, fell victim to several dubious American entre-preneurs in the 1960s, among them John Shaheen. The premier's decision to back Shaheen's plan for an oil refinery and petrochemical plant at Come By Chance prompted two of his most ambitious ministers, John Crosbie and Clyde Wells, to leave the Cabinet in 1968. Three years later, a revived Progressive Conservative Party under Frank Moores defeated Smallwood's government.

Although politicians liked to conjure up visions of an 'Atlantic Community', they often dis-agreed on how to achieve regional development. Prince Edward Island felt cheated when the Atlantic Provinces Adjustment Grant was divided on a 30:30:30:10 ratio, and each province had its own ideas about which capital projects should have priority if and when Ottawa could be induced to provide funding. By the early 1970s Labradorians were starting to resent what they perceived as their exploitation by a provincial government that otherwise ignored them. A Labrador flag was created in 1974, and the New Labrador Party was formed in time for the 1971 provincial election, where it proved to be the spoiler.

In 1964 Robichaud added yet another controversial project to the mix: union of the Atlantic provinces. His francophone supporters might well have opposed such a move, but it was popular in Ottawa, which was growing impatient with the region's proliferating demands. At Robichaud's urging, the three Maritime premiers—Smallwood remained aloof—established a commission in 1968 to study the issue. It was chaired by Queen's University professor John Deutsch, who recommended unification in his 1970 report. Not surprisingly, this advice was largely ignored. The commission's most important outcome was the creation of the Council of Maritime Premiers, established in 1971.

Social Adjustments

While political and business elites manoeuvred and negotiated, ordinary Atlantic Canadians were living the post-war revolution in their daily lives. The impact of economic restructuring is reflected in the statistics. During the 1950s alone, the numbers of people working in agriculture dropped by 49 per cent, in fishing and trapping by 37 per cent, in forestry by 24 per cent, and in mining by 22 per cent. The exit from primary pursuits continued through the 1960s. Each sector had its own cycle, but all were reshaped to meet the demands of an increasingly bureaucratized, centralized, mechanized, and, ultimately, computerized world.

Long an endangered species, the family farm survived only by adopting corporate practices. Quotas, marketing boards, and national standards spelled the end of part-time farming for any purpose apart from personal pleasure. Whereas one in five people had lived on farms in 1951, only one in 50 did so thirty years later. Apple growers in the Annapolis Valley, faced with the permanent closure of the British market, were encouraged by generous government subsidies to uproot their trees and convert their acreage to mixed crops for a regional market. Most of them got out of farming altogether.

In Prince Edward Island, the National Farmers Union and the Brothers and Sisters of Cornelius Howatt—named after the island's most famous nineteenth-century anti-Confederate—staged a protest in 1971 against development policies that they believed had contributed to the decline of family farming. At the height of tourist season, they jammed the highway between Charlottetown and Borden with their tractors, but general trends in agriculture were unaffected. Between 1951 and 1981, the proportion of Islanders employed in farming dropped from nearly 50 per cent to less than 10 per cent, and the number of farms from 10,137 to 3,154.

The story was the same in forestry, where mechanization had made it possible to fell and process more trees with fewer workers. In New Brunswick milling for the construction industry continued to thrive, but even there, as elsewhere in the region, the major product was pulpwood. By the 1980s the 19 pulp-and-paper operations in Atlantic Canada depended on foreign markets and faced intense competition. In the absence of tough environmental laws, companies were tempted to cut and run rather than follow the more costly forestry practices required to ensure a sustainable industry. A side effect of the over-exploitation of forest resources was a monoculture of softwood trees that invited periodic spruce budworm infestations.

In mining, restructuring produced mixed results. A growing demand for base metals such as lead, zinc, copper, and iron produced a mining boom in northern New Brunswick and western

Labrador. The most dramatic new frontier was offshore oil and natural gas, to which multinational investors were attracted by generous tax incentives. On the down side, the steady decline of the coal industry meant hard times for many communities. Mine disasters in Springhill in 1956 and 1958 tragically underlined the inadequacy of safety measures in superannuated mines. The fluor-spar industry on the Burin Peninsula appeared to be a success story, but the discovery that radon gas was causing cancer in workers, together with the availability of cheaper ore from Mexico, led to its closing in 1977.

Meanwhile, modernization and expansion in the fisheries set the stage for a dramatic collapse before the end of the century. In the early 1950s Europeans began sending freezer trawlers to the banks fishery, signalling a major transition in the region's oldest primary industry. With the emphasis on the offshore banks and fresh or frozen fish, on the plant rather than the fish stage, and overwhelmingly on the American market, salt fish production declined. Meanwhile, a record 810,000 tonnes of groundfish were taken in 1968. Eager to tap a resource on its own doorstep, the Canadian government declared a nine-mile limit in 1964, a 12-mile limit in 1970, then a 200-mile limit in 1977, and encouraged massive investment. The number of people engaged in the fisheries began to rise for the first time in over a century.

The expansion of employment in the fisheries notwithstanding, most of the jobs created in the new 'golden age' were in the burgeoning trade and service sectors, and often tied to state spending. By the early 1960s government employment accounted for over 100,000 jobs in the Atlantic region—more than forestry and mining combined. The Department of Defence, its budgets fattened by spending associated with the Korean War (1950–3) and the Cold War, employed 41,000 Atlantic Canadians in 1961. Many military bases received a new lease on life, and several new ones, such as CFB Gagetown in New Brunswick, were established. While Nova Scotia led the region in dependence on defence jobs—over 11 per cent of its labour force was employed in defence in 1961—all four Atlantic provinces benefited economically from the federal government's decision to locate more than one-quarter of the nation's armed forces on the east coast.

Many Atlantic Canadians had difficulty making the transition from primary to tertiary industries. Those displaced from farming, forestry, and mining industries often lacked the skills required by the available jobs and were obliged to find work outside the region. Increasingly, skilled employment went to qualified immigrants. Employment in areas traditionally dominated by women—clerical, teaching, nursing, social work—expanded rapidly. As more women entered the paid workforce, their subordinate positions and unfair wage scales caused concern, and some people began questioning gender relations within the family. At the same time the region's Aboriginal, Acadian, and African minorities voiced objections to their unequal access to new economic opportunities.

The human costs of economic transformation were alleviated in part by government intervention in the form of Ottawa's welfare-state policies: universal family allowances (1944), old-age pensions (1951), hospital insurance (1957), Medicare (1968), and Canada pension (1965) and social assistance (1966) plans. Unemployment insurance (now employment insurance) expanded in the post-war period to cover a growing number of Canadian workers, including the seasonally unemployed. For those who never had much disposable income, these programs often meant the difference between dignified subsistence and outright destitution.

Political leaders saw formal education as the key to success in the new economy and focused energy and funds on educational infrastructure. In the 1950s school enrolments in Atlantic

Canada grew from 338,364 to 485,051, with most of the so-called baby boomers attending large and new consolidated institutions. Vocational schools proliferated and universities were transformed. In the 1940s most Atlantic Canadian universities were small, private operations, often with religious affiliations. By 1970 Atlantic Canada boasted an impressive network of state-funded universities and a total enrolment of 15,820 students, up from just 5,811 a decade before. The Maritime Provinces Higher Education Commission was established to control escalating costs and duplication of programs, but university enrolments and budgets continued to rise, making higher education one of the most important industries in the region.

People's Politics

Businessmen, politicians, and bureaucrats were not the only ones responsible for the changes taking place in Atlantic Canada. Ordinary people also had an impact. Established organizations such as churches and unions adjusted to rapidly changing conditions, and new organizations to encourage reform sprouted like mushrooms across the Atlantic Canadian landscape.

Structural changes in the workforce were reflected in the fortunes of the labour movement. From a high of 32 per cent in 1953, union membership dropped to a low of 21 per cent in the early 1960s. As white-collar workers—teachers, nurses, and government employees—began signing union cards, the percentage rose again. Workers remaining in primary industries also organized more aggressively to protect their interests. By the 1980s Newfoundland had the highest proportion of organized labour in the region—37 per cent—primarily because of a 1971 decision to grant collective bargaining rights in the fishery. The Newfoundland Fishermen, Food, and Allied Workers, under its feisty leader Richard Cashin, fought two successful actions: a strike at Burgeo in 1971 and a massive work stoppage by trawler crews in 1974–5. In Canso a protracted strike led by the United Fishermen and Allied Workers' Union in 1970 won concessions in prices and berthing facilities, only to be challenged by the Canadian Food and Allied Workers Union, whose leaders were determined to represent workers in all facets of the fisheries.

The fact that the region's business and government leaders tended to treat ordinary people as just another natural resource helped to build support for the New Democratic Party (NDP). Created in 1961 through a marriage of the old CCF and organized labour, the NDP gradually gained strength in the region. Support came initially from Cape Breton but soon spread elsewhere, most notably in Halifax, as white-collar workers began reconsidering their traditional political allegiances.

By the early 1970s the voice of labour had strengthened considerably. When Nigadoo Mines near Bathurst, New Brunswick, announced in January 1972 that it was suspending operations and putting 300 employees out of work, it provoked an angry outburst from locals, who organized a 'Day of Concern'. Attended by Jean Marchand (the minister responsible for DREE), Premier Hatfield, and the leaders of both federal and provincial opposition parties, it sparked the creation of a $10-million temporary make-work program. Together, the protest and the response it received were testimony to the political climate of the day, when it was widely accepted that all levels of government had a responsibility to address poverty and unemployment.

The Day of Concern also reflected complex developments in New Brunswick's francophone community. While not all francophones in the Maritimes were descended from pre-Deportation Acadians, most identified with the deeply rooted Acadian heritage. Many working-class and younger francophones were becoming increasingly critical of the gradualist approach taken by their leaders. In 1968 the refusal of Moncton's mayor, Leonard Jones, to consider making the municipality bilingual precipitated a confrontation between the city council and students from the Université de Moncton. Student unrest flared again early in January 1972 after a showing of the National Film Board's *L'Acadie, l'Acadie* and, together with the mine closures, inspired the creation of the Parti Acadien. Although the new party's goal was to politicize francophones rather than to win seats, it fielded candidates in provincial elections between 1974 and 1984 and made headlines with its call for a francophone province—'Acadie'—in northeastern New Brunswick. Premier Hatfield's implementation of sections of the Official Languages Act helped to defuse some of the anger while confirming, once and for all, the bilingual character of the province.

Considerably fewer in numbers than their New Brunswick counterparts, francophones in Nova Scotia and Prince Edward Island had more reason to be concerned about their cultural survival. Some 90 per cent of those of French heritage in New Brunswick claimed French as their mother tongue in 1960, but only 45 per cent did so in Nova Scotia and Prince Edward Island. In 1967 francophones in Nova Scotia formed the Fédération Acadienne de la Nouvelle-Écosse in 1967, while the Société Saint-Thomas-d'Aquin, established in Prince Edward Island in 1919, took on a more active political role. The Island's legislature became officially bilingual in 1968, and all four provinces gradually made concessions in the area of French-language schooling. Francophone groups in Newfoundland and in Labrador began organizing in the early 1970s, forming the Fédération francophone de Terre-Neuve et du Labrador in 1973. With Moncton serving as the capital of the larger regional Acadie, French-language radio, television, arts, and cultural expression flourished.

As issues of human rights and social justice became part of the political agenda, members of the black minority stepped up their protests against second-class status. In 1954 the Nova Scotia government, spurred by the civil rights movement in the United States, quietly dropped a clause in the province's education act sanctioning separate black schools, and the last segregated school was closed in the early 1960s. New Brunswick's smaller black community formed its own Association for the Advancement of Coloured People in 1959, a counterpart to a similar organization established in Nova Scotia in 1945. In the 1960s all provinces in the region passed human rights legislation and established monitoring agencies. A federal Bill of Rights was passed in 1960, but it lacked the teeth necessary to force compliance.

Encouraged by the Black Power movement in the United States and galvanized by the decision of Halifax city council to demolish the black community of Africville, African Nova Scotians stepped up their efforts to fight discrimination and crippling poverty. The Black United Front (BUF) was founded in Halifax in 1969, after a visit to the city by Stokeley Carmichael and other leaders of the Black Panthers. Working with grants from both the federal and provincial governments, BUF leaders sponsored workshops and projects designed to help African Nova Scotians to increase both their self-esteem and their material well-being. The Black Cultural Society, established in 1977, accomplished one of its major goals in 1983 with the opening of the Black Cultural Centre in Dartmouth.

Like Africville, black communities near urban centres elsewhere in the region also disappeared in the twentieth century, the result of out-migration and galloping development. The black population living in Charlottetown's prosaically named Bog district, for instance, began to decline drastically in the first decade of the twentieth century, and in the 1960s a provincial government building was located on the site that in 1881 had been home to nearly 200 black Islanders.

Student unrest hit the Atlantic region in February 1968, when students at the Université de Moncton boycotted classes for 10 days to protest fee increases and then (with the silent blessing of university presidents) led a province-wide 'sit-in' at government offices in Fredericton. Centre d'études acadiennes Anselme-Chiasson, Université de Moncton. UM-008453, Centre d'études acadiennes Anselme-Chiasson, Université de Moncton.

As in earlier periods blacks in the region often found their prospects better elsewhere than in their native provinces. One example is Fredericton-born Willie O'Ree, who in 1958 became the first—and until 1986 the only—black player in the National Hockey League. Although blind in one eye (as a result of being hit by a puck), he was an exceptional left-winger and played in the junior leagues in Kitchener and Quebec City before being recruited to the Boston Bruins' farm team. He played in two Bruins' games in 1958 and for much of the 1961 season before being traded to other teams.

Aboriginal people also adopted a more activist approach. After three centuries of decline, their numbers in the region had finally begun to increase, reaching 18,000 by 1981. Revisions to the

Africville

The plight of blacks in Nova Scotia received international attention when the city of Halifax decided to demolish Africville. Located on the shores of Bedford Basin, Africville had been home to Halifax's black population since the mid-nineteenth century. The community had been shamefully neglected. The city provided no water and sewage services or garbage collection and had located the municipal dump nearby. Even after a serious fire in December 1947 drew attention to the lack of a water supply, the city authorities failed to act.

In 1962, without consulting the residents, the city council decided to relocate them and to use the site for industrial development. The residents' protests caught the attention of human rights activists. In 1965 both the CBC and *Maclean's* offered critical commentary, and in 1969 representatives of the US-based Black Panther movement arrived to lend support. Aaron Carvery, the last resident to reach a settlement with the city, was invited to City Hall in December 1969 and shown a 'suitcase full of money tied up in neat bundles'—$14,000—as an inducement to move.[7] He eventually received an apology for this outrageous attempt at a bribe, but the city pressed on with its plans for relocation. Most whites and a few blacks argued that urban renewal was a necessary prelude to a better future for all Haligonians.

Residents were compensated for their property and offered alternative housing, but they resented being treated as if they were unable to decide what was best for them. The use of garbage trucks instead of moving vans to relocate some members of the community seemed to symbolize the city's attitude. The residents also feared the loss of community, but, if anything, the destruction of Africville galvanized community spirit. Because of the prolonged struggle, Africville has not been forgotten and has been immortalized in books, films, and songs. Every year a picnic is held on the site of the former community, part of which is now a park.

Indian Act in 1951 eliminated some of its more repugnant features and finally granted women the right to vote in band elections. In 1960 status Indians were enfranchised. Ottawa's desire to abolish both the Indian Act and Indian status, articulated in a controversial 1969 White Paper, provoked a national effort to redress long-standing grievances and resist assimilation. By this time, the Union of New Brunswick Indians (1967) and Union of Nova Scotia Indians (1969) had been established.

In Labrador, more funds were invested in Aboriginal health, education, and housing. In the late 1950s, however, the provincial government decided, in concert with the Grenfell and Moravian missions, to close the northern Inuit settlements of Nutak and Hebron and move their residents to communities farther south. Neither the people who were to be relocated nor the people who were to receive them were consulted. As the Labrador Inuit Association has put it: 'The government told [us] that our social and economic welfare would be improved. Instead, a social, cultural and economic disintegration occurred, the effects of which can be felt to this day.'[8] In 2005 Premier Danny Williams issued a formal apology on behalf of the government for the way the decision was made and the difficulties that the people and their descendents experienced as a result of the move.

The consequences of relocation were perhaps even more devastating for the semi-nomadic Innu who in the 1960s were settled at Sheshatshiu and Davis Inlet. Arguably no Aboriginal group in the region suffered more in this period. The distress that accompanied the collapse of the fur trade was compounded by high rates of tuberculosis and the loss of traditional lands—without any compensation—to mining operations in western Labrador, military installations at Goose Bay, and the Churchill Falls project, including the enormous Smallwood Reservoir. In 1973 both the Labrador Inuit Association and the Federation of Newfoundland and Labrador Indians were formed. The latter soon split into island and Labrador components, and in 1990 the Labrador Innu adopted the name Innu Nation.

Despite its social difficulties and poor economic prospects, the Atlantic region continued to attract immigrants in the post-war period. War brides and their children, most of them of British background, were followed by refugees and displaced persons from Europe and domestic workers from the Caribbean. After Canada's immigration laws were liberalized in the 1960s, people from all over the world began arriving in Atlantic Canada. Their presence had little impact on the overall cultural mix, in part because many of them moved on. With the exception of the Dutch, who tended to take up farming, most of those who stayed settled in urban centres. During the Vietnam War (1965–75) 'draft dodgers' from the United States slipped across the border, and many of them took root.

In the Atlantic provinces as across North America, some of the most dramatic developments in the post-war period involved the changing status of women. Women flocked to jobs in the paid labour force and began entering university in unprecedented numbers. Meanwhile, the plummeting birth rate, escalating divorce rate, and increasing incidence of single motherhood prompted traditionalists to make dire predictions about the future of the family. Most women now had no more than two children, if they had any at all, and increasingly both parents worked outside the home.

In this period, Atlantic Canadian women joined their counterparts throughout North America in breaking down the barriers to achieving equality. Provincial branches of national women's organizations pushed for a variety of reforms. By the late 1960s, married women were eligible for civil service jobs that had previously been denied them, and quotas restricting women's entry into law, medical, and engineering schools had disappeared. The achievement of Helena Squires, who became the region's first elected female politician when she sat in the Newfoundland House of Assembly between 1930 and 1932, was finally matched in Nova Scotia when former Kentville mayor Gladys Porter was elected to the legislature in 1960. In 1953 Muriel Fergusson, Fredericton's first female alderperson, was named to the Senate, and in 1972 she became the first woman to be appointed Speaker. The Royal Commission on the Status of Women, which reported in 1970, eventually prompted provincial governments to establish commissions and advisory councils to address women's issues, to legislate equal pay and a fairer division of marital property upon divorce, and to fund women's centres and shelters.

Another issue that stimulated regional action was world peace, which was commonly threatened during the Cold War. In 1960 Halifax became one of the first cities in Canada to form a branch of the Voice of Women, an organization devoted to peace and disarmament. Three years earlier, Pugwash, Nova Scotia, had been the site of a unique effort to put an end to the nuclear madness that defined the Cold War. Twenty-two scientists from around the world, including the United States and the Soviet Union, converged on the summer home of the Nova Scotia-born industrialist Cyrus Eaton to discuss nuclear disarmament. In 1995 the Pugwash Conference on Science and World Affairs was awarded the Nobel Peace Prize for its efforts on behalf of world peace.

Environmental issues also inspired political activism. As early as 1962, in her groundbreaking book *Silent Spring*, Rachel Carson had singled out the 'rivers of death' created in New Brunswick by aerial pesticide spraying. In the 1970s Betty Keddy mobilized opposition to budworm spraying in New Brunswick, while Elizabeth May led a similar campaign in Cape Breton. At the same time, animal rights groups, especially the International Fund for Animal Welfare led by New Brunswick's Brian Davies, mounted a high-profile attack on the seal hunt, arguing in particular that the clubbing of seal pups was cruel and unnecessary. Greenpeace joined in, bringing French movie star Brigitte Bardot to the ice floes in 1977 and calling for boycotts of seal products in Europe and the United States. Newfoundlanders were outraged both by the threat the anti-sealing campaign posed for the rural economy and by what they saw as an unwarranted assault on their culture. Among the responses was a theatre production by The Mummers' Troupe in St John's entitled *They Club Seals, Don't They?*

Cultural Awakenings

For many Atlantic Canadians in this period, and especially for the baby boomers who came of age in the 1960s, life was defined as much by popular culture as it was by political developments. Elders were alarmed by what they saw as rampant hedonism, but there was little they could do to stem the tide of mass consumer culture that swept across North America from Hollywood, Nashville, New York, Montreal, and Toronto. Standoffs between teachers and students over the length of boys' hair (too long) and girls' skirts (too short) became common as did debates at home between parents and their teenage children over the rights and wrongs of pre-marital sex and the level of sound on radios and record players. In many recreational settings, the smell of marijuana smoke wafted gently on the air. It was the age of sex, drugs, and rock 'n roll.

The sexual revolution was sustained in large measure by the introduction of the birth control pill in the early 1960s. Despite the continuing proscription against the dissemination of birth control, doctors prescribed it, women embraced it, and the average size of families almost instantly declined. The proscription against birth control was finally dropped from the Criminal Code in 1969. At the same time, reforms of the law relating to homosexual relations, divorce, and abortion were introduced. Gays and lesbians began 'coming out of the closet', divorce rates skyrocketed, and the official rates of abortion increased dramatically.

This period also witnessed an unprecedented cultural expression. Improvements in education, nation-wide radio and television networks, and federal support for Canadian culture all fed into a cultural awakening that continues to generate excitement in the Atlantic region and beyond. In music the region produced a roster of stars that stretched back to the 1930s, when Don Messer and His Islanders began broadcasting from CFCY Charlottetown and Wilf Carter became a popular radio performer, better known in the United States as Montana Slim. Following the Second World War, Hank Snow became a regular at the Grand Ole Opry, and Anne Murray rose to international fame in 1969 with her rendition of 'Snowbird', composed by Prince Edward Island's Gene MacLellan. Carroll Baker won numerous Juno Awards, Stompin' Tom Connors became a Canadian icon, and although Stan Rogers grew up in Ontario, many of his songs were inspired by his Maritime roots. Edith Butler introduced Acadian folk songs to international audiences and, along with Prince Edward Island's Angèle Arsenault, composed new songs documenting the Acadian slant on the world. In their wake came a whole host of Acadian singers and songwriters. The Celtic traditions of Newfoundland and Cape Breton inspired a remarkable number of popular performers, starting with John Allan Cameron and Rita McNeil. They were soon followed by,

In 1944 the Nova Scotia-born contralto Portia White (1910–68), who had already won national acclaim, made her New York debut. She later toured the United States, Europe, and the Caribbean. LAC, PA-192783.

among others, The Wonderful Grand Band, Figgy Duff, Rawlins Cross, the Rankin Family, and Natalie MacMaster. Following the success of Portia White, a gifted contralto who performed at New York's Carnegie Hall in 1944, African Nova Scotian musicians, such as the a capella group Four the Moment, found enthusiastic audiences.

Halifax's Neptune Theatre opened in 1963, and in 1964, the centennial of the Charlottetown Conference, the Confederation Centre of the Arts (home of the Charlottetown Festival) opened in Charlottetown. Theatre New Brunswick followed in 1968. In St John's, the success of CODCO and the Mummers' Troupe, based in a former downtown union hall, laid the groundwork for the team that made *This Hour Has 22 Minutes*, a television phenomenon in the 1990s.

In the post-war period a new cultural maturity was being reflected in the regionally grounded work of poets and novelists such as Milton Acorn, Ernest Buckler, Harold Horwood, Percy Janes, Antonine Maillet, Alden Nowlan, and Ted Russell. They cleared the path for the next generation of literary greats, which included George Elliott Clarke, Wayne Johnston, Rita Joe, Ann-Marie MacDonald, Alistair MacLeod, David Adams Richards, Herménégilde Chiasson, and Maxine Tynes. Regional themes also inspired filmmakers. Don Shebib's award-winning film *Goin' Down the Road* (1970) exposed the plight of working-class Maritimers in Ontario, and Gordon Pinsent's *John and the Missus* (1974) was a gripping portrayal of outport resettlement in Newfoundland.

In this period, artists such as Alex Colville and his students at Mount Allison University, including Christopher Pratt, Mary Pratt, and Tom Forrestall, developed representational art in a direction that has come to be called 'Atlantic realism'. New Brunswick artists such as Miller Brittain often portrayed the harsher side of Maritime life. The same was true of David Blackwood, who gained widespread acclaim for his images of the seal hunt and other aspects of traditional life on Newfoundland's northeast coast. In Prince Edward Island, artists such as Erica Rutherford revealed new ways of looking at the island landscape. By the end of the twentieth century, Native artists who had long been excluded from formal channels of art education and marketing in the region began to exhibit their work, among them Ned Bear, Shirley Bear, Teresa Marshall, Leonard Paul, Jonathan Sark, Alan Syliboy, and Gilbert Hay. The region's self-taught folk artists, including Maud Lewis, Joseph Norris, Arch Williams, and Joseph Cullen, added yet another dimension of locally rooted artistic expression.

In Newfoundland in particular, a large part of the cultural awakening—dubbed 'the Newfoundland Renaissance' by Sandra Gwyn—involved questioning the assumption that

Antonine Maillet

Born in Bouctouche, New Brunswick, in 1929, Antonine Maillet gained international acclaim by giving an imaginative voice to Acadians in Atlantic Canada. Her plays, short stories, and novels were inspired by her Acadian roots, which offered plenty of drama for her creative genius.

Although her writing career began in the late 1950s, the research she conducted for her 1970 PhD dissertation in literature at Laval University deepened the quality of her work. Published in 1971 as *Rabelais et les traditions populaires en Acadie*, it catalogued over 500 archaic phrases and figures of speech from sixteenth-century French that were still used in the Acadian communities. She brought this knowledge to *La Sagouine* (1971), a series of humorous monologues by an old Acadian washerwoman. The play highlighted the unique Acadian dialect and was performed in both French and English throughout North America and Europe by Viola Leger. In 1972 Maillet followed up this success with the fantastic tale of *Don L'Orignal* (1972), which won the Governor General's Award for Fiction (French). Her 1979 epic novel *Pélagie-la Charette*, chronicling the story of the 10-year odyssey of a group of Acadians returning to their homeland 15 years after their expulsion, won her the prestigious French *Prix Goncourt*. Now living in Montreal, Maillet represents the best of the Acadian cultural revival that continues to inspire extraordinary talent.

Confederation was an unqualified good. By the mid-1970s, a new awareness of the province's history and culture was fuelling a sense of provincial nationalism that would have serious implications for federal–provincial relations.

Conclusion

If the period from 1949 to 1975 represents Atlantic Canada's golden age, it was gold-plated rather than pure metal. Although modernization had brought impressive changes, many of the old economic and social patterns remained in place. Out-migration was slowing but not halted, economic stagnation was confronted but not vanquished, and 'have-not' status was still an ever-present reality. What *was* striking about the period, in retrospect, was the conviction that progress was possible. The closing years of the twentieth century would test the convictions of even the most enduring optimist.

Further Readings

Acadiensis XXXV, 2 (Spring 2006), special issue on Atlantic Canada since 1939.

Bickerton, James P. 1990. *Nova Scotia, Ottawa, and the Politics of Regional Development*. Toronto: University of Toronto Press.

Conrad, Margaret. 1988. *George Nowlan: Maritime Conservative in Maritime Politics*. Toronto: University of Toronto Press.

Fingard, Judith, and Janet Guildford, eds. 2005. *Mothers of the Municipality: Women, Work, and Social Policy In Post-1945 Halifax*. Toronto: University of Toronto Press.

Fleming, Berkeley. 1988. *Beyond Anger and Longing: Community and Development in Atlantic Canada*. Sackville and Fredericton: Centre for Canadian Studies, Mount Allison University and Acadiensis Press.

Gwyn, Richard. 1999. *J. Smallwood, the Unlikely Revolutionary*. Toronto: McClelland and Stewart.

Overton, James. 1996. *Making A World of Difference: Essays on Tourism, Culture and Development in Newfoundland*. St John's: Institute of Social and Economic Research.

Smitheram, Verner, David Milne, and Satadal Dasgupta, eds. 1982. *The Garden Transformed: Prince Edward Island, 1945–1980*. Charlottetown: Ragweed Press.

Stanley, Della M.M. 1984. *Louis Robichaud: A Decade of Power*. Halifax: Nimbus Publishing.

Wright, Miriam. 2001. *A Fishery for Modern Times: The State and Industrialization of the Newfoundland Fishery, 1934–1968*. Don Mills: Oxford University Press.

Food For Thought

Adler, Judith. 1982. 'Tourism and the Pastoral: A Decade of Debate', in Verner Smitheram, David Milne, and Satadal Dasgupta, eds, *The Garden Transformed: Prince Edward Island, 1945-1980*. Charlottetown: Ragweed Press.

Recommended Websites

Black Cultural Centre for Nova Scotia
http://www.bccns.com/

Churchill Falls
http://www.heritage.nf.ca/law/cfimpacts.html

Chapter 15

The Atlantic Region in a Global Context, 1975 to the Present

In 1973 a global oil crisis precipitated by the Organization of Petroleum Exporting Countries (OPEC) brought an end to the post-war golden age. Two years later, rising government deficits and 'stagflation' prompted Ottawa to impose wage and price controls and to cut back on its spending. As neo-liberal economic arguments against government intervention, including assistance to the poor and to outlying regions, gradually became the conventional wisdom, policymakers across the political spectrum focused on 'restructuring' to accommodate a leaner and meaner reality. Atlantic Canadians had no option but to adjust to 'globalization'—the code word for the movement to impose free-market principles not merely on international trade relations but also on the internal affairs of nations around the world.

Atlantic Canada in the Global Village

The closing decades of the twentieth century brought dramatic changes in information and communications technologies (ICTs). With high-speed personal computers and the Internet connecting people around the world in seconds, the pace of change accelerated, human interaction became increasingly defined in 'virtual' networks, and e-mail emerged as the dominant form of communication. Finding information was now made easier by 'Googling', a reference to an Internet search engine that became popular early in the twenty-first century.

This stage was the only the latest in a process of globalization that had begun 500 years earlier, when Europeans began using new technologies to expand their power around the world. The invention of the printing press in the mid-fifteenth century, along with the construction of more seaworthy vessels, signalled a new stage in the compression of time and space—the short definition of the term 'globalization'. Printed texts in the form of pamphlets, books, and newspapers became powerful tools in determining knowledge and power and in supporting the activities of bureaucratic states and businesses. In the nineteenth century, railways, the telegraph, and the telephone further reduced the time it took to 'spread the word'.

By the end of the twentieth century people lived in what Canadian communications theorist Marshall McLuhan called a 'global village'. Events anywhere in the world were communicated instantaneously by radio, television, and increasingly the Internet. As Atlantic Canadians felt the impact of what pundits called the Information Age, they faced new challenges no less daunting than those that had accompanied the Industrial Revolution in the nineteenth century.

Contexts: National and International

The elections of Margaret Thatcher in Great Britain (1979), Ronald Reagan in the United States (1980), and Brian Mulroney in Canada (1984) signalled the emergence of a neo-liberal order in the major Western nations, which was reinforced in 1989 by the collapse of communism in Eastern Europe. A comprehensive Free Trade Agreement between Canada and the United States took effect the same year and was extended to Mexico in 1992. No longer sheltered by tariff walls, many companies moved their operations to countries that offered lower wages and fewer regulations. All the while, neo-liberals hammered home their message to politicians in the Atlantic region and elsewhere that lower taxes, less bureaucratic regulation, and greater power for private interests would have a more salutary impact than appealing to Ottawa for solutions to regional underdevelopment.

To make matters worse for 'have-not' provinces, Canadian federalism was facing serious challenges. They began with the 1976 election of the Parti Québécois, whose goal was to achieve independence for Quebec, and continued through the sovereignty referendum of 1980 and the years of constitutional turmoil that followed. By the mid-1980s, western Canada—already outraged by Trudeau's national energy strategy—had become so alienated by Ottawa's apparent preoccupation with central Canada that it was ready to embrace its own regionally oriented party. Founded in 1987, the Reform Party attracted so much support, especially in the two westernmost provinces, that in 1993 it effectively supplanted the Progressive Conservatives in Ottawa. Staunch proponents of the neo-liberal agenda, Reformers were outspoken in their criticism of government 'handouts' and those who received them, notably Atlantic Canadians.

In this hostile climate, Atlantic political leaders found it increasingly difficult to get their issues on the national agenda, especially once Ottawa started slashing transfer payments in an effort to bring the federal deficit under control. Beginning in the mid-1990s—just after the collapse of the cod fishery—these cutbacks had devastating consequences for a region with limited financial resources. Paul Martin, finance minister in the Jean Chrétien government, managed to rein in the deficit by the end of the 1990s and seemed poised to reopen the purse strings when he succeeded Chrétien as prime minister in 2003. Instead, after the June 2004 election, he became the leader of a shaky minority government that collapsed in the fall of 2005. In the ensuing contest the new Conservative Party, a coalition of the Progressive Conservatives and those who supported the Reform/Canadian Alliance Party, won the most seats but failed to secure a majority. The party's leader, Stephen Harper, was a neo-liberal ideologue from Alberta, who became notorious for claiming that Atlantic Canadians suffered from a 'culture of defeat'. Unless events intervened, the Atlantic provinces would not fare well in their efforts to seek federal assistance under a Harper regime.

Implementing this neo-liberal agenda was complicated by several events, including the terrorist attacks in the United States on 11 September 2001. Six weeks after this tragedy, US President George W. Bush authorized the invasion of Afghanistan because its government refused to surrender Osama bin Laden, the leader of al-Qaeda, a terrorist organization that appeared to be responsible for the attacks. The Taliban, Islamic extremists who ruled Afghanistan, refused to co-operate with Bush and made no secret of their determination to do anything they could to undermine Western domination.

In February 2003, the Chrétien government committed 140 members of the Princess Patricia's Canadian Light Infantry to assist the American occupation in Afghanistan and to help reconstruct war-torn communities. This response seemed entirely in line with Canada's many peacekeeping

Table 15.1	Timeline
1973	Global oil crisis ends post-war boom.
1976	Parti Québécois wins power in Quebec.
1977	200-mile limit declared.
1980	Quebec referendum on sovereignty-association.
1982	Constitution Act; 84 crew members lost on the Ocean Ranger.
1985	Atlantic Accord; Report of the Royal Commission on Canada's Economic Union and Development Prospects.
1987	Atlantic Canada Opportunities Agency established; Reform Party founded; Meech Lake Accord.
1988	Canada–US Free Trade Agreement signed.
1992	Cod moratorium; Charlottetown Accord; North American Free Trade Agreement signed.
1993	Westray Mine disaster kills 26 men.
1995	Second Quebec referendum.
1997	Confederation Bridge opens.
1999	Supreme Court decision in the Marshall case.
2001	Terrorists attack the World Trade Center and Pentagon.
2003	Royal Commission Report on Newfoundland and Labrador's Place in Canada; Supreme Court rules on undersea boundary between Nova Scotia and Newfoundland.
2005	Federal agreement with Nova Scotia and Newfoundland and Labrador on sharing royalties from offshore development; Nunatsiavut agreement.

missions around the world since the 1950s, except for the fact that it was not organized under the auspices of the United Nations.

In April 2003, the United States invaded Iraq to remove its dictatorial Islamic leader, Saddam Hussein, who was accused—incorrectly it was later discovered—by the Bush administration of stockpiling 'weapons of mass destruction'. Popular opposition to the invasion convinced Chrétien to resist making Canada a participant in the 'coalition of the willing', which included Great Britain. As a result relations with the United States became strained. In compensation for refusing to join the invasion of Iraq, the Chrétien government stepped up its contribution to the war in Afghanistan, where the Taliban were holding their own against the invaders. Canada participated in a NATO-led International Assistance force, sending nearly 2,000 troops into Afghanistan by May 2005. The Canadians were initially stationed primarily in the area around Kabul. Eight Canadian troops were killed in this deployment, four of them from 'friendly fire'.

When Canada agreed in May 2005 to send 1,250 troops to the Taliban stronghold of Kandahar, casualties began to mount. By the end of 2009 more than 130 Canadians had died and several times that number had been wounded in the war. The Canadian military had long served as a career option for job-starved Atlantic Canadians, but since the mid-1950s their missions were largely related to peacekeeping. With an alarming number of troops being seriously injured or losing their lives, it had become obvious that Canada's involvement in Afghanistan went beyond peacekeeping.

In the United States military spending mushroomed and deficits mounted. This, along with the deregulation of financial institutions in the United States and in many Western nations, led to a financial crisis that rumbled along through 2006 and 2007. It seemed initially to be confined to excessively loose mortgage-lending policies but, by the summer of 2008, it became clear that the problems went much deeper than the unusually large number of people defaulting on their mortgages. The whole global economy, integrated to a degree never before possible and reeling from an orgy of greed and irresponsibility, was in a state of crisis that threatened a depression equalled only in magnitude by the economic collapse of the 1930s.

Yet another impediment to the neo-liberal agenda was global warming's threat to the environment. For decades scientists had been issuing warnings about the impact of greenhouse gases on the earth's climate, the result of burning fossil fuels, intensive agriculture, and deforestation. Continuous increases in temperatures on land, sea, and permafrost threatened to melt Arctic ice, flood coastal areas, and ultimately extinguish the oxygen in the air. If the message was slow to sink in, it became more widely disseminated when former US vice-president Al Gore took the lead in sounding the alarm. His award-winning documentary, *An Inconvenient Truth* (2005), outlined in clear and dramatic terms the consequences of ignoring the signs of impending disaster. Since the onset of the Industrial Revolution, the level of greenhouse gases and the earth's human population had both increased alarmingly. At the end of the Second World War, the number of people living on the planet was 2.3 billion. By the beginning of the twenty-first century it was over 6 billion and would soon reach 9 billion. The pressure on the earth's resources, especially if everyone aspired to a North American lifestyle, would be too much to bear and all species, including humans, would be extinguished. To avoid such a calamity, Gore advised that greenhouse gas emissions must be reduced almost immediately by 90 per cent. This was an inconvenient truth, indeed, and one that demanded a timely response.

Variations on the Theme of Neo-liberalism

As the neo-liberal agenda descended in the 1970s, political leaders in the Atlantic region reluctantly adjusted to the prevailing winds. Like leaders in most underdeveloped areas and countries around the world, they felt more favourably disposed toward the post-war liberal consensus that included a helping hand from the state for those who needed it. That approach, it seemed, was no longer an option.

Most Western nations had tolerated the growing power of the state in the decades following the Second World War, but there had always been critics of this trend. Neo-liberals argued that Keynesian policies—deficit spending, tax incentives, transfer payments—created rigidities and inefficiencies that would cripple economic growth in a capitalist system. If governments simply reduced taxes, controlled inflation, and let the marketplace adjust to changing conditions, the economy would find an appropriate balance.

When inflation and economic stagnation arrived simultaneously in the 1970s, confidence in Keynes, planners, and interventionism declined. North American businesses, facing severe competition from Asian 'tigers', threatened to move their operations to developing countries unless taxes were reduced, environmental regulations relaxed, and social programs pared back. Now that satellite and computer communications made it possible to transfer assets instantaneously around the world, 'transnational' corporations could easily defy any one government's efforts to control their activities. This pattern was nothing new to Atlantic Canadians, who for nearly a century had watched the head offices of their banks, factories, and railways move to Montreal and Toronto, but this time the entire country seemed to be at risk. Ottawa was obliged to respond.

In 1982 the Trudeau government established a Royal Commission on Canada's Economic Union and Development Prospects, chaired by Donald Macdonald, a former Liberal finance minister. The commission's 1985 report supported neo-liberal demands for a more flexible economy capable of adjusting to global trends and to new technologies and recommended both free trade with the United States and an end to universal welfare-state programs. The commission's suggestions for mitigating the human costs of economic restructuring by providing a guaranteed minimum income were conveniently forgotten, and the principle of regional equity faded into the background. It was every man and woman—and each province—for themselves in the Information Age.

Atlantic premiers made no coordinated effort to influence the Macdonald Commission's findings or the way its recommendations were implemented. Instead, they tried to reposition their provinces to compete in a global market place. Motivated by the expansion of the fisheries and the discovery of the Hibernia oil field in the late 1970s, Premier Brian Peckford asserted Newfoundland's ownership of offshore resources on the basis of its status in international law before 1949 and insisted that the province should have equal control with Ottawa over offshore developments. The Trudeau government refused to relinquish federal control of offshore resources, and the Supreme Court in 1984 supported the contention that Ottawa had both ownership and exclusive jurisdiction.

The Progressive Conservatives, who came to power in 1984, were willing to negotiate. With the assistance of John Crosbie, the colourful and outspoken Newfoundland member of the Mulroney

The Costs of Development

In the winter of 1982, 84 crew members lost their lives when Mobil Oil's rig *Ocean Ranger* capsized in a fierce storm on the Hibernia oil field. This tragedy underscored the reality that new sea-based industries were no less life-threatening than the ones they had replaced. As in previous periods, human resources in the region were sometimes sacrificed to the gods of corporate investment.

This was certainly the case for the workers at the Westray coal mine in Pictou County, Nova Scotia, whose complaints about rock slides, cave-ins, and dangerous levels of methane gas had been largely ignored. When an explosion destroyed the mine in 1993, eight months into its operation, 26 men were killed. The mine owners were not held responsible for their negligence. Nor were company owners required to shoulder the environmental costs of their enterprises.

Among the worst legacies of industrial development in the Atlantic region are the Sydney Tar Ponds, reservoirs for the toxic brew of chemicals—benzene, kerosene, naphthalene, PCBs—produced as waste by the coke ovens and furnaces used in Sydney's steel processing industry for more than 80 years. The size of three city blocks, the tar ponds are especially troubling to the people living nearest to them, who have suffered a wide range of physical problems, including severe headaches, nosebleeds, breathing problems, birth defects, miscarriages, and cancer. Finally, in 2004, the federal and provincial governments announced that they would spend up to $400 million on a 10-year plan to clean up the site.

cabinet, accords were signed in 1985 with Newfoundland and Nova Scotia. While the agreements offered fewer benefits from offshore developments than Crosbie had hoped for, they signalled a less rigid attitude in Ottawa towards accommodating the interests of have-not provinces. The creation in 1987 of the Atlantic Canada Opportunities Agency (ACOA), which replaced the Department of Regional Industrial Expansion (DRIE) established five years earlier, was a further indication of Ottawa's intention to decentralize regional development efforts.

Federalism in Crisis

Federal–provincial relations were further complicated by the seemingly endless constitutional talks that followed the 1980 Quebec referendum on sovereignty-association. To blunt Quebec's desire for independence, Trudeau had promised constitutional reform. Since any change to Canada's constitution still had to be passed by the British Parliament, the power to amend the constitution had to be brought home to Canada and an amending formula worked out between the federal government and the provinces. Trudeau also wanted the new constitution to include a Charter of Rights and Freedoms—a proposal that Quebec and most other provinces perceived as an attempt to curtail provincial powers. Only two premiers, Richard Hatfield in New Brunswick and William Davis in Ontario, were initially prepared to support the legislation. Refusing to have his hands tied, Trudeau declared that he would proceed with or without provincial support, and the majority of premiers—fearing that Trudeau might get his reforms without making any concessions to the provinces—came to terms. The Constitution Act, 1982 passed. Quebec cried betrayal and refused to sign the deal.

In Atlantic Canada there was little opposition to the new constitutional arrangements. Most people embraced the Charter of Rights and Freedoms which enshrined in Canadian terms the basic human rights to freedom and equality that had informed public policy since the UN Declaration of 1948. A series of clauses in the Charter entrenched New Brunswick's bilingual character and the Constitution Act included a section obliging the federal government to support equal opportunities and services across the country.

The rights of provinces large and small were carefully calibrated in the formula relating to constitutional amendments. For amendments other than those affecting representation in the House of Commons, Senate, and the Supreme Court, which required unanimous consent, approval was needed of the federal Parliament plus two-thirds of the provinces representing 50 per cent of all Canadians. In addition any province that considered that its legislative or proprietary rights were compromised by an amendment could declare it null and void within its boundaries.

The adoption of the Constitution Act, 1982 did not end the controversy. Determined to better Trudeau, Mulroney set out to broker a deal that would 'bring Quebec into the constitution'. Ultimately, the Meech Lake Accord (1987–90) and Charlottetown Accord (1992) both failed, but Mulroney's efforts to secure a free trade agreement with the United States succeeded, ending more than a century of protectionism in Canadian trade policy.

The Atlantic premiers went their separate ways on constitutional and trade issues. New Brunswick's Liberal premier, Frank McKenna, whose party was elected by a landslide in 1987, found himself caught between powerful provincial interests opposed to the Meech Lake Accord as presented—Acadians were particularly concerned that special deals for Quebec would leave

The Constitution and Equalization

The Atlantic provinces played a central role, along with Manitoba and Saskatchewan, in securing a clause in the Constitution Act, 1982, entrenching Ottawa's obligation to support equalization as a means of muting regional disparities. Part III, article 36 of the Act reads:

EQUALIZATION AND REGIONAL DISPARITIES

I. Commitment to promote equal opportunities

(1) Without altering the legislative authority of Parliament or of the provincial legislatures, or the rights of any of them with respect to the exercise of their legislative authority, Parliament and the legislatures, together with the government of Canada and the provincial governments, are committed to

(a) promoting equal opportunities for the well-being of Canadians;

(b) furthering economic development to reduce disparity in opportunities; and

(c) providing essential public services of reasonable quality to all Canadians.

II. Commitment respecting public services

(1) Parliament and the government of Canada are committed to the principle of making equalization payments to ensure that provincial governments have sufficient revenues to provide reasonably comparable levels of public services at reasonably comparable levels of taxation.

To date there is little case law on this federal obligation, and wrangling over equalization remains a perennial feature of Canadian federalism.

---

them out in the cold——and his own inclination to support the measure. When Clyde Wells led the Liberals to victory in Newfoundland in 1989, he called into question the earlier acceptance of Meech Lake by the provincial legislature. Wells strongly opposed the accord, arguing that it trampled on provincial rights and failed to address regional disparities. The legislature rescinded its ratification and was preparing to hold a free vote when it became clear that Manitoba would not pass its legislation in time to save the accord from expiry.

Wells also opposed the Canada–United States Free Trade Agreement, but Maritime premiers took a different view. McKenna defied the federal wing of his party and many of his provincial supporters by endorsing the deal. Most Atlantic Canadians seemed to agree with Wells. In the 1988 federal election, voters in Atlantic Canada gave only 41 per cent of the popular vote and 12 of their 32 seats to the Progressive Conservatives. Once again the region was out of step with the rest of the country, and the agreement took effect on 1 January 1989.

The stranglehold of majority cultures on high political office in the region was broken in 1986 when Joe Ghiz, whose family came from Lebanon, was sworn in as Liberal premier of Prince Edward Island. He was a popular premier who, like Wells and McKenna, enjoyed the national stage. In 1992, Ghiz welcomed first ministers to the Island for the talks that produced the Charlottetown Accord. This time Newfoundland and Alberta held out for Senate reform that would recognize the equality of the provinces. When Quebec decided to submit the Accord to a binding referendum, Mulroney declared that all Canadians would have a voice. A national referendum was held on 26 October 1992. The Charlottetown Accord was rejected by the majority in all provinces except Newfoundland, New Brunswick, and Prince Edward Island, where voters apparently had had enough of constitutions.

Hard Times

In 1993 the Liberals returned to power under Jean Chrétien and continued along the same neo-liberal path taken by their Progressive Conservative predecessors. Social programs were cut, employment insurance became harder to get, and transfer payments decreased. Most provinces were forced to carry the ever-increasing costs of Medicare while slashing budgets for education, social services, and roads and by reducing public-sector employment. In Atlantic Canada, political leaders in some provinces outsourced school construction to private companies, built toll roads, and authorized universities to raise their fees to nearly double what students paid elsewhere in Canada. As a result the gap between rich and poor widened while the lines at food banks and welfare offices lengthened. Populations in the region's resource-based communities declined and local economies suffered, but this was the free market at work.

In this context regional politicians succumbed to the policy options developed by corporately funded think tanks such as the Halifax-based Atlantic Institute for Market Studies (AIMS). Under its founding director Brian Lee Crowley, business and political leaders were encouraged to make the Atlantic provinces the transportation and energy hub of 'Atlantica': a North Atlantic economic

Bruce MacKinnon, 'Oh Please, Oh Please', 1992. As this award-winning cartoon, published in the *Halifax Herald*, suggests, regional fortunes were increasingly tied to those of the United States following the Free Trade agreements of 1989 and 1992. Republished with permission from The Halifax Herald Limited.

zone that would include northern New England and southern Quebec—but not Labrador.[1] In a globalized world it seems that all things are possible.

Nowhere was the impact of such restructuring more keenly felt than in the Atlantic region's many fishing communities. When a 200-mile (370 kilometre) limit was declared in 1977, it looked as if the fisheries would have a bright future. With foreign vessels forbidden to fish within 200 miles of shore, governments had the opportunity to conserve and rebuild fish stocks. At that point scientific estimates of the stock's size were still overly optimistic, so instead of scaling back the Canadian fishery, governments encouraged it to expand. Political considerations no doubt played a role in this decision, along with inflated quotas.

The number of Atlantic Canadians engaged in the fishing industry rose from roughly 31,000 in 1974 to nearly 55,000 in 1980. By the early 1980s Canada was the world's leading fish-exporting country, up from third in 1976, with the Atlantic provinces providing 65 per cent of the national total. At the same time, fishing by foreign fleets outside the 200-mile limit (and in the case of France, inside the limit) intensified. During the 1980s both inshore and offshore fishers began to sound the alarm, and scientists reconsidered their estimates. With the collapse of the fish stocks in the late 1980s, Canadian quotas were cut and processing plants shut down. Taking advantage of the disaster, two corporate giants, Fishery Products International and National Sea, swallowed up their hard-pressed competitors.

In 1992 Fisheries Minister John Crosbie announced a moratorium on cod fishing and stringent controls on the exploitation of other fish stocks. With 1,300 Atlantic communities almost entirely dependent on the fishery, its collapse precipitated a crisis of titanic proportions. In Newfoundland, where much of the expansion in the fisheries had occurred, nearly 20,000 people were thrown out of work and the survival of dozens of communities became doubtful.

The crisis in the domestic fishery heightened Atlantic Canadians' resentment of what appeared to be irresponsible overfishing by foreign (mainly European) trawlers in international waters just outside the 200-mile limit. Spanish and Portuguese vessels in particular were increasing their catch of turbot—a species that, according to scientists, was now endangered. When Spain and Portugal, backed by the European Union, refused in 1995 to accept the reduced quotas set by the Northwest Atlantic Fisheries Organization (NAFO), the Canadian government—in which Newfoundlander Brian Tobin was fisheries minister—decided to move aggressively to conserve the stocks. Tobin's much-publicized efforts to protect the lowly turbot led the Spanish to talk of piracy and even war. Eventually an agreement was reached to control fishing on the Grand Banks more effectively, but overfishing persists.

The major beneficiaries of the rigorous restructuring of the Atlantic Canadian economy were industries elsewhere, especially in oil-rich Alberta. Between 2001 and 2006, 33,000 Atlantic Canadians moved to Alberta to find employment, not including the estimated 25,000 oil patch commuters (most of them men) who worked in Fort McMurray. Air Canada and WestJet added new flights between Calgary and Halifax, Sydney, and St John's to accommodate the mobile workforce, while the women left behind in Glace Bay, Harbour Mille, and other hard-pressed communities added responsibilities such as firefighting and coaching Little Leagues teams to their already busy schedules. When jobs in the west began to disappear in 2008 as a result of the financial crisis, many workers returned home and the special flights were cancelled. Communities in Atlantic Canada that benefited from the remittance payment of their distant citizens also felt the pinch of the rising unemployment rate in Alberta.

Native Claims

A new factor in resource development in Atlantic Canada was the assertion of Aboriginal claims both to land and to specific hunting and fishing rights. In the Maritimes such claims were based on treaties signed with the British in 1725–6 and 1760–1 and on the possession of Aboriginal rights that had never been extinguished. While the Mi'kmaq and Wolastoqiyik found the courts receptive, Ottawa continues to ignore the demands of the Passamaquoddy for recognition. The Inuit and Innu of Labrador have no treaty rights, and whether Newfoundland Mi'kmaq are covered by the eighteenth-century treaties remains in dispute. Meanwhile, all First Nations in Canada have been sustained in their resolve to redress past injustices by a series of Supreme Court decisions and by Section 35c of the Constitution, which recognizes and affirms existing Aboriginal rights.

One of the most important Supreme Court rulings was brought down in 1990 (*R. v. Sparrow*), declaring that Aboriginal people had the right to fish for subsistence and ceremonial purposes unless the government could demonstrate why limitation was necessary. In response, Ottawa introduced an Aboriginal Fisheries Strategy whereby communal fishing licences were distributed to First Nations in Atlantic Canada and British Columbia. Two Mi'kmaq communities—Membertou and Afton—refused to sign licensing agreements, arguing that treaty rights secured in 1761 superseded federal fisheries legislation.

In 1993 the Department of Fisheries and Oceans (DFO) charged Donald Marshall Jr of Membertou with catching eels out of season and with fishing and selling eels without a licence. The case eventually reached the Supreme Court, which dismissed the charges. It was a landmark ruling, reaffirming the integrity of eighteenth-century treaties and confirming the Mi'kmaq right to make a moderate living from the fishery. By extension, the Mi'kmaq could claim access to other ocean resources and to hunting. The firestorm that followed this decision forced the Supreme Court to qualify its judgment to the extent of arguing that the federal government had the power to restrict even the right to a 'moderate livelihood' if the Crown could justify the regulation on the 'grounds of public importance'.[2]

DFO officials would now be obliged to negotiate fisheries agreements rather than impose them on the Mi'kmaq. Since the DFO was slow to respond, the Mi'kmaq in some areas began fishing lobster out of season. In St Mary's Bay, Nova Scotia, Native and non-Native fishers negotiated an agreement to jointly manage the lobster fishery. Elsewhere, conflict often prevailed. When the Mi'kmaq of Esgenoopetits (Burnt Church), New Brunswick, laid lobster traps in the fall of 1999, non-Natives responded by destroying their traps, attacking their property, and vandalizing fish plants that accepted lobsters from Native fishers. The federal government tried to establish quotas for both sides, but tensions continued.

Meanwhile, Thomas Peter Paul, a member of the Wolastoqiyik First Nation, tested the right of Aboriginal people to take forest resources from Crown land for commercial purposes. The New Brunswick Court of Appeal upheld Paul's conviction for cutting trees on Crown land, and the Supreme Court refused to accept an appeal. Undaunted by this development, Aboriginal people in the region continued to exercise what they saw as their treaty right to commercially exploit Crown timber resources. In July 2005 the Supreme Court handed down rulings in two cases relating to Mi'kmaq logging rights. The appeals by Stephen Frederick Marshall and 34 other Mi'kmaq in Nova Scotia and by Joshua Bernard in New Brunswick were denied on the grounds that there was no connection between the commercial cutting of timber and Aboriginal trading activities at the time the treaties were signed.

In 1996 the Conne River Mi'kmaq (Miawpukek) launched a claim to about 20 per cent of the island of Newfoundland in 1996. The Newfoundland and Labrador Supreme Court ruled in 2003 (in the case of *R. vs. Drew*) that there was insufficient evidence of a Mi'kmaq presence in the area before the arrival of Europeans to sustain the claim. The decision was appealed, but the original decision was upheld and application to appeal to the Supreme Court of Canada was dismissed.

A complex situation developed in Labrador. In 1977 the Innu Nation and the Labrador Inuit Association (LIA) filed overlapping land claims. Negotiations with the LIA began in 1988, but an agreement in principle was not reached until 2001. The settlement was no doubt encouraged by the

Nunatsiavut

Labrador boasts the first modern Native land claims settlement in Atlantic Canada. On 22 January 2005, after 30 years of negotiations, the Labrador Inuit signed an agreement with the federal and provincial governments covering 72,520 square kilometres of land, to be known as Nunatsiavut ('our beautiful land'). It includes Labrador north of Hamilton Inlet as well as substantial portions of the Atlantic coast to the south and on Hamilton Inlet. The agreement also included 44,030 square kilometres of sea rights.

Of the land area, the Inuit own 15,800 square kilometres designated as Labrador Inuit Lands. In the rest of the area, they enjoy special rights related to traditional land use. The agreement also established the Torngat Mountains National Park Reserve in the northern area of the land claim. The package included $130 million in compensation for the forced relocation of the Inuit from Hebron and elsewhere in the 1950s; provincial royalties for resources; land,

mineral, and marine rights; and $120 million to establish self-government.

The Nunatsiavut Government represents not only the residents (Inuit and non-Inuit) of the land claims area but also Labrador Inuit living elsewhere in Canada. Nunatsiavut remains part of Newfoundland and Labrador, but its government has authority over health, education, justice, cultural affairs, economic development, and natural resources. The government consists of an elected president (who appoints an executive council) and an assembly of 16 members representing seven constituencies. The assembly elects the first minister. In addition, there are elected municipal councils in each town, led by an 'angajukKâk'—the chief executive and mayor—who sits in the assembly.

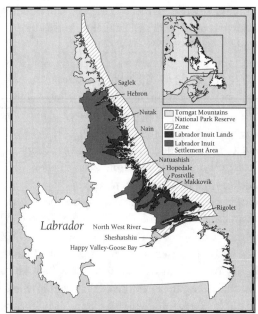

Map of Nunatsiavut.

Sandra Lovelace Nicholas

Sandra Lovelace Nicholas was born in 1947 on the Tobique Reserve, home to members of the Wolastoqiyik First Nation in New Brunswick. In 1970 she married an American, Bernard Lovelace, and moved to California. When her marriage ended a few years later, she and her children returned to Tobique, only to be denied access to housing and other rights provided under the Indian Act. Like all Native women subject to the Act, Sandra Lovelace had lost her Indian status when she married a non-Native man.

In co-operation with Native and non-Native women's organizations, Lovelace fought the case in the courts, and in 1979 she appealed to the United Nations. Two years later Canada was found in breach of the International Covenant on Civil and Political Rights. The Canadian government was slow to respond, in part because First Nations men opposed giving women equal rights to scarce reserve resources.

Under the Charter of Rights and Freedoms, double standards such as those sanctioned by the Indian Act could no longer be condoned. The Act was finally revised in 1985 to ensure that Native women who marry non-Native men and their children no longer lose their status. In 2005 Sandra Lovelace became the first Aboriginal person from Atlantic Canada to be appointed to the Canadian Senate.

discovery in 1993 of huge nickel deposits at Voisey's Bay, just south of the Inuit town of Nain. In January 2005 a treaty was signed that gave the Labrador Inuit substantial control over the northern coast, an area named Nunatsiavut. The Innu claim to a large part of Nitassinan (including Voisey's Bay)—their ancestral homeland in Labrador and Quebec—has proceeded even more slowly.

Both of these cases have been complicated by the intervention of the Labrador Métis Nation, founded in 1985, which in 1991 filed its own claim to Labrador south of Nain. The Métis people's claim to distinct Aboriginal status has been rejected by the provincial and federal governments and criticized by both Innu and Inuit. As a result, the validity of their land claim remains undecided.

Pulling Against Gravity

No matter what strategy its political leaders tried in this period, the region remained an area of high unemployment, low wages, and uncertain prospects. Governing a have-not province was, as political scientist Donald J. Savoie has suggested, like pulling against the forces of gravity.[3] Capital investment and human resources were irresistibly attracted to established centres of economic development. Try as they might, political leaders usually lost the tug-of-war with national and global economic forces—and the support of voters to boot.

In 1987 New Brunswick voters annihilated Richard Hatfield's Conservatives, giving every seat in the legislature to Frank McKenna's Liberals. McKenna was particularly aggressive in his efforts to attract call centres to the province, but such low-paying operations did little to change the overall economic picture. In the next provincial election the Liberals held on to most of the seats, but the Confederation of Regions (COR) Party, which attacked official bilingualism, managed to become the official opposition. Internal bickering soon made COR ineffective on the political scene. Following McKenna's resignation in 1997, the Liberal party collapsed and a reorganized Progressive Conservative Party swept back to power in 1999 under Bernard Lord. Unable to slay the dragon of underdevelopment and reluctant to stand up to private corporations that hiked insurance rates to obscene levels, Lord managed only a one-seat majority in the 2003 election.

Lord felt sufficiently confident in his grasp on power to call an early election in 2006. Although the Conservatives won the popular vote by a hair, Shawn Graham's Liberals won the majority of seats. Making a virtue out of necessity, Graham launched a 'self-sufficiency campaign', calculated to position New Brunswickers to go it alone in the face of federal cutbacks. He also embraced an aggressive industrial program that included building a second nuclear power plant, supporting an Irving-backed liquefied gas facility, and making Saint John a major hub in an Atlantic Gateway strategy designed to put the region at the centre of global trade.

Prince Edward Island experienced similar swings from the Progressive Conservatives to the Liberals and back again. In 1979 J. Angus MacLean, who had served as a cabinet minister in the Diefenbaker government, led the Progressive Conservatives to victory on a platform of 'rural renewal'. His efforts to slow the tide of modernity included a moratorium on new shopping malls, breaking a contract with New Brunswick to purchase energy from its Point Lepreau nuclear power plant (the only such station in Atlantic Canada), and a Land Protection Act that restricted individual land holdings to 1,000 acres (2,471 hectares) and corporate holdings to 3,000 acres (7,413 hectares). The latter policy was aimed specifically at another New Brunswick-based interest—the powerful Irvings—who were building up landholdings to support their processing operations.

When the Liberals, led by Catherine Callbeck, won the 1993 election, Prince Edward Island made history by becoming the first province to elect a woman as premier. (The leaders of both the other major parties were women as well.) Callbeck's victory was short-lived. Forced to deal with drastic federal cutbacks, she was blamed for the difficulties they caused in a province with a small tax base. In 1996 the Progressive Conservatives, under the leadership of Pat Binns, defeated the Liberals. A native of Saskatchewan, Binns was a farmer who managed to maintain voters' confidence in the primarily rural province through two more provincial elections.

In 2007 Binns sought an unprecedented fourth-term majority, running on a policy of continued good governance and job creation, but he was trounced by the Liberal Party, led by Robert Ghiz (the son of former premier Joe Ghiz). More than other premiers in the Maritimes, Ghiz caught the new wave of thinking in his 'Focus for Change' program that included an emphasis on environmentally-friendly energy sources. Given that global warming and the rising sea levels threatened the very existence of his low-lying island province, it was a timely initiative.

Nova Scotia's political fortunes in the late 1990s suggest the difficulties facing politicians in the two mainline parties. While the good-natured Progressive Conservative Premier John Buchanan managed to hold onto power from 1978 to 1990, his successor, Donald Cameron, quickly lost ground to Dr John Savage's Liberals, who won the 1993 provincial election. Savage also found it impossible to satisfy voter demands in an era defined by government downsizing, and in the next election his party was defeated by the Progressive Conservatives, led by another medical doctor, John Hamm. This time the election results were more complicated, with the NDP emerging as the official opposition. Hamm managed to hang on to power and to pass it on to Rodney MacDonald in 2006, but both men were obliged to walk a difficult tightrope. When the polls suggested that he might win a majority, MacDonald called an election for 13 June 2009. His lead over his rivals quickly evaporated during the campaign and the NDP lead by Darrell Dexter, the son of a sheet metal worker, finally broke the stranglehold of the two mainline parties on the region's provincial governments.

Determined not to suffer the fate of Liberal premiers elsewhere in the Atlantic region, Roger Grimes in Newfoundland and Labrador decided to deflect criticisms of his government by establishing a royal commission to explore how best to renew and strengthen his province's place in Canada. A telling feature of the inquiry was that the commissioners held hearings in Toronto and Fort McMurray, where so many of the province's citizens worked. Although the commission's report, tabled in the summer of 2003, clearly summarized the difficult economic situation and offered practical remedies, the response in Ottawa was a polite yawn. Grimes lost a provincial election later that fall to the Progressive Conservatives, led by Danny Williams, and the commission report was quietly buried.

Williams was more than just a new kid on the block. A Rhodes Scholar and self-made millionaire, Williams soon became a household name in Canada, something that could not be said of any other Atlantic premier of his generation. Utterly fearless, he appeared on the CNN program *Larry King Live* in the late winter of 2006 to debate former Beatle Paul McCartney and his then wife Heather Mills, who were in the Atlantic region to protest the seal hunt. By that time Williams was locked in a David and Goliath battle with Ottawa over equalization payments.

In the fall of 2004 Williams abruptly walked out of a federal–provincial conference on equalization policy, claiming that Liberal Prime Minister Paul Martin had reneged on his pre-election promise to give Newfoundland and Labrador and Nova Scotia a better deal on royalties from offshore development. After three months of posturing, an agreement was finally reached in January 2005 that gave the two have-not provinces most of what they wanted. Newfoundland and Labrador would receive $2 billion and Nova Scotia $830,000 over eight years to compensate them for equalization clawbacks, and the agreement could be extended for a further eight years if the provinces were still receiving equalization payments. When Stephen Harper later tried to reform equalization in a way that would penalize the Atlantic provinces, Williams stood up to him and even mobilized a highly effective campaign to defeat all Conservative candidates in Newfoundland and Labrador in the 2008 election.

Newfoundland and Labrador and Nova Scotia collaborated in their efforts to wrest royalty concessions from Ottawa, but they battled each other in the courts to determine the undersea boundary between the two provinces. There was a lot at stake. In 2002 an arbitration tribunal handed down a ruling that gave most of the potentially rich area in dispute to the former. Ottawa's distribution of scarce fish quotas in the Gulf of St Lawrence also produced tensions among competing fishers from Quebec, Newfoundland and Labrador, New Brunswick, and Prince Edward Island.

An Uncertain Future

As in the past, Atlantic Canadians adjusted as best they could to the economic and political forces swirling around them. Out-migration remained a common recourse for the unemployed, the young, and the upwardly mobile. During the 1990s Newfoundland and Labrador's population declined for the first time in recorded history. Other provinces held their own, but unevenly: in areas such as northeastern New Brunswick and Cape Breton the losses were just as precipitous as in Newfoundland and Labrador. In all four provinces, population and services alike increasingly

Table 15.2   Population of the Atlantic Provinces, 2001

Province	Total population	Urban population	% of total	Rural population	% of total
New Brunswick	729,498	367,902	50.4	361,596	49.6
Newfoundland	512,930	296,196	57.7	216,734	42.3
Nova Scotia	908,007	507,009	55.8	400,998	44.2
Prince Edward Island	135,294	60,675	44.8	74,619	55.2
Total	**2,285,729**	**1,231,782**	**53.9**	**1,053,947**	**46.1**

Source: Statistics Canada

Table 15.3   Cities with populations with over 20,000, 2001

Halifax, Nova Scotia	359,111
St John's, Newfoundland	99,182
Saint John, New Brunswick	69,661
Moncton, New Brunswick	61,046
Fredericton, New Brunswick	47,560
Charlottetown, Prince Edward Island	32,245
Sydney, Nova Scotia	26,083
Corner Brook, Newfoundland	20,103

Source: Statistics Canada

The Confederation Bridge finally linked the mainland to Prince Edward Island in 1997. BMPstock.com.

gravitated towards urban centres (see Tables 15.1 and 15.2).

Three cities in particular were targeted as 'growth centres': St John's, Moncton, and, above all, Halifax. Prosperous, lively, and expanding, Halifax emerged as a genuine metropolis, home to numerous corporate headquarters, regional federal offices, military installations, educational institutions, and health care facilities, as well as a centre for film and television production. Its hinterland consists of all four provinces, and the other capitals are becoming more or less resentful outports.

Elsewhere, Prince Edward Island was finally linked to the mainland with the completion of the Confederation Bridge in 1997. The structure is a magnificent engineering achievement and a rare example of a public service delegated to private initiative that seems to have succeeded. It is still too soon to say what impact improved communications will have on the island province.

History and Fiction

Over the past 30 years, fictional writers from Atlantic Canada have gone from strength to strength. One of their most important resources has been the region's history, which serves as a vast and fascinating storehouse of events just waiting for the touch of a creative writer. As a result, historical fiction has become a substantial literary genre in the Atlantic Provinces as much as anywhere.

This development has, in turn, prompted discussion about the relationship between academic history, where documentary evidence must be respected, and fictional accounts, where writers have more imaginative freedom. The latter can fill gaps in the historical record, create characters, dialogue, and incidents to move the narrative along, and accommodate different perspectives that may not have prevailed in the past. Even so, most writers will strive to create an accurate historical context. Newfoundland author Wayne Johnston is perhaps unusual in arguing that historical fiction should not be judged by its fidelity to actual fact, but by its quality as fiction, pure and simple. His novel *The Colony of Unrequited Dreams* (1998), which has Joseph Smallwood as its central character, was controversial precisely because the author did not consider himself fenced in by historical or geographical facts.

Other Newfoundland writers who have used 'real' history include John Steffler, whose *Afterlife of George Cartwright* (1992) is set in eighteenth-century Labrador; Michael Winter, who in *The Big Why* (2004) examines Rockwell Kent's unhappy stay in Brigus during the Great War; and Michael Crummey, who reinterprets the extinction of the Beothuk in *River Thieves* (2001), a subject also addressed by Bernice Morgan in *Cloud of Bone* (2007). The experience of the Newfoundland Regiment in the Great War is the subject of Kevin Major's *No Man's Land* (1995).

In the Maritimes, Antonine Maillet mines Acadian history to great advantage, while David Adams Richards, in a dozen novels written since 1981, draws upon his Miramichi roots to provide brilliant, if sometimes gloomy, depictions of rural society since the Second World War. George Elliott Clarke's novel about the Fredericton murder trial and execution of two of his cousins in 1949, *George & Rue* (2005), displays an exceptional blend of fact and fiction. Other examples include Carol Bruneau's *Glass Voices* (2007), which follows a Nova Scotia family from the Halifax Explosion to the 1960s. Stephen Kimber in *Reparations* (2006) looks at Africville, and Ami McKay's *The Birth House* (2006) was inspired by the experience of an early twentieth-century midwife in Scots Bay. Similarly, Sally Armstrong has fictionalized the life of a remarkable Miramichi ancestor in *The Nine Lives of Charlotte Taylor* (2007).

> A number of authors from Cape Breton also find inspiration from the past. The best known is Alistair MacLeod, many of whose short stories are set there, as is his award-winning novel, *No Great Mischief* (1999). Ann-Marie MacDonald's *Fall on Your Knees* (1996), a complex family saga set largely in New Waterford, was a best-seller, and Sheldon Currie has written stories, plays, and novels about the coal towns—*The Glace Bay Miners' Museum* (1979) was the basis for the movie *Margaret's Museum* (1995).
>
> The past is a common resource, which professional historians cannot (and should not) monopolize. Historical fiction can illuminate the past and expand the historical imagination, but the debate about boundaries should and will continue.

Essentially a city-state built around Charlottetown, Prince Edward Island remains the most cohesive of the Atlantic provinces, and polls suggest that, of all Canadians, Islanders are among those most satisfied with their worldly condition.

Whither Tending?

What the future holds for the Atlantic region as a whole is unclear. There are some who support Atlantic or Maritime union, but the preferred strategy, at least among political leaders, is to pursue closer collaboration while remaining separate entities. In 2000 the Council of Maritime Premiers evolved into the Council of Atlantic Premiers, with a renewed mandate for regional co-operation. The jury is still out on whether this strategy will pay dividends in negotiations with Ottawa and with capitalists eager to exploit what is left of the region's resources. While the financial meltdown in 2008 offered a grim reminder that unregulated capitalism fails to address many of the large issues facing humankind and may even contribute to present miseries, neo-liberal perspectives remain strong among corporate and political leaders. The ultimate irony for Atlantic Canadians, of course, is that as other areas of the country face the collapse of businesses and job losses, there is more interest in Ottawa in 'reforming' employment insurance and providing stimulus packages for faltering industries.

Most policy-makers concede that Confederation remains the preferred framework in which to help the Atlantic provinces close the gap between national and regional living standards. Although the gap has not disappeared, it has narrowed considerably since the 1950s. Indeed, economic growth in the region has kept pace, if at a distance, with the spectacular growth of the nation as a whole since the 1950s, and that in itself is a major achievement. So, too, is the emergence of new industries, including high-tech operations to support offshore development, fish farming, and wineries whose products win international competitions. Whether they can maintain the pace in an increasingly competitive and uncertain global context is difficult to predict.

Conclusion

Four centuries after the first permanent European settlements were established in the region, Atlantic Canadians face the prospect of responding yet again to forces centred elsewhere. Reform, retrenchment, and restructuring have been the mantra of the new world order, but Atlantic Canada has embraced them more out of necessity than conviction. While a few have been converted to the religion of the unshackled marketplace, many Atlantic Canadians regret the abandonment of the noble dream that made human welfare rather than corporate profits the measure of a civil society. 'Where are we,' asked the Newfoundland writer Moses Harvey in 1885, 'and whither tending?'[4] The answer remains obscure, but the region is undeniably at another turning point in its long history.

Further Readings

Candow, James E., and Carol Corbin, eds. 1997. *How Deep is the Ocean? Historical Essays on Canada's Atlantic Fishery*. Sydney: University College of Cape Breton Press.

Coates, Ken S. 2000. *The Marshall Decision and Native Rights*. Montreal: McGill-Queen's University Press.

Rose, George A. 2007. *The Ecological History of the North Atlantic Fisheries*. St John's: Breakwater Press.

Sandberg, Anders L., and Peter Clancy. 2000. *Against the Grain: Foresters and Politics in Nova Scotia*. Vancouver: UBC Press.

Savoie, Donald. 2001. *Pulling Against Gravity: Economic Development in New Brunswick During the McKenna Years*. Montreal: Institute for Research on Public Policy.

———. 2006. *Visiting Grandchildren: Economic Development in the Maritimes*. Toronto: University of Toronto Press.

Wicken, William C. 2002. *Mi'kmaq Treaties on Trial: History, Land, and Donald Marshall Junior*. Toronto: University of Toronto Press.

Food for Thought

Ommer, Rosemary, and Nancy J. Turner. 2004. 'Informal Rural Economies in History', *Labour/Le Travail* 53 (Spring): 127–57.

Recommended Websites

History of the Northern Cod Fishery
http://www.stemnet.nf.ca/cod/home1.htm

Nunatsiavut: Winds of Change
http://www.nunatsiavut.com/en/windsofchange.php

Selected Bibliography

The historical literature on Atlantic Canada is extensive, and making a selection of sources is difficult. Additional titles can be found in *Canadian History: A Readers' Guide*, 2 vols (Toronto: University of Toronto Press, 1994). *Volume 1: Beginnings to Confederation* (edited by M. Brook Taylor) is particularly useful for students of Atlantic Canada. The Atlantic Canada Portal (http://atlanticportal.hil.unb.ca) includes a searchable database of the *Acadiensis* bibliographies and an annotated list of websites devoted to Atlantic Canadian history and culture. Sources on the history of Newfoundland and Labrador to 1869 can be found on a website maintained by Olaf Uwe Janzen (http://www2.swgc.mun.ca/nfld_history/index.htm). See also Marguerite Maillet, *Bibliographie des publications de l'Acadie des provinces maritimes; livres et brochures, 1609–1996* (Moncton: les Éditions d'acadie, 1997) and Brian Douglas Tennyson, comp., *Cape Bretoniana: An Annotated Bibliography* (Toronto: University of Toronto Press, 2005). Articles on the region's history can be found in *Acadiensis* and *Newfoundland and Labrador Studies*, as well as *The Nova Scotia Historical Review*, *The Newfoundland Quarterly*, *Them Days*, *The Island Magazine*, *Les Cahiers de la Société historique acadienne*, and *The Cape Breton Magazine*.

General Works

Atlantic Geoscience Society. 2001. *The Last Billion Years: A Geological History of the Maritime Provinces*. Halifax: Nimbus.

Buckner, Phillip A., and John G. Reid, eds. 1994. *The Atlantic Region to Confederation: A History*. Toronto: University of Toronto Press.

Conrad, Margaret R., and James K. Hiller. 2001. *Atlantic Canada: A Region in the Making*. Toronto: Oxford University Press.

Forbes, E.R., and D.A. Muise, eds. 1993. *The Atlantic Provinces in Confederation*. Toronto: University of Toronto Press.

Hornsby, Stephen J. 2005. *British Atlantic, American Frontier: Spaces of Power in Early Modern British America*. Hanover: University Press of New England.

MacNutt, W.S. 1965. *The Atlantic Provinces: The Emergence of Colonial Society, 1712–1857*. Toronto: McClelland and Stewart.

Mancke, Elizabeth. 2005. *The Fault Lines of Empire: Political Differentiation in Massachusetts and Nova Scotia, ca. 1760–1830*. London: Routledge.

Reid, John G. 1987. *Six Crucial Decades: Times of Change in the History of the Maritimes*. Halifax: Nimbus.

Savoie, Donald. 2006. *Visiting Grandchildren: Economic Development in the Maritimes*. Toronto: University of Toronto Press.

General Essay Collections

Alexander, David. 1983. *Atlantic Canada and Confederation: Essays in Canadian Political Economy*, comp. Eric W. Sager, Lewis R. Fischer, and Stuart O. Pierson. Toronto: University of Toronto Press.

Bercuson, David Jay, and Phillip A. Buckner, eds. 1981. *Eastern and Western Perspectives, Papers from the Joint Atlantic Canada/Western Canadian Studies Conference*. Toronto: University of Toronto Press.

Bogaard, Paul A., ed. 1990. *Profiles of Science and Society in the Maritimes prior to 1914*. Fredericton: Acadiensis Press.

Brym, Robert J., and R. James Sacouman, eds. 1979. *Underdevelopment and Social Movements in Atlantic Canada*. Toronto: New Hogtown Press.

Buckner, P.A., and David Frank, eds. 1999. *Atlantic Canada before Confederation: The Acadiensis Reader*, Vol. 1, 3rd edn. Fredericton: Acadiensis Press.

———, eds. 1999. *Atlantic Canada after Confederation: The Acadiensis Reader*, Vol. 2, 3rd edn. Fredericton: Acadiensis Press.

Candow, James E., and Carol Corbin, eds. 1997. *How Deep is the Ocean? Historical Essays on Canada's Atlantic Fishery*. Sydney: University College of Cape Breton Press.

Davies, Gwendolyn. 1991. *Studies in Maritime Literary History*. Fredericton: Acadiensis Press.

Fleming, Berkeley, ed. 1988. *Beyond Anger and Longing: Community and Development in Atlantic Canada*. Sackville and Fredericton: Centre for Canadian Studies, Mount Allison University and Acadiensis Press.

Forbes, E.R. 1989. *Challenging the Regional Stereotype: Essays on the 20th Century Maritimes*. Fredericton: Acadiensis Press.

Frank, David, and Gregory S. Kealey, eds. 1995. *Labour and Working-Class History in Atlantic Canada: A Reader*. St John's: Institute of Social and Economic Research.

Guildford, Janet, and Suzanne Morton, eds. 1994. *Separate Spheres: Women's Worlds in the 19th Century Maritimes*. Fredericton: Acadiensis Press.

Inwood, Kris, ed. 1993. *Farm, Factory and Fortune: New Studies in the Economic History of the Maritime Provinces*. Fredericton: Acadiensis Press.

McCann, Larry, ed. 1987. *People and Place: Studies of Small Town Life in the Maritimes*. Fredericton: Acadiensis Press.

———, and Carrie MacMillan, eds. 1992. *The Sea and Culture of Atlantic Canada: A Multidisciplinary Sampler*. Sackville: Centre for Canadian Studies, Mount Allison University.

Martin, Ged, ed. 1990. *The Causes of Canadian Confederation*. Fredericton: Acadiensis Press.

Murphy, Terrence, and Cyril J. Byrne, eds. 1987. *Religion and Identity: The Experience of Irish and Scots Catholics in Atlantic Canada*. St John's: Jesperson Press.

Rawlyk, G.A., ed. 1967. *Historical Essays on the Atlantic Provinces*. Toronto: McClelland and Stewart.

———, ed. 1979. *The Atlantic Provinces and the Problems of Confederation*. St John's: Breakwater Press.

Reid, John G. 2008. *Essays on Northeastern North America, Seventeenth and Eighteenth Centuries*. Toronto: University of Toronto Press.

———, and Stephen J. Hornsby, eds. 2005. *New England and the Maritime Provinces: Connections and Comparisons*. Montreal: McGill-Queen's University Press.

Samson, Daniel, ed. 1994. *Contested Countryside: Rural Workers and Modern Society in Atlantic Canada*. Fredericton: Acadiensis Press.

Toner, Peter, ed. 1991. *The Irish in Atlantic Canada, 1780–1900*. Fredericton: New Ireland Press.

Regional Monographs

Beattie, Betsy. 2000. *Obligations and Opportunity: Single Maritime Women in Boston, 1870–1930*. Montreal: McGill-Queen's University Press.

Buckner, P.A. 1985. *The Transition to Responsible Government: British Policy in British North America, 1815–1850*. Westport CT: Greenwood.

Burrill, Gary. 1992. *Away: Maritimers in Massachusetts, Ontario, and Alberta*. Montreal: McGill-Queen's University Press.

Fingard, Judith. 1982. *Jack in Port: Sailortowns in Eastern Canada*. Toronto: University of Toronto Press.

Forbes, E.R. 1970. *The Maritime Rights Movement: 1919–1927: A Study in Canadian Regionalism*. Montreal: McGill-Queen's University Press.

Howell, Colin D. 1995. *Northern Sandlots: A Social History of Maritime Baseball*. Toronto: University of Toronto Press.

Innis, Harold. 1954 [1940 rev.]. *The Cod Fishery: The History of an International Economy*. Toronto: University of Toronto Press.

Keefer, Janice Kulyk. 1987. *Under Eastern Eyes: A Critical Reading of Maritime Fiction*. Toronto: University of Toronto Press.

Kert, Faye. 1997. *Prize and Prejudice: Privateering and Naval Prize in Atlantic Canada in the War of 1812*. St John's: International Maritime Economic History Association.

MacEachern, Alan. 2001. *Natural Selections: National Parks in Atlantic Canada, 1935–1970*. Montreal: McGill-Queen's University Press.

MacLeod, Malcolm. 2003. *Connections: Newfoundland's Pre-Confederation Links with Canada and the World*. St John's: Creative Publishers.

Ommer, Rosemary. 1991. *From Outpost to Outport: A Structural Analysis of the Jersey-Gaspé Cod Fishery, 1767–1914*. Montreal: McGill-Queen's University Press.

Sager, Eric W. 1989. *Seafaring Labour: The Merchant Marine in Atlantic Canada*. Montreal: McGill-Queen's University Press, 1989.

———, with Gerald E. Panting. 1990. *Maritime Capital: The Shipping Industry in Atlantic Canada, 1820–1914*. Montreal: McGill-Queen's University Press.

Saunders, S.A. 1984 [1939 rept]. *The Economic History of the Maritime Provinces*. Fredericton: Acadiensis Press.

Shyu, Larry N. 1997. *Chinese* (Peoples of the Maritimes Series). Halifax: Nimbus.

Taylor, M. Brook. 1989. *Promoters, Patriots and Partisans: Historiography in Nineteenth-Century English Canada*. Toronto: University of Toronto Press.

Thomas, Geraldine. 2000. *Greeks* (Peoples of the Maritimes Series). Tantallon: Four East Publications.

Thomas, Peter. 1986. *Strangers from a Secret Land: The Voyages of the Brig 'Albion' and the Founding of the First Welsh Settlements in Canada*. Toronto: University of Toronto Press.

Aboriginal Peoples

Bailey, A.G. 1969. *The Conflict of European and Eastern Algonkian Cultures, 1504–1700*, 2nd edn. Toronto: University of Toronto Press.

Blair, Susan. 2004. *Wolastoqiyik Ajemseg: The People of the Beautiful River at Jemseg*. Fredericton: New Brunswick Culture and Sport Secretariat.

Coates, Ken. 2000. *The Marshall Decision and Native Rights*. Toronto: General Publishing.

Davis, Stephen A. 1991. *The Micmac*. Tantallon: Four East Publications.

Deal, Michael, and Susan Deal. 1991. *Prehistoric Archaeology in the Maritime Provinces, Past and Present*. Research Reports in Archaeology No. 8. Fredericton: Council of Maritime Premiers Maritime Committee on Archaeological Cooperation.

Gould, G.P., and A.J. Semple, eds. 1980. *Our Land: The Maritimes*. Fredericton: Sainte Annes Point Press.

Henriksen, Georg. 1973. *Hunters in the Barrens: The Naskapi on the Edge of the White Man's World*. St John's: ISER.

Kleivan, Helge. 1966. *The Eskimos of Northeast Labrador: A History of Eskimo-White Relations, 1771–1955*. Oslo: Norsk Polarinstitutt.

McGhee, Robert. 1974. *The Native Peoples of Atlantic Canada: A History of Ethnic Interaction*. Toronto: McClelland and Stewart.

———. 1996. *Ancient People of the Arctic*. Vancouver: University of British Columbia Press.

———. 2004. *The Last Imaginary Place: A Human History of the Arctic World*. Toronto: Key Porter Books.

Maggo, Paulus. 1999. *Remembering the Years of My Life. Journeys of a Labrador Inuit Hunter*, ed. Carol Brice-Bennett. St John's: ISER.

Mailhot, José. 1997. *The People of Sheshatshit: In the Land of the Innu*. St John's: ISER.

Marshall, Ingeborg. 1996. *The History and Ethnography of the Beothuk*. Montreal: McGill-Queen's University Press.

Pastore, Ralph T. 1978. *The Newfoundland Micmacs: A History of their Traditional Life*. St John's: Newfoundland Historical Society, Pamphlet no. 5.

Paul, Daniel N. 2006. *We Were Not the Savages: A Mi'kmaq Perspective on the Collision Between Europe and North American Civilizations*, 3rd edn. Halifax: Fernwood.

Prins, Harold E.L. 1996. *The Mi'kmaq: Resistance, Accommodation, and Cultural Survival*. Fort Worth: Harcourt Brace College Publishers.

Reid, Jennifer. 1995. *Myth, Symbol, and Colonial Encounter: British and Mi'kmaq in Acadia, 1700–1867*. Ottawa: University of Ottawa Press.

Savoie, Donald J. 2000. *Aboriginal Economic Development in New Brunswick*. Moncton: Canadian Institute for Research on Regional Development.

Tuck, James A. 1976. *Newfoundland and Labrador Prehistory*. Ottawa: National Museum of Man, National Museums of Canada.

———. 1984. *Maritime Provinces Prehistory*. Ottawa: National Museum of Man, National Museums of Canada.

Upton, L.F.S. 1979. *Micmacs and Colonists: A Study of Imperial Relations, 1713–1760*. Vancouver: University of British Columbia Press.

Whitehead, Ruth Holmes. 1982. *Micmac Quillwork*. Halifax: Nova Scotia Museum.

———. 1991. *The Old Man Told Us: Excerpts from Micmac History, 1500–1950*. Halifax: Nimbus.

———. 2002. *Tracking Doctor Lonecloud: Showman to Legend Keeper*. Fredericton: Goose Lane.

Wicken, William C. 2002. *Mi'kmaq Treaties on Trial: History, Land and Donald Marshall Junior*. Toronto: University of Toronto Press.

European Exploration and Early Settlement

Bumsted, J.M. 1982. *The People's Clearance: Highland Emigration to British North America, 1770–1815*. Winnipeg: University of Manitoba Press.

Cell, Gillian T. 1969. *English Enterprise in Newfoundland, 1577–1660*. Toronto: University of Toronto Press.

———. 1982. *Newfoundland Discovered: English Attempts at Colonisation, 1610–1630*. London: Hakluyt Society.

Cook, Ramsay. 1993. *1492 and All That: Making a Garden Out of A Wilderness*. Toronto: Robarts Centre for Canadian Studies.

Handcock, W. Gordon. 1989. *'Soe Longe as there comes noe women': Origins of English Settlement in Newfoundland*. St John's: Breakwater Press.

Head, C. Grant. 1976. *Eighteenth Century Newfoundland: A Geographer's Perspective*. Toronto: McClelland and Stewart.

Jones, Elizabeth. 1986. *Gentlemen and Jesuits: Quests for Glory and Adventure in the Early Days of New France*. Toronto: University of Toronto Press.

Landry, Nicolas. 2008. *Plaisance (Terre-Neuve) 1650–1713: Une colonie française en Amerique*. Quebec: Septentrion.

Lewis-Simpson, Shannon, ed. 2003. *Vinland Revisited: The Norse World at the Turn of the First Millennium*. St John's: Historic Sites Association of Newfoundland and Labrador.

McGhee, Robert. 1991. *Canada Rediscovered*. Hull: Canadian Museum of Civilization.

Pope, Peter E. 1997. *The Many Landfalls of John Cabot*. Toronto: University of Toronto Press.

———. 2004. *Fish into Wine. The Newfoundland Plantation in the Seventeenth Century*. Chapel Hill: University of North Carolina Press.

Reid, John. 1981. *Acadia, Maine, and New Scotland: Marginal Colonies in the Seventeenth Century*. Toronto: University of Toronto Press.

Acadia and the Acadians

Arsenault, Georges. 1989. *The Island Acadians, 1720–1980*. Trans. Sally Ross. Charlottetown: Ragweed Press.

Basque, Maurice, et al. 2000. *Acadie au féminin: Un regard multidisciplinaire sur les Acadiennes et les Canadiens*. Moncton: Chaire d'études acadiennes, Université de Moncton.

———, and Jacques Paul Couturier, dirs. 2005. *Les Territoires de l'identité : perspectives acadiennes et françaises, XVIIe-XX siècles*. Moncton: Chaire d'études acadiennes, Université de Moncton.

———, with Eric Snow. 2006. *La Société Nationale de l'Acadie: Au cœur de la réuissite d'un peuple*. Moncton: Les Éditions de la Francophonie.

Brebner, John Bartlet. 1927. *New England's Outpost: Acadia Before the Conquest of Canada*. New York: Columbia University Press.

Clark, Andrew Hill. 1986. *The Geography of Early Nova Scotia to 1760*. Madison: University of Wisconsin Press.

Conrad, Margaret, ed. 1999. *Looking into Acadie: Three Illustrated Lectures*. Halifax: Nova Scotia Museum.

Couturier, Jacques Paul, and Phyllis E. LeBlanc, eds. 1996. *Économie et société en Acadie, 1850–1950*. Moncton: Éditions d'Acadie.

Daigle, Jean, ed. 1995. *Acadia of the Maritimes: Thematic Studies*. Moncton: Chaire d'études acadiennes, Université de Moncton.

Faragher, John Mack. 2005. *A Great and Noble Scheme: The Tragic Story of the Expulsion of the French Acadians from Their American Homeland*. New York: W.W. Norton.

Griffiths, N.E.S. 1973. *The Acadians: Creation of a People*. Toronto: McGraw Hill-Ryerson.

———. 1992. *The Contexts of Acadian History, 1686–1784*. Montreal: McGill-Queen's University Press.

———. 2004. *From Migrant to Acadian: A North American Border People 1604–1755*. Moncton and Montreal: Canadian Institute for Research on Public Policy and Public Administration, University of Moncton, and McGill-Queen's University Press.

Harvey, Fernand, and Gérard Beaulieu, dirs. 2000. *Les Relations entre le Quebec et l'Acadie de la tradition à la modernité*. Quebec: Éditions de l'IQRC/ Éditions d'Acadie.

Jobb, Dean. 2005. *The Acadians: A People's Story of Exile and Triumph*. Mississauga: Wiley and Sons.

Johnston, A.J.B. 1984. *Life and Religion at Louisbourg, 1713–1758*. Montreal: McGill-Queen's University Press.

———. 2001. *Control and Order in French Colonial Louisbourg, 1713–1758*. East Lansing: Michigan State University Press.

————. 2007. *Endgame 1758: The Promise, the Glory, and the Despair of Louisbourg's Last Decade*. Lincoln: University of Nebraska.

Landry, Nicolas. 1994. *Les pêches dans la péninsule acadienne, 1850–1900*. Moncton: Éditions d'Acadie.

————, and Nicole Lang. 2001. *Histoire de l'Acadie*. Sillery: Septentrion.

Laxer, James. 2006. *The Acadians in Search of a Homeland*. Toronto: Doubleday Canada.

LeBlanc, Barbara. 2003. *Postcards from Acadie: Grand Pré, Evangeline & the Acadian Identity*. Kentville: Gaspereau Press.

LeBlanc, Ronnie-Gilles, dir. 2005. *Du Grand Dérangement à la Déportation: Nouvelles perspectives historiques*. Moncton: Chaire d'études acadiennes, Université de Moncton.

McNeil, John Robert. 1985. *Atlantic Empires of France and Spain: Louisbourg and Havana, 1700–1763*. Chapel Hill: University of North Carolina Press.

Magord, André, dir. 2002. *Les Franco-Terreneuviens de la péninsule de Port-au-Port Évolution d'une identité franco-canadienne*. Moncton: Chaire d'études acadiennes, Université de Moncton.

Moore, Christopher. 1982. *Louisbourg Portraits: Life in an Eighteenth-Century Garrison Town*. Toronto: Macmillan.

Paratte, Dominique. 1998 [rev. edn.] *Acadians*. Halifax: Nimbus.

Reid, John G., et al. 2004. *The 'Conquest' of Acadia, 1710: Imperial, Colonial, and Aboriginal Constructions*. Toronto: University of Toronto Press.

Ross, Sally, and Alphonse Deveau. 1992. *The Acadians of Nova Scotia Past and Present*. Halifax: Nimbus.

Vanderlinden, Jacques. 1998. *Se marier en Acadie française, XVIIe et XVIIIe siècles*. Moncton: Chaire d'études acadiennes et Éditions d'Acadie.

New Brunswick

Acheson, T.W. 1985. *Saint John: The Making of an Urban Colonial Society*. Toronto: University of Toronto Press.

Bell, David G. 1983. *Early Loyalist Saint John: The Origins of New Brunswick Politics, 1783–1786*. Fredericton: New Ireland Press.

Condon, Ann Gorman. 1984. *The Loyalist Dream for New Brunswick: The Envy of the American States*. Fredericton: New Ireland Press.

Craig, Beatrice. 2009. *Backwoods Consumers and Homespun Capitalists: The Rise of a Market Culture in Eastern Canada*. Toronto: University of Toronto Press.

Dallison, Robert L. 2004. *Hope Restored: The American Revolution and the Founding of New Brunswick*. Fredericton: Goose Lane and the New Brunswick Military Heritage Series.

Hand, Chris M. 2003. *The Siege of Fort Beauséjour, 1755*. Fredericton: Goose Lane and the New Brunswick Military Heritage Series.

Kert, Faye. 2005. *Trimming Yankee Sails: Pirates and Privateers of New Brunswick*. Fredericton: Goose Lane and the New Brunswick Military Heritage Series.

MacDonald, M.A. 1990. *Rebels and Royalists: The Lives and Material Culture of New Brunswick's Early English Settlers, 1758–1783*. Fredericton: New Ireland Press.

MacNutt, W.S. 1984. *New Brunswick: A History*. Toronto: Macmillan.

Savoie, Donald J. 2001. *Pulling Against Gravity: Economic Development in New Brunswick during the McKenna Years*. Montreal: Institute for Research on Public Policy.

See, Scott W. 1993. *Riots in New Brunswick: Orange Nativism and Social Violence in the 1840s*. Toronto: University of Toronto Press.

Spray, William. 1972. *The Blacks in New Brunswick*. Fredericton: Brunswick Press.

Toner, Peter, ed. 1988. *New Ireland Remembered: Historical Essays on the Irish in New Brunswick*. Fredericton: New Ireland Press.

Van den Hoonaard, Will C. 1991. *Silent Ethnicity: The Dutch of New Brunswick*. Fredericton: New Ireland Press.

Wright, Esther Clark. 1955. *The Loyalists of New Brunswick*. Fredericton: Wright.

Wynn, Graeme. 1981. *Timber Colony: A Historical Geography of Early Nineteenth Century New Brunswick*. Toronto: University of Toronto Press.

Newfoundland and Labrador

Bannister, Jerry. 2004. *The Rule of the Admirals: Law, Custom, and Naval Government in Newfoundland, 1699–1832*. Toronto, University of Toronto Press for the Osgoode Society.

Blake, Raymond B. 1994. *Canadians at Last: Canada Integrates Newfoundland as a Province*. Toronto: University of Toronto Press.

Cadigan, Sean T. 1995. *Hope and Deception in Conception Bay: Merchant-Settler Relations in Newfoundland, 1785–1855*. Toronto: University of Toronto Press.

————. 2009. *Newfoundland and Labrador. A History*. Toronto: University of Toronto Press.

Cullum, Linda, Carmelita McGrath, and Marilyn Porter, eds. 2005. *Weather's Edge: Women in Newfoundland and Labrador, A Compendium*. St John's: Killick Press.

Duley, Margot I. 1993. *Where Once Our Mothers Stood We Stand: Women's Suffrage in Newfoundland, 1890–1925*. Charlottetown: gynergy books.

Fitzhugh, Lynne D. 1999. *The Labradorians: Voices from the Land of Cain*. St John's: Breakwater Press.

Greene, John P. 1999. *Between Damnation and Starvation: Priests and Merchants in Newfoundland Politics, 1745–1855*. Montreal: McGill-Queen's University Press.

Gwyn, Richard J. 1999. *Smallwood. The Unlikely Revolutionary*. Toronto: McClelland and Stewart.

Hiller, James, and Peter Neary, eds. 1980. *Newfoundland in the Nineteenth and Twentieth Centuries: Essays in Interpretation*. Toronto: University of Toronto Press.

————, and ———— eds. 1994. *Twentieth-Century Newfoundland: Explorations*. St John's: Breakwater Press.

————, and Christopher English, eds. 2007. *Newfoundland and the Entente Cordiale, 1904–2004*. St John's: Faculty of Arts Publications.

Kealey, Linda, ed. 1993. *Pursuing Equality: Historical Perspectives on Women in Newfoundland and Labrador*. St John's: Institute for Social and Economic Research.

Kennedy, John C. 1995. *People of the Bays and Island: Anthropological History and the Fate of Communities in the Unknown Labrador*. Toronto: University of Toronto Press.

Keough, Willeen G. 2006. *The Slender Thread: Irish Women on the Southern Avalon, 1750–1860*. New York: Gutenberg-e/Columbia University Press.

McCann, Philip. 1994. *Schooling in a Fishing Society: Education and Economic Conditions in Newfoundland and Labrador 1836–1986*. St John's: ISER.

McDonald, Ian D.H. 1987. *'To Each His Own': William Coaker and the Fishermen's Protective Union, 1908–1925*. St John's: ISER.

MacKenzie, David. 1986. *Inside the Atlantic Triangle: Canada and the Entrance of Newfoundland into Confederation, 1939–1949*. Toronto: University of Toronto Press.

Macpherson, Alan G., and Joyce Brown Macpherson. 1981. *The Natural Environment of Newfoundland, Past and Present*. St John's: Department of Geography, Memorial University of Newfoundland.

Mannion, John J., ed. 1977. *The Peopling of Newfoundland: Essays in Historical Geography*. St John's: Institute of Social and Economic Research.

Martin, Wendy. 1983. *Once Upon a Mine: The Story of Pre-Confederation Mines on the Island of Newfoundland*. Montreal: Canadian Institute of Mining and Metallurgy. E-Book: http://www.heritage.nf.ca/environment/mine/default.html.

Neary, Peter. 1988. *Newfoundland and the North Atlantic World, 1929–1949*. Montreal: McGill-Queen's University Press.

————, and Patrick O'Flaherty. 1974. *By Great Waters: A Newfoundland and Labrador Anthology*. Toronto: University of Toronto Press.

Newfoundland Historical Society. 2008. *A Short History of Newfoundland and Labrador*. Portugal Cove, NL: Boulder.

Noel, S.J.R. 1971. *Politics in Newfoundland*. Toronto: University of Toronto Press.

O'Flaherty, Patrick. 1979. *The Rock Observed: Studies in the Literature of Newfoundland*. Toronto: University of Toronto Press.

————. 1999. *Old Newfoundland: A History to 1843*. St John's: Long Beach Press.

————. 2005. *Lost Country: The Rise and Fall of Newfoundland, 1843–1933*. St John's: Long Beach Press.

Overton, James. 1996. *Making A World of Difference: Essays on Tourism, Culture and Development in Newfoundland*. St John's: ISER .

Porter, Marilyn. 1993. *Place and Persistence in the Lives of Newfoundland Women*. Aldershot: Avebury.

Rompkey, Bill. 2003. *The Story of Labrador*. Montreal: McGill-Queen's University Press.

Rompkey, Ronald. 1991. *Grenfell of Labrador: A Biography*. Toronto: University of Toronto Press.

Rose, George A. 2007. *Cod: The Ecological History of the North Atlantic Fisheries*. St John's: Breakwater Press.

Ryan, Shannon. 1994. *The Ice Hunters: A History of Newfoundland Sealing to 1914*. St John's: Breakwater Press.

————. n.d. *Fish Out of Water: The Newfoundland Saltfish Trade, 1814–1914*. St John's: Breakwater Press.

Stopp, Marianne P., ed. 2008. *The New Labrador Papers of Captain George Cartwright*. Montreal: McGill-Queen's University Press.

Thompson, F.F. 1961. *The French Shore Problem in Newfoundland: An Imperial Study*. Toronto: University of Toronto Press.

Webb, Jeff A. 2008. *The Voice of Newfoundland. A Social History of the Broadcasting Corporation of Newfoundland, 1939–1949*. Toronto: University of Toronto Press.

Nova Scotia

Barman, Jean. 2003. *Sojourning Sisters: The Lives and Letters of Jessie and Annie McQueen*. Toronto: University of Toronto Press.

Beck, J. Murray. 1982–3. *Joseph Howe*, 2 vols. Toronto: University of Toronto Press.

———. 1985–8. *The Politics of Nova Scotia*, 2 vols. Tantallon, NS: Four East Publications.

Bickerton, James P. 1990. *Nova Scotia, Ottawa, and the Politics of Regional Development*. Toronto: University of Toronto Press.

Brebner, John Bartlet. 1969. *The Neutral Yankees of Nova Scotia*. Toronto: McClelland and Stewart.

Brown, Robert Craig. 1975–80. *Robert Laird Borden: A Biography*, 2 vols. Toronto: University of Toronto Press.

Bruce, Harry. 1997. *An Illustrated History of Nova Scotia*. Halifax: Nimbus.

Campbell, D., and R.A. MacLean. 1974. *Beyond the Atlantic Roar: A Study of Nova Scotia Scots*. Toronto: McClelland and Stewart.

Candow, James, ed. 2001. *Industry and Society in Nova Scotia. An Illustrated History*. Halifax: Fernwood.

Conrad, Margaret. 1986. *George Nowlan: Maritime Conservative in Maritime Politics*. Toronto: University of Toronto Press.

———, Toni Laidlaw, and Donna Smyth. 1988. *No Place Like Home: The Diaries and Letters of Nova Scotia Women, 1771–1938*. Halifax: Formac.

———, ed. 1988. *They Planted Well: New England Planters in Maritime Canada*. Fredericton: Acadiensis Press, 1988.

———, ed. 1991. *Making Adjustments: Change and Continuity in Planter Nova Scotia, 1759–1800*. Fredericton: Acadiensis Press.

———, ed. 1995. *Intimate Relations: Family and Community in Planter Nova Scotia, 1759–1800*. Fredericton: Acadiensis Press.

———, and Barry Moody, eds. 2001. *Planter Links: Community and Culture in Colonial Nova Scotia*. Fredericton: Acadiensis Press.

Cuthbertson, Brian. 1994. *Johnny Bluenose at the Polls: Epic Nova Scotian Election Battles, 1758–1848*. Halifax: Formac.

Davies. Richard A. 2005. *Inventing Sam: A Biography of Thomas Chandler Haliburton*. Toronto: University of Toronto Press.

Donovan, Kenneth, ed. 1985. *Cape Breton at 200: Historical Essays in Honour of the Island's Bicentennial, 1785–1985*. Sydney: University College of Cape Breton Press.

———, ed. 1990. *The Island: New Perspectives on Cape Breton's History, 1713–1975*. Fredericton: Acadiensis Press.

Dunn, Brenda. 2000. *A History of Port-Royal/Annapolis Royal, 1605–1800*. Halifax: Nimbus.

Fingard, Judith. 1989. *The Dark Side of Life in Victorian Halifax*. Porters Lake, NS: Pottersfield Press.

———, and Janet Guildford, eds. 2005. *Mothers of the Municipality: Women, Work and Social Policy in Post-1945 Halifax*. Toronto: University of Toronto Press.

———, ———, and David Sutherland. 1999. *Halifax: The First 250 Years*. Halifax: Formac.

Frank, David. 1999. *J.B. McLachlan: A Biography*. Toronto: Lorimer.

Frost, James D. 2003. *Merchant Princes: Halifax's First Family of Finance, Ships and Steel*. Toronto: Lorimer.

Gerrits, G.H. 1996. *They Framed Well: The Dutch-Canadian Agricultural Community in Nova Scotia, 1945–1995*. Kentville: Vineland Press.

Grenier, John. 2008. *The Far Reaches of the Empire: War in Nova Scotia, 1710–1760*. Norman: University of Oklahoma Press.

Gwyn, Julian. 1998. *Excessive Expectations: Maritime Commerce and the Development of Nova Scotia, 1740–1870*. Montreal: McGill-Queen's University Press.

———. 2003. *Frigates and Foremasts: The North American Squadron in Nova Scotia Waters, 1745–1815*. Vancouver: University of British Columbia Press.

———. 2004. *Ashore and Afloat: The British Navy and the Halifax Naval Yard Before 1820*. Ottawa: University of Ottawa Press.

Henderson, T. Stephen. 2007. *Angus L. Macdonald: A Provincial Liberal*. Toronto: University of Toronto Press.

Hornsby, Stephen. 1992. *Nineteenth-Century Cape Breton: A Historical Geography*. Montreal: McGill-Queen's University Press.

Kimber, Stephen. 2008. *Loyalist and Layabouts: The Rapid Rise and Faster Fall of Shelburne, Nova Scotia, 1783 -1792*. Toronto: Doubleday Canada.

Macgillivray, Donald, and Brian Tennyson, eds. 1980. *Cape Breton Historical Essays*. Sydney: University College of Cape Breton Press.

McKay, Ian. 1994. *The Quest of the Folk: Antimodernism and Cultural Selection in Twentieth-Century Nova Scotia*. Montreal: McGill-Queen's University Press.

MacKinnon, Neil. 1989. *This Unfriendly Soil: The Loyalist Experience in Nova Scotia, 1783–1791*. Montreal: McGill-Queen's University Press.

Mann, Susan. 2005. *Margaret Macdonald: Imperial Daughter*. Montreal: McGill-Queen's University Press.

Morgan, Robert J. 2008. *Rise Again! The Story of Cape Breton Island*. Sydney: Breton Books.

Morton, Suzanne. 1995. *Ideal Surroundings: Domestic Life in a Working-Class Suburb in the 1920s*. Toronto: University of Toronto Press.

Neal, Rusty. 1999. *Brotherhood Economics: Women and Cooperatives in Nova Scotia*. Sydney: University of Cape Breton Press.

Pachai, Bridgal. 2007. *The Nova Scotia Black Experience Through the Centuries*. Halifax: Nimbus.

Pryke, K.G. 1979. *Nova Scotia and Confederation, 1864–74*. Toronto: University of Toronto Press.

Rawlyk, G.A. 1973. *Nova Scotia's Massachusetts: A Study of Massachusetts-Nova Scotia Relations, 1630 to 1784*. Montreal: McGill-Queen's University Press.

Ross, Sally, and Alphonse Deveau. 1992. *The Acadians of Nova Scotia Past and Present*. Halifax: Nimbus.

Samson, Daniel. 2008. *The Spirit of Industry and Improvement: Liberal Government and Rural-Industrial Society, Nova Scotia, 1790–1862*. Montreal: McGill-Queen's University Press.

Sandberg, L. Anders, and Peter Clancy. 2000. *Against the Grain: Foresters and Politics in Nova Scotia*. Vancouver: UBC Press.

Taylor, M. Brook. 2006. *A Camera on the Banks: Frederick William Wallace and the Fishermen of Nova Scotia*. Fredericton: Goose Lane.

Tennyson, Brian, and Roger Sarty. 2000. *Guardian of the Gulf: Sydney, Cape Breton and the Atlantic Wars*. Toronto: University of Toronto Press.

Waite, P.B. 1985. *The Man from Halifax: Sir John Thompson, Prime Minister*. Toronto: University of Toronto Press.

Walker, James W. St G. 1992. *The Black Loyalists: The Search for a Promised Land in Nova Scotia and Sierra Leone*, 2nd edn. Toronto: University of Toronto Press.

Whitfield, Harvey Amani. 2006. *Blacks on the Border: The Black Refugees in British North America, 1815–1860*. Burlington: University of Vermont Press.

Prince Edward Island

Arsenault, Georges. 1989. *The Island Acadians, 1720–1980*. Trans. Sally Ross. Charlottetown: Ragweed Press.

Baldwin, Douglas. 1998. *Land of the Red Soil. A Popular History of Prince Edward Island*. Charlottetown: Ragweed.

———, and Thomas Spira. 1988. *Gaslights, Epidemics and Vagabond Cows: Charlottetown in the Victorian Era*. Charlottetown: Ragweed Press.

Bitterman, Rusty. 2006. *Rural Protest on Prince Edward Island: From British Colonization to the Escheat Movement*. Toronto: University of Toronto Press.

———, and Margaret McCallum. 2008. *Lady Landlords of Prince Edward Island*. Toronto: University of Toronto Press.

Bolger, Francis. 1973. *Canada's Smallest Province: A History of PEI*. Charlottetown: Prince Edward Island Centennial Commission.

Bruce, Marian, and Elizabeth Cran, eds. 2004. *Working Together: Two Centuries of the Co-operative Movement on Prince Edward Island*. Charlottetown: Island Studies Press.

Bumsted, J.M. 1987. *Land, Settlement, and Politics in Eighteenth-Century Prince Edward Island*. Montreal: McGill-Queen's University Press.

Chiang, Hung-Min. 2006. *Chinese Islanders: Making A Home in the New World*. Charlottetown: Island Studies Press.

Clark, Andrew Hill. 1959. *Three Centuries and the Island: A Historical Geography of Settlement and Agriculture in Prince Edward Island*. Toronto: University of Toronto Press.

de Jong, Nicolas, and Marven E. Moore. 1994. *Shipbuilding on Prince Edward Island: Enterprise in a Maritime Setting, 1787–1920*. Mercury Series Paper 46. Ottawa: Canadian Museum of Civilization.

Greenhill, Basil, and Ann Giffard. 1967. *Westcountrymen in Prince Edward's Isle: A Fragment of the Great Migration*. Toronto: University of Toronto Press.

Hornby, Jim. 1991. *Black Islanders*. Island Studies Series No. 3. Charlottetown: Institute of Island Studies.

Ives, Edward D. 1999. *Drive Dull Care Away: Folksongs from Prince Edward Island*. Charlottetown: Institute of Island Studies.

MacDonald, Edward. 2000. *If You're Stronghearted: Prince Edward Island in the Twentieth Century*. Charlottetown: Museum and Heritage Foundation.

MacEachern, Alan. 2003. *Institute of Man and Resources: An Environmental Fable*. Charlottetown: Island Studies Press.

MacKinnon, Frank. 1951. *The Government of Prince Edward Island*. Toronto: University of Toronto Press.

O'Grady, Brendan. 2004. *Exiles and Islanders: The Irish Settlement of Prince Edward Island*. Montreal: McGill-Queen's University Press.

Rider, Peter. 2009. *Charlottetown: A History*. Charlottetown and Ottawa: Museum and Heritage Prince Edward Island and Canadian Museum of Civilization.

Robertson, Ian Ross. 1996. *The Tenant League of Prince Edward Island: Leasehold Tenure in the New World*. Toronto: University of Toronto Press.

———. 2008. *Sir Andrew Macphail: The Life and Legacy of a Man of Letters*. Montreal: McGill-Queen's University Press.

Rubio, Mary Henley. 2009. *Lucy Maud Montgomery: The Gift of Wings*. Toronto: Doubleday Canada.

Smitheram, Verner, David Milne, and Satadal Dasgupta, eds. 1982. *The Garden Transformed: Prince Edward Island, 1945–1980*. Charlottetown: Ragweed Press.

Weale, David. 1988. *A Stream Out of Lebanon: An Introduction to the Coming of the Syrian/Lebanese Emigrants to Prince Edward Island*. Charlottetown: Institute of Island Studies.

———. 1992. *Them Times*. Charlottetown: Institute of Island Studies.

Wells, Kennedy. 1986. *The Fishery of Prince Edward Island*. Charlottetown: Ragweed Press.

Websites

Websites are also listed at the end of each chapter. The following is a list of national websites that include valuable information on the Atlantic region.

The Atlas of Canada
http://atlas.gc.ca/site/index.html
Developed by Natural Resources Canada, this bilingual online atlas offers a collection of maps and related information about all regions of Canada.

Canada's Digital Collections
http://collections.ic.gc.ca
Canada's Digital Collections is one of the largest sources of Canadian content on the Internet, featuring over 600 collections celebrating Canada's history, geography, science, technology, and culture.

Canada's National History Society
http://www.historysociety.ca
The publisher of *The Beaver, Canada's History Magazine*, and *Kayak, Canada's History Magazine for Kids*, Canada's National History Society hosts a website that includes past issues of *The Beaver*.

The Canadian Encyclopedia
http://www.thecanadianencyclopedia.com
This electronic version of the *Canadian Encyclopedia* offers a variety of interactive activities and links.

Canadian Heritage Information Network
http://www.chin.gc.ca
The Canadian Heritage Information Network works with Canadian museums to create, present, and manage Canadian digital content.

Centre for the Study of Historical Consciousness
http://www.cshc.ubc.ca
This site includes academic articles on matters relating to historical understanding and the teaching of history as well as a comprehensive bibliography on these topics.

The Champlain Society
http://www.champlainsociety.ca/
The collection contains 83 of the Champlain Society's most important volumes (over 41,000 printed pages) dealing with exploration and discovery over three centuries.

Dictionary of Canadian Biography
http://www.biographi.ca
Hosted by the Library and Archives of Canada, this electronic version of the *Dictionary of Canadian Biography* facilitates searching across the 15 volumes of the dictionary currently in print.

Early Canadiana Online
http://www.canadiana.org/eco.php
Early Canadiana Online is a digital library providing access to works comprising nearly three million pages published from the time of the first European settlers up to the early twentieth century.

Geological Survey of Canada-Atlantic
http://gsc.nrcan.gc.ca/org/atlantic/index_e.php
This website includes information on the region's coastal and offshore resources.

Historica
http://www.histori.ca
This is the home page of Historica, a foundation whose mandate is to provide Canadians with a deeper understanding of their history and its importance in shaping their future.

The Historical Atlas of Canada
http://www.historicalatlas.ca/website/hacolp/
This website provides a wealth of information, including the maps and much of the research data from the award-winning three-volume *Historical Atlas of Canada*.

Library and Archives Canada
http://www.collectionscanada.ca
Library and Archives Canada hosts the largest collection of materials related to the nation's history. The site includes electronic resources and research tools.

Our Roots
http://www.ourroots.ca
The Our Roots project is designed to present an online coast-to-coast record of Canadian local histories.

Parks Canada
http://www.pc.gc.ca
The online home of Parks Canada includes information on Canada's national historic sites.

Statistics Canada
http://www.statcan.gc.ca
The Statistics Canada website contains a remarkable amount of historical and contemporary data.

Virtual Museum of Canada
http://www.virtualmuseum.ca
This site showcases the distinct culture entrusted in Canadian museums and includes a series of attractive virtual exhibits and an image gallery.

Notes

Introduction: A Region in the Making

1. On the challenges of writing on Atlantic Canada, see Ian McKay, 'A Note on "Region" in Writing the History of Atlantic Canada', *Acadiensis* XXIX, 2 (Spring 2000): 89–101, and James K. Hiller, 'Is Atlantic Canadian History Possible?' *Acadiensis* XXX, 1 (Autumn 2000): 16–22.

2. Alan Wilson, 'Crosscurrents in Maritime Regionalism', in Bruce Hodgins et al., *Federalism in Canada and Australia: Historical Perspectives, 1920–1988* (Peterborough: Frost Centre for Canadian Heritage and Development Studies, 1989), 366.

3. Phillip A. Buckner and John G. Reid, eds, *The Atlantic Region to Confederation: A History* (Toronto and Fredericton: University of Toronto Press and Acadiensis Press, 1994); E.R. Forbes and D.A. Muise, eds, *The Atlantic Provinces in Confederation* (Toronto and Fredericton: University of Toronto Press and Acadiensis Press, 1993).

4. J. Murray Beck, 'An Atlantic Region Political Culture: A Chimera', in David Jay Bercuson and Phillip A. Buckner, eds, *Eastern and Western Perspectives: Papers from the Joint Atlantic Canada/ Western Canadian Studies Conference* (Toronto: University of Toronto Press, 1981), 147–68.

5. Janice Kulyk Keefer, *Under Eastern Eyes: A Critical Reading of Maritime Fiction* (Toronto: University of Toronto Press, 1987), 10.

6. Patrick O'Flaherty, *The Rock Observed: Studies in the Literature of Newfoundland* (Toronto: University of Toronto Press, 1979), 100.

7. Edward MacDonald, *If You're Stronghearted: Prince Edward Island in the Twentieth Century* (Charlottetown: PEI Museum & Heritage Foundation, Summerside: Willliams and Crue, Ltd., 2000).

8. Ian McKay, 'Of Karl Marx and the Bluenose: Colin Campbell McKay and the Legacy of Maritime Socialism', *Acadiensis* XXVII, 2 (Spring 1998): 3.

9. Barry Cooper, 'Regionalism, Political Culture, and Canadian Political Myths', in Lisa Young and Keith Archer, eds, *Regionalism and Party Politics in Canada* (Toronto: Oxford University Press, 2002), 97.

10. Ian McKay, *The Quest of the Folk: Antimodernism and Cultural Selection in Twentieth-Century Nova Scotia* (Montreal: McGill-Queen's University Press, 1994).

11. Francis Bolger and Elizabeth R. Epperly, eds, *My Dear Mr. M: Letters to G.B. MacMillan from L.M. Montgomery* (Toronto: McGraw-Hill Ryerson, 1980), 65.

12. Gary Burrill, *Away: Maritimers in Massachusetts, Ontario, and Alberta* (Montreal: McGill-Queen's University Press, 1992).

13. Stephen H. Ullman, 'Nationalism and Regionalism in the Political Socialization of Cape Breton Whites and Indians', *The American Review of Canadian Studies* 5, 1 (Spring 1975): 66–97.

14. Marilyn Porter, *Place and Persistence in the Lives of Newfoundland Women* (Aldershot: Avebury, 1993).

15. E.R. Forbes, *Challenging the Regional Stereotype: Essays on the 20th Century Maritimes* (Fredericton: Acadiensis Press, 1989); Donald J. Savoie, *Visiting Grandchildren: Economic Development in the Maritimes* (Toronto: University of Toronto Press, 2006).

16. Sean T. Cadigan, 'Regional Politics are Class Politics: A Newfoundland and Labrador Perspective on Region', *Acadiensis* XXXV, 2 (Spring 2006): 168.

17. Donald J. Savoie, *Regional Economic Development: Canada's Search for Solutions*, 2nd edn (Toronto: University of Toronto Press, 1992), 233–8. For example, all four Atlantic Provinces in 2007 had a higher rate of home ownership without a mortgage

than the national average: Canada 30.6 per cent; NL 45.8 per cent; NB 37.8 per cent; NS 36.0 per cent; PEI 34.9 per cent (Statistics Canada, CANSIM Table 203–0019, Housing Tenure, 2007).

18. David Alexander, 'New Notions of Happiness: Nationalism, Regionalism, and Atlantic Canada', *Journal of Canadian Studies* 15, 2 (Summer 1980): 29–42.

Chapter 1: Beginnings

1. Ruth Holmes Whitehead, *Stories from the Six Worlds: Micmac Legends* (Halifax: Nimbus Publishing, 1988), 166–7.

2. Atlantic Geoscience Society, *The Last Billion Years: A Geological History of the Maritime Provinces* (Halifax: Nimbus Publishing, 2001), 62.

3. A useful summary of scholarship on this period of the region's history can be found in Stephen A. Davis, 'Early Societies: Sequences of Change', in Phillip A. Buckner and John G. Reid, eds, *The Atlantic Region to Confederation* (Toronto and Fredericton: University of Toronto and Acadiensis Press, 1994), 3–21.

4. Susan Blair, ed., *Wolastoqiyik Ajemseg: The People of Beautiful River at Jemseg*, Vol 2: *Archaeological Results* (Fredericton: Archaeological Services, Heritage Branch, Culture and Sports Secretariat, 2004).

5. James A. Tuck, 'The Archaic Period in the Maritime Provinces', in Michael Deal and Susan Blair, eds, *Prehistoric Archaeology in the Maritime Provinces: Past and Present Research* (Fredericton: Council of Maritime Premiers, 1991).

6. Bruce J. Bourque, *Diversity and Complexity in Prehistoric Maritime Societies* (New York: Plenum Press, 1995).

7. Lisa Rankin, 'Native Peoples from the Ice Age to the Extinction of the Beothuk', in *A Short History of Newfoundland and Labrador* (Portugal Cove–St Philip's: Bolder Publications, 2008), 7. See also Kevin McAleese, 'Ancient Uses of Ramah Chert', available at www.heritage.nl.ca/environment/landscape_ramah.html. [Map and colour photos].

8. Robert McGhee, *Ancient Peoples of the Arctic* (Vancouver: University of British Columbia Press, 1996).

Chapter 2: Aboriginal Peoples

1. Olive Patricia Dickason, *Canada's First Nations: A History of Founding Peoples from Earliest Times* (Toronto: McClelland and Stewart, 1992), 12.

2. For various perspectives on the numbers of Mi'kmaq at the time of contact see: Daniel N. Paul, *We Were Not the Savages*, 2nd edn (Halifax: Fernwood Publishing, 2000), 45–6; Virginia P. Miller, 'Aboriginal Micmac Population: A Review of the Evidence', *Ethnohistory* 23, 2 (Spring 1976): 117–27, and 'The Decline of the Nova Scotia Micmac Population, AD 1600–1850', *Culture* 2, 3 (1982): 107–20; Harald E.L. Prins, *The Mi'kmaq: Resistance, Accommodation, and Cultural Survival* (Fort Worth: Harcourt Brace College Publishers, 1996), 27; Ralph Pastore, 'The Sixteenth Century: Aboriginal Peoples and European Contact', in Phillip A. Buckner and John G. Reid, eds, *The Atlantic Region to Confederation: A History* (Toronto: University of Toronto Press, 1994), 24. See also John D. Daniels, 'The Indian Population of North America in 1492', *The William and Mary Quarterly*, 3rd series 49, 2 (April 1992): 298–320.

3. Nicolas Denys, *The Description and Natural History of the Coasts of North America*, ed. William F. Ganong (Toronto: Champlain Society, 1908), 401.

4. Cited in Ruth Holmes Whitehead, *The Old Man Told Us: Excerpts from Micmac History, 1500–1950* (Halifax: Nimbus Publishing, 1991), 11–12; translated by Margaret Anne Hamelin from a 'Lettre à Madame de Drucourt', n.d [c. 1750], in *Les Soirées Canadiennes* (Quebec: Brousseau Frères, 1863), 300–1.

5. Father Chrestien Le Clercq, *New Relation of Gaspesia With the Customs and Religion of the Gaspesian Indians*, 2nd edn, ed. and trans. William F. Ganong (Toronto: Champlain Society, 1910), 239.

6. Prins, *The Mi'kmaq*, 39–41.

7. Vincent O. Erickson, 'Maliseet-Passamaquoddy', in *Northeast*, ed. Bruce G. Trigger. Vol. 15, *Handbook of North American Indians*, ed. William C. Sturtevant (Washington, DC: Smithsonian Institution, 1978).

8. Nain station diary, 5 November 1772. Quoted in J.K. Hiller, 'The Foundation and the Early Years of the Moravian Mission in Labrador, 1752–1805' (MA thesis, Memorial University, 1967), 163.

9. Translation from W.C. Sturtevant, 'The First Inuit Depiction by Europeans', *Études/Inuit/Studies* 4, 1–2 (1980): 47–9.

10. Pastore, 34–5.

Chapter 3: European Encounters, 1000–1598

1. Josiah Jeremy to Silas Rand, 26 September 1869. Cited in Ruth Holmes Whitehead, *The Old Man Told Us: Excerpts from Micmac History* (Halifax: Nimbus, 1991), 8.
2. Birgitta Wallace, 'The Norse in Newfoundland: L'Anse aux Meadows and Vinland', *Newfoundland Studies* 19, 1 (2003): 5–43.
3. R.A. Skelton, 'Cabot, John', 'Cabot, Sebastian', *Dictionary of Canadian Biography Online*; Peter E. Pope, *The Many Landfalls of John Cabot* (Toronto: University of Toronto Press, 1997).
4. James Axtell, 'At the Water's Edge: Trading in the 16th Century', in *After Columbus: Essays in the Ethnohistory of Colonial North America* (New York: Oxford University Press, 1988), 145.
5. Cited in Harald E.L. Prins, *The Mi'kmaq: Resistance, Accommodation, and Cultural Survival* (Fort Worth: Harcourt Brace College Publishers, 1996), 50.
6. As translated in Sally Ross and Alphonse Deveau, *The Acadians of Nova Scotia, Past and Present* (Halifax: Nimbus, 1992), 3–4.
7. Cited in D.B. Quinn, *North American World*, Vol. 4 (New York: Arno Press, 1979), 64–5.
8. Axtell, 'At the Water's Edge', 177.

Chapter 4: Colonial Experiments, 1598–1632

1. Cited in Patrick O'Flaherty, *The Rock Observed: Studies in the Literature of Newfoundland* (Toronto: University of Toronto Press, 1979), 10.
2. Elizabeth Jones, *Gentlemen and Jesuits: Quests for Glory and Adventure in the Early Days of New France* (Toronto: University of Toronto Press, 1986), 29.
3. Lucien Campeau, 'Membertou, Henri', *Dictionary of Canadian Biography Online*.
4. Cited in Jones, *Gentlemen and Jesuits*, 92–3.
5. C. Bruce Fergusson, 'Stewart, James', in *Dictionary of Canadian Biography Online*; Andrew D. Nicholls, '"The purpois is honorabill, and may conduce to the good of our service": Lord Ochiltree and the Cape Breton Colony, 1629–1631', *Acadiensis* XXXIV, 2 (Spring 2005): 109–23.
6. Peter Pope, 'Six Letters from the Early Colony of Avalon', *Avalon Chronicles* 1 (1996): 6.
7. George Calvert to King Charles I, 19 August 1629, quoted in Gillian Cell, *Newfoundland Discovered: English Attempts at Colonization, 1610–1630* (London: Hakluyt Society, 1982), 295–6.

8. Ramsay Cook, '1492 and All That: Making a Garden out of a Wilderness', in Chad Gaffield and Pam Gaffield, eds, *Consuming Canada: Readings in Environmental History* (Toronto: Copp Clark, Ltd., 1995), 62–80.
9. Cited in Ruth Holmes Whitehead, *The Old Man Told Us: Excerpts from Micmac History, 1500–1950* (Halifax: Nimbus, 1991), 39.
10. Cited in Peter Neary and Patrick O'Flaherty, *By Great Waters: A Newfoundland and Labrador Anthology* (Toronto: University of Toronto Press, 1974), 10.

Chapter 5: Colonial Communities, 1632–1713

1. Andrew Hill Clark, *Acadia: The Geography of Early Nova Scotia to 1760* (Madison: University of Wisconsin Press, 1968), 90.
2. Sieur de Dièreville, *Relation of the Voyage to Port Royal in Acadia or New France*, ed. John Clarence Webster (Toronto: Champlain Society, 1933), 94–5.
3. N.E.S. Griffiths, 'The Acadians', *Dictionary of Canadian Biography Online*. For a more detailed discussion, see Naomi E.S. Griffiths, *The Contexts of Acadian History, 1686–1784* (Montreal and Kingston: McGill-Queen's University Press, 1992), and *From Migrant to Acadian: A North American Border People, 1604–1755* (Montreal and Kingston: McGill-Queen's University Press, 2005).
4. Peter E. Pope, *Fish into Wine: The Newfoundland Plantation in the Seventeenth Century* (Chapel Hill: University of North Carolina Press, 2004), 300.
5. Gordon Handcock, *'Soe longe as there comes noe women': Origins of English Settlement in Newfoundland* (St John's: Breakwater Press, 1989), 37.
6. Maurice Basque, 'Family and Political Culture in Pre-Conquest Acadia', in John G. Reid et al., *The 'Conquest' of Acadia, 1710: Imperial, Colonial and Aboriginal Constructions* (Toronto: University of Toronto Press, 2004), 58.
7. William C. Wicken, *Mi'kmaq Treaties on Trial: History, Land, and Donald Marshall Junior* (Toronto: University of Toronto Press, 2002), 56–7.
8. Alan F. Williams, *Father Baudoin's War: D'Iberville's Campaigns in Acadia and Newfoundland, 1696, 1697* (St John's: Memorial University, 1987), 33.
9. Williams, 48.
10. William Wicken, 'Mi'kmaq Decisions: Antoine Tecouenemac, the Conquest, and the Treaty of Utrecht', in John G. Reid et al., *The 'Conquest' of Acadia, 1710*, 86–100.

Chapter 6: Renegotiating the Atlantic Region, 1713–63

1. John G. Reid et al., *The 'Conquest' of Acadia, 1710: Imperial, Colonial, and Aboriginal Constructions* (Toronto: University of Toronto Press, 2004), 208.
2. Jerry Bannister, *The Rule of the Admirals: Laws, Custom, and Naval Government, 1699–1832* (Toronto: University of Toronto Press, 2003).
3. Brenda Dunn, *A History of Port-Royal/Annapolis Royal, 1605–1800* (Halifax: Nimbus, 2004), 106.
4. Kenneth Donovan, 'Slaves and Their Owners in Île Royale, 1713–1760', *Acadiensis* 25, 1 (Autumn 1995): 3–32.
5. N.E.S. Griffiths, 'The Golden Age: Acadian Life, 1713–1748', *Histoire Sociale* 17, 33 (May 1984): 21–34.
6. Cited in John G. Reid, 'Imperial Intrusions, 1686–1720', in Phillip A. Buckner and John G. Reid, eds, *The Atlantic Region to Confederation: A History* (Toronto and Fredericton: University of Toronto Press and Acadiensis Press, 1994), 100.
7. The National Archives, London, Colonial Office Series 217/5: 3r-5r. Cited in William C. Wicken, *Mi'kmaq Treaties on Trial: History, Land, and Donald Marshall Junior* (Toronto: University of Toronto Press, 2002), 61–2.
8. The National Archives, London, Colonial Office Series 217/4: doc 321. Cited in William C. Wicken, *Mi'kmaq Treaties on Trial*, 63–4.
9. Cited in Gérard Finn, 'Le Loutre, Jean-Louis', *Dictionary of Canadian Biography Online*.
10. Maurice Basque makes an obvious but often overlooked point that Acadians were not a monolithic group and that some Acadians had built ties with the British and others with the French in the period after 1713. See 'The Third Acadia: Political Adaptation and Societal Change', in John G. Reid et al., *The 'Conquest' of Acadia, 1710.*
11. Stephen A. White, 'The True Number of Acadians', in Ronnie-Gilles LeBlanc, dir., *Du Grand dérangement à la Déportation: Nouvelles perspectives historiques* (Moncton: Chaire d'études acadiennes, Université de Moncton, 2005), 21–56; Earle Lockerby, 'The Deportation of the Acadians from Ile St-Jean, 1758', *Acadiensis* 27, 2 (Spring 1998): 45–94.
12. Warren Perrin, *Acadian Redemption* (Erath, LA: Acadian Heritage and Cultural Foundation, Inc, 2004); James Laxer, *The Acadians in Search of a Homeland* (Toronto: Doubleday Canada, 2006), 103–10.
13. Stephen E. Patterson, 'Colonial Wars and Aboriginal Peoples, 1744–1763', in *The Atlantic Region to Confederation: A History*, 147.
14. A.J.B. Johnston, *Endgame 1758: The Promise, the Glory, and the Despair of Louisbourg's Last Decade* (Lincoln: University of Nebraska Press, 2007), 1.
15. Cited in M.A. MacDonald, *Rebels and Royalists: The Lives and Material Culture of New Brunswick's Early English-Speaking Settlers, 1758–1783* (Fredericton: New Ireland Press, 1990), 21.
16. G.P. Gould and A.J. Semple, eds, *Our Land: The Maritimes* (Fredericton: Sainte Annes Point Press, 1980), 177.

Chapter 7: Community Formation, 1749–1815

1. John Reid, 'Pax Britannica or Pax Indigena? Planter Nova Scotia (1760–1782) and competing Strategies of Pacification', *Canadian Historical Review* 85, 4 (December 2004): 669–93; Julian Gwyn, *Excessive Expectations: Maritime Commerce and the Development of Nova Scotia, 1740–1870* (Montreal and Kingston: McGill-Queen's University Press, 1998).
2. J. Garth Taylor, 'The Two World of Mikak', *The Beaver* 314, 3 (1984): 4–13; and 314, 4 (1984): 18–25. See also entries on Francis Lucas in *Dictionary of Canadian Biography Online*; and on Mikak and Tuglavina in *Dictionary of Canadian Biography Online*.
3. Quoted in C. Grant Head, *Eighteenth Century Newfoundland: A Geographer's Perspective* (Toronto: McClelland and Stewart, 1976), 198.
4. Michael Francklin to Lord George Germaine, 21 November 1780. Cited in W.D. Hamilton and W.A. Spray, eds, *Source Materials Relating to the New Brunswick Indian* (Fredericton: Centennial Press and Litho Ltd, 1976), 58–9.
5. Ann Gorman Condon, '1783–1800. Loyalist Arrival, Acadian Return, Imperial Reform', in Phillip A. Buckner and John G. Reid, eds, *The Atlantic Region to Confederation: A History* (Toronto and Fredericton: University of Toronto and Acadiensis Press, 1994), 192.
6. Edward Winslow to Ward Chipman, 7 July 1783, University of New Brunswick Archives, Harriet Irving Library, Winslow Family Papers, MG H2, Vol. 2, Part 2, p. 104 available in *The Edward*

Winslow Letters, 1783–1785, Atlantic Canada Virtual Archives, http://atlanticportal.hil.unb.ca/acva.

7. James W. St G. Walker, 'Peters (Petters), Thomas', *Dictionary of Canadian Biography Online*; 'Black Loyalists in New Brunswick, 1783–1854', Atlantic Canada Virtual Archives, http://atlanticportal. unb.hil.ca/acva.

8. Graeme Wynn, *Timber Colony: A Historical Geography of Early Nineteenth Century New Brunswick* (Toronto: University of Toronto Press, 1981).

9. Keith Mercer, 'The Murder of Lieutenant Lawry: A Case Study of British Naval Impressment in Newfoundland, 1794', *Newfoundland and Labrador Studies* 21, 2 (Fall 2006): 255–89.

Chapter 8: Maturing Colonial Societies, 1815–60

1. Joseph Howe, 'The Blue Nose', in M.G. Parks, ed., *Joseph Howe: Poems and Essays* (Toronto: University of Toronto Press, 1973), 145–6.

2. Karl Polanyi, *The Great Transformation: The Political and Economic Origins of Our Times* (Boston: Beacon Press, 1957).

3. Ronald Hyam, *Britain's Imperial Century, 1815–1914. A Study of Empire and Expansion* (London: Macmillan, 1993), 49.

4. Cited in D.C. Harvey, ed., *Journeys to the Island of St. John* (Toronto: Macmillan, 1955), 105.

5. Cited in Jennifer Reid, *Myth, Symbol, and Colonial Encounter: British and Mi'kmaq in Acadia, 1700–1867* (Ottawa: University of Ottawa Press, 1995), 36.

6. 'Statement of the Indian Delegation, 23 June 1842', cited in W.D. Hamilton and W.A. Spray, eds, *Source Materials Relating to the New Brunswick Indian* (Fredericton: Centennial Print and Litho Ltd., 1976), 112.

7. Eric W. Sager with Gerald E. Panting, *Maritime Capital: The Shipping Industry in Atlantic Canada, 1820–1914* (Montreal: McGill-Queen's University Press, 1990), 17.

8. T.W. Acheson, 'The 1840s: Decade of Tribulation', in Phillip A. Buckner and John G. Reid, eds, *The Atlantic Region to Confederation: A History* (Toronto and Fredericton: University of Toronto and Acadiensis Press, 1994), 307–32.

9. Cited in J.G. Millais, *Newfoundland and its Untrodden Ways* (London, 1907), 41.

10. Sean T. Cadigan, *Hope and Deception in Conception Bay: Merchant-Settler Relations in Newfoundland, 1785–1855* (Toronto: University of Toronto Press, 1995).

11. Gwynneth C.D. Jones, 'Gisborne, Frederic Newton', *Dictionary of Canadian Biography Online*.

12. A.J. Sandy Young, *Beyond Heroes: A Sport History of Nova Scotia*, Vol. 2 (Hantsport: Lancelot Press, 1991), 15.

13. Patrick O'Flaherty, 'Carson, William', *Dictionary of Canadian Biography Online*.

14. Rusty Bittermann and Margaret McCallum, 'When Private Rights become Private Wrongs: Property and the State in Prince Edward Island in the 1830s', in John McLaren, A.R. Buck, and Nancy Wright, eds, *Despotic Dominion: Property Rights and British Settler Societies* (Vancouver: University of British Columbia Press, 2005).

15. Ian McKay, 'The Liberal Order Framework: A Prospectus for a Reconnaissance of Canadian History', *Canadian Historical Review* 81, 4 (December 2000): 617–45.

16. Jerry Bannister, 'Canada as Counter-Revolution: The Loyalist Order Framework in Canadian History', in Jean-François Constant and Michel Ducharme, eds, *Liberalism and Hegemony: Debating the Canadian Liberal Revolution* (Toronto: University of Toronto Press, 2008); Ruth Sandwell, 'The Limits of Liberalism: The Liberal Reconnaissance and the History of the Family in Canada', *Canadian Historical Review* 83, 3 (September 2003): 423–50.

Chapter 9: Confronting Confederation, 1860–73

1. Greg Marquis, *In Armageddon's Shadow: The Civil War and Canada's Maritime Provinces* (Montreal: McGill-Queen's University Press, 1998).

2. Ian Ross Robertson, ed., *The Prince Edward Island Land Commission of 1860* (Fredericton: Acadiensis Press, 1988), 69–70.

3. Andrew Smith, *British Businessmen and Canadian Confederation: Constitution Making in an Age of Anglo-Globalization* (Montreal: McGill-Queen's University Press, 2008), 3.

4. Phillip A. Buckner, 'The 1860s: An End and a Beginning', in Phillip A. Buckner and John G. Reid, eds, *The Atlantic Region to Confederation: A History* (Toronto and Fredericton: University of Toronto Press and Acadiensis Press, 1994), 377.

5. Cited in J. Murray Beck, ed., *Joseph Howe: Voice of Nova Scotia* (Toronto: Carleton Library/McClelland & Stewart, 1964), 175.

6. C.M. Wallace, 'Tilley, Sir Samuel Leonard', *Dictionary of Canadian Biography Online*.
7. Cited in Kenneth G. Pryke, *Nova Scotia and Confederation, 1864–74* (Toronto: University of Toronto Press, 1978), 41.
8. Donald Warner, *The Idea of Continental Union: Agitation for the Annexation of Canada to the United States, 1849–1893* (University of Kentucky Press, 1960), 814.
9. David G. Alexander, 'Economic Growth in the Atlantic Region, 1880–1940', in Eric W. Sager, Lewis R. Fischer, Stuart O. Pierson, comps, *Atlantic Canada and Confederation: Essays in Canadian Political Economy* (St John's and Toronto: Memorial University and University of Toronto Press, 1983), 74.
10. James K. Hiller, 'Confederation Defeated: The Newfoundland Election of 1869', in James K. Hiller and Peter Neary, eds, *Newfoundland in the Nineteenth and Twentieth Centuries: Essays in Interpretation* (Toronto: University of Toronto Press, 1980).
11. Ian Ross Robertson, *The Tenant League of Prince Edward Island, 1864–1867: Leasehold Tenure in the New World* (Toronto: University of Toronto Press, 1996), 273.

Chapter 10: The Industrial Challenge, 1873–1901

1. D. Murray Young, 'Gibson, Alexander', *Dictionary of Canadian Biography Online*.
2. T.W. Acheson, 'The National Policy and the Industrialization of the Maritimes, 1880–1910', *Acadiensis* 1, 2 (Spring 1972): 3–28.
3. Greg Kealey, ed., *Canada Investigates Industrialism* (Toronto: University of Toronto Press, 1973), 395–6.
4. Judith Fingard, 'The 1880s: Paradoxes of Progress', in E.R. Forbes and D.A. Muise, eds, *The Atlantic Provinces in Confederation* (Toronto: University of Toronto Press, 1993), 97.
5. Naomi Griffiths, 'Evangeline: A Tale of Acadie', *The Canadian Encyclopedia*, 2nd edn (Edmonton: Hurtig, 1988), II, 729.
6. *Moniteur Acadien*, 10 June 1880. Cited in Georges Arsenault, *The Island Acadians, 1720–1980* (Charlottetown: Ragweed Press, 1989), 155.
7. Ronald Rompkey, *Grenfell of Labrador: A Biography* (Toronto: University of Toronto Press, 1991).
8. *The McQueen Family Letters, 1866–1934*, Atlantic Canada Virtual Archives, http://atlanticportal.hil.

unb.ca; Jean Barman, *Sojourning Sisters: The Lives and Letters of Jessie and Annie McQueen* (Toronto: University of Toronto Press, 2003).
9. Nancy Christie, ed., *Transatlantic Subjects: Ideas, Institutions, and Social Experience in Post Revolutionary British North America* (Montreal: McGill-Queen's University Press, 2008).
10. Alan Brookes, ed., 'The Provincials by Albert Kennedy', *Acadiensis* IV, 2 (Spring 1975): 94.

Chapter 11: The Promise and Peril of a New Century, 1901–19

1. David Frank, 'The Cape Breton Coal Industry and the Rise and Fall of the British Empire Steel Corporation', in Don Macgillivray and Brian Tennyson, eds, *Cape Breton Historical Essays* (Sydney: College of Cape Breton Press, 1980), 114–15.
2. *Fishermen's Advocate*, 29 October 1910. Quoted in Ian D.H. McDonald, *'To Each His Own.' William Coaker and the Fishermen's Protective Union in Newfoundland Politics, 1908–1925* (St John's, 1987), 21–2.
3. Quoted in S.J.R. Noel, *Politics in Newfoundland* (Toronto: University of Toronto Press, 1971), 88.
4. Mary Rubio and Elizabeth Waterston, eds, *The Selected Journals of L.M. Montgomery*, 5 vols (Toronto: Oxford University Press, 1987–2004).
5. Ian McKay, 'The Five Ages of Nova Scotian Tourism', *New Maritimes* 5, 11–12 (1987): 8.
6. Gerald L. Pocius, 'Tourists, Health Seekers and Sportsmen: Luring Americans to Newfoundland in the Early Twentieth Century', in James Hiller and Peter Neary, eds, *Twentieth-Century Newfoundland: Explorations* (St John's: Breakwater Press, 1994), 47–78.
7. Janet F. Kitz, *Shattered City: The Halifax Explosion and the Road to Recovery* (Halifax: Nimbus, 1989), 82, 96–104.
8. Major A. Rayley, 'Beaumont Hamel', *Veterans' Magazine* 1, 3 (1921): 37.
9. Ian McKay, 'The 1910s: The Stillborn Triumph of Progressive Reform', in E.R. Forbes and D.A. Muise, eds, *The Atlantic Provinces in Confederation* (Toronto and Fredericton: University of Toronto Press and Acadiensis Press, 1993), 229.
10. Extract from Periodical Accounts relating to the Missions of the Church of the United Brethren, 1919, in Helge Kleivan, *The Eskimos of Northeast Labrador: A History of Eskimo-White Relations,*

1771–1955 (Oslo: Norsk Polarinstitutt, 1966), 181.

11. Sylvia Bashevkin, *Toeing the Lines: Women and Party Politics in English Canada*, 2nd edn (Toronto: University of Toronto Press, 1993), 5.

Chapter 12: Between the Wars, 1919–39

1. S.A. Saunders, *The Economic History of the Maritime Provinces*, ed. T.W. Acheson (Fredericton: Acadiensis Press, 1984), 38.

2. E.R. Forbes, *The Maritime Rights Movement, 1919–1927: A Study in Canadian Regionalism* (Montreal: McGill-Queen's University Press, 1979), 176.

3. Douglas O. Baldwin, *She Answered Every Call: The Life of Public Health Nurse, Mona Gordon Wilson (1894–1981)* (Charlottetown: Indigo Press, 1997), 299.

4. Ken Coates, *The Marshall Decision and Native Rights* (Montreal: McGill-Queen's University Press), 82–3.

5. Daniel N. Paul, *We Were Not the Savages: A Mi'kmaq Perspective on the Collision between European and Native American Civilizations* (Halifax: Fernwood Publishing 2000), 270–1.

6. Ruth Holmes Whitehead, *Tracking Doctor Lonecloud: Showman to Legend Keeper* (Fredericton: Goose Lane, 2002).

7. Ian McKay, 'Among the Fisherfolk: J.F.B. Livesay and the Invention of Peggy's Cove', *Journal of Canadian Studies* 23, 1–2 (1988): 23–45.

8. Gwendolyn Davies, 'Frank Parker Day's Rockbound', in *Studies in Maritime Literary History* (Fredericton: Acadiensis Press, 1991), 174.

9. Kirk Niergarth, '"Missionary for Culture": Walter Abell, Maritime Art and Cultural Democracy, 1928–1944', *Acadiensis* XXXVI, 1 (Autumn 2006): 3–28; Sandra Paikowsky, '"From Away" The Carnegie Corporation, Walter Abell, and American Strategies for Art in the Maritimes from the 1920s to the 1940s', *The Journal of Canadian Art History* XXVII (2006): 36–72.

10. L.M. Grayson and Michael Bliss, eds, *The Wretched of Canada: Letters to R.B. Bennett, 1930–1935* (Toronto: University of Toronto Press, 1971), 37–38, 51, 113–14, 122–23.

11. Quoted in William C. Gilmore, *Newfoundland and Dominion Status: The External Affairs Competence and International Law Status of Newfoundland, 1855–1934* (Toronto: Carswell, 1988), 102.

12. Lady Hope Simpson to Ian Hope Simpson, 25 May 1935, in Peter Neary, ed., *White Tie and Decorations: Sir John and Lady Hope Simpson in Newfoundland, 1934–1936* (Toronto: University of Toronto Press, 1996), 158–160.

13. Cited in Jim Lotz, *The Humble Giant: Moses Coady, Canada's Rural Revolutionary* (Toronto: Novalis, 2005), 34.

14. James Overton, 'Brown Flour and Beri-beri: The Politics of Dietary and Health Reform in Newfoundland in the First Half of the Twentieth Century', *Newfoundland Studies* 14, 1 (1998): 15.

Chapter 13: The Emergence of an Atlantic Region, 1939–49

1. Gerry Harrop, *Clarie: Clarence Gillis, M.P., 1940–1957* (Hantsport, NS: Lancelot, 1987); Paul MacEwan, *Miners and Steelworkers: Labour in Cape Breton* (Toronto: Samuel Stevens Hakkert, 1976).

2. Georges Arsenault, *The Island Acadians, 1720–1980*, trans. Sally Ross (Charlottetown: Ragweed Press, 1989), 242.

3. The Universal Declaration of Human Rights, http://www.un.org/Overview/rights.html.

4. J.R. Smallwood, 'An Appeal', 31 May 1948. Cited in Peter Neary, ed., *The Political Economy of Newfoundland, 1929–1972* (Toronto: Copp Clark, 1973), 142.

5. Quoted in Jeff A. Webb, 'The Responsible Government League and the Confederation Campaigns of 1948', *Newfoundland Studies* 5, 2 (1989): 214.

6. Quoted in Jeff A. Webb, *The Voice of Newfoundland: A Social History of the Broadcasting Corporation of Newfoundland, 1939–1949* (Toronto: University of Toronto Press, 2008), 142.

7. Adrian Tanner, 'The Aboriginal Peoples of Newfoundland and Labrador and Confederation', *Newfoundland Studies* 14, 2 (1998): 238–52.

8. Cited in Corey Slumkoski, 'The Maritime Reaction to Newfoundland's Entry into Confederation' (PhD dissertation, University of New Brunswick, 2009), 57.

Chapter 14: The Real Golden Age? 1949–75

1. Eric Hobsbawm, *Age of Extremes: The Short Twentieth Century, 1914–1991* (London: Abacus, 1995), 6.

2. W.S. MacNutt, 'The Atlantic Revolution', *Atlantic Advocate* (June 1957): 11–13.

3. Dalton Camp, *Gentlemen, Players and Politicians* (Toronto: McClelland and Stewart, 1970), 329–30.

4. James P. Feehan and Melvin Baker, 'The Origins of a Coming Crisis: Renewal of the Churchill Falls Contract', *Dalhousie Law Journal* 30, 1 (2007): 242.

5. Della Stanley and M.M. Stanley, *Louis Robichaud: A Decade of Power* (Halifax: Nimbus Publishing, 1984), 93.

6. Edward MacDonald, *If You're Stronghearted: Prince Edward Island in the Twentieth Century* (Charlottetown: Prince Edward Island Museum and Heritage Foundation, 2000), 297–307.

7. Africville Genealogical Society, *The Spirit of Africville* (Halifax: Formac, 1992), 70.

8. Labrador Inuit Association, 'Nunatsiavut News', accessed 15 July 2005 at www.nunatsiavut.com/en/windsofchange.php.

Chapter 15: The Atlantic Region in a Global Context, 1975–2005

1. Brian Lee Crowley, *Atlantic Institute for Market Studies* (AIMS), http://www.aims.ca/library/atlanticapart1.pdf.

2. Ken S. Coates, *The Marshall Decision and Native Rights* (Montreal: McGill-Queen's University Press, 2000), 83.

3. Donald J. Savoie, *Pulling Against Gravity: Economic Development in New Brunswick During the McKenna Years* (Montreal: Institute for Research on Public Policy, 2001).

4. Moses Harvey, *Where Are We and Whither Tending? Three Lectures on the Reality and Worth of Human Progress* (Boston: Doyle and Whittle, 1886).

Index